SCHOOL AND COMMUNITY

THE PHILOSOPHY, PROCEDURES, AND PROBLEMS OF COMMUNITY STUDY AND SERVICE THROUGH SCHOOLS AND COLLEGES

By

EDWARD G. OLSEN
DIRECTOR OF SCHOOL AND COMMUNITY RELATIONS
WASHINGTON STATE
DEPARTMENT OF EDUCATION

In Coöperation With

JULIAN C. ALDRICH   ELDON W. MASON

EDMUND deS. BRUNNER   NATHAN K. MENDELSOHN

LOIS M. CLARK   MORRIS R. MITCHELL

VIVIAN EDMISTON   ALVIN B. ROBERTS

MARGARET O. KOOPMAN   JOHN ROTHSCHILD

CHARLES UGER

New York   **PRENTICE-HALL, INC.**   *1946*

PRENTICE–HALL EDUCATION SERIES

E. George Payne, Editor

First Printing................April, 1945
Second Printing............August, 1946

To

CLARENCE V. HOWELL

**FOUNDER AND DIRECTOR OF THE RECONCILIATION TRIPS
IN NEW YORK CITY**

**COURAGEOUS, DEVOTED, AND SUCCESSFUL PIONEER
IN AMERICAN INTERCULTURAL EDUCATION**

HIGHLIGHTING THIS VOLUME

OUR NEED

"Many schools are literally insulated in their communities. They are pedagogic islands, cut off by channels of convention from the world which surrounds them, and the inhabitants of these islands rarely venture to cross these channels during school hours. To be sure, they read about the surrounding world in books, and they return to live on the mainland when school is out. Few schools, however, have built bridges over which people may freely pass back and forth between school and community."—EDUCATIONAL POLICIES COMMISSION.

OUR PURPOSE

"The circumstances of our times make it imperative that the school should offer children more than book learning in the classrooms. It must, indeed, make use of all the community's resources for providing children with direct and valuable contacts with environmental reality. Experimentation along this line has already begun in schools at every level but it needs to be extended with great rapidity. Every community offers many opportunities to the schools for such experimentation. These should be vigorously uncovered and the school should take the initiative in persuading the community to make them available."—COMMISSION ON TEACHER EDUCATION OF THE AMERICAN COUNCIL ON EDUCATION.

OUR APPROACH

"In undertaking to prepare teachers for their responsibility to society we cannot expect to be successful if we work alone and through only those channels that are recognized in academic tradition. The teacher and the school need the help of the community, which can provide a favorable and sympathetic atmosphere, and the help of local organizations and of parents. The teacher in service will not make the fullest use of such assistance unless, during his pre-service education, he has learned how to establish helpful relations with the community to which he belongs, on and off the campus. He will not lead his pupils into effective citizenship unless he knows and understands their background and out of his own experience can show them where their initiative and their urge to be useful can find expression in service."—COMMITTEE ON TEACHER EDUCATION OF THE ASSOCIATION OF COLLEGES AND UNIVERSITIES OF THE STATE OF NEW YORK.

Preface

FROM many sources one learns that all life is educative, that the democratic school must become definitely concerned with the improvement of community and social living, that the major areas and problems of life should give direction to the curriculum, that functional education requires active participation in constructive community activities, and that in this air age the community must be thought of as local, regional, national, and world-wide in scope. All of these emphases are dominant in American educational thinking today.

Although the need for greatly expanded community study and service is clearly apparent, there has not hitherto existed a comprehensive treatment of procedures in this new and challenging field. This book therefore offers a compact, authoritative overview of the community education movement, detailed descriptions of those major community analysis, study, and service techniques which have been proved effective in actual practice, and an array of tested suggestions for successfully meeting the general problems thus involved. It is hoped that the volume may serve to meet a widespread demand for valid "know-how" in the area of community education at all school levels from kindergarten through adult education, and in all teaching fields from art to zoology. For surely there was profound wisdom in the words of Montaigne when he remarked that:

I would have the world to be the book my young gentlemen should study with most attention. Many strange humors, many sects, many judgments, opinions, laws, and customs teach us to judge rightly of our own actions, to correct our faults, and to inform our understanding, which is no trivial lesson.

No trivial lesson that, but the true essence of liberal education itself!

This book can serve as basic text for such courses as School and Community, Utilization of Community Resources in the Educational Program, The Community School, Education as Social Process, Teacher and Community, School-Community Relationships, and the like. It will also be useful as source reading in more conventional courses such as Elementary or Secondary Education, Methods of Teaching, Educational Sociology, Foundations of Education, Philosophy of Education, and many others. Finally, the book is designed to be an equally worthwhile reference guidebook for those numerous teachers, school administrators, and members of the general public who wish to work more intelligently in the promotion of better education than we have had in the past.

Identified below are the contributing authors, with the chapters for which each has been responsible:

Julian C. Aldrich, Northwest Missouri State Teachers College: *Chapters 14 and 15*

Edmund deS. Brunner, Teachers College, Columbia University: *Chapter 4 (with N. K. Mendelsohn)*

Lois M. Clark, Pennsylvania Department of Public Instruction: *Chapter 3*

Vivian Edmiston, New York State Education Department: *Chapter 16*

Margaret O. Koopman, Central Michigan College of Education: *Chapters 6, 17, and 20*

Eldon W. Mason, American Junior Red Cross: *Chapters 7 and 9*

Nathan K. Mendelsohn: *Chapter 4 (with E. deS. Brunner)*

Morris R. Mitchell, Macedonia Cooperative Community (Georgia): *Chapters 12 and 13*

Edward G. Olsen, Washington State Department of Education: *Chapters 1, 2, 18, 19, and 21*

Alvin B. Roberts, Haw Creek Township High School (Illinois): *Chapter 5*

John Rothschild, Executive Director of the Open Road: *Chapter 10*

Charles Uger, Public School 5, New York City: *Chapters 8 and 11*

Thanks are due to all these men and women, for they have cooperated long and well in the preparation of this book. While each individual approved the final draft of the chapters attributed to him, the undersigned alone is responsible for the planning, organization, content and spirit of the volume as a whole.

Grateful acknowledgment is also made to Paul H. Sheats and to L. B. Sharp for their critical readings of Chapters 5 and 11 respectively, and to Francis J. Brown, who twice reviewed the entire manuscript and thereby greatly stimulated its general improvement. Numerous publishers and writers generously authorized the use of quotations from copyrighted materials; their contributions have added much to this book and are individually credited within the text itself. Special commendation goes also to Faith Elliott Olsen, who has shared with me the planning, analysis, and practical development of this project from its first conception to its present form. Her constant encouragement, critical judgment, and editorial aid are well reflected in every section of this volume.

EDWARD G. OLSEN

Troy, New York
February 12, 1945

Foreword

By WILLIAM G. CARR

ASSOCIATE SECRETARY
NATIONAL EDUCATION ASSOCIATION OF THE UNITED STATES

WHEN my friend, Edward Olsen, invited me to write a Foreword to this book, I was naturally flattered and pleased. It seemed easy to dash off a few polite paragraphs of solemn prose, mentioning, of course, the scholarly resourcefulness of the authors, the profound importance of the subject and, above all, the relation of the book to other treatments of the same subject. But when the galley-proof arrived, all illusions as to the facility with which a Foreword could be composed vanished. The planned paragraphs of suave and reserved introduction suddenly seemed inadequate.

For this book does not offer a cautious, unemotional hypothesis that the community school may be a rather desirable development. Not at all; the authors devoutly *believe* that the community school is the key to the solution of the problem of education in a democracy. They are looking for converts; they insist; they plead; they use exclamation marks. Like all people with a burning ideal, they are going to irritate some folks at first. They are excited, enthusiastic, and so will the reader become unless that reader's arteries are hardened by acute professional complacency.

It is now exactly eighty years since Edward Sheldon, the famous Oswego schoolmaster, returned home from a visit to an exposition in Toronto, laden with charts, books, balls, cards, pictures of animals, building blocks, silkworms, cocoons, cotton bolls, grains, pottery, glassware, and a great idea. Sheldon's idea, reduced to utmost simplicity, was that people learn best by the most direct contact possible with the things they are learning about. Out of that idea grew much of the improvement of American schools in the last half of the nineteenth century. That idea, in essence, is the main point of this book, but with this addition: that while Sheldon and the Oswego Movement sought to bring the world into the classroom, this volume asks us also to take the classroom into the world.

This book tells how to throw bridges across the deep moat which typically separates the school from its community. Each bridge will be a two-lane highway so that the community can utilize the resources of the school and the school can use the community.

The modern school must learn to use the community as a great living laboratory and textbook of civic and personal life. Good books are essential tools of learning, but there are many lessons that cannot be learned from books. There must be more and better community study under the auspices of educational authorities. Not only must the school learn to use the community as an effective means of education; it must also render service to the community. Youth wants to serve. This volume suggests many ways in which young people, with the encouragement of the school and under its auspices, may help to make life better in the community, the nation, and the world in which they live. What better training for useful citizenship than this could be provided?

Nor is this the only dimension of the road that must be built between the school and the community. The lights ought to burn later in the school buildings. The school grounds, and other facilities should be available for public use more hours a day, more days a week, and more weeks a year. Who has not felt a sense of indignation at passing fenced and locked school playgrounds during the summer months, while children and young people were playing dangerously in the streets nearby? Modern schools have shops, libraries, gymnasiums, swimming pools, playgrounds, auditoriums, little theaters, science laboratories, and a host of other facilities that ought to be at the service of the community when these facilities are not required for the formal education of children and youth. Schools should be planned and built with this community service in mind, and school budgets should provide the funds and the staff that will enable the school to offer these services to the community.

American schools are vastly different one from another. We Americans make of that variety a virtue. We stoutly resist federal control of our schools. We minimize even state control of education. We insist that we want the schools to reflect community needs and to be "close to the people." But this local autonomy for education has not great value unless it is used. Schools which are legally "close to the people" but actually out of touch with the needs of the people for light and leadership might almost as well be controlled and administered by some far away, impersonal national administrative agency. So, when this book pleads for real community schools, it is asking for schools that are not only better in the strictly pedagogical sense, but also for schools that are more effective instruments of the American way of life.

Contents

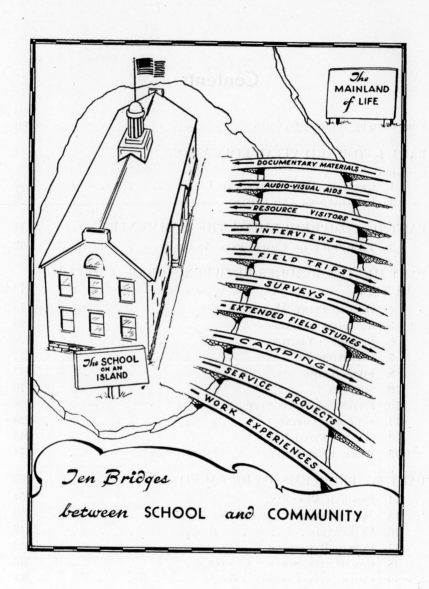

The
MAINLAND
of LIFE

DOCUMENTARY MATERIALS

AUDIO-VISUAL AIDS

RESOURCE VISITORS

INTERVIEWS

FIELD TRIPS

SURVEYS

EXTENDED FIELD STUDIES

CAMPING

SERVICE PROJECTS

WORK EXPERIENCES

The SCHOOL
ON AN
ISLAND

Ten Bridges

between SCHOOL *and* COMMUNITY

PART I

TOWARD VITAL EDUCATION

ALTHOUGH all of our children must some-how become reasonably competent partici-pators in the ongoing social processes of life, most children cannot master those processes upon the basis of verbal or printed descriptions alone. For words, we must remember, are highly abstract symbols; they are sheer verbalisms un-less given meaningful content by previous direct contact with reality. How, then, can we better teach our children than we have done in the book-centered school of the past?

*

THE GREAT PROBLEM

WE plead for an improved and enlarged education in order that there may be brought into ex-istence a society all of whose operations shall be more genuinely educative, conducive to the develop-ment of desire, judgment, and character. The desired education cannot occur within the four walls of a school shut off from life. Education must itself as-sume an increasing responsibility for participation in projecting ideas of social change and taking part in their execution in order to be educative. The great problem of American education is the discovery of methods and techniques by which this more direct and vital participation may be brought about.

JOHN DEWEY AND JOHN L. CHILDS

In W. H. Kilpatrick (ed.), *The Edu-cational Frontier.* By permission of The D. Appleton-Century Company, publishers.

1

SPIRITUAL PROLETARIAT

ALL over the world, but most particularly in the countries where civilization is supposed to be most advanced, there are collected in great cities huge masses of people who have lost their roots in the earth beneath them and their knowledge of the fixed stars in the heavens above them. They are the crowds that drift with all the winds that blow, and are caught up at last in the great hurricanes.

They are the people who eat but no longer know how their food is grown; who work and no longer see what they help to produce; who hear all the latest news and all the latest opinions but have no philosophy by which they can distinguish the true from the false, the credible from the incredible, the good from the bad.

Is it surprising that as civilization has become more streamlined, democracy has become more unworkable? For these masses without roots, these crowds without convictions, are the spiritual proletariat of the modern age, and the eruption of their volcanic and hysterical energy is the revolution that is shaking the world. They are the chaos in which the new Caesars are born.

. . . This feeling, which pervades the great urban centers, that all things are relative and impermanent and of no real importance, is merely the reflection of their own separation from the elementary experiences of humanity.

—WALTER LIPPMANN

From a syndicated article in the public press under date of Nov. 3, 1938. By permission of the *New York Herald Tribune.*

LEARNING THAT IS ALIVE

IN the community, boys and girls, whether in the everyday close concerns of their own neighborhood or in the almost equally close concerns of Norway and North Africa, can see firsthand the characteristics and needs of human society. The true meaning of whatever is learned is seen clearest in community action. Foreign language is spoken, mathematics is used, science is at work, the arts are being enjoyed, history and literature being lived. Learning comes alive in the community; and after the war we shall see more than we ever have before of learning that is alive. Factories, libraries, museums, welfare agencies, motion-pictures, radio, civic problems and city streets are the stuff of which tomorrow's textbooks will be made.

—BURTON P. FOWLER

In "Education for the Future." *Parents' Magazine,* February, 1944.

CHAPTER 1

Relating Our Schools to Life

The ivory tower is itself a casualty of war. Every period of great human conflict is also a time when educational workers begin to re-examine basic philosophies, question current school practices, plan new and better programs of instruction. Out of World War II is coming vigorous educational thinking and more objective planning for both public and private education. Once more a gigantic war effort has centered professional attention upon practical needs as never before—needs that are both individual and social; needs that are moral, emotional, and physical as well as intellectual. Education is increasingly accepting a philosophy which centers school instruction in community needs that are local, regional, national, and world-wide in scope, and teachers everywhere begin to conceive of true education as changed behavior within a democratic social order.

The future is ripe for change. Our times demand educational advance and reconstruction of a high order. But now, as always, the fundamental direction in which we seek to move toward that goal will assuredly determine the measure of our success in achieving it. How then shall we envision an education that is adequate to meet the imperative needs of this epoch?

What Is the Problem of Education?[1]

How can our modern schools—the American people's chief formal agency for mass education—best help all our youth to participate effectively and with personal satisfaction in the enduring processes of human living? How can we, earnest teachers of these needy youth, sensitize them to the intolerable disparities of human circumstance, stimulate in them a deep feeling of personal responsibility

---

[1] This section, several paragraphs following it, and the Chart on page 10 are somewhat adapted from their original presentation in the University of Pennsylvania Bulletin. *Education in a Nation at War:* Twenty-Ninth Annual Schoolmen's Week Proceedings, 1942. Used by permission.

for remedying the evils they perceive, give them the knowledge and skills necessary for intelligent judgment and action, acquaint them with the difficulties of arriving at truth in the social field, inculcate tolerance of honest differences in opinion, practice them in willing, cooperative group activity, and finally develop in them an unswerving loyalty to democratic ideals and practices? [2] How may teachers best aid these young people to *put down deep roots of personal responsibility for group welfare, of realistic social understanding, of intelligent civic loyalties whereby they may flexibly anchor their lives against the surging tides of social barbarism at home as well as abroad?* Is not this *the* educational problem of our generation?

Years Ago

The inescapable social fact of this century is that with the progress of industrialization and urbanization, human activities and relationships become steadily more specialized, more complex, more interdependent; yet at the very same time, less familiar and less personalized. Most children of even a generation ago shared directly and constantly in varied elementary experiences of humanity. They learned through early personal experience to till the soil, to tend farm animals, to make the bread, to care for younger children, to perform successfully the numerous necessary tasks of the rural household. Being held responsible for carrying farm or home responsibilities, they soon learned to accept definite personal responsibility, and to execute assignments promptly; to work in sustained fashion even at distasteful tasks. Meanwhile, they learned about politics from the arguments of their elders, they participated in the recreational activities of the local community, and they developed their ethical codes in home, church, and community where deeply conflicting patterns of moral behavior usually did not exist. And since they lived close to Nature, they often shared in the mating, birth-process, and death-watch of living things.

Elementary experiences of humanity these are—aiding life and battling death, growing food and building a home, governing and worshipping, educating and playing, doctoring and wondering . . . and it was through sharing intimately in basic human experiences such as these that children of this former day matured emotionally,

---

[2] These are the seven objectives of civic education, according to President Edmund E. Day of Cornell University. See his "How Can Our Schools Contribute to a Better Social Order?" in National Education Association, *Addresses and Proceedings,* Vol. 75 (1937), pp. 47–53.

developed personal character, and attached their emerging larger loyalties to personalized human values.

Under such conditions as these, children learned easily and well for they were motivated by genuine purposes of their own. They learned to do by doing, the processes in which they shared were consciously cooperative in nature, and the results of their work were demonstrably significant to themselves as well as to the adults of their own communities. No wonder, then, that the role of the common school, in their day, could be largely that of promoting simple literacy through intensive drill, and transmitting some of the social heritage through memorization of classic book-learning.

BUT TODAY

But what of many children today, especially those in our great metropolitan centers? Are they not the children of a "spiritual proletariat," crowded together and aimlessly drifting? These are the children who are indeed dispossessed for they help to grow no food; they rarely care for pets; their recreation is predominantly passive—through movies and radio; they have no real work experience even in adolescence; they are little concerned about political affairs; they remain shut away from the mysterious processes of birth and death. Whether they exist in squalid tenements or reside in luxurious apartments, their life-long separation from many elementary human experiences is precisely the same. Mistaking money for happiness, street address for success, and "getting by" for true achievement, they live their lives on the periphery of basic human experience rather than at its heart.

The city crowds people together physically even as it renders their wider associations less personalized. Meanwhile, talk about things increasingly supplants real experience with things. Just here lies one of the great challenges to education—to seek in every possible way to counteract the unfortunate but inevitable concomitants of urbanization by offering wider opportunities for direct experience in life processes. This same challenge, although in somewhat different form, confronts rural education also. . . . *Why do we teach what we teach?*

How Have Our Schools Responded?

Three major answers are commonly offered as solution to this primary problem of education today. It is noteworthy that each of these three answers reflects not only a different philosophic orientation with consequent varied educational program, but also constitutes a definite stage along the road from the school of yesterday to the school of tomorrow. Let us see how these three outlooks have been interpreted and expressed in our schools. To insure clear contrast, we shall sketch these outlooks starkly, recognizing as we do so that no school now exemplifies in full degree any one of these orientations.

THE ACADEMIC SCHOOL

An unforgettable portrait of the traditional schoolmaster is presented in Dickens' story, *Hard Times*. Here is pictured Professor Gradgrind, a teacher of the old school, an educational traditionalist to the core of his being. When the new girl, daughter of a horse trainer, appeared in his class for the first time, Gradgrind fixed her with an accusing eye and demanded that she define a horse. Define a horse? The girl was confused, stammering, unable to reply. To be sure, she had lived around horses all her life and she well knew how to manage and care for horses. But *defining* horses was something she had never before been asked to do, and so she hung her head in shame while the star pupil completed that assignment to the master's entire satisfaction:

"Horse: Quadruped. Graminiverous. Forty teeth, namely, twenty-four grinders, four eye-teeth and twelve incisive. Sheds coat in spring; in marshy country sheds hoofs, too. Hoofs hard, but requiring to be shod with iron. Age known by marks in mouth."

"Now, girl number twenty," said Mr. Gradgrind, "you know what a horse is." And so she did—in terms of the academic school's demand that pupils define, classify, construe, bound, tabulate, systematize, memorize, verbalize!

Although perhaps typical in Dickens' day, this satirical description is merely a caricature of what we now term the "traditional" school. Nevertheless, the fundamental orientation of that school has not basically changed; emphasis still falls primarily upon verbalistic learnings, logically organized, and imposed upon pupils with little real concern for individual differences in backgrounds, needs, or personal interests. This is true even though recent advances in teacher preparation, together with a slowly changing philosophy and practice of education, have done much to improve traditional schooling during the past quarter of a century.

THE PROGRESSIVE SCHOOL

In course of time a new conception of education emerged, largely in reaction against the academic character and repressive discipline of the academic school. This new conception found practical expression in the child-centered progressive school, and became for many educators the occasion for a veritable crusade. Some of the new devotees even proved themselves as doctrinaire and as fanatical as were any of the traditionalists against whose works they were in utter revolt. Define a horse? What nonsense! Here we try to help children who are interested in horses to comprehend horses, and to express fully their emotional reactions toward horses. We want our children to grow and grow in their conceptions and feelings about horses, until the basic horsiness of horses becomes a living, throbbing, vital aspect of their deepest beings!

Do not distort this emphasis. Progressive education has long since proved itself the most stimulating, most constructive educational philosophy of the past generation. Certainly it is more important to comprehend horses than to define them; more satisfying to express feelings aroused by horses than merely to tabulate and classify horses. But *comprehension* of horses, and *self-expression* about horses, are not sufficient for children who must live out their lives in this troubled twentieth century. These young people need to define and to comprehend, of course, but they must learn also how to *utilize* horses, so to speak, for improved human welfare if they hope to become competent, well-rounded, and tolerably civilized adults.

THE COMMUNITY SCHOOL

Within the past decade, however, progressive education has come of age. The Great Depression and the Global War forced the growing realization that life is real, life is urgent; life is not all sweetness and light in this best of all possible worlds, it is rather a towering problem of precarious existence within an unstable social order. Under the impact of that grave awareness, progressive educators are now carrying their movement forward into the second stage of its historic development. Having first opposed all aspects of the academic Traditional School on the general score that it overemphasized the training of the intellect while neglecting the interests and emotional needs of children, they are now conscious that certain grave defects were inherent in the earlier progressive

Activity School, and also that for all its limitations the Academic School did possess the virtue of systematic curriculum organization. In consequence of this twin realization, progressive educators are now developing the Community School as the best medium through which a higher synthesis of basic educational values may be achieved.

Organized knowledge, systematically mastered, is our greatest intellectual resource for both personal development and social improvement—always providing that such knowledge is functionally organized to meet life's problems and not merely mastered as an end in itself. It is clear also that child interests and self-expressions are splendid educational springboards to be used as such, but that they must never be mistaken for educational goals in themselves. Today we know that *practical school methods* must be evolved out of the psychological study of child nature. We are also now aware that *valid school purposes* can be discovered only through careful sociological analysis of the culture complex and of its ethical demands upon the individuals cradled within it. The Progressive Education Association, now renamed the American Education Fellowship, is officially cognizant of this fact, and has completely abandoned that older, almost anarchistic, emphasis upon the individual *qua* individual which generally characterized the movement in its initial stage. Definitely now emerging is a clear recognition that individual children, unique as each one is in personality and in potentiality, nevertheless possess certain common needs as members of society today and tomorrow. These needs, it is increasingly recognized, can be adequately met only through a functional interactivity between school and community, carefully planned for the achievement of broadly predetermined ends. The Fellowship has recently announced its new orientation partly as follows:

The American Education Fellowship proposes to give greater attention than heretofore to the whole life of the community—local, regional, national, international—within which the schools function and of which they are part.

It believes that, whereas the earlier period of progressive education was marked by strong concern for the interests and capacities of the individual child, and with group activities largely within the school itself, the period we are now entering should be marked by a more intimate and fruitful relationship with parents, interest groups, adult education—in short, with all aspects of the community which surround the child and curriculum, and which largely determine whether the schools are or are not to function as people's schools.

Without abandoning in slightest degree their primary emphasis upon child welfare, progressive educators have become generally aware that children, adolescents, and adults all live in a malfunctioning social order which must be democratically reconstructed, both domestically and internationally, if the majority of the people are to find reasonable opportunity and security in the future. American education stands today upon the very threshold of a wider and far more fruitful orientation than it has ever known: that of the community, life-centered, school.

The accompanying chart presents, in succinct form, a summary of the three basic educational orientations under discussion: the book-centered, child-centered, and life-centered schools. Although the chart may seem fairly obvious, two cautions should be observed when examining it critically.

1. *Oversimplification is necessarily characteristic of graphic contrast.* The data and descriptions should therefore be taken as indicating major emphases rather than definitive analyses. Sample: Even the three major categories themselves must be understood to overlap somewhat; as judged by actual practice, very few American schools today could be classified exclusively in any one category.

2. *Dates indicate the approximate periods of greatest theoretical acceptance by most leading educators,* not the peak period of practical, everyday expression in the nation's classrooms. There is always a considerable time lag between even the widespread acceptance of any theory and its consistent application in general practice. Illustration: Although most prominent educators now accept the philosophy of the life-centered, community school, it is probable that most school systems throughout the country are still predominantly academic and book-centered in their actual, regular teaching procedure.

There is more difference between the Academic School and the Progressive School than there is between the Progressive School and the Community School. The earlier Progressive School programs were largely developed in *reaction against* those of the Academic School; as John Dewey has pointed out, the Progressive School therefore tended in its antagonism to develop its own program negatively—upon the basis of what it opposed, rather than positively, through the constructive development of its own principles.[3] The Community School, on the other hand, represents a

---

[3] See John Dewey, *Experience and Education,* Ch. I. New York: Macmillan, 1938.

AMERICAN SCHOOL ORIENTATIONS IN BRIEF PERSPECTIVE

TYPE OF SCHOOL	ACADEMIC SCHOOL	PROGRESSIVE SCHOOL	COMMUNITY SCHOOL
BASIC ORIENTATION	Book-Centered	Child-Centered	Life-Centered
MAJOR INFLUENCE	to 1910	1920–1930	1940 on
IDEA OF HUMAN NATURE	Innately Evil (original sin)	Innately Good (original perfection)	Innately A-moral (environmental conditioning)
KEYNOTE OF METHOD	Repressive Discipline ("Spare the rod …")	Freedom from Restraint ("Allow natural growth")	Task Responsibility ("We have a job to do.")
BASIC AIMS	Memorization (define, classify)	Comprehension, Expression (understand, emotionalize)	Improved Control (manage, reconstruct)
CURRICULUM PATTERN	"Discipline" Subjects (grammar, history, mathematics, etc.)	Centers of Interest (Eskimos, story of paper, housing, etc.)	Social Processes (getting food, governing, protecting health, etc.)
LEARNING VALUES	All Deferred (no concern for child interests)	All Immediate (no concern for adult needs)	Both Deferred and Immediate (adult concerns become child interests)
RELATION TO LOCAL COMMUNITY	Ignored Completely (classroom is an ivory tower; community is ignored)	Utilized Incidentally (classroom is purified replica of life; community is source of materials and experiences)	Served Systematically (classroom is clearing house for experiences; community is laboratory for discovery and improvement)
TECHNIQUES FOR RELATING SCHOOL AND COMMUNITY	Documentary Materials Audio-visual Aids Resource Visitors	Documentary Materials Audio-visual Aids Resource Visitors Interviews Field Trips Surveys Extended Field Studies Camping	Documentary Materials Audio-visual Aids Resource Visitors Interviews Field Trips Surveys Extended Field Studies Camping Service Projects Work Experiences

positive and logical *development of* the Progressive School, together with intelligent utilization of certain educational values implicit in the program of the Academic School.

Yet the Community School is significantly different from the Progressive School because it operates according to certain additional principles which go much beyond those upon which the Progressive School is based. Although specific community schools differ widely in some respects, they are generally organized around six fundamental principles of purpose and program. For the Community School seeks to:

1. Evolve its purposes out of the interests and needs of the people.
2. Utilize a wide variety of community resources in its program.
3. Practice and promote democracy in all activities of school and community.
4. Build the curriculum core around the major processes and problems of human living.
5. Exercise definite leadership for the planned and cooperative improvement of group living in the community and larger areas.
6. Enlist children and adults in cooperative group projects of common interest and mutual concern.

While the first three of these principles may be found also in the Progressive School, it is the latter three which most significantly distinguish the Community School from its immediate predecessor. For it is these latter three principles which together provide that constructive social orientation whose absence constituted the chief defect of progressive education during the first phase of its development.

Thus has our professional sense of values changed: the *academic school,* with its insistence upon book-knowledge-set-out-to-be-learned, gave way to the *progressive school* with its emphasis upon child-interests-to-be-expressed, which now in turn yields philosophic first place to the *community school* which stresses a human-needs-to-be-met viewpoint. From a book-centered, through a child-centered, and into a life-centered school—this has been the progress of educational thought and experiment during these first four decades of the twentieth century.

What Is the Trend of Our Times?

Increasingly evident becomes the ultimate test of the teacher; in the symbolic words of Joseph K. Hart it is this:

"Does he know the city, old and new, and can he make the child see and understand the city: not in some fragment of the city nor many fragments, but the human community, broken yet still real, the background of his life and character and destiny?"[4]

Does the teacher know the community? Has he shared, under appropriate guidance, in personally satisfying and intellectually creative experiences with the basic community processes as they operate in the locality, region, nation, and world? Has he personally observed, participated in, and contributed toward such elementary experiences of humanity as properly challenge his interest and maturity level? Here rings the clarion call for realism in school education, for first-hand experience with the varied geographic, historical and contemporary factors which shape the human living of today! Here is that same bold challenge which permeates the work and writings of Comenius, Rousseau, Salzman, Pestalozzi, Spencer, Parker, Montessori, Dewey, Hart, Kilpatrick, Harold Rugg, Counts, Horne, Hanna, Carr, and many another prophetic educator from the seventeenth century to the present day. And here also is a basic philosophy of education that has been ignored or attacked in every generation by "ivory-towered" scholars who proudly exalt verbalistic renditions above tested sense experiencing, and who perchance deny the educational validity of the latter because they unconsciously fear its superior attraction over the former.

Although powerful voices are still raised in protest, serious, first-hand community study and participation is today widely considered an essential prerequisite to effective education in any society. Ever more clearly it becomes apparent that school education must be projected out of the sheltered classroom and into the living community which is the child's primary scene of present and future life activity. For education is inherently a social process, and if it is to be realistic, vital, and therefore defensible in the modern democratic world, its curricular program must be framed in terms of continuous, first-hand acquaintance with significant aspects of the physical, biological, and social environment. Thus the test of the teacher today is emphatically this: *Does he know the community* in its multiple historic and contemporary aspects, and can he lead children and youth into an ever-growing understanding, appreciation, and creative participation in that community . . . the inevitable background of his life, character, destiny?

---

[4] *A Social Interpretation of Education,* p. 44. New York: Henry Holt, 1929.

OTHER NATIONS ENCOURAGE FIELD STUDY

In some aspects of life-centered education, particularly that of extended field study, many foreign nations have pioneered far in advance of the United States. Perhaps this has been due to the fact that many of these nations are relatively small, live in close proximity to alien cultures, feel an intense national patriotism, or are genuinely devoted to popular enlightenment. Since several of these countries have encouraged community study programs which far overshadow anything yet attempted on a comparable scale in the United States, it may be worthwhile to note briefly some of the more significant developments which occurred prior to the outbreak of World War II.[5]

Austria. Established municipal lodging houses in the larger cities to provide low-cost eating and sleeping accommodations for visiting school pupils.

Czechoslovakia. The Ministry of Education required each student, as a condition of high school graduation, to have spent at least forty nights in youth hostels (low-cost hotels for overnight stops by young people engaged in extended field study).

England. The School Journey Association numbered 4,000 teacher-members, maintained (1935) 250 youth hostels, and escorted 60,000 school pupils on carefully planned excursions within England, on extended field trips to the Continent, and on cruises to other regions. The Secondary School Travel Trust arranged (1933–39) twelve foreign cruises through which some 15,000 boys and girls visited other countries, not only on the Continent, but also in North America, Africa, and even Australia.

Finland. An official school travel bureau provided information about possible field trips, costs, and accommodations.

France. The Ministry of Education strongly urged school excursions, and willingly permitted various local trips as well as two prolonged field journeys for each child each school year.

Germany. The Youth Hostel Association maintained (1933) more than 2,000 hostels, enrolled 128,000 paid members, and provided 4,600,000 night's lodgings. Of the visitors to the hostels (1926), thirty per cent were elementary school pupils, thirty-two per cent came from secondary schools and universities, while thirty-eight per cent belonged to the young working groups. Both the Weimar Republic and the Third Reich actively encouraged the widespread use of visual aids, excursions, extended field study, service activities, and work experience as effective forms of community-centered education.

Japan. All children went on school excursions during elementary and

---

[5] This information is taken largely from Henry C. Atyeo, *The Excursion as a Teaching Technique*, Ch. II. New York: Bureau of Publications, Teachers College, Columbia University, 1939.

secondary school years. Extended journeys to historic and religious shrines within the country were an integral part of the educative program at all academic levels.

Poland. The government established a special Commission to foster community study through educational tours, and subsidized inns and private home owners to provide inexpensive travel accommodations for students. Such excursion students were required to make careful preparation, conscientious observations, and individual reports of their experiences.

Russia. Eighty tourist stations were established for the accommodation of students and other travelers on their way to various centers of public and educational interest such as historical museums, cooperative farms, and industrial enterprises.

Vital means of education this is, in all these nations! First-hand experience, under competent adult guidance, has proved its technical worth to the youth of many countries abroad. This we must recognize, even as we deplore some of the goals thus sought. Here in the United States, our vast geographic distances, our cultural isolation, our traditions of localism, and our professional unconcern for social processes and problems have all combined to hinder the development of similar extensive life-centered education in this country. Nevertheless, we are witnessing a steadily growing recognition that American schools as well must speedily become more socially realistic if they expect to meet genuine youth needs with full effectiveness.

AMERICAN SCHOOLS BECOME COMMUNITY-MINDED

Just how extensive and influential is this life-centered movement in our American schools today? Although no definitive statement can be offered, it is clear that during the past decade, the study of the community through first-hand experience has received widespread emphasis at all school levels from kindergarten through university. Professional interest in life-centered education developed markedly after about 1935, and continues at a high level despite the war. Three separate and significant indications of that interest may well be noted by way of illustration.

1. *Expansion of the Literature: Thinking It Through*

The number of professional magazine articles devoted to a given field, over a period of years, is a fairly reliable index of that field's significance to the profession at large. It is therefore interesting to note that during the past several years there has been a steady and

marked increase in the number of such articles concerned with
various aspects of community study and participation. Careful
search through fifty leading educational journals, cross-checked by
reference to the *Education Index,* obviously does not exhaust the
evidence even as it discloses the rapid increase in the number of
such articles published during a single twelve-year period:

Years	Articles	Increase Over 1930–33
1930–33	37	—
1934–37	118	219 per cent
1938–41	402	986 per cent

This twelve-year period, here summarized by three-year intervals,
is that of January 1930 through December 1941—roughly from the
beginning of the Great Depression until America's entrance into
the Global War. Twelve years of nearly universal confusion, tension,
strife! Surely it is no accident that the increasing concern of American educators for realistic teaching in these troubled times should
have been reflected in a marked increase of professional articles
devoted to the subject of community-centered education. Many
bulletins, pamphlets, and books in the same field also appeared. In
the literature of their respective fields, many educators were beginning in these years to express their thoughts about realistic
community study.

2. *School Experimentation: Trying It Out*

Thought without subsequent action is both futile and frustrating.
It is no wonder, therefore, that a vast increase in school experimentation with various forms of life-centered education should
have paralleled the literary development just noted. Throughout
the nation, individual teachers, schools, school systems, colleges,
universities, and state education departments have established or
encouraged numerous programs of community study and participation as more or less integral aspects of the educative process under
their control. The scope and significance of these programs is indicated by three recent surveys covering developments throughout
the nation. Although each of these studies provides only a partial
picture of the total field, their reciprocal findings clearly indicate
the extent to which experimentation with life-centered curricula
is under way in the United States.

Public Schools Using the Excursion Technique. The United States
Office of Education found in 1936 that the "excursion" was then being used

as an instructional technique by more than four-fifths of **8800** schools and school systems, representing about two-thirds of the total public elementary and secondary school enrollment in the United States.[6]

High School Departments Utilizing Excursions. Atyeo discovered in 1936 that, in a national sampling of selected high schools using the excursion technique, more than half of these schools scheduled excursions to supplement instruction in science, social studies, and practical arts, while between a fourth and a half of these schools reported excursions in connection with commercial subjects, art, music, and English.[7]

Teacher Education in Community Study Techniques. Olsen found that in 1942 approximately one-third of America's fully accredited institutions educating teachers, made available to them some type of experience with the philosophy, procedures, and problems of life-centered education. Three chief types of experience were offered: *special courses* which emphasized community study methods and techniques, community structure and organization, or community relationships of the school; *aspects of conventional courses* whereby community study was given limited attention in Educational Sociology, General Methods, Rural Education, and so forth; and *informal and extracurricular experiences* such as those involved in scrap collection, gasoline rationing, service in social settlements, leadership of youth groups, and the like.[8]

Limited in scope as are all three of these national surveys, their findings nevertheless suggest that elementary schools, high schools, colleges, and universities throughout the country are beginning to experiment seriously with the possibilities of relating school instruction to community life in direct fashion. In many significant programs at every academic level, American teachers are trying out their thoughts about community study and participation.

3. *Decreed Program: Compelling Its Growth*

After a new educational development has been tested experimentally and adjudged valuable, state education authorities are likely to prescribe its inclusion in the professional curriculum for prospective teachers. Such prescription in the area of community study occurred in 1942, when the New York State Board of Regents adopted four major Criteria as standards to be used by the State Department of Education in appraising institutional programs of teacher education within the state. One Criterion requires, in part, that future teachers of the academic subjects in New York State high schools shall have developed

---

[6] *School Use of Visual Aids*, U. S. Office of Education Bulletin 1938, No. 4, pp. 23–25.

[7] Henry C. Atyeo, *The Excursion as a Teaching Technique*, Ch. IV.

[8] Edward G. Olsen, "National Survey of Teacher Education in Community Study Techniques," *Educational Record*, October 1943, pp. 421–35.

"An appreciation of the nature of contemporary society and the role of the schools in the sound promotion of the enduring interests of this society. This implies a much larger measure of actual participation in community life than has been characteristic of either teachers or young people attending school. . . .

"Such a study of society cannot be realistic if it is confined to the reading of books. It calls for active participation by the student in community or regional life and close contact with various representative public and private agencies. The resources and institutions of the local community or region should be used as a laboratory for the study of society. . . . Prospective teachers should be encouraged to understand measures which are taken to bring school and community into fruitful forms of cooperation and mutual service."[9]

Thus, does any important educational movement typically develop: local experiments are made and reported in the literature; these accounts inspire other experiments which, in turn, are described in print to become further additions to the literature and thereby stimulate improved experimentation elsewhere, and so on. Consciousness of need and programs designed to meet that need develop reciprocally until finally both are officially recognized, sanctioned, and even prescribed by responsible educational authorities. In precisely this manner has life-centered education developed in the United States during the past decade.

How Shall We Think of Life-Centered Education?

Out of all this thinking and experimentation, have emerged at least five major conceptions of what life-centered education should do.[10] These five conceptions are not mutually exclusive, but, broadly considered, represent the progression of emphases developed by leading community-minded educators during the past two or three decades. Viewpoints 1, 2, and 3, it will be observed, draw the community into the school; while viewpoints 4 and 5 take the school into the community.

FIVE VIEWPOINTS

1. **The school should operate as an educational center for adults.** Since education is a life-long, continuous process, the use of the school plant and facilities should be available to adults as well as to children.

---

[9] *Criteria for Teacher Education,* Committee on Teacher Education of the Association of Colleges and Universities of the State of New York, 1942.

[10] The material in this and the following section is taken largely from the author's article "Community and School" in the *Encyclopedia of Modern Education,* pp. 171–73. Used by permission.

There, in late afternoons and evenings, adults of the community should find their educational and social center wherein cultural subjects, arts and crafts, vocational training, civic forums, gymnasium, cafeteria, and the like are open to them.

2. **The school should utilize community resources to invigorate the conventional program.** In order to vitalize the curriculum and teaching methods, give depth of meaning to instruction, and provide for direct as well as vicarious learning experiences, the school should survey the educative resources of its community, catalog them, and utilize them when appropriate for its established educational purposes.

3. **The school should center its curriculum in a study of community structure, processes, and problems.** Every community is a microcosm of human experience, since within it go on the basic processes and related problems of making a living, sharing in citizenship, exchanging ideas, securing education, adjusting to people, maintaining life and health, enjoying beauty, meeting religious needs, engaging in recreation, and the like. The core curriculum should therefore be organized around a direct study of the local and regional community's physical setting, organization, class and caste structure, basic activities, climate of opinion, and needs and problems as these and similar factors affect individual and group welfare.

4. **The school should improve the community through participation in its activities.** Students, teachers, and civic-minded laymen should cooperatively plan and execute various service projects of a genuinely civic nature. Thus, youth will learn that the community has need of its service; and the community will discover that youth's contribution to the general welfare can be at once important, intelligent, and effective.

5. **The school should lead in coordinating the educative efforts of the community.** Since all life is educative, the role of the school in the total educational process is primarily a coordinating and a residual one. The school, therefore, should lead all the educational agencies of the community into an organized and cooperative program for the more effective education of youth and adults in school and out, and should itself provide only those aspects of a desirable education which people in such a program do not obtain elsewhere, or receive in insufficient degree.

Five outlooks! Five conceptions of what the community-minded school should do! Yet all too frequently we have become so enamoured of one conception—or so blind to possibilities in the others—that we ignore or neglect the remaining four. Some teachers, for example, are much concerned about the effective utilization of available resources (Orientation 2), but remain oblivious to the psychological and social significance of cooperative community service projects (Orientation 4). Other teachers, enthusiastically utilizing resources and developing service projects, are unaware that the school plant itself might well serve some genuine community needs (Orientation 1), that their own efforts would prove much more effective if coordinated with those of non-school educative agencies (Orientation 5), or that the school program itself might well be organized accordingly (Orientation 3). Rare indeed is the school in which all five outlooks are utilized in appropriate balance.

BALANCE AND INSIGHT ARE NEEDED

Although one or more of these five approaches to the community may be found in many conventional schools, it is only the Community School which is sufficiently functional and versatile to utilize them all in a balanced manner. Such a school operates as a full-time educational center for the entire community population, utilizes all appropriate community resources for instructional purposes, centers its curriculum in the community itself, actively serves the locality through direct attack upon some of its pressing problems, and leads in coordinating democratically all possible community agencies toward the common goal of more effective education in that region. These things it does because its supporters realize that education is basically a social process; that educational forms and functions must respond to the changing needs of human beings; that democratic education must be able as well as willing to honor its fundamental obligation of helping people to live more effectively and happily, both as individuals and as members of interdependent social groups.

Historically viewed, the great virtue of the academic school lies in its systematic organization of subject-matter; that of the progressive school is its driving concern for the all-around development of the individual child; that of the emergent Community School appears to be its emphasis upon social reconstruction through cooperative effort democratically organized. *All three* emphases, each transmuted in terms of present needs, must be maintained in the new school of tomorrow. Not otherwise are the twin educational goals of individual self-development and democratic social reconstruction likely to be successfully achieved.

Nor is this emphasis upon life-centered education necessarily a narrow or a provincial one. Visionless, indeed, is he who fails to perceive that in our time the local community is inextricably bound up with the regional, national, and world communities, and must be both studied and improved accordingly. Far from being provincial, therefore, the Community School which *begins* its operation in the service area of the school is *ultimately* as broad as the earth in its developing concerns and services. If it does not so expand and extend its vision, it is likely to be narrowly oriented at the very period in history when world-mindedness is so desperately essential. The local community is the intellectual starting point and the social service area, but it must always be understood as a point of departure and not as the ultimate terminal. Local community study and service is an intellectual starting point; it should usually be seriously related to social processes in the larger areas of region, nation, and the world at large.

Opportunity to Advance

Democracy as we have known it developed within a societal framework which was essentially agrarian, rural, and nationalistic. Under these conditions, it was not especially dangerous to society for our schools to emphasize individual success above all else— either through leisure class "culture" identified largely as book learning about the past, or through practical training in vocational skills whereby working class children might hope to climb higher upon the ladder of pecuniary success. This educational divorce between personal culture and vocational efficiency not only reflected the basic class structure of society, it also left recipients of liberal education unprepared to earn their livings (save as teachers) even as it doomed those skilled in vocational pursuits to a dwarfed intellectual life.

Beneath much of our political-social-economic confusion and strife today lies this fundamental yet wholly artificial dichotomy between liberal and practical education, between ideas and activities, between academic theories and their applications in everyday affairs. It is often evident that the most highly schooled amongst us are the most inexperienced in practical matters, while among the most powerful "practical" men are those most lacking in social vision and in a sense of personal responsibility for the common welfare.

It is only through realistic—and therefore through life-centered —education that this great gulf between thinking and doing, between school and community, can be permanently bridged and thereafter forgotten. And unless that gulf is speedily eliminated, democracy in the Global Air Age may not long endure. In a highly technological, urban, interdependent world society, the preservation of democracy even as a form of government necessitates the development of broad social understanding, humane personal attitudes, and specific civic skills upon the part of most citizens, regardless of their origins, status, and prospects. Such social-civic *competence,* be it noted, can be achieved only through intelligently-directed and personally satisfying experiences with the persistent processes and problems of living on this planet.

Although popular interest and school concern is properly centered upon the present war effort, there is every indication that even in wartime—and especially in wartime!—serious community study and participation by America's youth is rapidly increasing. And increase it must if American schools are to meet the social and psychological needs of youth today and in future years of political, economic, and social reconstruction.

The civic and educational values achieved by students in wartime through scrap collection, agricultural service, Victory Corps activities, intercultural projects, part-time work experience, global conceptions of strategy and organization, and the like must not be lost with the end of military hostilities. During World War I, the gulf between school and community was widely bridged in similar fashion, but only for that war's duration. There was then no enduring appreciation of the vital educational values inherent in continued school-community cooperation, and after 1918 the schools quickly reverted to academic isolation. Like the nation, the schools speedily returned to a socially disastrous "normalcy."

Today it is widely recognized that the persistent processes and problems of human living in local, regional, national and even international communities should constitute the core curriculum of the modern democratic school; that the ideas, attitudes, and skills necessary for successful living must be learned through active participation in the solving of significant personal and group problems; and that education becomes truly effective as it identifies individual and community problems as such, and then cooperatively attempts to deal with them constructively.[11] Much has been done during the past decade to implement these educational ideals in practical school programs. Although life-centered education has demonstrated its impressive possibilities, we must ever be conscious that these are only *possibilities;* that they will prove disappointing or even disastrous unless soberly developed by competent professional leadership. Life-centered education must not become such

---

[11] See Samuel Everett (ed.), *The Community School,* p. 461. New York: Appleton-Century, 1938.

a virtual fetish in this generation as did the child-centered school during the 1920's!

In the postwar world there will be a vast and deep concern for international education to hold and fully win the peace. Yet such education, as it develops, had better be far more *intimate and humanly realistic* than it was after World War I. It must include many first-hand friendly contacts with nationals of many countries, as well as carefully-planned intercultural relationships between divergent national and racial groups in this country. Unless these *personal experiences* are widely developed, there is real danger that postwar international education may once more be bookish and largely verbalistic.

The signs of the times are clear. They indicate simply that the community study and participation movement of the 1930's must be fully integrated with the intercultural and international movement of the 1940's. Only thus, and in no other way, can the American school make its fullest contribution to the winning of both war and peace in our time. Huxley has well said that "the great end of life is not knowledge, but action." Shall we not agree that the same is true of lifelike education?

SELECTED REFERENCES

Americans All: Studies in Intercultural Education. Sponsored by the Department of Supervisors and Directors of Instruction of the National Education Association, the National Council of Teachers of English, and the Society for Curriculum Study. Washington: National Education Association, 1942. Depicts the social necessity for improving intercultural relationships within the United States, describes twenty unusual school programs toward that end, identifies the role of the leader and the basic issues involved, and includes annotated bibliographies.

Apple, Joe A., "Culture, Environment and Education." *School and Society* 55: 683–87 (June 20, 1942). Urges that schools readjust their programs in the light of what cultural anthropology, ecology, organismic psychology, and pragmatic philosophy have discovered in recent years.

Barnard, Eunice F., "Food Joins the Three R's." *Survey Graphic* 32:428–31 (Nov. 1943). In the one-room schools of a Kentucky county, the basic school skills are now taught in terms of good food and better nutrition, goats and garden projects. In Vermont and Florida similar rigidly controlled experiments are under way to determine to what extent schools can actually raise living standards in their communities.

Clapp, Elsie R., *Community Schools in Action.* New York: The Viking Press, 1939. Detailed description of two experiments in developing a public school program, from kindergarten through adult education, adjusted to the needs and based upon the resources of the community. Includes a complete record of the curriculum for every grade.

Cook, Lloyd A., *Community Foundations of Education.* New York: McGraw-Hill,

1938. A textbook in educational sociology, stressing the relationship of the school and the community with particular reference to the community influences affecting youth.

Cook, Lloyd A., "Educating for Community Action and Unity." *Social Education* 6:304–08 (Nov. 1942). Shows how the age of cities and specialization has impersonalized human living, indicates the nature of needed community action today, and suggests what the schools may do to educate for community leadership.

Cook, Lloyd A. "School and Community." In Walter S. Monroe (ed.), *Encyclopedia of Educational Research*, pp. 1000–05. New York: Macmillan, 1941.

Dewey, John, *The School and Society*. Chicago: University of Chicago Press, 1910, rev. ed. Excellent background reading on the basic philosophy of community-centered education.

Dunn, Fannie W., "An Evaluation of the Educational Movement to Integrate the School and the Community." In Department of Rural Education, National Education Association, *Community Resources in Rural Schools*, Ch. VIII. Washington: The Association, 1939. Documents forty years development in the school-community movement, with particular reference to rural education.

Educational Policies Commission, *Education for All American Youth*. Washington: the Commission, 1944. Describes ideal rural and urban schools as they might and can be developed within the next few years. The essential orientation is that of the life-centered, community school.

Epler, Stephen E., "The Teacher, the School, and the Community." Washington: American Council on Education, 1941. An annotated directory of organizations and agencies concerned with community problems, and a selected bibliography covering books and pamphlets, motion pictures, and magazine articles.

Everett, Samuel (ed.), *The Community School*. New York: D. Appleton-Century, 1938. The philosophy of community education, the programs and principles of nine functioning community schools in both rural and urban regions, a survey of additional community programs, and an analysis of the programs in terms of basic issues.

Ferguson, Charles W., "Schools Out." *Readers Digest* 28:105–08 (March 1936). Popular account of how school excursions and extended field studies developed in Europe. Some American long trips are mentioned.

Fowler, Burton P., "Education for the Future." *Parents' Magazine* 28: 2: 17 plus. (Feb. 1944). Characterizes the community school of tomorrow, stressing community action, work experience, mental health clinics, community use of foreign languages, science, mathematics, the arts, and so forth.

Hanna, Paul R., "Capitalizing Educational Resources of the Community." *National Elementary Principal* 21:162–66 (April 1942). Sketches objectives of each grade in the elementary school, noting in each case what community resources would be useful for each grade.

Hart, Joseph K., *A Social Interpretation of Education*. New York: Henry Holt, 1929. Historical and philosophic background for understanding the traditional, activity, and community school viewpoints.

John Dewey Society, *Democracy and the Curriculum*, Ch. XIV. Third Yearbook. New York: D. Appleton-Century, 1939. Envisions a new school designed for the finest individual and community development, and states the general program of such a school.

Kilpatrick, William H., "Principles of Community Learning." In Samuel Everett (ed.), *The Community School*, Introduction. New York: D. Appleton-Century, 1938. States the more important principles of learning upon which community-centered education is built. Considers the social nature of the self, the needs of the culture, group interests and community enterprises, democratic education and leadership.

Krey, A. C., "The World At Home." In Ruth West (ed.), *Utilization of Community Resources in the Social Studies:* Ninth Yearbook, National Council for the Social Studies, pp. 173–81. Cambridge, Mass.: The Council, 1938. Personal documentation of the way in which a local community must be seen and understood in its historic development and as part of a modern world community.

Mitchell, Morris R., "Taking Dewey Seriously." *Progressive Education* 15:110–17 (Feb. 1938). A vivid description of the Lincoln School community participation project in Georgia, explained in terms of simple educational philosophy. Extended student comments are included. .

Olsen, Edward G., "Community and School." In Harry N. Rivlin and Herbert Schueler (eds.), *Encyclopedia of Modern Education,* pp. 171–73. New York: The Philosophical Library, 1943.

Olsen, Edward G., "Cro-Magnon Education: Then and Now." *New York State Education* 30:662–63, 714–15 (June 1943). Somewhat satirical account of how education was life-centered in pre-historic times, used extended field study, work experience, service projects, surveys, excursions, etc., but then entered into a formal school of words as civilization developed.

Parker District High School Faculty and the Staff of the Southern Association Study, "Parker High School Serves Its People." Greenville, South Carolina: Parker District Schools, 1942. Illustrated pamphlet detailing the philosophy, program and planning of the Parker District community school.

Pickett, Clarence E., "What Is a Community?" *Progressive Education* 15:91–96 (Feb. 1938). Any defensible society must maximize personal values. The old rural community did so; the modern city does not. Therefore the school of today must stress group cohesion as well as individual development.

Pierce, Paul R., *Developing a High School Curriculum.* New York: American Book Co., 1942. Developmental account of how the Wells High School in Chicago changed from a traditional into a community-centered school.

Reavis, William C. (ed.), *The School and the Urban Community.* Chicago: University of Chicago Press, 1942. Fifteen papers read at the Eleventh Annual Conference of Administrative Officers of Public and Private Schools, July 1942. Discusses numerous aspects of the school-community problem, and lists many vital issues involved.

"Schools Awake: A Cooperative Community Program in Van Buren County, Michigan." Battle Creek, Michigan: the W. K. Kellogg Foundation, 1942. Illustrated brochure showing how the citizens of one community moved toward cooperative solution of their school problems.

Spears, Harold, *The Emerging High-School Curriculum,* Chs. IV, VIII, IX, X. New York: American Book Co., 1940. Describes community-school developments in four well-known schools in Kentucky, Michigan, Tennessee, and Indiana.

Tidwell, R. E., "Planning Improvement in Rural Living Through the Schools." Studies in Education No. 4. University, Alabama: Bureau of Educational Research, College of Education, 1943. Reports on exploratory study of possibilities for improving living among rural people through the agency of the public schools.

Tyler, Ralph W., "Relations of the Urban Community and the Modern School." *Elementary School Journal* 43:14–22 (Sept. 1942). Characteristics of urbanism; implications for the city school's program, community contacts, and staff organization.

Vickery, William E., and Stewart G. Cole, *Intercultural Education in American*

Schools. New York: Harper, 1943. Proposed objectives and methods; suggested programs, materials, techniques and basic concepts.

Whitelaw, John B., "The School and Its Community." Brockport, New York: The Author, 1940. Distributed through the University of Chicago Bookstore. Introduction to school-community planning. Emphasizes philosophy, community analysis, school self-survey, study of pupils, effective action.

Wood, Hugh B., "The School Curriculum and Community Life." Eugene: University of Oregon. Philosophy of learning, principles of curriculum development, proposed educational program.

Woodward, Julian L., "Is the Community Emphasis Overdone in School Programs?" *Harvard Educational Review* 11:473–80 (Oct. 1941). Warns against the dangers of localism in community study, pointing out that world problems are more important than national problems, national problems more important than local problems, that schools must retain perspective in their teaching.

CHAPTER 2
Foundations and Goals

Traditional notions of how to make a school program are happily in flux today. Many teachers are literally reversing their conventional ways of thinking about this tremendous problem. In the past, they have usually thought somewhat along this line: *How can I teach my subject-field more effectively? What can I do to motivate student interest in the things I teach?* But now, under the challenge of modern psychology and the impact of this critical era in human history, they are beginning to ask instead: *What abilities and motives must people acquire in order to become well-rounded, efficient, and ethical participators in the ongoing life of a democratic society? How can I help people develop those necessary abilities?* This is indeed a reversal in basic orientation—precisely because its point of departure is the discovery of essential child, youth, and adult needs, rather than a projective defense of some logically organized academic field of knowledge. This new educational orientation values organized subject-matter quite as much as does the old, but it insists that appropriate subject-matter be used as a tool for more effective living (including deepest appreciations), not merely mastered as an exercise in mental discipline or in academic learning.

In terms of the community education movement, these two orientations may be expressed as follows:

TRADITIONAL PROGRAM (SUBJECT–CENTERED OUTLOOK)		MODERN PROGRAM (LIFE–CENTERED OUTLOOK)	
Utilize community resources to enrich and vitalize the teaching of conventional subjects such as	Geography Science Social Studies Literature Home Economics etc.	Lead students to study and serve the community in its varied	geographic, scientific, sociological, literary, home-making, etc.,	aspects, processes and relationships

Thus, it is evident that life-centered education is not just another device for enriching the traditional curriculum, for motivating the slothful student, or for making the teacher's job more interesting.

Although any well-managed program of community study and participation achieves these values in large measure, its primary purpose is far more comprehensive. It aims at nothing less than eventual organization of the whole school program around the general concept of the life-centered, community school. This broad concept, we should note, springs directly from the best we know today about the philosophy and science of modern education. Let us see how this can be.

What Are the Basic Criteria of Democratic Education Today?

Any program designed for the adequate education of youth must satisfy two fundamental criteria of value:

(a) **As content** (what shall we teach?) it must provide for the development of those abilities requisite to successful adjustment of the individual within his changing culture, and

(b) **As method** (how shall we teach?) it must operate according to known principles of effective learning.

The measure of genuine success achieved by any educational program will depend upon the degree to which that program satisfies these basic social and psychological criteria. Let us therefore examine the educational implications and imperatives of each in turn.

CRITERION OF CONTENT: SOCIAL REALISM

Ours is an age of instability, an era of universal stress and strife, a period of cataclysmic political, economic, and social upheaval unparalleled in history. Surely now if ever, it is clear that democratic education—viewed as consciously promoted behavior changes—is the only enduring basis for peaceful progress, whether in a tiny hamlet or throughout the whole world. The Damoclean menace of our age is not technological but social; freedom and security in this century have been threatened by no defect of Nature but simply by man's collective failure to establish human civilization upon an enduring basis of universal justice and hence of plenty and peace for all. If such an ideal civilization as we envision is ever to be built upon this planet, it will have to be underwritten by appropriate education at all academic levels in all nations around the globe.

School youth in particular must come to know that widespread unemployment and poverty existed in practically all industrialized nations during the 1930's primarily because the business arrangements of the time were not capable of widely distributing the relative abundance of the economic goods our modern technology was able to produce. Youth must realize that fascist aggression was able to terrorize mankind during the 1940's largely because the existing international system of sovereign political nations was incompatible with the planetary economy our world technology had created. Unless young people in this nation and abroad come to understand that modern poverty and war with their attendant evils are rooted in the lag of man's social institutions behind his technical achievements, they will remain intellectually baffled, emotionally frustrated, civically cynical.

Such is the great challenge to liberal education in our time. Somehow teachers must inflame youth with a burning belief that the obligation to diminish this social lag is their own; that the momentous civic opportunity of their generation is to invent new democratic patterns of domestic and international organization, so that the present threat of technology may become, instead, the universal realization of its glorious promise. Young people everywhere must develop an effective demand that man's technology be used for his mutual welfare and not for his exploitation or destruction. Unless youth can be motivated to help build a democratic world-wide culture that is as rational in its social arrangements as it already has become in its technological developments, they will remain uncomprehending victims of their own machines.

Imaginative young people, who frankly face these problems of our divided culture, know full well that the nineteenth century tradition of education as "mental discipline" or as "personal culture" is today inadequate and even tragic. Equally so is our growing twentieth century emphasis upon vocational training of a narrow type. If the thirty year sequence of World War I, Communism, Depression, Fascism, and World War II has taught us nothing else, it has surely written in letters of blood and tears the sternest educational imperative of our era: *learn to live as a human race together, or learn to die!*

It is increasingly clear that the American schools of our time must become speedily, directly, and intelligently concerned with major human values. For even when this global war is won on the field of battle, civilization will still be confronted by two gigantic and interrelated problems beside which all others—even that of war itself—pale into minor significance. Domestic economic reconstruction and international political reorganization—*these* are the overwhelming issues of our time! They are issues which must be faced and settled through democratic procedures, or else the very conditions which give them birth will continue to menace the existence of democracy everywhere. As two eminent educators have well phrased them, these are the problems which starkly confront each of us living today:

THE DOMESTIC ECONOMIC PROBLEM	THE INTERNATIONAL POLITICAL PROBLEM
"This is 'the American Problem': to bring forth on this continent—in the form of a coöperative commonwealth—the civilization of abundance, democratic behavior, and integrity of expression and of beauty which is now potentially available."[1]	"When you put aggressive nationalism behind the conception of the totalitarian State in a technological age, you have potentially the most destructive force the world has ever seen arrayed against civilization."[2]
—HAROLD RUGG	—CHRISTIAN GAUSS

Here are the most pressing social realities of this twentieth century! Implicit in them are more bitterly divisive political issues than any our people have faced since the Civil War. Yet faced and mastered they must be, for in our kind of highly industrialized, interdependent world there can be no enduring security for any person anywhere until the Four Freedoms are the common heritage of all men everywhere.

This is why the public school in our democracy dare not remain book-centered or child-centered; like organized society itself, the democratic school must speedily become genuinely life-centered in its basic orientation, outlook, purposes, curriculum, and methods. For today as never before in all human history, the *essential study of mankind is man*—his individual perplexities, his group procedures, his social problems. Now at last we must take ourselves and our students out of the crumbling ivory tower into the living community, there to study man and his problems in ways that are realistic, functional, vital!

All that we know today about the major social forces of our times drives home our first inescapable truth: that in a democratic, industrialized, interdependent civilization the people's school must prepare the people's children for more effective individual and collective living through continuing personal experience with the persistent processes of living. Not otherwise shall we satisfy the

---

[1] The John Dewey Society, *Democracy and the Curriculum*, p. 27. New York: Appleton-Century, 1939.

[2] *The New York Times,* Feb. 24, 1939.

first criterion of the democratic school: that its curriculum content be socially realistic.

CRITERION OF METHOD: PSYCHOLOGICAL VALIDITY

During the past thirty years, a host of practical experiments and scientific studies have provided, in their total significance, new and objective bases for our present ideas of human growth, development, and learning. Without becoming technical, let us simply summarize the most significant of these findings as follows: [3]

BASIC NATURE OF THE CHILD ...who therefore...	LEARNS BEST UNDER THESE CONDITIONS
1. The child is by nature dynamic	
Physical, emotional, and intellectual activity is natural and therefore satisfying to him; inactivity is definitely annoying.	His learning situations should call out appropriate motor, mental, and aesthetic activity on his part.
2. The child is a whole being	
The physical, mental and emotional aspects of his life are closely interrelated, and cannot actually be separated from each other.	His educational experiences should be so integrated as to provide for regular development and harmonious expression of all his powers.
3. The child is an intelligent being	
Thinking, investigating, questioning, discovering, and experimenting are all instinctive and hence are basically satisfying to him.	He needs constant opportunity to analyze problems, plan appropriate courses of action, execute his plans, and appraise the results.
4. The child lives in a culture complex	
His central outlooks, attitudes, ideals, interests, and purposes are all conditioned within him by the total environmental background out of which he comes.	His school experiences should lead him to analyze and to surmount the limitations of the particular group mores controlling his behavior.
5. The child is a creature of habit	
As his varied activities become routinized, they become habitual, and consequently satisfying as long as they remain adequate as adjustment forms. New learning occurs only when the habitual response is blocked or proved inadequate; that is, under the stimulus of some tension, felt need, or some perception of a problem situation.	His learning experiences should be such that they cannot be mastered upon the basis of previous habit alone, but require instead a creative reconstruction of experience in a new patterning in order to overcome the annoyance of the confronting tension.

[3] Seven of the ten following italicized statements were originally presented in the report of the Committee on a Democratic Method of Education at the Eighth International Conference of the New Education Fellowship. See *Progressive Education,* October 1941, pp. 323–24.

6. *The child is creative*

Since he is a dynamic, intelligent, and therefore imaginative being, it is natural that creative self-expression—through varied media—of his individual ideas and feelings should prove highly satisfying to him.

He needs adequate and constant opportunity to express artistically those surging emotions and gripping ideas which from time to time possess him deeply.

7. *The child has interests and purposes*

The child's own interests and purposes function as basic drives to his physical, mental, and emotional activity; as goals they motivate his behavior at all times.

His school experiences should be those in which he can take keen interest because they serve both to meet his felt needs and to recognize the present purposing in his own acts.

8. *The child's experiences give meaning to his language*

Words have real meaning to a person only as his own experiences provide accurate interpretations of those words. If a child is taught words without previous experiential content to give them meaning, he is acquiring verbalisms only.

His learning situations should provide for preliminary first-hand experiences with reality, followed by suitable vicarious or linguistic experiences to further interpret, clarify, and reinforce the meaning of those initially direct experiences.

9. *The child's growth is related to his maturity*

To a considerable degree, the integrity of a child's perceptions, viewpoints, attitudes, appreciations, ideals, and motives is dependent upon the extent of his physiological, social, and emotional maturation.

The extent of his given responsibilities and permitted freedoms should be consistent with the degree of his development toward true adult maturity.

10. *The child is learning to live in society*

For better or for worse, the child must learn to make at least minimum adjustment to the demands of modern life upon him, must learn to behave as a social being in such manner as will most fully benefit himself and others.

He needs constant stimulus and opportunity to make wise decisions, assume personal responsibilities, and cooperate constructively with others for common ends and public welfare.

All that we know today about the nature, growth, and learning abilities of human beings accentuates a second axiom: that effective learning situations must be those which enable the learner, acting as a dynamic, unified, intelligent, creative, and purposing being, to interact constructively with all the wholesome experiences of life to be found in the physical, biological, and social environment. Not otherwise shall we satisfy this second criterion of the democratic school: that its teaching methods be psychologically valid.

Social realism and psychological validity—basic standards by which to appraise the modern American school! That school—whether it be public or private, elementary, secondary, college or university—must successfully meet these two essential criteria if it hopes to serve the needs of youth in this troubled world. How, then, does the community-centered program satisfy these criteria, thereby proving itself a vital development in sound education rather than merely the latest pedagogical fad?

How Does Life-Centered Education Meet These Criteria?

The life-centered educational program—always provided that it is carefully planned and soundly administered—meets both social and psychological criteria with considerable success. This fact becomes apparent as we examine the close relationship which exists between the basic principles of democratic teaching and their expression in any well-managed community education program. These principles of effective teaching, it is well to note, are those which insistently emerge out of the social and psychological conclusions summarized above.

How Teaching Principles are Utilized in Community-Centered Education

Basic Principles of Successful Teaching at Any Academic Level

How Community-Centered Programs Utilize These Principles

(1) **Educate the whole child.** The child is not just a mind to be instructed: he is a physically, socially, emotionally, ethically, *and* intellectually growing person. If his powers are to develop in proper harmony, he needs learning activities which challenge his emerging interests and abilities in all the areas of his growth.

Integrated learning occurs. Well-planned community study projects necessarily involve not only intellectual understanding but, simultaneously, social poise, emotional control, physical activity, aesthetic response, and bodily skills. Pupils who explore a tenement house or a coal mine, for instance, develop all these aspects of the personality in unconscious integration.

(2) **Keep the program informal, flexible, and democratic.** Children are restless and need confidence in their own powers and achievements. They therefore need every chance to ask questions freely, confer with other children informally, share in planning their individual and group activities, carry personal responsibility for group projects, help to judge critically the results of their efforts. This requires that the entire classroom atmosphere be friendly and democratic as well as informal and flexible, and that children not be held in unfair competition with standards of performance beyond their possible ability to achieve.

Informality, flexibility, and democracy are essentials of any program. Interviews, excursions, surveys, service projects, camping, work experiences, and extended field studies cannot be standardized from pupil to pupil, from class to class, or from year to year. Every child who participates can discover facts and report findings valuable to the group, and hence, builds confidence in himself as he knowingly contributes to the advancement of the project. Group planning, shared responsibility, and mutual evaluation are possible in the highest degree.

Basic Principles of Successful Teaching at Any Academic Level	How Community-Centered Programs Utilize These Principles

Capitalize upon present pupil interests. It is of utmost importance that the teacher first discover what interests and purposes his students already have, and then use these drives as springboards to further desirable learning. Thus, limited interests may develop into wider interests, undesirable purposes into praiseworthy purposes, and the child's educational growth be best promoted.

(3) **Every child is interested in his own community.** He may not be much concerned with irregular verbs or with the life cycle of *bacillus typhosis,* but he is considerably interested in telling friends about his next-door playmate who is ill with typhoid fever. Beginning with these immediate interests, it is not hard for the alert teacher to stimulate class concern about the fact that the city does not inspect the milk supply, and that well-written letters of protest might be sent to the health commissioner and to the editor of the local newspaper.

Let motivation be intrinsic. Most learners find few desirable incentives in the traditional system of school marks, honors, and penalties. Their most moving incentives are those of real life itself: to explore the new and the interesting, to associate actively with other people, to manipulate and construct things, to compare opinions about matters which seem important, and to express one's self artistically.

(4) **The keynote is—"Let's find out!"** Let's find out where that frog lives . . . what a police reporter does . . . how to interview an employer . . . Life-centered projects, such as these, which actually develop out of students' interests, concerns, and needs, require little artificial stimulation for their initiation and development. The operating incentives are those which are natural in people's lives and fundamental in their interests; they are definitely not artificial or academic.

Make learning experiences vivid and direct. Generalizations will be mere verbalisms unless they are based upon meaningful personal experiences. That is why children need constant opportunity for motion pictures, radio programs, excursions, interviews, service projects, work experience, and the like. Through such media the children receive more concrete, interesting, and meaningful educational experiences than they are likely to receive through the printed page alone.

(5) **First-hand contact is ultimate realism.** "We read about slum housing in our textbook," remarked one student as she stood in the backyard of a legally condemned but still-occupied tenement, "but I never believed anything could be as bad as this! Why doesn't somebody *do* something about it?" Pupils who thus experience slum housing, or who watch a plasterer at work, or who visit the morgue to see what a drunken driver can do to himself are learning vivid lessons they will doubtless never forget.

Stress problem-solving, the basis of functional learning. Real education comes about when children intelligently attack real problems, think them through, and then do something to solve them. Every chance should therefore be given for pupils to discover, define, attack, solve, and interpret both personal and social problems within the limitations of their own present abilities, interests, and needs.

(6) **Real life abounds in problems.** These problems may be vast or trivial, personal or social, intimate or remote, but all of them are important to some people in some degree. Pupils who visit a public health clinic to learn the truth about the symptoms, detection, and treatment of tuberculosis are gaining valuable experience in problem-solving; so also are those who climb to the roof to visualize better the local village's transit development.

Basic Principles of Successful Teaching at Any Academic Level	*How Community-Centered Programs Utilize These Principles*
Provide for the achievement of lasting pupil satisfactions. Students who dislike their work learn little from it, and retain that little briefly. Every effort should therefore be made to maintain learning situations wherein children will achieve genuine success, find personal satisfaction therein, and thus grow intellectually, emotionally, socially.	(7) **Possible satisfactions are many and varied.** Children who discover for themselves how an elevator works, who aid in constructing a health exhibit for the county fair, or who help a neighboring farmer terrace his hillside can experience deep emotional satisfaction as well as increased intellectual understanding. Such projects bring feelings of success; success is satisfying; satisfaction brings increased enthusiasm; enthusiasm leads to further activity of the similarly creative and hence basically satisfying nature.
Let the curriculum mirror the community. Learning situations must reflect life in the pupil's own community if they are to be most effective. Since little transfer of training between diverse situations can be expected, it is essential that the core of the required curriculum directly reflect the basic social processes and problems of the community, rather than the logical subject areas of the traditional school, or the socially insignificant interest-units of many activity schools. Not otherwise will the curriculum relate functionally to the personal interests, experiences, and needs of young people today.	(8) **The community is used as a living laboratory.** Within every community, large or small, urban or rural, go on the basic social processes of getting a living, preserving health, sharing in citizenship, rearing children, seeking amusement, expressing religious impulses, and the like. When pupils study familiar though actually unknown processes, develop intellectual perspectives, improve emotional outlooks and serviceable personal skills as they observe and participate in these processes, they are discovering for themselves not only the problems they face, but also the resources they can utilize in attacking those problems. Thus life, as well as the school, becomes truly educative in their eyes.

Such are the broad and basic principles of democratic teaching upon which modern, functional education is based. But what, more specifically still, does the life-centered program seek to accomplish? Since true education must be defined in terms of behavior changes, just what kinds of educational achievement does the community-minded teacher hope to motivate in his students?

What Goals Are Sought?

To answer this query, let us note part of a recent statement analyzing three interrelated aims of modern community study and participation—aims which are likewise central to the philosophy of democratic education today:

1. UNDERSTANDING OUR EVOLVING CULTURE

"In every community, the basic social arrangements of our way of life are found in operation, and in each are reflected the climate of opinion and the value standards which dominate American life. While tools, techniques, ideologies, and values may vary somewhat from community to community, the mobility of population, the automobile, the metropolitan newspaper, the national periodical, the radio, and the motion picture have produced a large degree of similarity throughout America. Hence, the community offers the raw materials for an understanding of our total culture. No teacher should stop after developing a knowledge of the community situation, but a study of community activities can be used to make the data of books, pamphlets, and other sources of information concerning American and world cultures vital and interesting." [4]

Yet understanding is not enough. Knowledge without ethics is at best indifferent to values and at worst destructive of them. Accordingly, we cherish a second purpose, the

2. DEVELOPMENT OF A WHOLESOME FRAMEWORK OF VALUES

"As children and youth participate in community activities, they should not only be gaining an understanding of what *is*, but they should also be building a conception of what *ought to be*. Value standards cannot be established apart from life activities. The guidance of youth in community participation offers excellent opportunities to develop attitudes and ideals commensurate with the democratic way of life. Coming to grips with real problems enables youth to formulate intelligent purposes to which they can dedicate their lives." [4]

But even this will not suffice. Full knowledge one may have, and high ethics also, yet without personal skill in group work technique, he will remain ineffective and even blunderingly destructive. That is why we must search still further for our final major aim, that of

3. COMPETENCE IN SOCIAL PARTICIPATION

"As youth gain an understanding of our evolving culture and build a framework of values, they are also acquiring the social competence necessary to participate effectively in the activities of our culture, so that they can achieve the values they deem desirable . . . The attack upon community problems also gives youth an opportunity to learn to think by thinking. Problems are constantly recognized, analyzed, and defined; relevant data are collected, evaluated, and organized; and appropriate conclusions are formulated, verified, and applied." [4]

Understanding . . . ethics . . . group work skills . . . these factors together—and only *together*—can produce that community "know-how" which brings enduring, desirable results.

Thus can a community-centered educational program contribute

---

[4] James Quillen, "Education for Democratic Living," in Ruth West (ed.), *Utilization of Community Resources in the Social Studies,* p. 10. Ninth Yearbook, National Council for the Social Studies, 1938.

effectively to the attainment of that triple aim which lies at the very heart of modern, democratic, life-centered education:

Social Understanding—developing *knowledge* about our evolving human culture.

Social Attitudes—establishing *value standards* of judgment upon contemporary affairs.

Social Skills—increasing *personal competence* in effective community participation.

How Does Such a Community Study and Service Program Prove Its Value?

Experience indicates that comprehensively aimed, intelligently planned, and competently managed community study programs can in considerable measure achieve various important educational values which should be fundamental in the lives of all students, teachers, and interested laymen today. Let us examine these values in turn, noting as we do so that each succinct statement merits intensive analysis and illustration if it is to be fully meaningful.

COMMUNITY STUDY AND SERVICE VALUES FOR THE STUDENT

1. **Stimulates a realistic understanding of the natural and social environment,** of man's struggles in the past, problems of the present, and perplexities for the future.

2. **Heightens awareness of human solidarity** through identifying man's persistent processes of living as essentially the same throughout history and around the world.

3. **Develops sensitivity to the infinite complexity of human affairs,** to the interrelation of process and problem, to the growing need for co-operative planning for common welfare.

4. **Increases awareness of social lag:** of the fact that man's technical progress has far outstripped his social progress, and that in this situation, lies continuous threat to democracy as an organized way of life.

5. **Deepens respect for the essential dignity of human labor,** whether that labor be primarily physical or mental in nature.

6. **Challenges the civic patriotism of youth,** and thereby develops the significant psychological perception that the community needs service from youth as much as youth needs opportunity in the community.

7. **Provides means for a gradual, intelligent transition** from the unconcerned immaturity of childhood into the emotional, vocational, parental, and civic maturity of responsible adulthood.

8. **Arouses interests and ambitions,** and fosters intelligent choice of vocational career, character pattern, and life philosophy.

9. **Strengthens democratic behavior** by providing constant expe-

rience in planning, executing, and evaluating cooperative group projects, with requisite tolerance and appreciation in the process.

10. **Develops desirable personal character traits** such as those of initiative, courtesy, self-control, leadership, sympathy, tolerance, and social sensitivity.

11. **Stimulates development of the scientific, or problem-solving, habit,** since there is constant experience in facing a problem, projecting hypothetical solutions, collecting data, weighing evidence, verifying conclusions, and thinking constantly and critically about the whole procedure.

12. **Aids attainment of fundamental research skills** in the accurate observation, thoughtful interpretation, careful organization, and effective presentation of socially significant data.

13. **Makes concepts more accurate** by properly generalizing ideas only after considerable direct experience to give those generalizations their realistic personal significance.

14. **Reveals wider opportunities for growth,** through intimate acquaintance with those educational, vocational, and civic resources which may be utilized as future avenues of personal development and social service.

15. **Vitalizes school work** by providing genuine satisfaction in rich and varied learning experiences closely related to present personal interests and purposes, and thereby stimulates increased interest in, and respect for, systematic education of demonstrated worth.

Community Study and Service Values for the Teacher

(in addition to those listed above for students)

1. **Relates the teaching and learning process to significant life activities** as they are carried on in the locality, the region, the nation, the world.

2. **Improves pupil-teacher relationship as problems of discipline fade away** under the enthusiasms of cooperative sharing in challenging community situations.

3. **Provides a wealth of stimulating instructional material** which is useful in many classes, subject fields, and units of work.

4. **Motivates student learning,** since youth can perceive definite, present relationship between what they do in school and the persistent processes and problems of life they must face outside of school.

5. **Socializes class procedure** while minimizing the danger of classroom disorder which frequently accompanies socialization-around less significant pupil activities.

6. **Provides opportunity for creative experience by all students,** since abilities of many kinds are essential to successful, cooperative community-centered education.

7. **Allows easy correlation of subject matter,** because almost every real life situation under investigation must properly be approached from the varied perspectives of several academic fields.

8. **Establishes effective opportunity for guidance** along educa-

tional, vocational, and civic lines, since community study and participation are both informal and cooperative.

9. **Permits school cooperation with community leaders** toward the achievement of educational objectives deemed valid by both school and community.

10. **Promotes public goodwill toward the school** as parents and other laymen come to appreciate the realistic and functional nature of this effective education received by their children.

11. **Makes teaching a constant adventure** rather than a dull routine, since class work remains permanently meaningful, vivid, varied, and realistic.

12. **Enriches personality and improves teaching effectiveness,** for a deepened appreciation of varied beliefs and customs makes possible the emergence of broader social understanding, deeper human sympathy, and genuine tolerance of human differences.

COMMUNITY STUDY AND SERVICE VALUES FOR THE COOPERATING LAYMAN

1. **Provides opportunity to cooperate with youth and the school** in promoting effective education and improving community life.

2. **Permits informal contact with students and teachers** as together with laymen they participate in community processes and cooperatively tackle community problems.

3. **Makes effective a share in the common community obligation** to better relate school education with enduring life needs as they exist in the area.

4. **Enlists youthful energies and enthusiasms in constructive activities,** rather than allowing them to be dissipated in frivolous pursuits or in delinquent behavior.

5. **Produces an adult population which understands its basic community needs,** and which has had successful group experience in democratically utilizing available community resources for the more effective meeting of common community problems.

Students and teachers and laymen—cooperatively attacking real problems of personal interest and social concern! Here is modern education at its best, and here too is epitomized that emerging educational institution of the next generation, the life-centered, community school. For clearly it is that school which can most easily bridge the historic gulf between learning and living, and which can thereby best serve the common cause of democracy and education in our time.

SELECTED REFERENCES

Andrus, Ruth, "The Social Development of Children: How Children Live and Grow and Learn." In William E. Young (ed.), *The Social Studies in the Ele-*

mentary School: Twelfth Yearbook, National Council for the Social Studies, Ch. I. Washington: The Council, 1941. A clear statement of the nature of learning and the development of the self.

Corey, Stephen M., "For Vital Learning, Students Must Have Materials Related to Their Goals." In North Central Association of Colleges and Secondary Schools, *General Education in the American High School,* Ch. 5. Chicago: Scott, Foresman and Co., 1942. Defines learning as goal-seeking behavior changes, and shows the principles of educational method which necessarily follow.

Counts, George S., *The Social Foundations of Education.* Part IX: Report of the Commission on the Social Studies, American Historical Association. New York: Charles Scribner's Sons, 1934. Analyzes the fundamental social trends, tensions and problems of our culture, and suggests the appropriate role of the school in dealing with them.

John Dewey Society, *Democracy and the Curriculum,* Part I. Third Yearbook. New York: D. Appleton-Century, 1939. Characterizes the American social order and its fundamental needs and potentialities.

Friedman, Bertha B., "Learning." In Harry N. Rivlin and Herbert Schueler (eds.), *Encyclopedia of Modern Education,* pp. 444–49. New York: The Philosophical Library, 1943.

Gates, Arthur I., and others, *Educational Psychology,* Ch. XIII. New York: Macmillan, 1942. Analyzes the development of meanings, and shows the necessity of having a perceptual basis for generalizing.

Horn, Ernest, *Methods of Instruction in the Social Studies,* Chs. IV, V. Part XV: Report of the Commission on the Social Studies, American Historical Association. New York: Charles Scribner's Sons, 1937. The problem of meaning, the symbolic character of language, the relation of experience to reading.

Lynd, Robert S., *Knowledge for What?* Princeton, New Jersey: Princeton University Press, 1939. Urges that teachers and others not stop with the discovery of facts and the making of hypotheses, but that they go on to develop programs of action for social improvement.

Miel, Alice, "Living in a Modern World." In *Toward a New Curriculum:* 1944 Yearbook, Department of Supervision and Curriculum Development, National Education Association, Ch. 2. Washington: The Association, 1944. Outlines the kinds of experience considered necessary for effective living today, with desirable directions of curriculum change to provide such experiences.

Rugg, Harold. *Now Is the Moment.* New York: Duell, Sloan & Pearce, 1943. A rigorous analysis of our times, based upon a library of historical and contemporary evidence, and presented as the only valid approach to the designing of educational practice for the future. See also his "Educational Planning for Postwar Reconstruction" in *Frontiers of Democracy* for April and May, 1943.

Wilson, Howard E., "Developing Skill in Critical Thinking Through Participation in School and Community Life." In Howard R. Anderson (ed.), *Teaching Critical Thinking in the Social Studies:* Thirteenth Yearbook, National Council for the Social Studies, Part III. Washington: The Council, 1942. Various aspects of the thinking process are identified, with suggestions for utilizing school and community resources in developing them.

PART II

COMPREHENDING THE COMMUNITY

EDUCATIONAL bridges, many of them, are needed to connect the insular school with the community mainland. But before such bridges are utilized, constructed, or even designed, the educational worker must become acquainted with that mainland topography. He must know its underlying strata, its basic patterns, its essential structure, its operating processes, its stresses, strains and problems, its organized institutions, and its major agencies. He must gain intelligent perspective upon community life as a whole, seeing it as a structural and functional unity possessing internal organization and meaning. Until this fundamental orientation is secured, ambitious builders of pedagogic bridges will lack both direction and skill; their labors, however devoted, will achieve at best only partial success. Adequate community analysis is always essential to community understanding and activity.

*

SUBSTANCE OF LIFE

NO child can escape his community. He may not like his parents, or the neighbors or the ways of the world. He may groan under the processes of living, and wish he were dead. But he goes on living, and he goes on living in the community. The life of the community flows about him, foul or pure: he swims in it, drinks it, goes to sleep in it, and wakes to the new day to find it still about him. He belongs to it: it nourishes him, or starves him, or poisons him: it gives him the substance of his life. And in the long run it takes its toll of him, and all he is.

—JOSEPH K. HART

Adult Education. By permission of the Thomas Y. Crowell Company, publishers

FIRST IN THE DRAMA

FIRST and foremost in the drama of education is the social scene in which it is enacted. The school is in the midst of all the elements of this scene—the soil and climate; the land, the streams, minerals and timber; the people, black and white; their homes, farms, factories, shops and roads; their work and play; their houses and gardens; their food and clothing, their amusements and folkways; their government; their problems of disease and crime; their poverty, their wealth; their vanishing natural resources; their economic uncertainty; their insecurity of position or place; their joys and sorrows; their children, and anxieties for the future.

—ALABAMA EDUCATION ASSOCIATION

In "Social and Economic Conditions in Alabama and Their Implications for Education," p. v. Montgomery: Alabama Education Association, 1937.

EXAMINATION OF SOCIETY

IT is clear that any group, charged with the task of shaping educational theory or practice for any people, should begin with an examination of the society to be served—its natural surroundings, its major trends and tensions, its controlling ideals, values, and interests.

—GEORGE S. COUNTS

In *The Social Foundations of Education*, p. 1. By permission of Charles Scribner's Sons, publishers.

INSEPARABLE FACTORS

AMERICAN schools are beginning to concern themselves with the latent resources of education for democracy in the community. Their leaders are seeking to understand local cultures which influence individuals, school, family, church, and the like, and consequently contribute to distinctive patterns of community life. Such educators are employing a principle originally set forth by William James: that person and community are poles of *one* social process. If individual and culture groups are inseparable factors in community life, they need to be related intelligently in order to assure the maximum of democratic advantages to all parties involved.

—STEWART G. COLE

In William E. Vickery and Stewart G. Cole, *Intercultural Education in American Schools*, p. 2. By permission of Harper & Brothers, publishers.

CHAPTER 3

Technique of Community Analysis

A child's first awareness of his community is likely to be experienced in terms of some minute or fragmentary phase of its total life. He grows up thinking of his community, when he thinks of it at all, merely as the place where he lives. As time goes on and his interests widen, he comes to know many other aspects of community life, but not usually with clear comprehension of their interrelation and significance. To achieve such understanding, he must fit together the fragmentary insights of his experience, add to and interpret them, and thus develop a conceptual pattern which emphasizes the unity as well as the complexity of the community.

Conversely, the student of human society who seeks to comprehend community life must experience its varied aspects as a means of understanding the whole. He must know its physical setting, its people, its historic development, its institutional structure, its social processes and emergent problems, its existing agencies. Such comprehension requires both observation and analysis, each closely related to the other, and both preceded, as well as followed, by an ordered overview without which perspective is likely to be lost.

Community Structure

Though the community is usually complex in nature with an extent and scope difficult to delimit, it is a tangible concept which can be defined. The word "community" derives from the same roots as do "common" and "communal" and suggests a sharing in common. We recognize this sense of sharing in our feeling of belonging to a particular community, even though we are often only vaguely aware of just what it is that we share.

FUNCTIONAL ELEMENTS

Cook's definition of community clarifies this sense of what is shared.[1] He thinks of a community as "(1) a population aggregate,

---

[1] See Lloyd A. Cook, "The Meaning of Community," *Educational Method,* March 1939, pp. 259–62.

(2) inhabiting a contiguous territory, (3) integrated through past experiences, (4) possessing a number of basic service institutions, (5) conscious of its unity, and (6) able to act in a corporate capacity in meeting recurring life crises." We see, then, that a community occupies a particular space on the land, and that its people must have had a history which they recognize as theirs and in which they feel pride. They must be conscious that they belong together as a community. They must have service institutions sufficient in number and type to meet their basic human needs and to make group persistence possible. And finally, they must be able to act together to meet whatever crises may arise and to solve problems involving their public welfare. Such are the basic elements, interaction of which makes a community.

COMMUNITY AREAS

Customarily we think of a community as centering in a particular village, town, or city, or perhaps in a neighborhood within such a city. Yet most smaller towns and villages are no longer self-sufficient, and even large cities are dependent for many products and services upon areas and agencies far removed in space or time. If our concept of the community is to be realistic and of practical value in the education of our children, this trend toward larger spatial areas must be recognized, and the community concept reinterpreted to include them. Let us therefore consider the *service area of the school as the local community,* and with this as a base, distinguish four major community areas, as follows:

1. **Local community:** the service area of the school—the village, town, or city; the township, parish, or county.
2. **Regional community:** the next larger political or geographic unit—the state or a regional grouping of states.
3. **National community:** the nation considered as a whole.
4. **International community:** national groupings as linked by close political, economic, or cultural ties—including a potentially possible world state.

Now it is evident that in our modern complex society, each individual, each family, or each school "belongs" to several overlapping communities, and that membership in each may serve different purposes, or the same purpose under differing circumstances. Furthermore, these community areas are not fixed and permanent, as the case of a mid-western farm family will illustrate.

A quarter century ago, this family was served by a one-teacher elementary school located a short distance to the south of its dwelling; received its mail, voted, and obtained its groceries and fuel from a small village two and a half miles west; attended an open-country church, two and a half miles to the northeast; did its banking and bought clothing and hardware in a small city ten miles to the south. The older children attended high school in another village six miles to the northwest. When the country church closed, the family affiliated with a church in another village seven miles to the west, where the younger children also attended high school. Farm produce was sold and farm supplies and dry goods were bought in any one of three centers. Certain types of business were transacted in the county seat, twenty-five miles distant. The services of the State Agricultural College were utilized, and many purchases were made from the catalogues of mail-order houses located hundreds of miles away. In all these and other ways, this rural family was aware of its membership in state and national as well as in local and regional communities. It is significant that this family never lacked a definite sense of "belonging," even though its community areas overlapped so much.

COMMUNITY LEVELS

Still another aspect of the community pattern must be considered. There are strata or levels of the community's culture which roughly coincide with degrees of difficulty in studying community life. These community levels should therefore be clearly recognized in order that the levels selected for study may be appropriate to the abilities and maturity of the group planning a community study.

Rugg has identified three levels of community [2] which may be designated as (1) the material level, (2) the institutional level, and (3) the psychological level. Let us see what these levels are, and when they might be investigated.

1. **Material level.** This is the external civilization, the *things* people use or have made, as well as the people themselves. This level includes a community's natural resources, the industries and service occupations which produce and distribute goods and services, the physical setting of the community—its housing, streets and transportation system, its parks and playgrounds, its water supply and sanitation service, its communication facilities, its protective services, its coal mines, bee hives, lakes, fire engines, housing projects and the like. Children in the elementary school

---

[2] See Harold Rugg, *American Life and the School Curriculum*, pp. 20–24. Boston: Ginn, 1936.

may appropriately undertake community study on this primary level, beginning with its simpler and more tangible aspects.

2. Institutional level. Here are the organized ways of living, the *mass habits* of the people. This second level is less tangible, but extremely significant in determining community behavior; it is the "cradle of custom" into which each child is born. Marriage customs, family form, governmental practices, religious rituals, the language used, the number system followed, the common arrangements for economic exchange and monetary usage—all illustrate institutions of different types. Community study at this institutional level should usually be delayed until the high school years bring greater maturity of intelligence.

3. Psychological level. Determining both the customs and the material creations of the community are the *motivations* of the people. These are the desires that produce activity, the fears which inhibit behavior, the attitudes which pattern acceptable conduct, the stereotypes, ideas, ideals, loyalties, values, and taboos which influence and direct human behavior. Obviously this psychological level is an area of study which only mature minds should seek to penetrate.

Having thus identified the community's *structure* in terms of its basic elements, areas, and levels, we now proceed to examine its second major aspect, that is, its *setting*.

Community Setting

Where is the community located with respect to natural features, climatic conditions, and relation to other communities? How large is it? How is it arranged on the earth's surface? Who are its people? Where did they come from? Why are they here? Such are some of the queries subsumed under the two chief aspects of any community's setting: (1) its physical setting (geography), and (2) its human setting (people).

PHYSICAL SETTING

Every community has a physical setting, a base on the land. The size, topography, and natural features of the place it occupies may influence markedly the life of the community. This fact is most familiar to us through its extreme cases, but it is equally (if not always as strikingly) true of the more numerous communities we are likely to consider as "typical" or "average." The particular physical features which most directly affect the pattern of a community and which should be singled out for first study will vary. In general, however, certain basic aspects of the geographic setting can be suggested.

1. **Climate** is a vital factor. In its extremes, it affects the productiveness of the community, and within its more temperate limits, it influences the daily life of the people in subtle as well as in direct ways. Temperature range affects agricultural production, recreational participation, and numerous other phases of community life. The length of time completely free from frost is of special importance to farmers in the temperate zones, where a difference of a few weeks in the season's length is a major factor in determining what crops can be successfully grown. The amount and seasonal distribution of precipitation is important. Even the wind makes a difference, particularly in those regions where storms are frequent or may approach hurricane proportions.

2. **Size** is significant, whether the community be a large city, a compact village, a town-centered rural area, or a sprawling open-country region. Size always affects face-to-face relationships, and also helps to determine the types of services a community can offer its residents.

3. **Topography** affects ease of access to and from a community, and thus profoundly influences the mores and customs of the people as well as determining their occupations, recreational activities, and the like.

4. **Soil type and fertility** are especially significant in rural areas devoted to agriculture and related industries. Soil drainage is important in both rural and urban communities, and in urban areas the distance of the bedrock from the earth's surface is of great significance. In New Orleans, for example, few houses with basements are built, and underground burial in cemeteries is impractical because of the high water-table. In New York City, both the extensive subway system and the great number of extremely tall buildings are made possible—or at least simpler—by the proximity of the bedrock to the surface.

5. **Water resources** constitute a major aspect which should be considered from the viewpoints of water supply for drinking purposes, drainage needs, industrial use, irrigation, and transportation.

6. **Mineral deposits,** including building rock, greatly influence a community's occupations, wealth, housing standards, and the like.

7. **Forest and animal resources** have likewise helped to shape the social patterns of many communities.

Climate, topography, and natural resources may be thought of as the natural inheritance of a particular locality, but the picture of a community's geographic setting is not complete until we see what has been done with this inheritance and how the land has been used. A few city-communities in this country have had the benefit of careful planning to guide their growth in a spatial pattern; most of them, however, have expanded more or less spontaneously, with little or no preplanning. Many communities have tried in more recent years to establish some pattern of physical growth that will gradually correct poor land usage and prevent it entirely in the future. The zoning plans of a city or area should be studied in connection with the problem of past and present land use.

Effort should be made to visualize clearly, and in some detail, the spatial location of the community's typical industries and facilities, their relation to the natural features of the community, and their interrelatedness with each other. A social base map, such as is described in Chapter 5, should be procured, and land use indicated thereon through the medium of different colorings.

Having located or "spotted" these various types of land use on the map, it will be fruitful to study it further. What relation is there between the community's shape, land utilization pattern, site, and topography? How are the various parts of the area related to each other? For example, where is the poorer residential section with respect to the manufactural area? What relationship exists between the location of the waterfront or railroad and the commercial area? How are the several land utilization areas located with respect to land values? These are typical of the types of relationships within the community which might well be examined. Similar relationships with other areas and other communities should likewise be explored.

HUMAN SETTING

Communities with similar geographic settings may vary widely in their over-all patterns of living. Such differences frequently result because people of different types inhabit those community areas. The next step in analyzing the setting of a community is therefore to learn about its people—who they are and what they are like.

1. **Population number** is the first factor to be considered. Number is significant both in an absolute sense and in relation to the past, to other nearby communities, and to land area covered. A population of 10,000 scattered over a large rural area in the Southwest, for example, has a very different significance from that of a similar number concentrated within a few square miles in urban Rhode Island; likewise, a present population of 10,000 is one thing for a community which last year numbered 1,800, and quite another for a community which recently numbered 15,000 residents.

2. **Age and sex composition** may profoundly affect a community's organized life. Many rural communities, for example, find themselves with a relatively high proportion of very young and very old people; this situation imposes a heavy economic burden upon the community because a smaller proportion of people at productive ages must support a larger percentage of dependents. Obviously, too, a community with a disproportionately large male population may face problems quite different

from one having a surplus of females. Similarly, the marital status of the population will be a significant factor influencing sex mores.

3. **Educational status** will greatly affect community welfare, particularly in its civic, social, and vocational aspects. A high proportion of illiteracy within a community will have its real influence, as will the presence within the population of many college graduates.

4. **Occupational status** is closely related to educational level, and has similar community effects. Land-owning farmers are different people from tenant-farmers, just as unskilled workers live differently in many respects from industrial technicians and professional persons. The way in which community residents get their living is thus very significant.

5. **Nationality pattern** is of special importance in the United States, because this country is populated largely by immigrants and their children. Some communities are composed almost entirely of so-called "native-stock," that is, of white people from specified national backgrounds whose ancestors have lived here for many generations. Other communities have many foreign-born, or first- and second-generation descendants of foreign-born whites. In the latter case, one such nationality group may predominate in the community, or many such groups may be represented. Where population mixtures exist, it is important to know what proportion of the population is of so-called "foreign" descent, whether this proportion is changing and if so in what direction, what the leading nationalities are in point of number and relative proportion, and the citizenship status of foreign-born persons. The extent to which "foreign" people have established neighborhood colonies which remain relatively free from "Americanizing" influences will also be worth knowing.

6. **Racial minority groups** present problems not unlike those of nationality groups, except that their problems may be more baffling since a question of caste is also involved. These groups differ, moreover, in that their status depends less upon the recency of their migration to this country and more upon the fact of race or color, with its caste connotations and its economic and social disadvantagements. As with nationality groups, it will be important to learn what the ratio of colored (such as the Chinese, Japanese, Filipinos, Indians, Negroes) and other racially variant populations is to the whole, whether this ratio is changing, and if so, in which direction.

7. **Class and caste structure** is closely related to the whole matter of racial and nationality groupings. Class differences exist within the strictly white populations, but with the colored races class distinctions are reinforced and made more burdensome by the added fact of caste. This has the effect of concentrating most lower caste persons in the lower classes and making it difficult for them to move upward in the social scale.

As social patterns, class and caste affect those whom they disadvantage in tangible ways. Work opportunities are limited both in type and in availability; and wage discriminations often exist. The result is that the whole economic position of the group is insecure. Such insecurity shows itself in the physical setting of the community through such aspects as poor housing and sanitation. Further effects of class and caste discrimination are apparent at the institutional level, where schools, libraries, recreational facilities, hospitals, etc. either do not exist or are inferior to those provided for more privileged groups. It is at the psychological level, however, that the great power of class and caste discrimination is most apparent.

All seven of these factors must be investigated if we are to understand the people of any community. All seven are highly significant to that people's conceptions and practices in matters of everyday living. All, in different ways, are reflected in a thousand community activities every day, particularly at the institutional and psychological levels where community factors are highly potent even though physically invisible.

Community Processes and Problems

Community activities are always carried on by people for the fulfillment of their basic human needs. The *social processes* which make up the ongoing life of the community directly reflect these needs and are maintained to satisfy them. To the degree that needs are adequately met through satisfactorily operating social processes, the community is successfully performing its basic functions. Where these processes are not functioning satisfactorily, that fact is indicated by the existence in the community of resulting *social problems*. To understand the community, therefore, it is essential that we comprehend the social processes at work, and also recognize those problems which emerge from their failure. The illustrative descriptions of community functioning which follow therefore include suggestive analyses of (a) social processes (adjustment: positive), and (b) related social problems (maladjustment: negative) whose existence indicates some type of failure in the process. Each of twelve basic processes will be described briefly, and will be followed by still briefer portrayals of typical emergent problems.

1. UTILIZING NATURAL ENVIRONMENT

People find different ways of adjusting to quite similar environments. Sometimes this flows from the uniqueness of human personality, from the fact that we are each somewhat different from everyone else. Often it is for reasons arising out of our backgrounds and ideals. One group of people moves into a locality with a particular type of soil and climate, and becomes a share-cropping tenantry in a one-crop farming program; these people remain ill-fed, ill-housed, and ill-clothed. Another group comes onto similar land near by and becomes a farm-owning community, practices diversified farming, preserves its own foodstuffs during the growing season; is reasonably prosperous. The geographic setting for these two communities is similar, but the people's ways of adjusting to that setting are markedly different.

Adjustment to the physical environment may take many forms, and involves the practice of mastering as well as submitting to that environment. The kinds of homes that are built, the "sky line" of a city, how the people distribute themselves in relation to the natural features of the community such as rivers or hills, what use they make of land features, location, and natural resources in developing ways of making a living—these are a few among many possible evidences of how environment is utilized by the people. Such utilization may be simple and direct or complex and circuitous; it may prove highly successful or hopelessly inadequate.

Poor Utilization of Natural Environment Brings Social Problems:

1. Faulty use of land. Failure to put land to its best use—for agriculture, building sites, parks and playgrounds, etc.—may prevent the adequate functioning of other social processes such as making a living, maintaining health, improving family life, and the like.

2. Waste of natural resources. Failure to plan for wise use, conservation, and possible restoration of natural resources may menace both the present and the future well-being of any community.

2. Appreciating the Past

Human beings need to have roots, to feel that they "belong." Part of this satisfaction comes from the day-to-day group life of the community, part from psychological identification with family and community traditions. A community's present outlooks, values, and ideals are themselves outgrowths of tradition. It follows that a community can be better understood when its essential history is known: how long it has existed, how it came into being, who settled it, why they came, what institutions and enterprises they established, what ideals they upheld, who their leaders were, what common crises arose and what adjustments to those crises were made. To this knowledge should be added understanding of the extent to which the community is constantly keeping alive in popular thought the significant developments of its history and the lives of its heroes.

Improper Appreciation of the Past Brings Social Problems:

a. Ancestor worship and cultural imperialism. Pride in the history of one's community may become so exalted that those sharing it come to feel that all things must be appraised in terms of earlier customs and standards; that present guardians of past tradition have an almost divine responsibility to force those traditions upon all others in the community. Intolerance of new ideas brings social stagnation; community failure may well result if such intolerance is characteristic of the whole community population. Where an "old families" group resists change, struggle and conflict are inevitable, but growth is still possible.

b. Social instability. A community may have too little sense of identity with its past, thereby lacking a powerful stabilizing and morale-strengthening force which is essential to continued mutual activity in the common interest.

3. ADJUSTING TO PEOPLE

The adjustments which people of a community make to each other influence the whole community pattern of life. Such adjustments may be simple or complex, easy or difficult, direct or remote—all depending upon the community's physical setting, social structure, and basic mores. Where there is great homogeneity of population, adjustments will vary with the abilities of individuals to "get along" with others. Where there is marked heterogeneity, class and caste differences will create more general difficulties. The heterogeneous situation may involve the presence of different racial groups in the community, the movement of new groups or "outlanders" into districts where old residents have long held traditional leadership, the existence of divergent occupational classes including owners and workers—these and many other factors may divide the people and produce conflicts within a community.

Now the presence of such differences within a community is not, in itself, undesirable. Variations and contrasts may lead to the stimulation and enrichment of personal and community life. But deep-seated differences may, on the other hand, prove seriously disruptive of effective community living. Therefore the student of the community will need to discover what the divisive factors in the population pattern are, what organizations deliberately or unwittingly promote group conflict, and what agencies are at work to bring about wholesome group adjustments. The new school emphasis upon intercultural education is one reflection of growing awareness of this need.

Failure to Adjust to People Brings Social Problems:

a. Personality conflicts. Such conflicts may affect community life only in limited personal ways, or, if persons in authoritative positions are involved, they may influence it through official or semi-official action of far-reaching consequences.

b. Racial, national, and class hostility. Here root the most vexing of all human problems. Group suspicion, fear, hatred, and even open conflict exist in many communities; even when surface appearances are quiet the underlying tensions are there and may readily be provoked into overt antagonisms.

4. EXCHANGING IDEAS

Communication with one's fellows is necessary, not only to gratify a fundamental desire for this type of human association, but also in order that people may function more effectively in carrying on other social processes. The efficiency with which the people of a community are able to understand each other, and their ability to improve their thinking and practices through the various media of communication available to them, are both important attributes of the community's development.

The basic medium for the exchange of ideas is, of course, language. Thus it is desirable to know the community's status with respect to both oral and written languages. Is it a one-language community, or are there groups to which a foreign language is still the habitual tongue? Is there opportunity for adequate exchange of opinion between them and other groups in the community? Whether one or many languages are spoken, how literate are the people? To what extent do they use books, magazines, and newspapers to secure information and to reach understanding about matters which concern them?

In modern life, the exchange of ideas depends not only on language, but also upon the devices which have been developed as aids to communication. The telephone and telegraph, the radio, press, movies, and the like serve as common means of communication between people distant from each other. It is therefore desirable for the student of community life to be aware of what communication aids are available; how widely they are used; and what their effects, both actual and potential, may be.

Communication does something more than meet a personal need of individuals and serve as a means of exchanging information. It is the means by which public opinion is formed, and public opinion is an extremely potent force in determining what individuals or groups think and do, as well as in influencing group action on vital issues. "Public opinion" is in reality a crystallization of the ideas and values which the dominant groups accept and uphold. In part, it is the product of many informal and unorganized influences —the cultural traditions of the community, its economic interests, the informal interchange of ideas among its people—these and many others. In part, it may also be the product of carefully organized efforts by special interest groups, who either seek converts to altruistic ideals or who wish to exploit the people for personal gain. A complete study of a community will thus require attention to the significant elements of its public opinion, and will seek to understand what forces or agencies—pulpit, press, business interests, political groups, labor organizations, patriotic associations, and so forth—are creating or influencing that opinion.

Malfunctioning in the Exchange of Ideas Brings Social Problems:

a. Stereotyped thinking and action. There may be such exchange of ideas (or lack of it) that there is no real stimulus to creative thought, and new problems are analyzed according to the same old patterns so that they are never realistically faced, or their elements of newness even understood.

b. Evil propaganda. The agencies of communication can be easily diverted to the purposes of those who want to use other people to achieve their own ends. Such use of these agencies thwarts full and sound functioning of many social processes, since it distorts or even falsifies truth.

5. Making a Living

The physical needs of all people for food, clothing, and shelter must be met, and such additional goods and services provided as have come to be considered desirable by the community group in question. In a primitive community, these physical needs are provided directly by each individual or family unit, or at most by the clan. Today our economic life has become so complex, and the work a man does may be so many stages removed from the actual feeding, clothing, and sheltering of his family, that the process of "making a living" has come to involve many intricately interrelated aspects of community life. Anything which relates to the production, distribution, or consumption of economic goods is a part of "making a living." A study of how a community makes its living should therefore include such various items as the following:

Occupations

What do the people do, either to produce directly what they need or to secure the means with which to purchase it? Does their work go on within the community area, or does it take them elsewhere? Is this a one-industry community, or are the occupations numerous and diversified? Who works—only men and unmarried women, or are children and women with families employed? Communities may have widely varying occupational patterns. They may be single-industry communities in which most of the people are unskilled or semi-skilled laborers. They may be largely residence communities for professional workers with just enough other workers to maintain the basic services which characterize any community. There are probably as many variations in occupational patterns as there are local communities, for each community has its own particular pattern, developed through the interplay of many factors and forces. That pattern is always significant to the person desiring full understanding of the community life itself.

Industries, Commerce, Professional Services

Direct attention should be given to a study of the community's industries, to its financial and trade operations, and to the specialized services that are carried on. This will include the manufacturing plants, wholesale and retail stores, public utilities, banks and finance companies, transportation and communication services, professional services, food production and distribution services, garages, laundries, dry cleaners, and the like. For many of these, it will be important to know how long they have existed in the community; whether they are locally owned and operated, or are branches of larger companies centered elsewhere; why they were located in this particular community area, and so on.

Placement Services

At times when a labor shortage exists the question of placement seems relatively easy of solution, but when there are more workers than jobs, the securing of employment becomes a serious matter to the community as well as to the individual worker. The organization and regulation of job placement, first through state and local services and then through the United States Employment Service, has been an effort to develop an effective placement system operating solely in the public interest. Some educational institutions have

given their students some vocational guidance, including attention
to the technique of finding a job. The effectiveness of the placement service in any community depends not alone on the existence
of such service, but also upon its quality—on how these services
are administered, whether staffs are well trained and carefully
selected, whether offices are adequate in facilities for interviewing,
and in location and hours of service, and so forth. The practices of
community employers in hiring need to be known, particularly with
respect to racial groups, ages of workers, sex, and other factors
upon which employment distinctions may be based.

Conditions of Work

Both the safeguards established by law and the actual conditions
existing locally should be known. These include such matters as
safety, sanitation, wages, hours of labor, compensation for industrial injury and for unemployment, and special safeguards to working women and children. The conditions of work in nearby areas
may also need to be investigated for their effect upon the local
community, either in the setting of standards or in determining
the availability of workers.

Labor Organizations

It is important to discover whether any labor organization has
jurisdiction over workers in the community, and the effect which
the presence or absence of unionism has upon making a living.
Doubtless considerable variation occurs in the adequacy with which
unions serve their members and in their effects upon the communities in which they operate. In studying their role in the community, attention should be given to what unions do to other aspects
of community life as well as to their direct effect upon employment policies and practices.

Business Organizations

Such organizations as chambers of commerce, manufacturers' associations, employers' and merchants' associations, and the like may
have both a direct and an indirect influence upon community life.
This may be illustrated quickly through the case of a city where
a manpower shortage was developing, but where the usual evidences
of need for child-care programs to release mothers for employment
had not developed. Investigation disclosed the fact that agreements reached by the local organization of personnel directors had

prevented this problem from emerging as it would otherwise have done had there been no unified, community-wide policy to cover it. Here the influence of a business group was affecting family living, limiting the necessity for a public service, and meeting an employer's problem. Such is typical of the varied ways in which such business associations influence the functioning of many social processes in the community.

Technological Trends

Technological developments have created many changes in ways of making a living, sometimes by so simplifying and specializing a job that it has lost the creative challenge formerly inherent in it, sometimes by actually destroying work opportunities for some persons thus making them less able to buy available goods. Technology plays an important part in the growth and expansion of particular communities, and in the decline of others. The development of complex machines has necessitated greater capital investment, and thereby affected the extent of local ownership and control over the community's business enterprises. Industries without roots in a local community have not hesitated to move out when conditions elsewhere seemed more promising. All these and many other results of technological change have added to the potential richness of human life, but, at the same time, have made the problem of getting a living more complex for the individual worker. In studying the community, it will be important to know to what extent it has already adjusted to technological changes successfully, how aware it is of the need for such adjustment, and how able to face still further adjustments. This will be one measure of the community's ability to act corporately in meeting one of the crises which may be expected to occur.

Assistance to the Needy and Dependent

Those persons who, for one reason or another, are incapable of making a living or who are denied opportunity to do so are still faced with the necessity of securing a living of at least minimum standard. Therefore, what the community does through unemployment insurance, old-age benefits, widows' pensions, mothers' assistance, and the like, should be considered under making a living as well as in its more civic aspects.

So important and so rapidly changing is the process of making a living that many crucial problems have arisen in this area. Without relating these problems specifically to the various aspects of making a living outlined above, let us merely note some of the problems which exist today.

Malfunctioning with Respect to Making a Living Brings Social Problems:

a. Unemployment. Apart from the idleness of the truly unemployable, most unemployment is directly traceable to the malfunctioning of the economic system—to unstable business conditions, to exploitation of labor and consumers, to restriction of work opportunities by union organizations, to restriction of production on the part of employers. In studying unemployment within the community, it is necessary not only to ascertain its causes in the local situation, but also to discover the related problems which unemployment has in turn created—problems of family living, of warped personalities, and of poor citizenship.

b. Poverty and insecurity. These may be outgrowths of unemployment, of working conditions which permit inadequate wages, of failure in individual capacity, or of inadequate skill or training. Again, the effects of this twin problem must be considered along with its causes.

c. Exploitation of labor. Where exploitation brings such evils as inadequate wages, unduly long hours, or unsafe or unhealthful conditions of work, its effects upon health, family living, and upon opportunity to share in other elements of a satisfying life can be extremely harmful.

d. Capital-labor conflict. Such conflict always reflects failure to develop economic arrangements satisfactory to all parties concerned. Often, each group is fearful of exploitation by the other. The extent of this conflict, the degree to which the community's industries have been able to resolve it, and their means of attacking the problem should all be studied.

e. Waste of natural resources. Where private enterprise controls the use of natural resources, the long-time needs of the community—local, regional, national, world community—may be and often are ignored. One of the community's corporate responsibilities is to supply this long view and see that available resources are properly utilized.

f. Inadequate production. The community may be failing with respect to making a living because it is not producing sufficient goods and economic services to meet minimum needs. This failure may sometimes result from accidental causes—from "act of God;" usually, however, it flows from man-made factors such as failure to utilize technological advances, failure to settle labor disputes, or deliberate restriction of production in the interests of higher profits to the producers, both capitalists and organized workers.

6. Sharing in Citizenship

In one sense, citizenship is the quality of daily living by people in the community—how they meet their responsibilities, get along with their neighbors, and contribute to the maintenance of needed services. In another sense, citizenship is a more formal matter of personal participation in the political activities of the community —membership in a political party, campaigning, voting, and office-holding. Both aspects of citizenship are important, and each affects the other. The latter, however, is the more public aspect and the more easily studied objectively; it usually indicates also the adequacy of the community's corporate functioning.

In most communities four or more governments are in simultaneous operation: municipal, town or township, county, state, and federal. In some states, school districts, water districts, and other special political subdivisions form additional political units. The boundaries of each of these, the extent of its authority, its form of organization, the officials who hold office, the interrelationships among governments, and the effectiveness of those governments are all factors which contribute to the common community life, and which should be studied by the student interested in knowing his community.

Governments are organized to provide social services which cannot be as adequately maintained by individual citizens or by smaller groups of people. The effectiveness with which a community shares in citizenship is thus evidenced by the adequacy of the services it renders in such areas as protection and public safety, health, welfare, education, and community planning, and by its success in keeping governmental costs at levels commensurate with the quality of the services rendered.

Citizenship has a still further responsibility, which is to improve the process and the conditions of group living. Since our nation is founded upon the belief that the democratic process is the best means of achieving the greatest good for the most people, and since this process is not yet perfected and must be constantly strengthened and adapted to changing conditions, every American community shares in the responsibility of improving that democratic process. That is why it is well to observe whether the community's citizens contribute positively to this strengthening process, or whether they weaken it through indifference or even active opposition.

Inadequate Sharing in Citizenship Brings Social Problems:

a. **Public indifference.** Many people do not work actively at their citizenship, even to the minimum extent of voting or of keeping informed concerning action contemplated by government bodies. The result of such civic indifference is that the worst elements of society may govern it.

b. **Political corruption and graft.** Government office is sometimes used by individuals or political organizations to increase their power or wealth, regardless of genuine public interest. Ineffective service, witl. waste or misuse of public funds, results.

c. **Crime, vice, delinquency.** Such evils are partly the result of failure by families and other institutions to perform their functions effectively. In large measure, however, they reflect community failure to provide adequate social safeguards and effective rehabilitative measures.

7. MAINTAINING HEALTH AND SAFETY

The community's health status is disclosed by statistics on infant and maternal mortality, incidence of disease, number of deaths from various diseases, average length of life, the accident rate, the insanity rate, and the like. General health status may be affected by particular occupational diseases, as well as by the economic status of the people, the standards of living maintained, and the provisions made by the community to safeguard and improve public health.

Community authority is usually necessary to maintain a safe water supply, safe standards of purity in the milk and food supply, adequate sewage and refuse disposal, and protection against hazards to life and safety. Such controls are also essential in preventing the spread of communicable disease and in maintaining satisfactory housing conditions.

The community also needs facilities for health service and medical care. These facilities include hospitals, clinics, and dispensaries; physicians, dentists, and other such medical specialists; registered and practical nurses; and some type of general community health program. With regard to health and medical service personnel, it is important to know what their training has been, their standing in their professions, and the legal safeguards governing practice of these professions. How hospital services are organized and administered, how competently they are staffed, what services they offer, and to whom their services are available should be known to the community investigator. So also should the general program of public health, its scope both as to inclusion and to persons reached, the quality of the service including its program of health education for children and for the adult population. Nutrition education should be a part of such a general educational program.

In analyzing health status in a community, its services to the physically and mentally handicapped must not be ignored. The incidence of mental illness, mental defectiveness, blindness, deafness, and physical crippling are all factors to be investigated, as are the provisions available for the care and special treatment of all such handicapped persons in the community.

Provisions for the public safety include police protection and traffic supervision, fire prevention and control, accident prevention and first-aid facilities. Communities will differ markedly in their provisions for public safety, as they do in all other aspects of community life.

Inadequate Maintenance of Health and Safety Brings Social Problems:

a. Physical unfitness. Anything which destroys or reduces the individual's physical fitness is of proper concern to the community at large. Individual illness affects general welfare in two chief ways: it requires the use of medical supplies, facilities, and personnel, and it limits the individual's productive power. Malnourishment as well as overt illness and accidents are thus both individual and community problems.

b. Mental unfitness. Mental illness and serious emotional instability are likewise of general public concern, and for exactly the same reasons as those indicated above.

c. Slums. Slums are a social problem in multifarious ways. They are a cause of poor health, not merely a symptom of it, and should be so regarded in studying the community's health status.

8. IMPROVING FAMILY LIFE

The community promotes family life by setting up legal controls to govern the establishment and dissolution of family units, that is, to regulate marriage and annulment or divorce. It may further protect and promote family living by offering opportunities for pre-marital instruction, and by providing guidance in family affairs to persons desiring it after marriage. Further strengthening of family life results from public assistance with such special problems as maternal health, child spacing and care, home management, budgeting and finance, and selection and preparation of food.

Marriage laws and customs should therefore be examined to determine their effect upon the family. What are the laws governing age and other requirements for marriage? Are blood tests required prior to marriage in order to establish freedom from venereal disease? Is marriage regarded by the community as a serious undertaking, or do the conditions under which marriage ceremonies occur detract from its dignity? Is birth control endorsed, tolerated, or opposed by dominant public opinion? What is the community's attitude toward divorce? Are divorces frequent? On what grounds are they obtainable? Are there special courts to hear divorce cases, and is any really scientific attempt at reconciliation made before divorces are granted?

What family service agencies operate in the community? If none, are there any useful informal aids such as those sometimes offered by qualified teachers or clergymen? Does the community have a sound and extensive parent education program? Is training in child care available? What about education in consumer buying? What provision does the community make to help broken families maintain a high quality of family living? All of these and many similar questions need to be asked and answered before an understanding of the community's family life can be achieved.

Failure in Promoting Family Living Brings Social Problems:

a. Marital discord and divorce. Although these problems are intensely personal, they also reflect community failure, particularly in terms of previous school education and present welfare facilities.

b. Neglected children. Whenever children are neglected, and regardless of the situation, either a family or the community or both are at fault.

c. Consumer exploitation. This indicates family failure on the economic side rather than in social adjustment. Since individual families will not usually be able to overcome such exploitation, it must be considered as a community problem and attacked as such through public education and governmental activity.

9. SECURING EDUCATION

The community's provisions for education include not only the schools, but also many other institutions and services which go beyond formal education and which serve adults as well as youth. The public schools, however, play a major and easily definable role, so a study of educational services might well begin with them. Significant information which should be readily obtainable includes: length of school term, ages between which children are required to attend school, for what age children schools are actually maintained, types of educational services offered; qualifications and methods of election of school board members; qualifications, methods of selection, salaries, and terms of office of school superintendent, principals, supervisors, and teachers; pupil-teacher ratio; extent and condition of school plant, and the like. Information concerning the curriculum will be exceptionally valuable, particularly with respect to changes made to adapt it to new personal and civic needs.

Private institutions for learning should also be surveyed. These may include parochial schools, private day schools catering to the well-to-do, so-called boarding schools, experimental schools, business and trade schools, and schools serving handicapped children. It will be important to know the extent to which each of these is supervised or regulated by the State Department of Education.

The community may include institutions of higher learning whose auspices, types of curriculum, and professional rating may be studied. Libraries, museums, public forums, Americanization programs, and organized adult education programs should also be investigated to secure a well-rounded orientation in the area of education.

Failure to Provide Suitable Educational Opportunities Brings Social Problems:

a. Illiteracy. The presence of illiteracy among people capable of learning is serious evidence of failure in one of the community's major responsibilities. The handicaps it imposes upon otherwise competent adults are obvious; this personal inadequacy is always reflected in community affairs, both civic and vocational.

b. Waste of intellectual resources. Schools sometimes establish their curricular programs to satisfy students of average mental ability, and thus fail to meet the needs of those who deviate considerably from that average. Many schools now make special provisions for the handicapped, but there is still widespread failure to adapt programs to the abilities of the more able pupils. Such failure constitutes a serious individual and social loss, for superior minds are any community's greatest resource.

10. MEETING RELIGIOUS NEEDS

The tangible aspects of a community's religious life include its organized churches and missions, and its social-religious agencies such as the Salvation Army, Volunteers of America, Young Men's Christian Association, Catholic Youth Organization, Young Men's Hebrew Association, Newman Club, Young Women's Hebrew Association, and Young Women's Christian Association. The number and location of churches and missions, their denominational affiliations, the counseling and guidance services they offer to congregational members and non-members, and their programs of religious education might all be examined. Is a program of week-day religious instruction carried on? If so, under whose auspices and through what arrangements are these programs carried out? What professional training do church leaders and religious educators receive? Is there any coordination of religious programs among the churches? How large a proportion of the population is actively served by the

churches? Such are typical of the queries to be investigated in connection with this process of community living.

Malfunctioning or Inadequacy in Religious Activities
Brings Social Problems:

a. **Superstition.** Religious gullibility and the cherishing of ideas and
practices having anti-social implications is both a personal and a community affair.

b. **Bigotry and intolerance.** Community life is menaced whenever
psychological barriers between groups or individuals prevent frank facing of facts related to current problems.

11. ENJOYING BEAUTY

People need opportunities to enjoy beauty in music, in the
graphic arts, in architecture, landscaping and other scenic arts, in
craftsmanship, and in nature itself. Such opportunities depend upon
the presence of beauty within the community, and also upon the
development of the people's capacity for seeing, preserving, and
creating beauty. Any review of the community's artistic interests
and resources should therefore include a survey of all these factors,
as well as a survey of public art collections, a study of the degree
to which homes in the community reflect interest in and appreciation of beauty, and information concerning the extent to which education for appreciation and participation in the creative arts is
provided in the community.

Failure to Enjoy Beauty Brings Social Problems:

a. **Community ugliness.** Littered streets, unkept lawns and shrubbery, unpainted buildings, and other evidences of unconcern for community beauty are both an aesthetic and a civic problem. Such tolerance of unnecessary ugliness is reflected in lowered land values as well
as in lessened community morale.

12. ENGAGING IN RECREATION

Much of the recreational activity in the typical community is informal, developed by the individual himself and centering in the
family and in small groups of friends. The play of little children,
the reading of newspapers, magazines, and books, listening to the
radio, going to the movies, taking a hike, having a picnic, gathering
at the drug store for a coke—all these recreational activities occur
without community planning. Self-direction is important to any
good recreational program, but complete dependence upon informal

and unplanned activities is undesirable since many people may and do enter into leisure time activities which are distinctly harmful to them.

Organized recreational activities are usually of two kinds: those provided by public or private agencies and not operated for profit, and those organized by commercial agencies. Among the former may be community parks and playgrounds with volunteer or paid supervisors, musical organizations offering participation and entertainment, arts and crafts programs, little theaters, hobby clubs, swimming pools, libraries, museums, community festivals, and the like. Commercial recreation may include the movies, skating rinks, dance halls, night clubs, swimming, golf, or tennis clubs, traveling circuses, professional baseball, football, or hockey, pool halls, or any similar activities and facilities.

As all such facilities are investigated, attention should be given to the extent, quality, and availability of the services they provide, and especially to the standards which they maintain. The degree to which any recreational activity is harmful or beneficial depends in large measure upon the moral and ethical standards maintained within it.

Undesirable or Inadequate Recreation Brings Social Problems:

a. **Waste or poor use of leisure time.** "Killing time" is not true recreation, since it is not an activity which positively re-creates the individual's energy and poise. Failure to experience such genuine re-creation means failure to remain at one's best level of health, happiness, and productive efficiency; furthermore, it may lead into unwholesome ways of spending time.

b. **Exploitation by commercial agencies.** Youth is particularly susceptible to such exploitation because in its great desire for glamorous activity it is not always discriminating as to recreational facilities used. If community organizations fail to provide suitable constructive facilities, youth will often spend its money upon whatever activities are available, however undesirable they may actually be from a moral standpoint.

Such are the twelve fundamental social processes which go on in some form or another in every community large or small, urban or rural, near or remote, historic or contemporary. Such also are some among the typical social problems which emerge in contemporary American communities as these basic processes prove inadequate or fail to function with full effectiveness.

Community Time Period

Any adequate analysis of the community requires also that the time factor be recognized and understood. So far in our analysis of community structure, setting, processes, and problems we have tacitly assumed a purely contemporary approach; that is, we have sought to discover how these community aspects function *now*. Yet it is obvious that current phenomena have not leaped full-blown into being; rather they have emerged out of historic struggle and crisis, defeat and victory, growth and decline. All of a community's past thus influences its present, and at the same time, conditions its hopes and plans for the future. That is why no community analysis which is focused exclusively upon contemporary events can ever be satisfactory. Community analysts therefore need to consider all three temporal aspects of the community's life, each in its interrelationship with both of the others:

1. **Historic:** what has happened already?
2. **Contemporary:** what is happening now?
3. **Future:** what will, might, should, or should not happen in days to come?

Only in this way can perspective be retained, trends discerned, and future possibilities projected. At all times the community analyst must remain sensitive to the fact that community origins and development most powerfully influence a community's aspirations for the future as well as its current life. Indeed, contemporary events can hardly be understood at all without constant reference to both their historic development and their future potentialities. Man lives today on his hopes for the future as well as on his memories of the past.

Community Agencies

The community picture will not be complete until one final factor is considered: that of the many agencies which operate in and for the community. These agencies are always inextricably related to each social process since they constitute the organized expression of those processes in everyday life. Many agencies are themselves interrelated; often they form a veritable web of community organizations which cut across the social processes in such ways that they need to be examined and understood on their own account. A brief discussion may clarify this point.

Types of Agencies and Organizations

Communities are served by at least three types of agencies and organizations. These may be designated as follows:

1. Governmental: agencies created by law, regulated by law or official pronouncement, and supported through taxation. Examples: the legislature, post office, police force, rationing board, public school, public library, Bureau of Standards.

2. Commercial: agencies operated privately for purposes of profit-making. Illustrations: store, factory, newspaper plant, beauty parlor, railroad, peanut stand, chamber of commerce.

3. Private non-commercial: agencies organized voluntarily by private groups to serve specific purposes, controlled by their own members, and financed by subscriptions, membership fees, gifts, and bequests. Samples: political party, medical association, service club, church, planned parenthood center, community coordinating council.

These three general types of agency may be illustrated further in relation to any one of the social processes described above. With respect to making a living, for example, there are both Federal and state agencies which have authority to regulate and enforce standards concerning conditions of work; there are trade associations and labor unions seeking to advance the financial interests of their members; and there are private welfare organizations through whose facilities workers may increase their vocational competence.

Both governmental and commercial agencies are relatively easy to discover in the community, but often the private non-commercial organizations are more difficult to find since many of them may not be registered with any central clearinghouse. In such cases, councils of social agencies and other organizations having an over-all concern with particular aspects of community life may have the needed information, or may be helpful in securing it.

Scope of Service

An agency may have been created to perform but one simple and clear-cut service, or it may offer many and varied services. Some organizations gather to themselves new responsibilities as they grow and develop, so that eventually they function in areas far beyond those originally envisioned. Most agencies soon develop feelings of "vested rights" within a particular field, and are characteristically unwilling to abandon it even though their services are no longer really needed or could be better provided by some other organization. That is why the actual functions performed by an agency, as well as its interrelationships with other organizations, must be known if the community picture is to be a complete and accurate one.

Agencies and organizations vary also in the areas they serve. Government agencies serve the political areas by and for which they were created; such areas may be local, county-wide, state-wide, nationwide, or international in scope. Non-commercial agencies may also serve areas as small as a neighborhood or as large as an entire hemisphere or even the whole world. Some agencies which offer a nationwide or international service do so only generally, through their national organizations. Others serve through units or subdivisions in the region, state, and local community. The American Red Cross is a notable example of a private, non-commercial organization which functions effectively in all community areas: in tiny hamlets, in counties, states, regions, nations, and between nations through the International Red Cross.

COMMUNITY PLANNING

There is growing public realization that in a society as complex as ours, deliberate public planning is essential if we are to establish and maintain a satisfactory quality of living for all our people. Community planning, which is one expression of this development, is in a sense a civic responsibility, and was so indicated in this chapter. Yet many private and non-commercial agencies operate in this field, and since much valuable planning is done informally, quite apart from any official action by government, it is apparent that community planning is a proper function of all three types of agencies listed above. Any study of community agencies should therefore seek to discover what is being done to coordinate all community activities directed toward improvement of the general welfare through conscious planning of future programs, and also what efforts are being made to stimulate wider awareness of this general need.

To Summarize

Community analysis, however interesting its procedures and findings, should never be considered an end in itself. Sociological analysis, like medical diagnosis, is properly only the intelligent basis for prescriptive action.

We have already seen (Chapter 1) that the fundamental purpose

IN LIFE-CENTERED EDUCATION

COMMUNITY LIFE AND NEEDS

(Essential Curriculum Content)														
Geography & Topography		COMMUNITY SETTING											Population Composition & Status	
COMMUNITY AREAS	SOCIAL PROCESSES AND PROBLEMS												COMMUNITY LEVELS	
	1	2	3	4	5	6	7	8	9	10	11	12		
Local	Utilizing Natural Environment	Appreciating the Past	Adjusting to People	Exchanging Ideas	Making a Living	Sharing in Citizenship	Maintaining Health & Safety	Improving Family Living	Securing Education	Meeting Religious Needs	Enjoying Beauty	Engaging in Recreation	Material / Institutional / Psychological	
Regional													Material / Institutional / Psychological	
National													Material / Institutional / Psychological	
International													Material / Institutional / Psychological	

ARE INTERPRETED FOR THE CHILD BY THE SCHOOL

(Basic Educational Methods)									
Documentary Materials	Audio-Visual Aids	Resource Visitors	Interviews	Field Trips	Surveys	Extended Field Studies	Camping	Service Projects	Work Experiences

TO MEET HIS VITAL NEED FOR ADULT COMPETENCE

(The Goal) — Attitudes ↔ Skills ↔ Understanding — SUCCESSFUL LIVING

THUS RELATING SCHOOL INSTRUCTION WITH COMMUNITY LIFE NEEDS

of life-centered education is to help students attain ever-increasing ability to face life's perplexing problems with success and satisfaction. We have understood (Chapter 2) that such ability requires the development, through first-hand experiences, intellectually analyzed, of appropriate community understandings, attitudes, and skills. And finally we have recognized (Chapter 3) that the community itself must be understood in terms of its primary structure, setting, processes and problems, agencies, and historic development before active exploration of that community becomes educationally desirable.

Parts I and II of this volume have thus established for us the necessary general prerequisites to successful community study and participation through organized school programs. Now we are ready for Part III, wherein we shall examine the nature, values, types, tested procedures, and limitations of ten distinctive "bridges" which may be used to link school instruction with community life itself. First, however, the accompanying chart should be examined for its summary of Parts I and II and its preview of Part III. Here we note that in life-centered education, the *processes and problems of human living* (the essential curriculum content) *are interpreted through vicarious and first-hand experiences* (basic educational methods) *in order to meet the child's need for genuine competence in successful living* (fundamental goal of all education). In the light of this perspective, let us now begin to examine the techniques of building pedagogic bridges between the insular school and the mainland of life.

SELECTED REFERENCES

Bingham, Florence C. (ed.), *Community Life in a Democracy*. Chicago: National Congress of Parents and Teachers, 1942. A handbook of practical suggestions for democratically improving daily life in American communities.

Colcord, Joanna C., *Your Community: Its Provision for Health, Education, Safety, and Welfare*. New York: Russell Sage Foundation, 1941. Detailed suggestions for making non-technical studies of a community.

Cook, Lloyd A., *Community Backgrounds of Education*. New York: McGraw-Hill, 1938. Sociological interpretation of community life, with particular reference to community patterns and influences which surround youth and condition the work of the schools.

Cook, Lloyd A., "The Meaning of Community." *Educational Method* 28:259–62 (March 1939). Functional criteria by which to define a true community in terms of a locality group plus its culture.

Croad, J. Russell, "Learning Experiences Based Upon Community Life." *California Journal of Elementary Education* 11:103–17 (Nov. 1942). Describes the historical background, population, industries and occupations, government, topography and natural resources of Monterey city to illustrate community analysis.

Georgia Program for the Improvement of Instruction in the Public Schools, "The Community as a Source of Materials of Instruction." Atlanta: State Department of Education, 1938. Practical advice for utilizing community resources in the school program. Especially useful are the suggested questions concerning community needs and resources, together with possible ways of investigating them.

Green, Mildred, "Community Life—Today and Yesterday." *National Education Association Journal* 29:52 (Feb. 1940). How a group of slow, underprivileged sixth-graders analyzed their community in studying how civilization has developed.

Greenough, Katherine C., "Know Your County." Washington: National League of Women Voters, 1937. Handbook for the study of county government by its various functions.

Hall, Robert B., "Local Inventory and Regional Planning in the School Curriculum." *Journal of Geography* 33:17–22 (Jan. 1934). The educational values of local community mapping, with specific suggestions for such mapping.

Junker, Buford H., and Martin B. Loeb, "The School and Social Structure in a Mid-western Community." *School Review* 50:686–95 (Dec. 1942). Excellent non-technical study of one community in terms of population, class stratification, participation of teachers, influence of social differentiation in high school, differing attitudes toward education, and the like. A good model for introductory community analysis.

Karlin, Jules (ed.), *Field Manual for Teachers*, Chs. II, VI. Chicago: Werkman's Book House, 1941. Outlines for the classification of community resources and for the systematic study of a community.

Koopman, Margaret O., *Social Processes*. Mount Pleasant, Michigan: Central Michigan College of Education, 1939. Mimeographed activity workbook and directions for prospective teachers engaged in community study at the College.

Lynch, Helen, "City Planners from Little Children Grow." *School Executive* 63: 35–36 (Oct. 1943). Seventh-graders study problem of planning as it appears in their own district, prepare an assembly program of findings, and with the city planning commission emphasize the importance of a city-wide focusing of community study upon city planning.

Morgan, Arthur E., *The Small Community*. New York: Harper, 1942. Points out the primary significance of the local community in human affairs; analyzes forms of community organization, especially the community council; describes various community processes and problems; and summarizes general observations.

National League of Women Voters, "Know Your Town." Washington: 1941. Selected questions to be used in studying a town's history, population, industry, workers, public welfare, education, health, recreation, courts, streets, housing, government, etc.

Parker, Edith P., "Geography and the Community." *Journal of Geography* 40: 98–108 (March 1941). How to analyze a community, make a community map, carry out simple fieldwork, see meaning and "wholeness," and think about what a better community would be like.

Riggs, M. J., "Geography Field Work in the Small City." *Journal of Geography* 37:28–31 (Jan. 1938). Useful suggestions for studying the spatial pattern of any city, and for generalizing upon its meaning.

Santa Barbara County Teacher's Guide for Use of Community Resources. Santa Barbara, California: The Schauer Printing Studio, Inc., 1941. A guide in building units of study centering around local community processes and resources. Excellent correlation of problems and pupil activities.

Smith, T. Lynn, "The Role of the Community in American Rural Life." *Journal of Educational Sociology* 14:387–400 (March 1941). Defines the community and the neighborhood, notes trends in the structure and role of the community, and suggests how educational programs can capitalize on the natural social units of rural America.

United States Office of Education, "Know Your Community." Leaflet 57, Know Your School Series. Washington: Government Printing Office, 1941. Significant orientation, questions, and references for studying size of the community, location, history, people, making a living, community organization and government, health, recreation and cultural opportunities, housing, and welfare services.

Wale, Fred G., "Twin Oaks: A Community Coming of Age." *Progressive Education* 19:270–77 (May 1942). Colloquial monologue describing how the people of a West Virginia village-rural area became conscious of their needs, went about meeting them cooperatively, and found their school program just what they needed.

PART III
TEN BRIDGES BETWEEN SCHOOL AND COMMUNITY

SINCE the turn of the century the rising demand for social and psychological realism in American schools has found expression in many schools of varied philosophy and practice. Scrutiny of their basic curricular programs reveals the use of ten major approaches to community life, each of which may be considered as one step nearer the first-hand, comprehensive experiencing of reality than was its immediate predecessor. Ranged in ascending order those ten bridges between school and community are these: Documentary Materials, Audio-visual Aids, Resource Visitors, Interviews, Field Trips, Surveys, Extended Field Studies, Camping, Service Projects, and Work Experiences. In this section we shall examine each such bridge in turn.

*

VISION OF THE BEST EDUCATION

AN actual situation responsibly faced is the ideal unit of educative experience; of all possible situations, no other is quite so educative as one that prompts the responsible leaders of the community to join with the young in carrying forward an enterprise in which all really share, and in which each can have his own responsible part. This is the education in which democracy can most rejoice, particularly in these times when we must learn to put the public welfare first in point of time and importance. In solemn fact, *cooperative activities for community improvement* form the vision of the best education yet conceived.

—WILLIAM H. KILPATRICK

In Paul R. Hanna and Research Staff, *Youth Serves the Community*. By permission of the D. Appleton-Century Company, publishers.

THE BOOK HABIT

IT is not exaggerating to say that the book habit is so firmly fixed that very many pupils, otherwise intelligent, have a positive aversion to directing their attention to things themselves—it seems so much simpler to occupy the mind with what someone else has said about these things. While it is mere stupidity not to make judicious use of the discoveries and attainments of others, the substitution of the seeing of others for the use of one's own eyes is such a self-contradictory principle as to require no criticism.

—JOHN DEWEY

In "The Primary-Education Fetich."
The Forum, May, 1898.

EDUCATION CEASES TO FUNCTION

IN a rapidly changing world education ceases to function as a vital force—and therefore ceases to be education—unless it proves itself able to meet new conditions.

—HAROLD SPEARS

In *Experiences in Building a Curriculum*, p. 19. By permission of the Macmillan Company, publishers.

CANNOT OPERATE WITHIN FOUR WALLS

THE important part about the social aspect of education is that educational institutions cannot operate within four walls. They must, to be effective, be identified with their supporting communities. They must utilize these communities in their work . . . The more closely an educational institution responds to the need of its community, the more effective it will be.

—ERNEST O. MELBY

In "A Concept of Dynamic Education." *Educational Trends*, June–July, 1938.

THE STUFF THAT MAKES EDUCATION REAL

CHILDREN who come into the schoolhouse to learn must leave the schoolhouse to learn—they must find in the outside world the stuff that makes education real. Book learning—even learning from pictures and talks—is detached, ungrounded, unless it grows out of substantial experience with the real world.

—CARLETON WASHBURNE

In *A Living Philosophy of Education*, p. 395. By permission of the John Day Company, publishers.

CHAPTER 4

Utilize Documentary Materials

CRIME AND THE SCHOOL BUDGET

Heated, almost bitter debate marked the annual meeting of the Falville Board of Selectmen. The police report had just revealed a 26 per cent increase in crime as measured by total arrests, and the town leaders hotly traded "causes" and "cures" without agreement concerning either. As the situation became tense and baffling, a visiting educator offered to study the problem and report upon it at a later special meeting of the Board. His offer was accepted, and the session adjourned to await his findings.

The investigator turned to the annual Town Reports as his chief source of information. These Reports made detailed analysis of the activities of the various town departments and other sub-divisions. A breakdown of the crime statistics by age groupings indicated that the bulk of the crime increase had occurred among boys of high school age. This fact immediately raised certain questions about the efficiency of the school system.

He next discovered that although high school enrollment had increased 42 per cent during the past six years, total school expenditures had declined more than 9 per cent in the same period, while per pupil costs had dropped from $117 to $98, or 16 per cent. Although this per pupil cost was still above the national average, the investigator was able—in view of the community's relatively high economic standing—to ask pointedly whether there might be some relation between the reduction in the school budget and the increase in crime statistics. He noted further that the school report indicated an abnormally high degree of retardation in Falville schools.

Upon the basis of these findings, the educator recommended that the Board authorize a special survey of school retardation and its causes. For if such retardation could be measurably decreased, he suggested, many a child would be spared that dangerous, predelinquent attitude of discouragement, frustration, and resentment, often developed by a lively sense of failure in school. Then the delinquency and crime rates would doubtless be reduced, and in addition, the schools would save money through elimination of most classroom "repeaters."

The Board was much impressed by this lucid analysis and recommen-

---

[1] Much of this chapter's material originally appeared in Edmund deS. Brunner, "The School and Its Community," in Staff of Division I, Teachers College, Columbia University, *Readings in the Foundations of Education,* Vol. I, pp. 209–26; also in his "How to Study a Community," *Teachers College Record,* March 1941, pp. 483–92. Used by permission.

dation, and promptly took favorable action upon it. The town's Annual Reports, it appeared, had proved to be of more than mere historical value.

What Are Documentary Materials?

"Documentary materials" is a generic term applied to all written or printed sources of information, but not including maps, charts, photographs, or other such visual aids. Among the chief kinds of documentary materials are books, magazines, newspapers, pamphlets, diaries, school and library records, deeds, abstracts, tax receipts, bank statements, bills of lading, and the like.

How May Documentary Materials Prove Useful?

The school is an institution of the community. Its fortunes ebb and flow with those of the community. School-community interaction is inevitable, and thus, by the same token, intimate and extensive knowledge of the community is a *sine qua non* of successful school teaching and administration. Perhaps the primary approach to the attainment of that knowledge is through the wise use of written source materials. Documentary materials, well used, can:

1. Provide interesting teaching materials for many academic fields such as those of civics, economics, history, sociology, science, home economics, industrial arts, and the like.

2. Promote development of the scientific attitude in the analysis of community traditions, interests, outlooks, and so forth, since of all informational sources, the printed page may be the most impersonal and least emotional.

3. Stimulate needed perspective by providing comparable data from communities distant in either space or time or both.

4. Permit intelligent solution of community problems by basing both analysis and policy-making upon accurate data objectively gathered.

For every community, regardless of size, there are available many kinds of documentary materials whereby school instruction can be made more interesting and functional. And every teacher, whatever his subject field, can enrich and vitalize his own procedures through appropriate use of available documentary sources. Such is one practical method of bridging the gulf between school and community life.

What Are the Major Sources of Documentary Materials?

Such materials are procurable from four chief sources: standard publishers, governments, civic associations, and business organizations. Let us note some typical contributions of each in turn.

1. Standard Publishers

Numerous commercial publishing houses (including university presses and newspapers) issue considerable material useful in community study and service. Many of these publications are valuable as general background for local situations, for making comparisons between local conditions and those elsewhere, and for basic study of larger community areas. No comprehensive list of such materials could be presented here, but the following items are perhaps suggestive:

Encyclopedias

1. *Americana*
2. *Britannica*
3. *Catholic Encyclopedia*
4. *Jewish Encyclopedia*
5. *Encyclopedia of Religion and Ethics*
6. *Encyclopedia of the Social Sciences*

Biographical Dictionaries

1. *Dictionary of American Biography*
2. *Who's Who*
3. *Who's Who in America*

Cumulative Indexes

1. *Education Index*
2. *International Index to Periodicals*
3. *New York Times Index*
4. *Public Affairs Information Service*
5. *Readers Guide to Periodical Literature*

Annuals, Handbooks, and Yearbooks

1. *American Year Book*. Excellent narrative accounts of the year's developments in such broad fields as history, economics, public resources, social conditions, government, literature, education, science, religion, etc. Lists of relevant periodical references and of related organizations are included.

2. *Book of the States*. An authoritative summary of governmental affairs in each of the forty-eight states. Tabular comparisons are made for such items as state election laws, state expenditures, state employees and payrolls, industrial relations, marriage laws, crime control legislation, motor vehicle regulation, etc. Rosters of state administrative officials are included.

3. *Municipal Year Book*. Annual résumé of activities and statistical data for most American cities. Gives comparable data on such matters as crime rates, population shifts, accident deaths, library expenditures, school enrollment, tax rates, names of chief administrative officers, etc.

4. *Social Work Yearbook.* Authoritative articles on all aspects of social work such as city planning, housing, youth problems, unemployment, and so forth.

5. *Statesman's Year Book.* Concise and readable manual of descriptive and statistical information about governments of all countries in the world. For each country, it gives data on government, education, religion, justice, social welfare, industry, etc. Valuable bibliographies are included.

6. *Statistical Abstract of the United States.* Official statistics covering social, economic, and governmental aspects of the nation.

7. *United States Government Manual.* Describes the creation, organization, functions, and activities of all branches of the federal government. Organization charts are included, and so are the names and titles of all administrative officials.

8. *World Almanac.* The most comprehensive and useful handbook of miscellaneous information. Contains much data on industry, government, history, education, religion, biography, and similar subjects.

State Yearbooks such as the *New York Red Book,* the *Oregon Blue Book,* are issued by many of the forty-eight states. These provide official information concerning such matters as state legislation, school system, law enforcement, planning and housing, names and titles of state officials, and the like.

Pamphlets

1. *America's Town Meeting of the Air.* Printed transcriptions of weekly radio discussions centering around current issues of popular interest. Some recent issues discussed are: *Let's Face the Race Question, Freedom of Speech on the Air, Does Bureaucracy Menace America? Will Wage Incentives Eliminate Conflict Between Labor and Management? Is a World Federation Government Desirable and Possible?* Address: Town Hall, New York, N. Y.

2. *Building America.* Illustrated unit studies of modern problems. Eight study units are published each academic year. Typical topics are: *Housing, Movies, Seeing America, Civil Liberties, Community Planning, Rubber, America Discovers Its Songs, War Against Inflation, Italian-Americans.* Address: 2 West 45th St., New York 19, N. Y.

3. *Foreign Policy Association's Headline Series.* Factual, authoritative, and graphic analyses of current issues and backgrounds in American foreign policy. Recent topics treated were: *Mexico, Russia at War, Struggle for World Order, War on the Short Wave, Shadow Over Asia, Look at Latin America, The Changing Far East.* Address: 22 East 38th St., New York 16, N. Y.

4. *Public Affairs Pamphlets.* Unit treatments of timely social, economic, political, and educational problems by recognized authorities. Suggestive titles: *Saving Our Soil, What the New Census Means, Prostitution and the War, Vitamins for Health, Cooperatives in the U. S., The Negro and the War, Races of Mankind.* Address: 30 Rockefeller Plaza, New York 20, N. Y.

5. *University of Chicago Round Table.* Transcribed reports of weekly

radio discussions of current interest topics. Recent titles are: *Anti-Semitism, War Medicine, Strategy of Food, Morals in Wartime, Where's Bunker Hill?* Address: University of Chicago Press, Chicago 37, Ill.

2. GOVERNMENTS

Federal, state, and local governments publish much valuable material in addition to the few sources cited above. Many such items are either free or very inexpensive, thus putting them within financial reach of most teachers and all schools.

Many federal agencies, for example, issue documentary materials which may provide useful information concerning the national, regional, and even local community areas. Especially noteworthy are these Departments and sub-divisions:

1. Agriculture
2. Commerce
3. Justice
4. Labor (Children's Bureau, Women's Bureau, Bureau of Labor Statistics)
5. Federal Security Agency (Social Security Board, Office of Education, Public Health Service).

Lists of publications issued by these and other Departments may be obtained without charge, upon application to the Superintendent of Documents, Government Printing Office, Washington, D. C.

A majority of the states issue annual or biennial handbooks such as those already mentioned for New York and Oregon. The teacher should communicate with the relevant state agency concerning the availability of such reviews. From these, it is possible to discover how one's own county, and often one's local community, compares with others in the state. Information of this sort shows some of the services that the state offers its citizens, and also makes direct and concrete the more generalized content of school textbooks.

Counties and even municipalities often publish comparable reports, the latter especially in New England. In one Massachusetts town, this report runs to three hundred pages and is sent to the citizens. It provides detailed financial data for all departments such as fire, police, health and sanitation, education, libraries, highways, charities, recreation, unemployment, debt, and interest. It lists all appropriations, reports on assessments and tax collections. It presents, in addition to this financial data, careful discussion of the work and accomplishments of each department, as well as other significant data. For the schools, the training, salary and years of service in the town of each teacher, supervisor, and administrator are recorded; detailed information on enrollment and attendance is set forth by grades in each school; school expenditures are listed under forty-eight headings and the proportion each gets of the total budget is shown; age-grade tables are worked out. Other municipal departments are similarly reported upon.

Even if such local reports are not published, they are almost invariably prepared for submission to higher authorities and are locally filed and available for consultation.

City directories are common and very useful sources of information in metropolitan areas. New York City's "Little Green Book," for example, boasts over five hundred pages of "bible paper," is a veritable encyclopedia of information about the city government, and is a local best-seller at fifty cents a copy.

3. BUSINESS ORGANIZATIONS

A major source of documentary materials are the business organizations of the community. Despite the private character and interested nature of their activities, such agencies should not be overlooked as sources of community information.

While chambers of commerce, in the nature of the case, try to put the best foot forward, they do frequently gather and record valuable information, particularly in the area of economic and business conditions. Labor unions, too, may offer fruitful source materials. Large unions especially have educational departments which collect a great amount of local data in their attempts to develop workers' understanding and public support. In large cities, the telephone company will have data on population trends, home ownership, and other related matters useful to it in planning for the location of telephone centrals and in forecasting demands for service. Such information may be equally pertinent for such a public agency as the school. This data is not made available to the general public, but may usually be obtained by responsible school officials.

Real estate boards and trade associations are other important business organizations which frequently collect data on local economic conditions, and may often make it available for school use.

4. CIVIC ASSOCIATIONS

Many local and state agencies of an essentially civic character assemble vital information about their communities. Among the many such agencies whose findings and records are valuable in community study are these:

Historical societies	Housing authorities
Patriotic associations	Civic planning agencies
Social agencies	Farm and home bureaus
Fraternal and service clubs	Women's civic organizations
Cultural minority associations	Selective Service boards
Churches	Schools and colleges

The larger the community, the better and more complete all these sources of information are likely to be. Here and there, educational authorities are themselves beginning to prepare excellent handbooks, specifically designed as guides to selected aspects of local community life. Typical of these are the Los Angeles City School District's *Community Life Series:* "Parks and Recreational Centers," "The Civic Center," etc.; the Los Angeles County Schools' *Industrial Units Series:* "The Petroleum Industry," "The Walnut Industry," etc.; Philadelphia's *Curriculum Reference Pamphlets:* "Speaking of Elections," "They Carry the Mail," etc. and its *Educational Bulletins:* "Building the School into the Community," "Home and School Relations," "Health and Human Relations," etc.; Syracuse University's Community Study Handbooks: "Community Planning," "The Structure of Local Government," "Financing Local Government," "Parties and Politics in the Local Community," etc. (titles tentative at this writing); and Clarence V. Howell's *Let's Go to Church,* an interpretative guide to the many and varied religious centers of New York City.[2] Yet even in small communities, it is surprising how much material of local social significance exists in easily obtainable form. The formula for obtaining it lies simply in knowing where to go for the kind of information desired.

What Information Can Documentary Materials Provide?

Very few communities have been exhaustively studied like Middletown. In this respect rural America is more fortunate than urban, for the rural sociologists, especially in the agricultural colleges, have made some thousands of studies of communities and of many aspects of community life such as standards of living, social

---

[2] Published by Reconciliation Trips, Inc., 417 West 121 St., New York City.

organizations, recreational and library facilities, health, housing, cooperatives, social aspects of farm tenancy, the social contribution
of the consolidated school problem, the status of youth, and so on.
Some urban universities have also conducted extensive surveys of
their communities. While all such studies are a first resource, if
only as a guide to method, it is obvious that most communities have
not been so placed under a social microscope, and that the teacher
must therefore rely largely upon his own investigations.

It will perhaps be most fruitful to classify the main documentary
sources according to the kinds of information sought. Let us therefore see what typical documentary materials are available for the
investigation of population data, history, geography, economic conditions, cultural status, social welfare, and public planning. We
shall consider each of these areas in turn.

POPULATION DATA

A primary source as to population is the United States Census.[3]
The amount of information available for any given community depends chiefly upon its size. The Census is most complete for all cities
of over 100,000 population, somewhat less complete for those of
10,000 to 100,000, and for places below 1,000 only the total population with its age and sex distribution is published.[4] There is, however, a mass of data, relating to small units such as towns, counties,
and small population groups, which is tabulated but not printed,
and which is of particular value in making local studies. For the
kind of tabulated but unpublished data available, one should consult C. Luther Fry's "Making Use of Census Data." [5]

The Bureau of the Census will furnish answers to questions of
considerable scope about any community. This service is free of
charge if the request can be taken care of by one clerk in a day
or less, and at cost if it takes longer. The requested information
can be supplied, if desired, by the so-called enumeration districts,
the small basic units, carefully mapped, for which the data are
recorded and tabulated. The usefulness of these units is illustrated
by the situation in one quite homogeneous community where a bit-

---

[3] For a topical listing of what each Census volume since 1870 contains, see P. W.
Maynard, "The Use of Local Statistics in High School Courses in Sociology and
Social Problems." *Social Studies* 31:22 (Jan. 1940).

[4] For unincorporated places the Census Bureau publishes only approximate population figures in response to requests.

[5] *American Statistical Association Journal* 25:129–38 (Jan. 1930).

ter fight broke out as to whether or not to build a new school and where to locate it, if built. An outside consultant discovered that 70 per cent of the actual and 75 per cent of the potential school enrollment resided in three enumeration districts, the rest in the other ten. This fact explained the reason for the conflict and furnished part of the basis for its settlement.

Among other important items the population census gives data concerning:

Age and sex composition of the population.
Number of foreign-born by country of origin.
Number of native-born of foreign parentage.
Marital status of the population.
School attendance by ages under twenty-one years.
Educational status of population 25 years of age and over.
Color of population.
Number of persons born outside the state.
Number of persons ten years old and over engaged in gainful occupations by sex and industry groups.
Migration.

Much of this information is available by wards in large cities, by the separate counties of each state, and also for the urban, rural-farm, and rural non-farm population groups.[6]

How can such information be useful to the student of school and community? Suppose he found that in a given community, children ten to fourteen years of age make up 8.5 per cent of the population, those five to nine years, 8.0 per cent, and those under five, 7.3 per cent. With these simple facts before him, he could make reasonable deductions as to the birth rate of the community and the probable trend in school enrollment during the next several years. The picture in another community, where the percentages for the three age groups were respectively 9.6, 9.5, and 9.6 would show quite a different probable school attendance in the future. In such a case, the community whose school population was maintaining itself would probably be a more logical locus for a new consolidated school than would the community with declining school enrollment.

Occupational data may reveal important social and educational forces operating in a community. Consider this illustration:

---

[6] It is important to note any changes in procedure which may make earlier census figures not strictly comparable with the later. The introductory sections of Census volumes contain explanations of such changes.

NUMBER AND PER CENT OF MARRIED WOMEN 15 AND OVER
GAINFULLY OCCUPIED, FOR CITIES OF 100,000 OR MORE

City	Total	Number Gainfully Occupied	Per Cent Gainfully Occupied
New York, N. Y. . . .	1,485,155	174,882	11.8
Bronx	285,444	23,839	8.4
Brooklyn	542,845	47,193	8.7
Manhattan	369,986	74,585	20.2
Queens	254,839	26,432	10.4
Richmond	32,492	2,833	8.7

From these figures, significant clues can be obtained as to size of
family, family life of school children, and the like. We can deduce
that Manhattan, for example, would tend to have smaller families
than the other boroughs. Page 59 of the Family Census Volume
shows us that the median size family for Manhattan (all families)
is 2.80, while it varies from 3.39 for Queens, 3.54 for Bronx, 3.63
for Brooklyn, to 3.67 for Richmond. The implications are varied—
but one educational consequence might very well be the presence
in Manhattan schools of many more problems, on the average, relating to the "only child." (This example, be it noted, is picked at
random and no attempt has been made to check the clue further. All
such interpretations must be considered merely as hypotheses to be
checked by further intensive analysis before even tentative acceptance.)

In addition to the population census, the family census presents [7]
among other valuable data that on size of family; number of families with no children, one child, two, three, four, five, and more
children; value or rental of houses; income, and possession of radios
and specified household appliances. As one example of how part of
these data may be used, let us compare town R with the adjoining
town L, and with the county B, in respect to size of family. Thus we
find:

PROPORTION OF FAMILIES HAVING

	No Children under 10	1 Child under 10	2 Children under 10	3 or More under 10	Median Size of Family
Town R	66.9%	19.7%	10.3%	3.1%	3.37
Town L	53.4	23.3	13.4	9.9	3.76
County B . . .	58.2	22.2	12.5	7.1	3.54

[7] Some data contained in the family census, 1930, appears in the Housing and
Population reports of the 1940 census.

These figures suggest that the high school occupies a relatively more important place in town R's system than it does in either the neighboring town or in the county. This diagnosis may be checked by noting the percentage of different age groups attending school in the same three areas:

SCHOOL ATTENDANCE—PER CENT ATTENDING

	Ages			
	7 to 13	*14 to 15*	*16 to 17*	*19 to 20*
Town R	98.6%	97.7%	77.1%	37.1%
Town L	98.6	77.3	37.6	11.8
County B	97.9	91.3	55.8	18.2

Such further data not only confirm the relative importance of the high school years in town R, but at the same time offer indirect evidence of the community's economic strength—for only a community that can afford to do so retains large proportions of its youth in school after sixteen years of age.

In a number of major cities the census data has been published by local census committees in very detailed form for extremely small units. These units are called "census tracts," or "sanitary districts." Such census tracts—of which there are some 10,461 in or adjacent to sixty cities, including all cities of 250,000 or more— are generally constant from one census period to another. Within such cities, this makes possible accurate comparison of school neighborhoods and thus provides basis for modification of individual school programs.

History and Geography

Primary sources in this area are numerous. Local and county histories and legal records, documents preserved in libraries, newspaper files, minutes of proceedings of local governing bodies, old letters, memoirs—all these and many similar materials should yield a good account of the community's early settlement, noteworthy crises, noted leaders, and high points of development.

State histories often contain detailed references to particular local communities. These histories, when they are not available in print, are sometimes obtainable in manuscript form from the State Library or the State Historical Association. The federal census may also be useful in this connection, particularly in its data on nativity and interstate migration. The Illinois State Planning Commission, for example, has drawn from the census returns an interesting analysis of how interstate migration has affected the composition of that state's population in recent years.

The Writers' Program of the old Works Projects Administration compiled and had published much valuable data portraying the story of our American heritage. These publications include the *American Guide Series* and the *American Life Series* of books, together with scores of leaflets, pamphlets, and booklets dealing with many aspects of local communities' history, culture and life.

The Government Printing Office publishes many inexpensive books and pamphlets dealing with national, regional and local history, biography, geography, geology, climate, flora and fauna, and the like. Price lists of such materials may be secured without charge from the Superintendent of Documents, Washington, D. C.

Historical fiction and popular biography, particularly if centered in actual local communities or regions, can well be used to infuse the breath of real life into otherwise musty records and dry statistics. Yet precisely because such materials are fictional in character, they must be carefully scrutinized for general authenticity. Among the best of such historical fiction are the books of Hervey Allen for the Colonial frontier, Walter Edmonds for New York State, Joseph Lincoln for Cape Cod, Ellen Glasgow and Erskine Caldwell for the South, Willa Cather and Zona Gale for the midwest, Edgar Lee Masters for Illinois, Walter Havighurst for the Great Lakes region, Zane Grey, Rex Beach, James Oliver Curwood, and Vardis Fisher for the West. There are also books like Partridge's *Country Lawyer,* Hough's *Country Editor,* and Della Lutes' *Country School-ma'am* which provide rich insight into earlier community life and its human values.

ECONOMIC CONDITIONS

Many data concerning the economic status of the community are available. There is, first of all, much information on occupations and incomes. One whole census volume presents occupational data by states, including a classification of workers in more important occupations by color, nativity, and age.

A socio-economic scale readily applicable to the occupational distribution has been devised by Dr. Heba Edwards of the Census Bureau. This scale classifies occupations within nine major categories: (1) Proprietors, officials, and managers, (2) Clerks, (3)

Skilled workers, (4) Semi-skilled workers, (5) Laborers, (6) Servants, (7–8) Public and Semi-official public employees, (9) Professional.

The Census Bureau in 1930, 1933, 1935, and 1940 undertook censuses of American business, wholesale and retail. The retail census is especially valuable for purposes of community study. It gives total retail sales, number of stores, sales, employees, and total wages by type of store. This data should prove most valuable to the vocational teacher in the new area of distributive occupations. It is presented by states, counties, and municipalities of over 2,500 population. The data on per capita retail sales is perhaps the best single index of community wealth. Such an index may be used in varied ways; for example, comparisons may be made between counties or cities as to their respective per capita retail sales and their per pupil expenditures for schools. Or again, the effect of depression or recovery or war conditions upon a single community may be studied by observing how its per capita sales have fluctuated from state and national averages and from census to census. In such manner can the general economic strength of a community be estimated.

Similar, but less use can be made of the Biennial Census of Manufactures. This census presents (for all counties and cities of 10,000 population and over) statistics on such items as total number of manufacturing plants, value of products, number of employees, and wages paid.

In rural areas the census of agriculture, taken twice each decade, is most useful. It gives data on farm income, earnings off the farm, the number of farmers by tenure and color, farm population and its mobility, size and type of farms, the number and wages of agricultural laborers, and a wide variety of technical agricultural information.

By using this census, a class in Allen County, Kansas, for example, could learn that in 1935 their county had 2,155 farms with about 8,000 people living on them; that there were 5,016 sheep and lambs of all ages in the county as against 5,820 in 1930; that in 1934 the county raised 351,992 chickens who produced 1,363,932 dozens of eggs; that the value of farm garden vegetables dropped from $52,039 in 1929 from 1,296 farms to $6,507 in 1934 from 833 farms. The effect of a disastrous drought is evident in these figures, and could be still more clearly illustrated by extending the figures further. Genuine motivation for a thorough study of drought and plans for dealing with it is thus attained.

Interesting classroom use can also be made of the statistics on number of bushels of apples, cherries, peaches, and other fruits produced by the county's farmers. Totals can be divided by the county population, or by number of families, and enlightening discussion thereby started about how many bushels each person or family could theoretically have, the problems of exchanging these commodities for others necessary, and related questions.

Implications of the agricultural statistics are quite varied. Size of farms obviously affects density of population and, therefore, the spacing and enrollment of schools. A high proportion of tenancy is often associated with a high mobility of population, and especially, but not exclusively in the South, with low farm income and a high degree of pupil retardation in the schools. A high proportion of agricultural laborers in the farm population usually means corporation or other large-scale and mechanized farming together with the employment of purely seasonal labor; this suggests, as in California, the presence of a disadvantaged, immigrant labor group with the galaxy of problems it produces for schools and other social agencies. These and other similar factors clearly influence the type of school and affect its program, both in terms of its curriculum and with respect to its community relations and services. This latter problem is one of many studied by colleges in some of the states most concerned. There is also a two-volume report upon it by the United States Department of Labor.

Unemployment is another major economic problem to which separate census volumes have been devoted. In using unemployment data, however, particular care is necessary because of lack of uniformity in the use and meaning of the term "unemployed."

Another useful source of economic information is the *Market Data Handbook* of the Department of Commerce, of which there have been four issues since the first in 1929. The current issue is dated 1939. It reports upon 82 items by states for every county and municipality of over 2,500 population. Among the items are six on population and families, nine on volume and type of business, thirteen on employment and payrolls, over thirty on retail trade by major types, and over twenty on indicators of consumer purchasing power. These data are valuable for administrators, home economists, and teachers of social studies. In using the *Handbook*, however, certain cautions are in order. Many of the items in the 1939 volume are computed on the basis of 1930 Census results (e.g., per cent of white population, per cent owning homes, per cent of United States total population), thus raising the question as to whether 1930 figures serve the purposes of the inquiry. The statis-tics for sales per capita are based on 1935 sales and 1930 population, for example. In one Texas county the 1930 population was 15,778. Discovery of oil doubled that figure by 1935. The per capita sales figure, based on 1935 sales and 1930 population, is thus $1,474 as compared with a state average of $221! Such cases as this merely serve to dramatize the eternal necessity of scrutinizing with ut-most care, all the assumptions upon which any statistical data are based.

Cultural Status

The cultural tastes, interests, and problems of a community may be approached through many media. Magazine circulation or local newsstand sales is suggestive of the cultural level of a community; library circulation, measured by both quantity and quality, may also tell much about characteristic attitudes and tastes. Local news-papers, especially in their editorials, offer other worthwhile insights in this area.

Statistics on voting will indicate not only the political com-plexion of the community, but will also suggest something of local civic-consciousness as that is reflected in the size of the voting population.

Local laws and ordinances may reveal a community's interpreta-tion of civil rights, particularly for minority groups within its bor-ders. As background material in this area, the publications of the American Civil Liberties Union are especially valuable; so also are the reported activities and publications of various organizations seeking to improve or to disrupt existing intercultural relations. Such agencies in the interracial area may be epitomized by the National Association for the Advancement of Colored People on the one hand, and by the Ku Klux Klan on the other.[8]

Information concerning the religious denominations in the com-munity, with their proportionate memberships, may be found in the United States Census of Religious Bodies. Local religious activities are generally well publicized in the press; while denominational beliefs and rituals may be better understood through consultation

---

[8] For an extended list of constructive organizations, some with numerous local branches, see W. E. Vickery and S. G. Cole, *Intercultural Education in American Schools*, pp. 212–14. New York: Harpers, 1943.

of appropriate articles in standard encyclopedias, including the *Catholic Encyclopedia,* the *Jewish Encyclopedia,* and the *Encyclopedia of Religion and Ethics.*

SOCIAL WELFARE

Accurate data concerning community health, recreation, housing, social organization, and the like is all-important to the alert teacher or school administrator. Although information on such items in their local aspects is more difficult to secure than are facts about population or economic life, it can often be found, even for small communities. Some information on housing, for example, is contained in the United States Family Census. The 1940 Census included a separate housing and household inquiry covering such items as conditions of housing and plumbing facilities, type of structure, number of rooms, number of persons per room, tenure, and value or rental. Many communities participated in a W.P.A. housing survey in 1935. At about the same time, there was a national health survey, supervised by the Federal Public Health Service, which, though conducted on a sampling basis, had a wide coverage. It secured data from nearly 800,000 families in 89 cities and a number of rural areas, and reported upon the amount and kinds of illnesses and also the relation between disease and underlying socio-economic and other conditions.

The real importance of such integrated analysis is underlined by one case selected from a 1939 report of the Public Health Service. This report shows that of 10,717 cases of pellagra reported for the United States as a whole, 4,428—more than 40 per cent—occurred in the single state of Mississippi. We would therefore expect Mississippi educators to take account of this startling fact in the school curriculum, just as we would expect educators anywhere to take similar account of outstanding problems in their own communities. In a recent Massachusetts Town Report, for example, the Board of Health reports 46 cases of dog bite during a single year—an unusually high number for a small community. Might not this fact deserve some special attention in the schools of that community?

By using census material and data from the American Medical Association, it would be possible to get accurate estimates of how well a community's health needs are served by physicians and other health personnel. Comparisons between communities on the basis of per capita medical service would thus be simple to make. The

Association issues an annual directory of physicians in the United States, which would be available at the County Medical Society where one exists.

A detailed study of consumer income and standards of living in 58 representative cities, and in many more villages and rural communities in every region of the country was recently made under the auspices of the Bureau of Home Economics of the United States Department of Agriculture. Regional reports were issued through 1940 and 1941, and some are still in process. The volume on family expenditures for housing and household operation, to illustrate one of the reports, describes the dwellings of families studied, the number of rooms, persons per room, presence of electricity, central furnace, hot and cold water and other sanitary facilities.

Although these studies were concerned with only a fraction of the communities in the nation, they do give some indication of the situation within states and regions, and on some of the economic items the comparison may be sharpened, if no other data exists, by assuming that local variations from reported results will vary somewhat in proportion to per capita retail sales.[9] One very useful reference for comparative study of regional and smaller areas is R. A. Mangus' *Rural Regions of the United States,* a special report of the W.P.A.'s Division of Research.

Many cities have a Council of Social Agencies. Some of these councils have very useful research departments. Nearly all of them will have a "directory of social agencies," and can have access to member agencies' reports. Even where such a council is lacking, the executives of community chests, employment agencies, family welfare bureaus, commissioners of public welfare, visiting nurses associations, and other social welfare agencies can provide much reliable data concerning local social welfare. Sometimes local studies of health conditions, housing, zoning, and so forth have been reported only in local newspapers or even solely in a typewritten manuscript. Often public and university libraries may have such studies on file.

Information on juvenile delinquency can be obtained from the judge of the juvenile court, the police, or from social workers such as probation officers. If local community maps are plotted to show

---

[9] An estimate of rural retail sales in the Middle West in 1928, based on standard of living studies by colleges of agriculture, varied only two per cent from the total secured by the United States Census of Retail Sales in 1929.

the delinquents' residences, and also such other factors as racial distribution of the population, the value or rental of homes, locations of youth-serving agencies, distribution of relief cases and similar data, significant associations—both positive and negative—are usually discovered. Urban data of this sort are most useful to social agencies as well as to the school, since such information facilitates intelligent cooperation between them.

Knowledge of a community's social patterning is more difficult to acquire. The problem differs somewhat with the size of the community. In larger cities it is often sufficient to keep in touch with the various councils—such as those dealing with social work, adult education, labor unions, and recreation—and, through them, to learn what agencies are operating in any given neighborhood, and what services and facilities each offers. In smaller cities, towns, and villages, constant reading of the local newspapers will provide useful clues, as will constant touch with the socially alert clergy.

Civic agencies and organizations are of two main types: (a) *general interest*—those which represent the entire community so far as their area of interest and service is concerned (such as a League of Women Voters, Chamber of Commerce, or a Council of Social Agencies)—and (b) *special interest*—those which are chiefly concerned with some particular aspect or segment of community life (a ski club, an historical society, a maternal health center). To the teacher, the importance of knowing both types of organizations lies not merely in their programs and objectives. It goes further, for the memberships of these organizations often represent the influential groups in the community itself, and through contact with such members, access can often be had to other and perhaps wider groups. Moreover, such organizations frequently ask favors from the school, whose administrator needs to know how to evaluate such requests for cooperation. The wise school administrator thus has an additional reason for maintaining a complete card file of all local agencies such as is described in Chapter 18.

PUBLIC PLANNING

In this age of interdependence, government planning for public welfare is increasingly essential. The National Resources Planning Board, State Planning Boards in 46 of the 48 states, numerous county agricultural planning committees, and nearly 500 municipal planning boards, now operating, all indicate the significance of this new area.

The surveys and reports made by these various boards cover a wide range of social and economic data. The Illinois State Board, for example, has made the following among a much larger number of studies: Population trends and a 1960 population forecast for each city, village, and rural area; analysis of Illinois' education costs and estimates of future school needs as based on prospective age composition of the population; an inventory of recreational facilities and needs, and a study of leisure-time activities; the economic status of the state's population based upon occupations, farm and wage income, employment and unemployment, value of owned homes, retail sales, and relief load; a comprehensive inventory of mineral resources and of mineral production, marketing, and research; industrial trends in production, decentralization, cost elements, employment, and wages.

There is a growing recognition in the nation, in the state, in the counties, and in the cities that accurate, objective data are essential as a basis for intelligent public planning. In accord with this recognition, these many planning boards are accumulating an impressive amount of material, much of which is highly significant and easily available to the interested school-community investigator. A letter to one's own State Planning Board will bring full information concerning reports available.

How Can Documentary Materials Be Used Successfully?

All of the above suggestions merely emphasize the advantage of utilizing whatever documentary materials are available and pertinent to the immediate subject of investigation. The teacher should be especially alert to make full use of government agencies whose business it is to know all the documentary materials available in any given subject and community area. Certainly the teacher should own catalogues of publications issued by such federal Departments as those of Agriculture, Interior, Labor, and Commerce. To illustrate, the teacher who knows the Department of Agriculture publications will be aware that the Department's experiment stations have mapped types of soil and relative productivity for most counties on soil survey maps and have made these maps available for distribution. That teacher will know that for small areas—communities and even neighborhoods—the records of the Agricultural Adjustment Administration, available in the local office, are useful for such data as types of land tenure, crops, and livestock products. Again, the teacher who is acquainted with the federal Office of Education publications knows that it issues regular statistics on comparative school attendance, number of teachers and pupil-teacher ratios, teachers' salaries, financial support of education, school expenditures, value of school property, comparative statistics for Negro and White, and for urban and rural schools. And since many governmental materials are distributed without charge, they are especially useful for classroom purposes. Not only do they serve immediate teaching needs, but in the long view the pupils' resulting insights into the activities of local and state or national governments may be even more important educationally.

In working with any documentary materials, certain cautions should be observed. Let us therefore note four suggestions in this connection:

1. Decide Exactly What You Want to Find Out

The number and kinds of documentary sources used should be determined by what we want to know. Every source will tell us something about our community. No source or combination of sources will tell us everything—nor do we want to know everything. Rather, we want to know everything relevant to a particular problem. We must therefore go to sources with definite questions to be answered. We may want a rough, general estimate of the status of a particular community, or a detailed understanding of one special aspect of community life, or a well-rounded picture of the community as a functioning whole.

Each of these wants requires a different procedure in the use of available documentary materials. For one it may suffice to consult a few indices, e.g. total retail sales, per cent of the population in one or another of the "dependent" classes, and so on. For the next, every source pertaining to the special aspect in question will have to be studied, for clearly no quick check of such things as total retail sales, the number on relief, and existing land values will give us a full insight into the economic status of the community. One must learn to recognize the many degrees of fullness of analysis possible, and then to adjust the scope and intensity of research to the degree of completeness required.

2. Determine Who Will Use the Materials, and for What Purposes

Which documentary materials are to be used will depend to a considerable extent upon who is going to use them and why. For example, a civics class studying its community would probably not use local school records as a source, although an educator or a graduate student might very well do so.

3. REMEMBER THAT MATERIALS VARY GREATLY IN RELIABILITY

We must always check carefully, particularly when objective data are essential, upon the source or author of the material, the purpose for which it was prepared, and the methodology used. Newspapers, for example, always have a point of view which frequently reflects the attitudes of special interest groups, and it is important to learn this viewpoint in order to make full allowance for it. Chamber of commerce and labor union material will similarly show a bias, although more so on some questions than on others.

Many problems relating to methodology arise. We must know something of the conditions and assumptions under which the source materials were prepared. As a single example, we must be sure that terms used are truly comparable before we attempt to make contrasts between one community and another. In one city, to illustrate this point, birth data collected are based upon live births, while in another city such data include all births whether live or stillborn. Uncritical comparisons of birth rates in these two cities would obviously be quite misleading.

4. DON'T JUMP AT CONCLUSIONS

Social phenomena are complex and caution us never to generalize widely from limited and insufficient data. Professional integrity and public welfare alike demand that conclusions reached be restricted in scope and enthusiasm to implications reasonably inherent in the data itself.

Careful observance of such cautions as these will make the use of documentary materials in community study both profitable and interesting. Furthermore, it will do much to point the truth of that old cliché to the effect that even though liars figure, figures do not lie.

What Are the Limitations of Documentary Materials?

Despite their obvious values, the use of documentary materials in community study has certain marked limitations. Among these limitations there are three of major significance:

1. **Impersonality is characteristic of most printed materials,** and is particularly evident in such statistical items as census reports and sur-

vey summaries. Such materials definitely repel many people by their very lack of human "warmth."

2. Gullibility concerning the written word is unfortunately very prevalent. Many persons tend to accept as true whatever appears in print. The inherent authority of the printed page is still so great that it is genuinely hard to make immature readers critical of the assumptions and attitudes underlying the materials they use.

3. Difficulty of apprehending full meaning from written words alone. Words are highly abstract symbols, and frequently arouse quite different meanings in different minds. And since written words are necessarily inflexible in the sense that their author is not present to interpret, amplify, or clarify *his* meaning, it is evident that documentary materials must be used with exceeding care if their true meaning is to be commonly understood by all readers.

How may we overcome these limitations and proceed to study the community in ways that are more personalized, vivid, and meaningful? In answering these questions we may perhaps find a suggestion in the old Chinese saying that "one picture is worth a thousand words." Might this be the case in community study? Yes, often! Let us now proceed to consider that suggestion in the chapter following.

SELECTED REFERENCES

Andersen, Ruth, "Town Reports Are Useful." *Social Education* 6:265–66 (Oct. 1942). Suggestions for using New England Town Reports as local documentary materials in that region.

Calkin, Homer L., "Local History: A Means of Better Understanding United States History." *School Review* 50:53–60 (Jan. 1942). Many examples of local newspapers, diaries, journals, account books, manuscripts, etc. as local source materials.

Farr, Henry L., "Collecting and Using Current Materials." *Social Education* 4:174–76 (March 1940). Suggestions for assembling many kinds of documentary and other materials, and for using them effectively in the classroom.

Hubbard, Frank W., "How the Principal May Use the 1940 Census." In Department of Elementary School Principals, "How to Know and How to Use Your Community," pp. 37–41. Washington: National Education Association, 1941–42. Facts available in the Census, how to get such facts and use them, common misconceptions about government documents and census data.

Karlin, Jules (ed.), *Field Manual for Teachers*, Ch. VIII. Chicago: Werkman's Book House, 1941. Detailed and illustrated advice on using census data in local community study.

Mackintosh, Helen K., "Pen-and-Ink Friendships for the Americas." *School Life* 26:297–98 (July 1941). Names, locates, and characterizes nine American agencies through which letter-writing contacts with foreign students may be made.

Reeves, Floyd W., "Regional and National Resources of Use to Localities in Solving School and Community Problems." In William C. Reavis (ed.), *The School and the Urban Community*, pp. 215–27. Chicago: University of Chicago

Press, 1942. Comments on useful publications of six private organizations, and on those of several federal government bureaus.

Ridley, Clarence E., and Herbert A. Simon, "The Citizen Looks at His Local Government." *Social Education* 4:94–98 (Feb. 1940). Informal suggestions for looking critically at local administration in terms of such factors as tax rate, streets and housing, city hall records, public health reports, etc.

Sanders, Mary F., "Producing Curriculum Materials About the Community." *Elementary School Journal* 43:601–06 (June 1943). Reasons why the local community is often neglected, some community concepts needed by the child, and the problems each school faces in preparing its own instructional material on the community.

United States Bureau of the Census, "Uses of the 1940 Census Data in Schools." Washington: Government Printing Office, 1942. Designed for use particularly in rural high schools. Tells how photostatic copies of census data on townships and other minor civil divisions may be obtained and utilized.

Works Progress Administration, Writers' Program, *American Guide Series.* "Includes a uniform guide to each of the States, Alaska, Puerto Rico, and the District of Columbia. Each State and Territorial guide covers major motor highways mile by mile, with descriptions of towns and villages, inland and coastal waterways, recreation areas, historic shrines, and contemporary and historical points of interest. Separate chapters present the major cities, and an introductory section describes the background of the State or Territory— its history, archeology, geology, climate, industrial development, labor movement, architecture, literature," etc. There are also "guides to major cities, regions, counties, and towns; recreational pamphlets, pictorial guides, and others."

Works Progress Administration, Writers' Program, *American Life Series.* This series "includes books dealing with American life and customs, natural history, the American Indian, the Negro, military and maritime history, folklore, ethnic groups, national defense, and other significant subjects."

CHAPTER 5

Audio-Visual Aids

COMMUNITY STUDY IN A RURAL SCHOOL

Community study through audio-visual aids is systematically carried on in the rural schools of McDonough County, Illinois. Here a five-year experimental program is stressing the study of local community resources as one vital basis for a better understanding of regional, national, and international problems. This program is built around an outline guide which is used to give both direction and integration to the classroom activities. Three sections only of that guide are here reproduced by way of illustration.[1]

We Study Our Community

Outline of Activities Carried Out in McDonough Co.	Suggested Additional Audio-Visual Aids	Audio-Visual Aids for Correlating Our Community with Larger Areas
I Community History	(Note: All starred films were available in the county at stated times during the study and were used in schools where electricity was available at that time.)	
A Historical development traced through study of		
1 County histories		
2 Atlases		
3 Interviews with older residents		
4 Maps showing location of homes of early settlers		Films: *First Americans* *Colonial Children* *Mohawk Valley* (Eastman)
5 Old pictures, deeds, land grants, etc.		
6 U. S. map showing routes traveled by present inhabitants	* Color film on U. S. travel—*This Amazing America*	*Boone Trail* (Eastman)
7 Stories of early settlers and their homes	* Color film on construction—*The Making of American Homes*	*Kentucky Pioneers* (Erpi) *Flatboat Pioneers* (Erpi)
8 Dramatizations	Broadcasts from the homes of great literary figures of America— "American Pilgrimage" by Ted Malone.	

---

[1] Adapted from Dorothy I. Dixon, "Community Resources Pave the Way," *Educational Screen*, February 1943, pp. 47–51.

Outline of Activities Carried Out in McDonough Co.	Suggested Additional Audio-Visual Aids	Audio-Visual Aids for Correlating Our Community with Larger Areas
B History of the school pictured by		
1 Pictures of original building, present building, and any changes that may have occurred in the interim		
2 Reports, records, and minutes of the early schools	An opaque projector could be used to present these pictures for study by the pupils, or for community or P.T.A. meetings.	
3 Story of origin of present name of the school		
4 Exhibit of old textbooks		
5 Copy of original deed of land for school purposes. (May be secured at Co. Recorder's Office.)	To project this copy of the original deed on the screen would make possible a much more detailed study by a large group.	Glass Slides: *Beyond the Mississippi*
C Population trends and occupational development depicted by		Films: *Territorial Expansion of the United States* *Alaska* (Eastman) *The Old South* (Eastman)
1 Maps or charts showing population of community at time of first school and at the present		
2 Charts showing occupations of the early peoples, compared to those of today.	* Films on Food: *Meat for America, Exploring the African Continent Algonquin Waters Behind the Cup*	*From Seed to Cloth* (Produced by Pathe in cooperation with Harvard) *From Flax to Linen* (Eastman)
	* Film on Modern Homemaking: *Come Out of the Kitchen*	*From Fleece to Fabric* (Erpi) *Timber Front* (Canadian)
	* Film on Clothing Manufacturing: *Botany Clothes the Nation*	*New England Fisherman* (Eastman) *Romance of Silk* *Pacific Coast Salmon*
D Interesting residents—then and now—studied through		
1 Newspaper articles		
2 Pictures	Interesting filmstrips showing the people, their hobbies and interests,	Film: *Birthplace of America*
3 Stories related by present residents		

Outline of Activities Carried Out in McDonough Co.

Suggested Additional Audio-Visual Aids

Audio-Visual Aids for Correlating Our Community with Larger Areas

4 Old letters written by former residents now participating in state or national affairs
5 Snapshots

could be prepared by the children.

V Community Occupations
A Types of farming studied
1 General
2 Dairy
3 Grain
4 Livestock
5 Truck

B Charts and graphs showing employment of local residents, employment of city workers on farms, and the number of farm people employed elsewhere.

C Charts or graphs showing percentage of land owners engaged in farming and the percentage of farms being cultivated by tenants.

Lantern slides depicting the complete story of any type of farming—i.e.
From Seed to Loaf, or *The Proper Care of Cows*
* Film
A Planter of Colonial Virginia (Erpi)

Films:
Wheat to Bread
Corn Farmer
Miracle of the Meadows
Milk and Health
Market Gardening (Eastman)

Limestone and Marble (Eastman)
Arts and Crafts of Mexico
Pottery Making
Sand and Clay (Eastman)
Furniture Making (Eastman)
Anthracite Coal (Eastman)
Bituminous Coal (Eastman)

Glass Slides:
Community Helpers
Importance of Agriculture
Corn, America's Greatest Crop

IX Community Health
A Studied through survey of health resources and needs of community
1 Number of doctors, dentists, hospitals, and clinics in community
2 Playgrounds and recreational resources
3 Community water supply
4 Health needs in the community.

Have test made of water supply of school and homes by member of the State Health Department.
Show lantern slides, prepared to picture results of survey regarding health needs and water supply, at community or P.T.A. meetings.

Films:
Blindness and Saving Sight
Carbon Monoxide: The Unseen Danger
Care of the Teeth (Eastman)
Cancer, Its Cure and Prevention (March of Time)
City Water Supply
Heart Disease (March of Time)
The House Fly (Erpi)

What Are Audio-Visual Aids?

"Audio-visual aids" are mechanical teaching devices which appeal directly to the physical senses, particularly those of hearing and of sight. The audio aids are those designed to impart information, mold attitudes, and otherwise influence behavior through sound impressions. Records, transcriptions, and the radio are the most important aids in this audio group. The visual aids are those which have been developed to utilize the eye as a primary channel of sensory experience. The chart, graph, map, object, specimen, model, picture, stereograph, glass slide, slidefilm, and motion picture are all included in this category. Sometimes the two types are combined, as in the case of the dramatic skit, the sound slidefilm, the sound motion picture, or television.

What Special Values Have Audio-Visual Aids?

Some of the most valuable audio-visual aids are relatively new, and have not yet been widely used as learning aids. The educational value of competent audio-visual instruction, however, has been fully demonstrated, particularly during the past decade which has witnessed a tremendous development in this field. The ever-increasing number of colleges and universities offering special courses in the audio-visual field is a further indication of recognized value. In community study—of all areas and all levels—these aids may:

1. **Furnish vivid experiences** which are the essential basis for intellectual analysis, comparison, and generalization about the world of things and people.
2. **Provide a simplified view of complex data,** and thereby render complicated physical, social, and aesthetic situations more easily intelligible.
3. **Personalize geographically distant scenes and events** as they almost literally "bring the world into the classroom."
4. **Make real the past** as they recreate for the student dramatic and authentic episodes of history.
5. **Economize time** by presenting a wealth of impressions to the students in a well-organized, concise, and intrinsically interesting manner.

Literally hundreds of different audio-visual items are available to enrich and actualize the community study program. Here, then, is another fruitful method of linking school instruction to the larger community life, both past and present.

What Audio-Visual Aids Are Useful in Community Study?

Audio-visual aids intended to give students a better understanding of the community—whether that community be local, regional, national, or even world-wide in scope—must be selected carefully and used with intelligence and discrimination. To do otherwise is to dissipate valuable interest, effort, time, and money.

Two general classes of audio-visual aids are available for purposes of community study. The first group will include many materials collected or constructed by the teacher and students as they study the local community area. The second group will include, almost wholly, materials prepared by governmental, commercial, or civic agencies. These latter aids will be used primarily in studying the regional, national, and international communities. In utilizing both types, however, we must keep foremost in mind the two prime essentials of success in the use of any audio or visual aid: *1. Remember that it is an aid to good teaching and not a substitute for teaching, and 2. Be sure that the chosen aid directly contributes in maximum degree to achievement of the exact educational objectives sought.*

1. GRAPHIC DOCUMENTS ARE VITAL

Although charts, graphs, and maps are in one sense documentary materials, they are listed here because they all involve a greater degree of visual perception than do printed and written words alone. All are schematic representations of reality rather than verbal descriptions of it; they are therefore properly included among other visual aids intended to help students interpret meaningfully the community.

Table charts, organization charts, map charts, pictographs, line graphs, bar graphs, area graphs, physical maps, population maps, historical maps, literary maps, health maps, and relief maps are all among the various kinds of graphic documents which may be used to picture such categories of community data as the following:

Population: Sex, age, racial and national composition; changes in numbers and types; present residential areas.

History: Early settlements, community growth and extension, chronology of dates, location of existing historical sites and buildings, genealogy of famous families, etc.

Geography: Land use and productivity in relation to natural factors such as mountains and plains, waterways, climatic conditions, vegetation, animal life, soil composition, scenic areas, mineral and oil deposits, etc.

Political Organization: Political areas and boundaries, seats of government, principal cities, relationships between governmental divisions, lines of administrative authority and responsibility, etc.

Economic Conditions: Land ownership and values, industrial development, agricultural regions and products, changes in price level, financial balance sheet, American productive capacity, division of the national income, unemployment by years, etc.

Public Welfare: Occupational distributions, delinquency areas, housing conditions, racial and national residential groupings, health conditions, illiteracy rate, recreational facilities, life expectancy in different regions, frequency of accidents, welfare agencies, etc.

Transportation Facilities: Streets and highways, railroads, bus lines, ship and aviation routes, locations of terminals, etc.

Artistic Heritage: Homes and habitations of famous authors, dramatists, musicians, painters, poets, playwrights, actors, sculptors, etc.

Specific directions for preparing most types of graphic documents need not be given here. Three newer varieties of the graphic document, however, do merit brief mention at this point because they are so very appropriate to the community study field. Let us therefore consider the techniques of fashioning pictorial charts, land use maps, and social base maps.

Pictorial Chart

Sometimes called a "pictograph," this chart is an arrangement of realistic or symbolic pictures in such manner as to tell a statistical story. To make a pictorial chart, standardized symbols appropriate to the subject matter are either purchased or drawn. These symbols are cut out and pasted upon a paper or cardboard background, which is then properly lettered and titled. Excellent examples of this technique may be found in the Public Affairs Pamphlets and in the University of Chicago Round Table Transcripts.

Sheets of standardized pictorial symbols have been especially prepared for schools, and may be purchased at small cost from Pictorial Statistics, Inc., 142 Lexington Ave., New York 16, N. Y. This organization also publishes for school use an inexpensive and useful booklet entitled *Instructions for Chartmakers.* Interested teachers will find a much more comprehensive treatment of pictographic possibilities in Rudolph Modley's *How to Use Pictorial Statistics.*[2]

Land Use Map

This is a special type of map, constructed to show just how the land space of a given area is utilized for productive (or nonpro-

---

[2] New York: Harper, 1937.

ductive) purposes. It is an original drawing, done to scale upon the basis of actual field investigations, and is best finished according to some such symbolic representation:

LAND USE AND COLOR DESIGNATIONS*

Type of Land Use	Suggested Color	Pencil Number		
		A. W. Faber Castell	Dixon's Best	American Pencil, Unique
Forest	Dark Green	17	354	1208
Water Areas	Light Blue	21	320½	1216
Farm Land	Golden Yellow	6	353	1229
Dwellings (1–2 family)	Orange	9	324	1214
Dwellings (multiple) .	Light Brown	47	335½	1239
Commercial Buildings	Red	36	321	1207
Industry—light . . .	Violet	30	323	1210
Industry—heavy . .	Purple	29	323½	1225
Transportation . . .	Black	no number	no number	no number
Public Buildings and Grounds	Pink	31	322	1217
National Monuments .	Dark Blue	24	330	1236
Recreational Areas .	Lemon Yellow	3	353½	1209
Welfare Institutions .	Dark Brown	54	343	1224
Vacant Land . . .	White	no number	no number	no number

*Adapted from the National Resources Committee, "Suggested Symbols for Plans, Maps, and Charts." Washington: The Committee, 1938. (Order from the Superintendent of Documents.)

Often it will be necessary to differentiate land use within one or more of these major categories, e.g. to distinguish superior, average, and inferior housing areas, or to indicate agricultural land devoted to corn in contrast to that sown in wheat. In such cases, subdivide the map accordingly, and then color the subdivisions with contrasting hatching rather than solidly throughout. Six or more different subdivisions may thus be identified through the use of parallel vertical lines, horizontal lines, diagonal lines, intersecting diagonal lines, lines of different widths, and by means of dots of different sizes.

Land use mapping may be facilitated by the preliminary use of a good topographic map of the area in question. The United States Geological Survey (Department of the Interior, Washington, D. C.) has published large-scale topographic maps, size 16½ by 20 inches, for over half of the country. An index map of any state, listing the local topographic maps available for that state, will be furnished by the Survey upon request and without charge.

Social Base Map

This map is similar in general nature to the land use map just described. It differs, however, in that its chief purpose is to locate specifically the various *agencies* serving a local community or a neighborhood, rather than to visualize the general purposes to which the land surface of an area is put.

To make this useful community-study aid, a large-scale outline map of the area in question is necessary. Such a map may be drawn in the school, but it is preferable to purchase it if one can be found. For an urban area, a large-scale map can sometimes be secured from the city or county department of engineering, health, or taxa-tion, or from the local Council of Social Agencies. Rural area maps of sufficiently small scale are more difficult to find; lacking others, however, the Rural Delivery Maps issued by the Post Office Department may be used even though their scale of one inch to the mile is rather small for most effective results as a social base map.[3]

The next step is to procure or make a number of small graphic symbols to indicate the generic types and geographic locations of different governmental, educational, religious, welfare, social, recreational, commercial, and other community agencies. The Russell Sage Foundation [4] has developed a series of standard symbols, and sells them at 5 cents per sheet, single sample copies free. Pins or thumbtacks with variously colored heads may also be used to designate major types of agencies. Their chief disadvantages are that the agencies they represent are not self-evident—as they are in the case of the printed symbols—and also that in order to affix them the map must be mounted in some rigid fashion.

The final step is to attach the chosen symbols in their proper places upon the map, and to add appropriate captions and a descriptive legend. Then the map is ready for display and use.

The construction of such a local land use or social base map often stimulates student interest in the larger community areas, and in their relationships to the immediate locality. To illustrate: if the

---

[3] The Superintendent of Documents reports that "1,585 county maps are available, a list of which will be furnished upon application to the Disbursing Clerk, Post Office Department. Each county map shows all post offices within the county, all roads, houses, schools, and churches known at the time the map was originally drawn, and an outline of the drainage. Blue-line prints of these county maps are sold .... Rural routes emanating from post offices in counties for which county maps have not been drawn are shown on local maps. Each of these maps shows the area covered by rural delivery routes from a single post office."

[4] 130 East 22nd St., New York 10, N. Y.

map is designed to show the community's important industries, the questions will arise: "Where do these industries get their raw materials? And where do the finished products go?" The answer to these and other similar questions calls for study of larger and larger areas, and of other local communities both near and far away. Thus the pupil-made maps of their own immediate locality become a nucleus for the further study of regional, national, and international resources, relationships, needs and problems.

2. EXHIBITS SPUR INTEREST

Literally thousands of material objects, specimens, and models can be used to enrich and amplify the community study program. Such exhibits are widely available through purchase, donation, loan, and excursion viewing. The following list suggests merely a few of these many exhibits that can fruitfully be used to deepen classroom understanding of the physical, biological, and social environment:

Anatomical: skulls, bones, claws, organs, feathers, teeth, skins.
Animals: rats, mice, rabbits, kittens, squirrels, chickens.
Apiary: drones, workers, and queen bees; comb honey, beeswax.
Aquarium: fish, tadpoles, frogs, turtles, snails, water plants.
Art: pictures, paintings, sculptures, posters, advertising illustrations.
Beverages: cocoa, coffee, tea, soft drinks, liquors.
Building material: brick, tile, wood, metal, paint, nails, asbestos, hardware.
Clothing: period and costume; hats, shoes, dresses, coats, trousers, gloves.
Coins, money, and stamps: domestic and foreign; ancient and modern.
Communication: ancient methods and materials; telephone, telegraph, radio.
Cooking and serving equipment: dishes, utensils, devices.
Documentary materials: books, bulletins, magazines, newspapers, diaries, deeds.
Dolls: ancient and modern; domestic and foreign; clothing, equipment.
Fabrics: ancient and modern; domestic and foreign.
Flowers: local and national; wild and domesticated; fresh and pressed.
Foods and food products: domestic and foreign.
Foreign articles: money, foods, clothing, posters, pictures, games, stamps.
Fuels: wood, oil, anthracite and bituminous coal, peat.
Fungi: mosses, lichens, and galls.
Furniture: beds, chairs, tables, etc., ancient and modern.
Grass: grasses and grass seeds.
Indian relics: arrowheads, flints, celts, hatchets, fishhooks, harpoon, pottery.
Insects: bugs, moths, butterflies, grasshoppers, flies, larvae, eggs.
Jewelry: ancient and modern.
Leaves: twigs, nuts, seeds, galls.
Metals: pure and alloy.
Nests: bird, rabbit, wasp, mud-dauber.
Pictures: paintings, drawings, sketches, daguerreotypes, photographs.
Plants: flowers, ferns, grains, cacti, vegetables, bulbs.
Plastics: anatomical models, scale-sized reproductions of buildings, terrain.
Post cards and travel folders: domestic and foreign.
Pottery: vases, bowls, birdbaths, water bottles, ash trays, pitchers.
Radio: equipment and materials; obsolete and modern.
Raw materials: cotton, flax, silk, latex, foodstuffs.

Reptiles: snakes, lizards, salamanders.
Rocks: stones, minerals, ores, fossils, petrified woods.
Seasoning: salt, sugar, pepper, spices, nutmeg, cinnamon, vinegar, sage, cloves.
Seeds and grains: domestic and foreign, imported and exported, large and small.
Shells: conch, scallop, oyster, clam, crab, snail, coral.
Timepieces: devices, watches, clocks; ancient and modern.
Tools and implements: ancient and modern.
Toys and playthings: ancient and modern, domestic and foreign.
Weeds and weed seeds: types, control methods, commercial uses.
Wood: various kinds, cut to show grain; knots, bark, burls, cones, nuts, buds, pulp, sawdust, diseases, unusual growths, petrification.

Exhibits such as the above may be procured from varied sources such as pupils' homes, industrial and commercial concerns, fairs and public exhibitions, city and state chambers of commerce, public and private museums, school supply houses, and from other schools through exchange or loan.

Some items may be obtained for permanent exhibition, while others can be borrowed for temporary use. Many useful models can be made by the students themselves, either in the school classroom or shop, or in their own homes for display in school. Steel construction sets, for example, may easily be utilized to build working models of machinery and mechanical appliances. Lifelike papier-mâché models may easily be constructed from newspapers, plaster, and a little paint.[5]

While this is not the place for detailed descriptions of how to make exhibits, a few general suggestions may be given to indicate some of the simpler possibilities.

Metals, ores, leaves, shells, woods, and similar objects and specimens can be wired, nailed, glued, or screwed onto mounting boards (either made or purchased) of wood, plywood, Beaverboard, or Celotex, or onto the bottom of shallow boxes or drawers.

Butterflies, moths, and insects may be placed on cotton in shallow glass-covered boxes or frames.

Seeds and grains may be displayed in jars or bottles; *live insects*, in moist earth and twig-supplied glass jars with perforated lids; *toads, snakes, and lizards*, in screened boxes supplied with rocks, earth, and moss; *nests*, on enclosed shelves; and *fish, tadpoles, and water plants*, in a bowl or aquarium.

Working models should be mounted on a wooden or metal base.

Fragile items, such as old letters, newspapers, pictures and other documents, fabrics, pressed flowers, etc., should be protected by glass or other transparent material. They may be placed in a frame, case, celluloid jacket or envelope, or on the table under a piece of plate glass. Cellophane

---

[5] For instructions, see Elizabeth Gray, "Model Making in Biology," *School Science and Mathematics*, December 1943, pp. 828–36.

is also satisfactory as a protective medium, provided it is handled carefully and fastened securely.

Evolutionary exhibits can be easily and effectively planned and executed. Typical demonstrations are the life cycle of the butterfly, moth, dragonfly, or Japanese beetle; the reduction of ores; the fabrication of alloys; the growth of plants and flowers; the manufacture of soap; the preparation of sugar; the stages of man's development from prehistoric times; the progression in artificial lighting or of water, land or air transportation, showing the process from the raw material or the beginning through the stages of growth or manufacture to the final product.

Students may even design and execute more complicated exhibits such as a habitat or similar natural group. A habitat composed of earth, water, shrubs, trees, grass, and insects may be constructed upon a suitable board base. The water is represented by a piece of window glass painted on the underside. Soil is shown by pebbles, sand, and sifted earth on glue; irregular heights by plaster of paris on pieces of propped-up screen; grass by hemp, bristles, flax, dried grass, or excelsior glued in holes in the base and properly trimmed and colored; trees and shrubs are cut from sponges or constructed of twigs and glued-on paper leaves. Insects, and even birds and beasts, can be suitably set, mounted, or suspended. A painted background, preferably semi-circular in shape, helps to give a realistic appearance to the group setting. The exhibit should then be placed in a covered and glass-enclosed case and may, if desired, be electrically lighted.

In a similar manner, such other exhibits as these may be developed: Eskimo village (snow is made by spraying melted paraffin), Indian village, primitive village, aquarium (dry aquarium with frogs and suspended fish and tadpoles, and plants, sand, rocks, bugs, etc.), soil erosion, irrigation projects, models of famous buildings, or groups of other buildings (made from plaster of paris on built-up frames of lollipop or other small sticks, pieces of wicker, wax, paraffin, or putty models of fences, animals, men, walks, stones, etc.), and relief maps.

Every school should and can have its own museum of materials illustrating community life. It is well-known that many persons, adults as well as children, enjoy collecting items of various kinds, and that many students already possess item collections of their own. If it is appropriately suggested to them, they will probably react most favorably to the idea of having a school museum, and will cooperate enthusiastically in developing it. Such a group project is both intriguing and educative to students and faculty alike. Co-operative planning, accepting and discharging individual responsibility, doing the necessary research in obtaining, understanding, classifying, mounting, and labeling exhibits, evaluating one's own and one's neighbors' efforts, and generally working together for the common good, bring pronounced educational benefits.

The school museum is not completed when the exhibits have been made and labeled; they must also be located accessibly and displayed attractively if they are to become effective educational agents. The exhibits may therefore be placed in the corridors, in the library or another centrally-located room, scattered about in the various classrooms, or located in a special wing of the building or even in a separate building. Under varying conditions, any or all of these locations would be satisfactory. The important thing is to locate the exhibits where they can be used easily and without formality, utilized without disturbing other students and teachers, easily moved to various classrooms, suitably protected and indexed, and grouped to represent an artistic appearance. But whatever the location chosen for the school museum, care and discrimination should always be used to the end that only truly educative materials be collected or constructed. We must always keep in mind the fact that a good museum is not merely a collection of miscellaneous items gathered at random from the community; it is rather a usable collection of significant community realia.

3. PICTURES ILLUMINE

Photographs, sketches, cartoons, paintings, pictures clipped from magazines and newspapers, and many other similar "flat pictures" provide a wealth of valuable information about a community, whether that community is near or far in either time or space. Such pictures are easily available from many sources, inexpensive and convenient to collect, make, mount, and use. Having been mounted and titled, they may then be passed about among the students or displayed upon a convenient bulletin board. The predominant picture magazines such as *Life, Look,* the *National Geographic,* and others offer good clipping possibilities. Many inexpensive sets and series of prepared instructional pictures are also available from various commercial publishing houses.

Pictorial materials should always be properly mounted in order to enhance their attractiveness, make them more usable, and preserve them better. A well-mounted picture, photographic print, or silhouette is more interesting and significant than an unmounted one, and it is also more artistic because of the pleasing contrast between the item and its mount or the agreeable blending of the two. Being mounted, it is more easily passed around, handled, and otherwise used by students; it can be laid down perfectly flat, stood upright, or hung upon the wall. It is more easily preserved from wrinkling, bending, tearing, or soiling, and it can be more conveniently filed than an unmounted item. Furthermore, it is often desirable to mount several items together so as to show comparisons, contrasts, or continuities. Needless to say, the mounting must be carefully done in order to achieve these values. A poorly mounted picture—one inaccurately cut, inartistically located, carelessly glued, or crudely labeled—represents a comparable loss of desirable educational results.

4. Stereographs Are Vivid

The stereograph is essentially a tool for individual instruction, so it is best to have the pupils use it during the study period. Because of the many details brought out by the third dimension, the student will find that the stereograph requires more time for mastery or even for appreciation than does a photograph or other flat picture. Only a few stereographs should therefore be used at one time, especially if the scene under view is new material to the pupil. More may be used, of course, if they are viewed for purposes of rapid preview or review.

Carefully prepared plans for the use of stereographs are necessary if maximum learning is to occur. Pertinent questions concerning each scene will stimulate the child to study specifically rather than merely to view generally. And as is true of all visual aids, the stereographs should be as readily available to the interested students as is any other kind of community-study reference material.

5. Slides and Slidefilms Appeal

Slides and slidefilms are particularly useful in community-centered education since many thousands of them, covering all aspects of the environment, are available from commercial and professional agencies, on a sale or loan basis, and because they can readily be made by students and teachers. As a general rule, photographic slides, regardless of size and type, may be classed in two groups: (1) those prepared by local amateurs for the study of the immediate community, and (2) those produced by technical experts to reflect the larger regional, national, and world areas. Since sources of slides and slidefilms in class 2 are indicated on pages 123–25, we shall confine attention here to the amateur productions of class 1. Accordingly, we shall consider how local community study may be vivified by the making and using of photographic and hand-drawn slides, and also slidefilms.

Photographic Slides

Photographic slides are of two sizes: "standard" and "2 × 2," which incorporate a transparent image secured through previous photography and appropriately fixed upon or between glass protectors.

The photographic slide is a splendid medium for reproducing many such community-interest items as the following:

1. Old documents: Maps, original manuscripts, blueprints, deeds of sale, photographs, etc., may be found in every community and photographed for projection purposes in the school. To take such pictures successfully, however, most cameras will have to be fitted with special accessories costing several dollars or more.

2. Slides made from old negatives: Since the introduction of the roll film the camera has become almost a household article. Community activities of many kinds are frequently photographed by local camera fans, who will be glad to loan desired negatives for reproduction as slides. Likewise, scenes of many years past may be found in the files of long-established commercial studios and may also be borrowed.

3. Current photographs: The various scenes which may be currently photographed even by amateurs are too numerous to mention. When we consider the many natural sites, scenic points, industries, occupations, means of transportation, special celebrations, etc., we shall begin to grasp the possibilities of slide-making for local community study.

Hand-drawn Standard Slides

Home-made slides of several types may be used in presenting a wealth of ideas pertaining to the community. Since these slides are so adaptable to a wide range of materials, the most commonly used forms are listed here, with brief instructions for making them.

1. Etched-glass slides: This type is most often used to reproduce maps, charts, graphs, diagrams, and other material of a similar graphic nature. The etched slide is simply a plain piece of glass, roughened on one side with acid so that one can draw or write on it with pencil, colored pencils, or ink. The image or picture is traced or drawn on paper so that it will come within the $3\frac{1}{4}'' \times 4''$ dimension of the standard slide. The glass, roughened side up, is placed over the image to be reproduced, and the tracing is made. The slide is then ready for use.

2. India ink slides: A bright and clear outline or diagram may be produced by using India ink on a plain cover glass. A thin coat of shellac on the glass makes a better surface on which to draw.

3. Cellophane slides: This type of slide is used most frequently for projecting written material. To prepare it, cut a piece of cellophane the size of the slide. Then cut a piece of good carbon paper 6½" by 8" in size, and fold the carboned sides together. Place the cellophane inside the folded carbon, and write or type the desired copy. Remove the cellophane on which the words now appear, and mount it between cover glasses to protect and give it rigidity.

4. Silhouette and paper cutout slides: Slides of this type are of special interest to the teacher of lower grades. The figure to be reproduced is cut out of opaque paper and then inserted between two cover glasses. If the figure itself is used, the silhouette is obtained when the slide is projected. But if the paper from which the figure was cut out is utilized, all of the slide surface except that of the figure will be dark. Such "cutout" slides may be made more attractive by using colored cellophane. Sometimes several colors may be used to advantage, either together or in slide sequence.

Slidefilms

The slidefilm is a 35-mm. continuous film strip carrying a number of photographs called "frames" or pictures. It is prepared either by reversing the original negative image during the developing process, or by contact printing of a positive strip from the negative film. Slidefilms have become increasingly popular in recent years, and are especially useful for easy amateur recording of field trip scenes, later to be projected in the classroom as part of the trip report. Such slidefilms can be shown with accompanying oral comment, or the spoken explanations, complete with musical and other sound effects, may be transcribed upon phonograph records for synchronized use with the projection itself.

6. MOTION PICTURES STIMULATE

Through motion pictures, we can almost literally bring the world into the classroom. By using different types of photography, such as the time lapse, slow motion animation cartoon, microphotography, miniature, and the like, practically every form of physical phenomena and life activity may be realistically reproduced.

As in the case of slides and slidefilms, motion picture films for community study may be grouped in two broad divisions according to their general availability: (1) those useful in the study of the local or immediate environment, and (2) those which reproduce features of more remote community areas. In this section, we shall notice significant examples of both types.

Local Community Films

Many useful and interesting films of this kind may be produced by schools, school classes, individual teachers, or mature students. The preparation of a local film always arouses widespread interest and at the same time provides many significant learning experiences and excellent technical training for all members of the producing group. Preparing the script, planning the scenes (approximately seventy to eighty for a four-hundred foot reel), placing the people or objects in each scene, preparing the titles, writing the lecture (if a sound film), acting the parts, arranging photographic equipment and "shooting" the pictures—all these activities provide rich and vital experiences.

The following list of school-made films will indicate the wide variety of possible subject materials for local community study through motion pictures at all school levels.

TITLE OF FILM	SCHOOL WHICH PRODUCED IT	FACULTY SPONSOR
Patrol Protection	Fourth Street Elementary School, Columbus, Ohio	Charles A. Vance
Columbia River Cavalcade	John Rodgers High School, Spokane, Wash.	E. T. Becher
We Discover China	Manual Arts High School, Los Angeles, Cal.	Helen M. Bail
Clocks and Watches—How They Are Made	Bristol High School, Bristol, Conn.	E. F. Wheeler
Is There Room for Us?	University of Minnesota	Milton Hahn
Science Serves the Farmer	University of New Hampshire	Donald W. Smith
Dawn of Art	Antioch College	Raymond S. Stites

In making local films such as these, emphasis generally centers about three aspects of the school-community relationship: (1) Interpreting the community to the school students, (2) interpreting the school program to the community residents, and (3) depicting other time periods or important events of the community.[6]

Larger Community Films

Films useful in the study of nonlocal community areas are usually produced by commercial sources although they may be taken by teachers and other amateurs in the course of their travels. In gen-

---

[6] For an interesting example of local community interpretation through films, see Harrison U. Wood, "Local Industries Help Make Film Material," *Occupations*, December 1940, pp. 180–83; *Education Digest*, February 1941, pp. 10–12.

eral, there are two broad types of films: complete story films and problem films. In either of these areas any one or a combination of three basic techniques may be used: documentary, animation, and professional actors. The essential character of the documentary film is that it reports natural phenomena and the activities of real people who are not professional actors. A brief mention of both major types of films, with a few suggestive titles in each category, will indicate the numerous uses of the motion picture in the study of the regional, national, and international community areas, as well as of local events and natural processes.

COMPLETE STORY FILMS

NATURAL EVENTS

Eclipse of the Sun
Electrons and Current Flow
Seed Dispersal

The Indian Elephant
The Endocrine Glands
Reproduction Among Mammals

LIFE IN OTHER LANDS

Children of China
Down the Yukon River
Dwellers in Cold Countries

Fjords of Norway
Life in the Sahara
Women of Many Lands

LIFE AT OTHER TIMES

World a Million Years Ago
From Clay to Bronze
Medieval Village

The Crusades
Flat Boat Pioneers
Mormon Trail

BIOGRAPHIES

Columbus
Master Will Shakespeare
Thomas Jefferson

The Heart of Lincoln
The Life of Pasteur
Story of Dr. Carver

LITERARY, MUSICAL, AND DANCE CLASSICS

Hamlet
Les Miserables
The Scarlet Letter

Dance of the Hours
Music of the Nations
Songs of the Range

OCCUPATIONS AND INDUSTRIES

Alaska's Silver Millions
Our Inland Waterways
Petroleum Geology

Singing Wheels
Wonder World of Chemistry
Woolen Industry

TECHNICAL PROCESSES

From Flax to Linen
Guidance in the Public Schools
Refining Crude Oil

Story of Gasoline
Tree to Newspaper
Water Purifying

TRAVELOGUES

Bonnie Scotland
Cavalcade of Texas
Colorful Sweden

Daylighting the Padres Trail
Heart of Australia
Southern Arizona

PROBLEM FILMS

Bill of Rights	*The Plow That Broke the Plains*
Black Legion	*The Right to Work*
Captains Courageous	*The River*
Dead End	*The Spanish Earth*
Juvenile Delinquency	*World in Flames*
Machine: Master or Slave?	*Youth Gets a Break*

7. RADIO IMPRESSES

All of the major networks and many local stations regularly broadcast programs of a superior educational nature. Among these, the majority may be utilized in the study of the community, particularly in its regional, national, and international relationships. But the radio is not only a resource to be used for purposes of school instruction; it is also an excellent medium whereby the students can publicize in the community their own findings concerning community life, developments, and problems.

Local Community Broadcasts

Within the past few years, many communities have constructed and are maintaining their own broadcasting stations. Although purely local in coverage (apart from network programs), these stations generally have a large audience within the region served. Many colleges and universities either maintain their own stations, or have access to local broadcasting resources. The programs of all such local stations may often include scripts dealing with the history, growth, industries, occupations, social needs, and other concerns of local radio listeners.

Many schools, conversely, are using local radio stations to acquaint their patrons with the school activities, especially those involving or reporting upon school-community relationships and programs. Such school-sponsored programs provide valuable training for the students in several important ways:

1. *The fact that the program is to be "on the air"* makes preparation for it much more interesting, exciting, and vital.

2. *The material must be presented in a competent manner.* This calls for a well-written script, interesting and adapted to the prospective audience, and for excellent enunciation and accurate timing.

3. *Actual experience in a radio program is a memorable personal event,* and may lead to further career explorations of the field.

Schools might well arrange a series of radio programs, covering both school activities and local community affairs as they impinge upon the curricular program. Broadcasts portraying early events, describing historic buildings and sites, interviews with leading citizens and with technical specialists in varied fields, analyses of local occupations and social problems are all suggestive of the programs which might be presented. Such programs will serve the double purpose of better acquainting the students with their community, and of better informing the community about its schools.

Many schools, however, will not have opportunities to utilize a radio station, and among those who do, active broadcasting will of necessity be restricted to a relatively few students. An alternative plan of lesser but still marked value is to let students present similar programs to their own classes or to the student body. This is done through the medium of a microphone connected to the sound projector or to the school's public address system. Recordings may easily be used to provide musical backgrounds and interludes with either of these systems. In any case, however, the students who are "on the air" should be in a separate room from the audience in order to maintain the radio illusion.

Larger Community Radio

Many of the programs presented by the great networks and widely broadcast are well-suited for use in the study and appreciation of more remote community areas, processes, and problems. Some such programs will also fit into the school study of some local communities. These network programs are of two chief types: those arranged primarily for the general radio audience, and those especially prepared for school instructional purposes.

For General Listening

Little need be said about the nature and purposes of the standard commercially sponsored and the familiar sustaining programs. While all of these programs entertain, many of them also deal dramatically with significant social processes and problems, and as such, may be extremely useful in modern educational institutions. Although many of these programs are on the air during the evening hours or on Saturdays and Sundays, they may frequently be recaptured by means of transcriptions. Programs such as the following are typical of the better offerings which merit attention in regional, national, and world community study:

American Forum of the Air	*Chicago Theater of the Air*
America's Town Meeting of the Air	*Great Plays*
Army Hour	*Information Please*
Cavalcade of America	*Invitation to Learning*

Keep Up With the World	*Pacific Story*
March of Time	*People's Platform*
Meet Your Navy	*Radio Newsreel*
Metropolitan Opera	*Report to the Nation*
NBC Symphony	*Transatlantic Call*
New York Philharmonic Symphony	*University of Chicago Roundtable*

For School Instruction

Far fewer are the educational programs specifically designed for broadcasting to school students during regular instructional hours. Among these, perhaps the best and most widely used have been Walter Damrosch's *Music Appreciation Hour,* presented over a period of many years by NBC, and CBS's *American School of the Air,* "now taken by 177,000 classrooms in the United States, beamed to Latin America and overseas and utilized by the Office of War Information as the official channel of dissemination to school pupils and teachers. Through the cooperation of the War Department, the science and geography broadcasts are recorded and flown to 400 stations of the Armed Forces Radio Service for rebroadcast throughout the world wherever American servicemen are stationed. Veterans' hospitals are also receiving the programs for the re-education and rehabilitation of wounded and ill servicemen."[7] This *American School of the Air* presents a different broadcast every school day, with the same day each week devoted to one basic area of instruction. The 1944–45 schedule illustrates this general program:

Mondays—*Science Frontiers: Careers in science*
Tuesdays—*Gateways to Music: From folk song to symphony*
Wednesdays—*New Horizons: World geography*
Thursdays—*Tales from Far and Near: Modern and classical stories dramatized*
Fridays—*This Living World: Current events and postwar problems*

FM Broadcasting

So-called "staticless" radio broadcasting is the newest development in this field, and is apparently destined to supplant present broadcasting within a few years. This greatly improved medium is already of considerable interest to the educational world, as the large number of applications for school and college broadcasting rights bears witness. The technical advantages of FM are explained in a recent pamphlet entitled *FM Broadcasting,*[8] and the educational literature is currently discussing educational possibilities inherent in FM radio.

---

[7] *School and Society,* September 30, 1944.
[8] Radio Corporation of America, Camden, New Jersey.

8. RECORDINGS ENLIVEN

Community study may now be immensely enriched through the considered use of phonograph records and transcriptions. Literally hundreds of excellent recordings and broadcast transcriptions are suitable for serious instructional use at the elementary, secondary, college, and university levels. Among these recordings are many which are especially appropriate to the regional, national, and international community areas, to the institutional and psychological levels, and to the historic, contemporary, and future time periods. Schools which are equipped to make their own recordings will find numerous opportunities for more realistic local community study and public reporting through this interesting medium.

Some of the larger broadcasting companies now provide transcriptions of outstanding programs originating with them. The United States Office of Education maintains a free loan service whereby hundreds of radio transcriptions may be borrowed by educational agencies without even transportation costs to the user.[9] Various audio-visual libraries, often operating under university sponsorship, also serve as inexpensive loan or sale centers. The Recordings Division of the New York University Film Library and the American Council on Education, for example, lists 1000 educational recordings on social and economic problems, literature, languages, history, science, and so forth, which may be purchased or rented.[10]

Suggestive of the wide variety of programs now available are the following transcriptions and recordings listed by the two distributing agencies just mentioned:

U. S. Office of Education (series titles)	New York University (disc titles)
Americans All—Immigrants All	*Challenge of the Four Freedoms*
Freedom's People	*A Council for Youth*
The Ballad Hunter	*Valley Forge*
This Is History	*Susan B. Anthony*
Life for Wildlife	*Walt Whitman*
Health for America	*A Christmas Carol*
What Are We Fighting For?	*Macbeth*
Historic War Speeches	*Silas Marner*
Adventures in Research	*Tale of Two Cities*

[9] Transcriptions generally require the use of special playback equipment operating at a speed of 33 revolutions per minute. This slower speed, in contrast to the conventional phonograph which runs at 78 r.p.m., is designed to encompass a fifteen-minute program upon each side of a 16-inch record.

[10] 71 Washington Square South, New York 12, N. Y.

9. DRAMATICS ARE FUN

Pageants, plays, and skits all have their place in the community-centered curricular program. They serve especially well as culminating activities for large units of work; since they require considerable physical, emotional, and mental activity, they are excellent media for developing both intellectual understandings and emotionalized attitudes. Dramatics integrate logical fact with emotional feeling; they simultaneously impart information and cultivate attitudes.

Brief skits, longer plays, extensive pageants are all suitable for the dramatic treatment of many themes which are central in the lifelike school curriculum. The history of the community, scenes of pioneer life, origins of national holidays, minority contributions to public welfare, the ideals and problems of democracy—all these but suggest topics of interest and vital concern in life-centered education. Full-length plays and pageants obviously require more elaborate staging and preparation; they may therefore best be presented on important school occasions and as part of community festivals. Skits and one-act plays obviously require less preparation and may be well utilized for classroom or assembly portrayals of more limited theme situations.[11]

10. TELEVISION ENTHRALLS

The educational potentialities of television are still largely unexplored, but as increasing social use is made of our advancing technology, we may find this among the greatest of all audio-visual aids to school instruction. Instantaneous viewing of historic events may become commonplace; visible interviews with prominent personalities in all fields of endeavor may be a regular part of the school curriculum; master lecturers upon any conceivable subject may be freely utilized; televised laboratory experiments may be clearly demonstrated to scores or hundreds of students simultaneously; television excursions into industrial plants, technical laboratories, museums, art galleries, churches, welfare centers, historic sites, community festivals, engineering projects, cooperative communities, experimental schools, and a host of other such com-

---

[11] The Council for Democracy, 285 Madison Avenue, New York, N. Y., distributes a series of short, vital, professionally-written plays dealing with the nature and problems of realistic democratic citizenship today. These plays may be freely used, without royalties, by young Americans all over the country.

munity centers may await the flick of a switch. All these possibilities are already within the range of technical achievement, and await only their extensive development as educational aids to vivid community study.

Varied indeed are the ten basic audio-visual aids we have noted! Graphic documents, exhibits, direct-view pictures, machine-viewed pictures, projected still pictures, motion pictures, radio broadcasts, recordings, dramatic productions, and television—each type has its special advantages and its particular limitations, all depending in turn upon the time, the place, and the equipment available, and upon the student's own needs and interests. All of these ten aids can and should be used, at appropriate occasions and under suitable circumstances, in the systematic or the informal study of local, regional, national and international community areas. To do this, is to take proper advantage of modern technology's contributions to education; to do less, is to fail in making modern education fully worthwhile in terms of both content and method.

How Should Audio-Visual Aids Be Used?

Specific directions for utilizing each of the audio-visual aids just mentioned is beyond the province of this book. Readers who are not already familiar with the tested techniques of utilizing such aids to maximum educational advantage should consult any good handbook in the field of audio-visual aids. Yet some general suggestions are in order here, and will be presented as fundamental principles which must obviously be applied to specific situations. These principles have been drawn out of much practical experience with audio-visual aids on all school levels, and their observance should enable the teacher to utilize such aids to community study with full confidence and success.

1. Choose Sensory Aids with Care

Like any other classroom aids, audio-visual equipment and materials must be carefully chosen in the light of the specific educational objectives sought. The purchase of equipment, as well as the classroom use of films, slides, charts, maps, and the like should be critically judged in the light of such basic criteria as these:

1. For what educational purposes is it designed?
2. To what extent will it probably accomplish these purposes?
3. Can it be used effectively by or for the students for whom it is designed?

4. Is it easily and conveniently operated, manipulated, handled, or used?

5. Is it well-made mechanically? Is it durable?

6. To what extent is it guaranteed, if this is essential?

7. Is the price reasonable? How does it compare with the prices of other similar products?

8. Can repairs and replacements be obtained easily?

9. Is there any possibility of danger in the using of it?

10. Will it represent an attractive and respected piece of equipment?

11. Is the company that produces it fully reliable?

12. Is the material it presents authentic? Interesting? Comprehensible? Concrete? Clear? Concise? Natural?

13. Does it suggest new questions, problems, materials, activities, implications, applications, and experiences?

2. Know Specific Functions of the Various Aids

Every conceivable audio-visual aid is undoubtedly valuable— for certain purposes, with selected groups, under given conditions. But under different conditions, with different groups, with different purposes, any such aid may conceivably prove useless or even harmful. Teachers must ever bear in mind the fact that educational techniques are only relatively valuable, and that there is thus no "best" type of audio or visual aid for all purposes, groups, and conditions. It is therefore highly important to understand the specific possibilities of each different aid if all are to be used with maximum success.

3. Select Aids Which Are Appropriate to the Group

An aid can be so called only if and when it really aids. And it will never aid maximally unless it is suited to the backgrounds, abilities, interests, and needs of the pupils using it. Every aid must be chosen and utilized in terms of its appropriateness to the physical, intellectual, emotional, and social development of the group with which it is to be used. If it is too difficult, it will handicap ready learning; if it is too simple, it will create undesirable student attitudes. And it is entirely possible, with even the same group of pupils, for a given aid to be appropriate in one type of educational situation and unsuitable in another.

4. Actively Use Audio-Visual Material; Do Not Merely Display It

Merely looking at a photograph, diagram, or motion picture, or simply listening to a phonograph record or a radio broadcast, will not produce maximum educational results. Sensory aids are not mystical devices through the use of which the student becomes instantly and completely educated. At best, they are still only "aids" to instruction. Even though their use constitutes valuable pupil experience, that experience is still primarily a second-hand one. In other words, audio-visual aids are supplementary and not substitutive; they do not represent complete educational experiences in themselves. It follows, therefore, that the teacher should have very definite purposes for the use of any aid, and that he should carefully integrate the contribution of that aid with the larger purposes of the course, unit, or lesson.

5. MAKE THOROUGH PREPARATION FOR USING THE SELECTED AID

In no type of teaching activity is previous preparation more necessary than in sensory instruction. Precisely because of the dramatic quality associated with audio-visual materials, there is always danger of an interesting but undiscriminating experience in their use. This educational hazard can be avoided only by thorough planning and preparation on the part of both the teacher and the class. The instructor must be familiar with the chosen device and must comprehend the true nature of its potential contribution to the class experience. He must know just how the aid can stimulate a better understanding and appreciation of the group's past, present, and probable future educational experiences. He must know how to operate the aid with the utmost utility and economy. The students, meanwhile, must feel a sense of need or lack which they know can be met through the selected aid. Such a felt need, with anticipation of satisfying it, provides the best possible learning attitude.

6. AVOID USING TOO MANY AIDS

The successful class lesson will be an integrated experience in which the central purpose is approached from several directions, all of which are consciously related to each other as well as to that primary objective itself. Obviously, therefore, only a few sensory aids should be utilized during a conventional class period. This time limitation, as well as the educational requirements themselves, thus compel judicious selection among the various available aids.

*

These six general principles of use must be carefully observed if audio-visual aids are to be used successfully as one type of bridge between school and community. We must never forget that audio-visual materials are *aids to learning,* and must therefore be used as teaching tools and not as substitutes for teaching.

Where Can We Get Audio-Visual Materials?

Successful use of audio-visual aids in community study obviously requires familiarity with the sources which supply these many teaching materials. And because a *continuing* familiarity is essential to prevent instructional obsolescence, it is important that we be generally acquainted with the standard and cumulative sources of information in this field. Periodic reference to the following primary books, magazines, and agencies will best enable one to keep abreast of new materials and equipment as well as to discriminate intelligently among the old.

STANDARD REFERENCE BOOKS

American Council on Education, *Selected Educational Motion Pictures: A Descriptive Encyclopedia.* Washington: the Council, 1942.

Nearly 500 carefully selected films are listed and described, each in terms of grade placement, sources, appraisal, and detailed content description. Periodical supplements to this volume are planned by the Council.

Cook, Dorothy E., and Eva Rahbek Smith, *Educational Film Catalog.* New York: H. W. Wilson Company, 1944.

This is a cumulative service, since quarterly and yearly supplements are issued regularly. Some 3,000 films that have been prepared for classroom use have now been listed according to the Dewey Decimal System of classification. In each case, the film is annotated to include mention of the producer, grade placement, description of contents, and distributive source.

Dent, E. C., *The Audio-Visual Handbook.* Chicago: Society for Visual Education, 1944.

A considerable portion of this volume is devoted to different audio-visual materials and equipment, and to the companies producing them.

McKown, H. C., and A. B. Roberts, *Audio-visual Aids to Instruction.* New York: McGraw-Hill, 1940.

Chapter 16, "Sources of Materials and Equipment," gives extended attention to sources of museum materials, maps, charts, and other non-projected materials.

Miles, J. Robert, *Recordings for School Use.* Yonkers, New York: World Book Company, 1942.

This is probably the most complete single source of records suitable for school use. The recordings are listed according to academic subject fields, with a paragraph describing the content of each. Suggestions are also given as to the proper grade placement of each record.

1000 and One: The Blue Book of Non-Theatrical Films. Chicago: *The Educational Screen,* annual publication.

Over 5,000 films are very briefly described. Since very little information about the films is given, this handbook is chiefly useful as a quick source for locating desired films under subject classification.

United States Office of Education, *Sources of Visual Aids for Instructional Use in Schools.* Washington: Government Printing Office, 1941.

Nearly 1,200 agencies and organizations supplying audio-visual materials and equipment are listed by name and address. All are classified under various headings such as charts and graphs, exhibits, lantern slides, motion pictures, objects, specimens, models, pictures, photographs, stereographs, cameras, projectors, etc.

United States Office of Education, *Transcriptions for Victory.* Washington: The Office. Mimeographed and frequently revised.

Lists and annotates several hundred broadcast transcriptions which are available to educational agencies on a free loan basis. Each transcription is characterized, the playing time of the total program is given, and suggestions for use are made.

MAGAZINES

Educational Screen. 64 East Lake Street, Chicago, Illinois.

A professional magazine devoted exclusively to audio-visual education, materials, and equipment.

Film and Radio Discussion Guide. 172 Renner Avenue, Newark, New Jersey.

An illustrated periodical describing current and impending developments in radio and motion pictures, both commercial and educational.

Scholastic, Social Education, The School Executive, The Nation's Schools, and *Secondary Education* are among the educational journals which maintain regular departments or otherwise give space to descriptions of new materials of an audio-visual nature.

AGENCIES AND ORGANIZATIONS

The United States Office of Education issues descriptive and research bulletins from time to time; these are excellent sources of information concerning developments and sources in the audio-visual area.

New Tools for Learning (280 Madison Ave., New York 16, N. Y.) represents the New York University Film Library and Recordings Division, the University of Chicago Round Table, the Public Affairs Committee, Inc., and the New York Institute on Postwar Reconstruction. This agency is prepared to assist teachers in locating films, pamphlets, and recordings related to units of study in the school curriculum. A pamphlet listing these materials by topics and subject-matter areas is available without charge.

The Teaching Materials Service (205 East 42nd St., New York 17, N. Y.) sells many objects, specimens and models such as foreign flags, samples of cotton, anatomical figures, etc.

State Education Departments often publish lists of materials and sources specifically available or suitable to schools within their jurisdictions.

Large museums and universities often maintain audio-visual libraries from which qualified institutions may borrow exhibits, slides, films, recordings, documentary materials, and the like.

No comprehensive listing of agencies, magazines, or books can or should be attempted in a volume of this nature. The above suggestions, however, will enable the interested teacher to write directly to whatever sources of materials and equipment seem worthwhile. This procedure, together with current periodical reading in the field, will enable him easily to know what materials he wishes to use, and where to procure them.

What Are the Limitations of Audio-Visual Aids?

Audio-visual aids are indeed most valuable adjuncts to learning. Yet they do possess definite limitations which should be carefully noted by those who use them for purposes of serious community study through the schools. Among the limitations characteristic of audio-visual aids as a group are four:

1. **Entertainment function.** The intrinsic interest of these aids, in contrast with traditional classroom procedures and equipment, may permit them to become ends in themselves, rather than means to other and superior educational purposes.

2. **Substitute for direct experience.** Closely related to the first limitation, is the danger that reproduced reality in the classroom may be habitually substituted for direct experience with that reality. Projected pictures of birds, in lieu of an excursion to a nearby aviary, would be most inappropriate in that situation. All audio-visual aids are supplementary experiences only.

3. **Over-simplification of complex situations.** These aids, being largely representations of reality, may present a deceptively easy picture of man's environment, activities, and problems.

4. **Propaganda.** Since practically all aids are "edited" in some fashion —by the very choice of subject matter, at least—they easily become media for unconscious or deliberate propaganda. American nationalists, for example, prefer the Mercator projection of the world map, while proponents of full international responsibility utilize the newer "polar view" projections.

Realizing these limitations, how may we provide experiences for pupils in other than mechanical ways? In particular, might we arrange for students to confer with other living persons than their teachers, and thus begin to enjoy more direct learning and socializing experiences? Would that be possible? Surely it would! The technique for doing it is therefore presented in the chapter to follow.

SELECTED REFERENCES

Since the audio-visual field is so extensive, specific periodical references are omitted from the following list:

American School of the Air, "Teachers Manual." Columbia Broadcasting System, 485 Madison Avenue, New York 22, N. Y. A current guide to Columbia's "School of the Air" programs.

Bathhurst, Effie G., "Phonograph Records as an Aid to Learning in Rural Elementary Schools." Albany, New York: University of the State of New York, State Education Department, 1943. A handbook for teachers and supervisors, based upon an extensive experiment in the use of phonograph records in nature study, English, and regional study.

Brunstetter, M. R., *How to Use the Educational Sound Film.* Chicago: University of Chicago Press, 1937. Specific methods for using the sound film for maximum success.

Child, Eleanor D., and Hardy R. Finch, *Producing School Movies.* Chicago: National Council of Teachers of English, 1941. A manual of detailed instructions for teachers and students who wish to produce amateur films.

Dale, Edgar, and Charles F. Hoban, Jr., "Visual Education." In Walter S. Monroe (ed.), *Encyclopedia of Educational Research,* pp. 1323–34. New York: Macmillan, 1941.

Dent, Ellsworth C., *The Audio-Visual Handbook.* Chicago: Society for Visual Education, Inc., 1944. Practical and detailed treatment of nearly all aspects of the field.

Educational Screen Magazine. 64 East Lake Street, Chicago, Illinois. Devoted exclusively to audio-visual aids in education.

Federal Radio Education Committee, *Service Bulletin.* Washington: United States Office of Education. Monthly bulletin of radio development news.

Harrison, Margaret, *Radio in the Classroom.* New York: Prentice-Hall, 1938. Objectives, principles and practices of radio as a supplementary tool, especially in rural and small-town schools. Discusses classroom use, equipment and supervision; radio's contributions to the activity program; and illustrates with teaching units.

Hoban, Charles F., Jr., *Focus on Learning.* Washington: American Council on Education, 1942. Reviews the role of motion pictures in education, analyzes the types of educational films and their contributions to the learning process, and outlines the teacher's responsibility in selecting and using films.

Hoban, Charles F., Charles F. Hoban, Jr., and Samuel B. Zisman, *Visualizing the Curriculum.* New York: The Cordon Company, 1937. Comprehensive and illustrated treatment of the whole audio-visual field. Basic principles are stressed, followed by suggestions for using objects, models, school museum, motion pictures, still pictures, slides, slidefilms, cartoons, posters, charts, graphs, etc. Procedures for administering a visual aids program are detailed.

Inter-American University of the Air. National Broadcasting Company, 30 Rockefeller Plaza, New York, N. Y. Write for programs and materials.

McKown, H. C., and Alvin B. Roberts, *Audio-Visual Aids to Instruction.* New

York: McGraw-Hill, 1940. Outlines principles to be observed in establishing an audio-visual program. Three chapters are devoted to detailed lesson plans suggesting ways of utilizing aids.

Modley, Rudolf, *How to Use Pictorial Statistics*. New York: Harper, 1937. Comprehensive treatment, well illustrated, of the history and use of pictorial symbols in statistics.

Modley, Rudolf, "Maps, Charts, Graphs, and Pictures As Aids in Economic Education." In Harold F. Clark (ed.), *Economic Education:* Eleventh Yearbook of the National Council for the Social Studies, Ch. VIII. Washington: The Council, 1940. Illustrated uses, advantages, and disadvantages of each type of aid. Easily generalized from economics to other fields of education.

Moore, Eleanor M., *Youth in Museums*. Philadelphia: University of Pennsylvania Press, 1941. Reports programs in over a hundred museums, with special concern for methods of improving their usefulness to youth. Relationships to schools, activities for enriching the school curriculum, the interrelation between such activities and other community resources, etc. are explored.

National Resources Committee, "Suggested Symbols for Plans, Maps, and Charts." Washington: Government Printing Office, 1938. Detailed suggestions for presenting all types of data graphically, designed to encourage standardization of such symbols in the interest of general intelligibility.

Powel, Lydia, *The Art Museum Comes to the School*. New York: Harper, 1944. How art museums in several cities have worked with public schools, and how schools and museums generally can collaborate to stimulate a wider appreciation of art.

Ramsay, Grace F., *Educational Work in Museums of the United States*. H. W. Wilson, 1939. Especially useful for its chapters on teacher education in museums, suggested educational activities with school classes, museums and the radio, and museum excursions.

United States Office of Education, "F–M for Education." Washington: The Office, 1944. Describe F–M radio, the ways in which an F–M educational station can be used, and the steps to be taken in acquiring a station.

Woelfel, Norman, and Irving Robbins, "School-Wide Use of Radio." Washington: Federal Radio Education Committee, U. S. Office of Education, 1942. Reports findings and recommendations of an experimental study made in an Ohio junior high school.

CHAPTER 6

Resource Visitors

THE SPINNER

"Come see the spinning wheel! A lady is really going to spin wool for us! She's in the next room!"

The bright-eyed, ten-year-old youngster danced in eagerness as we followed him to the adjoining classroom. There at her spinning wheel sat Mrs. Helm, an immigrant farm woman, talking easily to a group of attentive boys and girls assembling around her. Yes, this was nice fresh wool and would spin well. Did Mary get it from the Farmer's Co-op? Had the children washed it? This is the way you card the wool, combing out the fibers.

Breathless with suspense, the children watched as she prepared the wheel for spinning. Finally she placed her foot upon the tread and began to spin, showing how the thread could be made thin as gossamer or thick and sturdy by the skillful use of one's hands. As the spinning continued, she chatted with the children about life on the farm, the number of fleeces she kept, when the wool was sold, the things she knitted for her husband, children, and grandchildren. She explained how she had bought her little spinning wheel from Sears Roebuck, and how it had become rickety with years of constant use. To the children from urban homes, it was startling to discover that in some Scandinavian and German homes of their own community spinning was by no means a lost art.

What Are Resource Visitors?

The term "resource visitors" is applied to people who can demonstrate special accomplishments or particular abilities which are of interest and value to school pupils, and who are also both able and willing to display, discuss, or otherwise present their attainments before a student group. Resource visitors are generally utilized for serious educational purposes rather than for mere entertainment.

Why Are Resource Visitors Worthwhile?

The human resources of the community can be used to great advantage in any school. In every locality, there are people of rich

128

and varied backgrounds who can be invited into the school to help make its program vital and realistic. This technique:

1. **Permits vital and realistic experiences** when excursions are not feasible because of distance, cost, transportation, hazards involved, size of class, school regulations, or refusal of factories, laboratories, agencies, and the like to admit visitors.

2. **Helps students realize** that people as well as books are desirable sources of information and inspiration.

3. **Creates better understanding** of many different types of people and helps students identify themselves with other people and their problems.

4. **Promotes social experiences** shared by youth and adults to their mutual interest and satisfaction, thereby increasing the respect of each age group for the other.

5. **Provides opportunity for developing social skills** in real life situations—letter writing, telephoning, making introductions, receiving guests, carrying on a conversation, interviewing, listening attentively, leading discussions.

6. **Allows adults to learn, through their own experience,** what modern teachers are trying to do for students.

Every community, however small or isolated, has within it some resource persons who can make classroom learning more realistic and vital. School programs can therefore be greatly enriched through careful use of appropriate resources people.

What Kinds of Resource People Are There?

Human resources are not limited to any particular area of learning or to any special age group. An art class may wish to see a potter demonstrate his craft; a home economics group may want to watch a mother bathe a baby; a science class may ask an electrician to tell about his work; a group of future farmers may find out from a farmer the secret of a bumper sugar beet yield.

The technique of bringing visitors into the school is one which requires considerable talking by the guest speaker and searching questions on the part of the class. It is therefore a technique more suitable to older boys and girls and adults than to very young children. And it is a technique requiring warmth, informality, and careful preparation by the speaker. Only when carefully controlled as to time, vocabulary, ideas and demonstration procedures, is the experience recommended for children in the early elementary grades.

It is a safe rule to bring resource people into the classroom only when they can make some contribution which has direct bearing upon the activity, problem, or unit which the pupils are planning or working upon. The exceptions are in the case of an outstanding personage or an important event in which there is general interest, or when there is definite likelihood of broadening children's outlooks and interests. Such general needs are most often met through assembly programs. Below are listed types of experience which resource people might provide for either school or classroom groups.

General Assemblies

1. **Special day observance**: speakers for Armistice Day, Book Week, Lincoln's birthday, I-Am-an-American Day, Bill of Rights Week, etc.

2. **General interest topics**: talks by experts on civilian defense, health, sports, safety, postwar problems.

3. **Community celebrations**: programs in connection with Farmers' Week, Old Settlers' Day, Community Festival, Agricultural Fair, Flower Show, Play Day.

4. **Intercultural education**: talks, music, dances by representatives of minority cultural groups, recognition of newly naturalized citizens, talks by persons who have lived with other cultural groups.

5. **All-school problems**: panels, roundtables, and discussions of the recreational program, beautifying the grounds, school conservation, boy-girl relationships, the school camp, the curriculum, school government, the Victory Corps.

6. **Aesthetics**: concerts, dance programs, art exhibits.

7. **Hobbies**: talks and exhibitions of hobbies such as making flies and casting for trout, hunting Indian relics, training animals, collecting dolls, old-fashioned dances, folk ballads.

In the Classroom

1. **Early settlers** to describe pioneer days, changes in the community, contrasts between old and new in home life, school procedures, recreational customs, dress, beliefs.

2. **Patrons** of the school to discuss community problems such as relation of school to community life, what schools can do for boys and girls, school and home relationships.

3. **Leaders in non-school educational agencies:**

   a. *Parents* to discuss problems and responsibilities of the home.

   b. *Recreation Director* to analyze community recreation, to solicit and instruct volunteer workers, to correlate school and community recreational programs.

   c. *Public Health Nurse* to discuss health in the community, build wholesome attitudes toward the public health program, solicit cooperation in specific health projects, advise on school health problems.

   d. *City Manager* to explain functions of government, local civic problems.

e. *Community Council members* to interpret the function of the Council and explain its plans for improving community living.

f. *Conservation Officer* to show movies and discuss reforestation, soil erosion control, plant diseases, conserving wild life, how schools can cooperate in the conservation program.

g. *Red Cross Worker* to explain the services rendered by the organization, to organize a Junior Red Cross program, to teach classes in first aid, home nursing, child care, nutrition.

h. *Minister* to describe social services of the churches, to analyze community problems, to solicit volunteer workers for community projects in social welfare.

i. *Theater Manager* to talk about film selection, how to appreciate motion pictures, how movie equipment works, new developments in motion picture making, outstanding movies.

j. *Librarian* to discuss services of the county or city library, new books of interest to the group, how to use the library; to tell stories and interest children in the library story hour; to discuss the work of a librarian.

k. *Newspaper Editor* to describe how news is gathered and how a newspaper is printed; to discuss what makes a good newspaper, advertising, vocations in the field of journalism, how to read a newspaper; to encourage individual and class groups to write for the paper, and to try out for various jobs in printing shops and newspaper offices.

l. *Civic art officials* such as directors of musical organizations, playhouses, museums, art studios, etc. to explain their work and encourage interested students to participate.

4. **Leaders in other community organizations:**

a. *Farmers,* dairymen, fruitgrowers, agricultural workers to analyze problems related to farming and country life.

b. *Industrialists* to discuss technical processes, relation of industries to the community, labor policies.

c. *Labor organizers* to explain problems of the worker, reasons for organizing, social security, government and labor; to describe the work they do; to explain training required for unskilled, semiskilled, skilled, and technical workers.

d. *Business people* to talk about price ceilings, rationing, priorities, distribution problems, wise buying, cooperatives, vocations in merchandising.

e. *White-collar workers* to explain job opportunities, wages, training required.

f. *Scientific workers* to talk about their positions, their scientific processes, the scientific and social significance of their labor.

g. *Social workers* to discuss actual cases, types of aid available, the Social Security Act, social service as a career.

h. *Director of the U. S. Employment Office* to describe the activities of the office, shortages and surpluses of labor, movement of workers between areas and industries, the war and manpower.

The general function of any resource person is to contribute to the solution of problems, to help enrich and broaden meanings, to awaken and help build worthwhile interests, to acquaint students with varied aspects of their social and physical environment, and to develop deepened sensitivity to people, their ways of living, accomplishments, and problems.

How Can Resource People Be Used?

When a situation arises wherein a group feels the need of outside assistance, it is well for the teacher to do some exploratory planning. What kind of resource person will meet the need of the group? Who is available? Who is most suitable in terms of his background and the maturity level of the pupils? Are there any problems involved, such as cost of transportation, advance arrangements, difficulty of making contacts, and the like? Answers to these and similar queries should be available in the school's card index of community resources, such as is described in Chapter 18.

Preparing for the Visitor

In planning the use of resource people, the following steps should be taken by teacher and students working cooperatively:

1. Determine the Major Purpose

Discuss such questions as why an outside person is needed at this juncture, how his general area of competence fits into the class program, what he might contribute to the group's understanding, attitudes, interests, or skills.

2. Identify Specific Problems

Decide just what should be found out from the expected visitor. Formulate a few significant questions for him, and perhaps allocate responsibility for asking them to various class members.

3. Decide Whom to Invite

This decision may have to be taken in some cases before that of step 2 above. Consult the card file, and canvass the group for additional suggestions.

4. Plan the Form of Presentation Desired

This might be an exhibit and informal talk, a demonstration with explanations, a panel discussion of several people including some from the student group, a luncheon meeting with conversation afterward, a formal talk followed by open forum, a planned interview before the class, an illustrated talk, or the like.

5. Issue the Invitation

This should be done well in advance. If an invitation is extended and accepted orally, it should be confirmed in writing immediately afterward.

6. Inform the Speaker about the Class Group

Before the event, send to the resource person a statement containing such information as the age level, academic grade and class, and number of students in the group, the date, time and place of meeting, any needed traveling instructions, length of time for the meeting, name of person in charge, and names and positions of any other participants in the program, a statement of the group's general purpose, problem, or need, and, in some circumstances, a list of questions which will be asked by the students.

7. Plan Where, When, and How to Receive the Guest at the School

Also arrange for any necessary entertainment after the class session if he does not plan to leave the school or town immediately.

8. Make Clear Arrangements for Equipment

Special rooms, projectors and screens, maps, tables, etc. may be needed; if so, be sure that they will be ready at the designated time and place.

9. Agree upon Standards

The group might agree that each member will be prepared for the activity, will pay careful attention to the speaker, try to participate if opportunity offers, be fully responsible if asked to assume responsibility such as arranging the room, telephoning, greeting the guest, acting as chairman, or the like.

10. Choose a Chairman and a Recorder

The recorder's function is to write a factual account of the meeting as it progresses. It is generally better to have one student or a small committee act as recorder since a better summary results, and the group as a whole can give undivided attention to the speaker.

11. Decide How to Thank the Guest Afterward

Appreciation may be expressed by applause, orally by the chairman for the group, in later conversation, by letter, or by a combination of these approaches.

12. Check All Arrangements One Day before the Visit

Remind the speaker by letter or telephone call, and be sure that all needed equipment and services will be ready on time.

It is imperative that the group be well prepared for the situation into which an outside person is brought. In the case of an assembly speaker, interest can be generated through the school council, homeroom meetings, bulletin-board notices, posters, articles in the school and community papers, and through student participation in planning. When a resource person is to be used with a class group, the planning outlined above will furnish both motivation and meaning for the experience.

The Visit

At appropriate times, the activities already planned by the group should be carried out by them. This will involve meeting and welcoming the visitor, and being thoughtful of his wraps, his desire for last-minute grooming, and his wish to see the room before he talks in it. Before introducing him to the group, be sure you know enough about his background and accomplishments to make a personalized introduction. Be very sure to pronounce his name clearly and correctly. After the talk or other presentation, escort the visitor to the exit from the building, or to whatever further entertainment has been planned for him.

13. Be Ever Conscious of Public Relations

Students should be fully aware that such a visit is more than an educational experience for themselves; it is also a venture in public relations on the part of the school. The care with which they plan, their cordiality and receptiveness, their participation, the use they make of the experience in the school and in the community —all such factors will surely impress the lay visitor for good or ill, and will mould his opinion of both the character and effectiveness of the entire school.

Interpreting the Experience

As soon as possible after the visit, the teacher and students together should analyze its value, decide upon next steps, and record their impressions in some tangible form. The group's planning should be appraised, as well as the guest's contribution and the participation of the students.

14. PLAN APPROPRIATE FOLLOW-UP

Opportunities for constructive follow-up activities in classroom, school, and community should be explored, and plans made while enthusiasm is still strong. Some record of the speaker with a general evalution should be placed in the community resource file, and a description of the whole experience might well be written for class use and for publicity purposes.

Through such a process, the resource visitor's contribution is better understood and appreciated by the class, and is more likely to lead into further educational activities. Frequently the outside person stimulates the group to creative participation in community processes, or perhaps provides some entrée into local activities. The alert teacher will capitalize to the full upon all such opportunities.

What Are the Limitations of Resource Visitors?

Despite its evident value, the technique of using resource visitors has certain important limitations, of which these two are the most significant:

1. **Inability of many an otherwise competent adult** to speak successfully to students, particularly when he is in their environment rather than his own.

2. **Lack of that "atmosphere"** which naturally surrounds the speaker when he is at ease in his own familiar environment or location.

If only boys and girls might go outside their schoolrooms to talk with resource people at work in their own everyday situations—how much more realistic *that* would be! Can it be done? Of course! And the basic technique for doing it is analyzed in the chapter to follow.

SELECTED REFERENCES

Brown, Inga E., "Use of Community Resources in Rural Schools." *Social Education* 5:520–24 (Nov. 1941). Vivid account of how early settlers, immigrants, state officials, etc. may be utilized as stimulating resource visitors.

Carper, M. L., "Out-of-School Teachers." *Educational Leadership* I:350–53 (March 1944). Musicians, actors, lumberjacks and many other people from the community help to teach school in a Virginia community.

Emerich, Tom P., "Vitalized Economics in the Junior College." *Junior College Journal* 10:27–31 (Sept. 1939). A bank president came into the classroom to lecture on the making of loans, a credit bureau manager explained how they kept files on 750,000 different people, the head of a labor union told how his organization operates, the director of the local U. S. Employment Service explained his work, etc.

Solem, Lyl R., "Tailor Comes to School." *Clearing House* 14:294–96 (Jan. 1940). An expert tailor came to class to explain how suits are made; a cobbler demonstrated shoe-construction and repair; a furrier put together a woman's fur coat before the class. All such experiences were preceded and followed by appropriate study and activities.

Studer, Norman, "Local History: A Neglected Resource." *Progressive Education* 19:8–11 (Jan. 1942). Emphasizes the importance and possibilities of utilizing resource people in the study of local history.

CHAPTER 7

Interviews[1]

Portland's 600 Dutch Uncles

When Ralph Dugdale became superintendent of schools in Portland, Oregon, he launched a survey to find out what seniors in the 11 city high schools expected to do after graduating. What he learned appalled him. Three out of four were not going to college, and expected to "look for a job;" in what business or trade, nine out of ten hadn't the slightest idea. Many who did have a preference mentioned occupations which can absorb only a few of our high school graduates. Almost none had ever talked with a business or a professional man about work.

Dugdale told 300 Portland Rotarians about his occupational survey of their sons' and daughters' job hopes. "I wish each of you could take on half a dozen boys and talk like Dutch uncles to them about what it takes to get and hold a job," he suggested.

The chairman of the meeting met the challenge. "I'll bet there isn't a man in this room," he said, "who wouldn't talk with any boy you sent to his office."

"I'll bet there isn't a boy in the senior class," replied Dugdale, "who wouldn't be tickled to talk with a successful business man."

That was the beginning of Portland's "Dutch Uncle" plan. Today 600 business and professional men, Kiwanians, Rotarians, and others, are helping to put boys—and girls, too—on the right job track. At first the interviews were mostly duds; the boys, ignorant of business, were ill at ease and unable to ask the right questions. So school authorities sent out a staff member to do some interviewing and prepare a series of brief monographs on "What People Do." One, for example, tells what a pharmacist has to know, how much money he may expect to make, and so on. Sixty businesses and trades have been covered so far, each monograph carefully checked for accuracy. Mimeographed at first, the monographs are now printed. Every high school has complete sets on file, for consultation, and seniors have copies to keep.

Kiwanis backed this project and also the making of a motion picture, *How to Ask for a Job.* In it boys and girls from each Portland high school are shown going to local businessmen and asking for work, demonstrating both the right and the wrong way to do it. Every senior sees this picture before calling on a businessman.

---

[1] Some material in this chapter was written by Howard E. Wilson and at his request is used without specific acknowledgment but with much appreciation.

School authorities selected teachers in each school to act as counselors, and worked out a system of appointments for the 3600 boys and girls in the graduating class. Dugdale discovered, with something of a shock, that many of his teachers had only the vaguest ideas of job requirements. So, to educate the counselors, the service clubs now send two businessmen each week to spend an afternoon with the 60 teachers assigned to coach the boys and girls for their interviews.

The guidance program is proving effective even in the trade schools. Bill Thomas of Benson Trade School, where a score of trades are taught, was directed away from all of these to—of all pursuits—cooking! He had been ashamed to admit his fondness for it, because cooking was something girls did. "Not always," replied the teacher. "Most of the chefs of the big hotels are men. How would you like to talk with the chef of the Multnomah Hotel?" Bill's eyes glowed. He spent an afternoon in the Multnomah's kitchen, found out what opportunities there were for good chefs, and soon *knew* what he wanted to do.

Bill's classmate, George, wanted to be a timberman. He thought he might start as a forester, so arrangements were made for George to spend a week-end with a forester in the nearby mountains. The glamour George had expected wasn't there and he came home cured of the idea. Superintendent Dugdale feels that George's interview was as successful as Bill's; it kept George from making a wrong start.

Some seniors talk with ten or a dozen businessmen, but most of them find their line after two or three interviews, and many hit it right the first time. Where a boy shows real interest, the businessman often invites him to come back from time to time and talk things over. . . .

It was an eye opener to the boys and girls to discover how punctilious businessmen are about appointments and how graciously they receive people. The eyes of some of the businessmen have been opened too. They used to groan about the sins of modern youth. Now they say: "I always told you this younger generation has the stuff." [2]

What Are Interviews?

"Interviews" are informal personal conferences wherein one or more students question an adult to get authoritative opinion or information of some sort. As a method of community study, the interview technique is similar to that of using resource people. It nevertheless differs from it in two notable respects: (a) the interview is held in the expert's usual place of work or residence, rather than in the school classroom, and (b) the interview is primarily a question-and-answer procedure; it does not require of the interviewee a prepared talk, demonstration, or other type of organized

---

[2] From Frank J. Taylor, "Portland's 600 Dutch Uncles," *The Forum and Century,* June 1940; *Reader's Digest,* July 1940, pp. 109–11.

program. The interview, in short, utilizes resource persons for educational purposes, but does so under different conditions from those described in the previous chapter.

What Advantages Have Field Interviews?

In every community there are individual citizens whose experiences, interests, knowledge, points of view, or characteristics are worth knowing about; yet who cannot for one reason or another conveniently be brought into the school as resource persons. They may, however, be interviewed in their own locale. The interview technique:

1. **Gives students a personalized view** of community living and of some of the values and ends toward which selected residents would direct it. Through their eyes, and in man-to-man intimacy, young people may see community processes in operation; with these adults they may assess human relations.

2. **Provides experience in meeting people,** which is itself an important social quality. The adolescent who has talked successfully with a mature person about matters of common concern has himself advanced toward maturity.

In every community there are adults who can speak with authority about their work, interests, or hobbies. Every school can thus enrich its teaching program by encouraging students to interview local residents.

How Can the Interview Be Utilized?

The values of an interview are matched by its dangers, none the less real because they are complex, elusive, hard to observe. Illustrative of what may happen is the case of one interview in which a thoughtless and prejudiced adult belabored a pupil with his personal animosity toward the school administration. That pupil's adjustment to society was definitely retarded by that act. Of equal misfortune is the case of another interview in which one student's bumptious aggressiveness was considerably increased by the indulgent pampering of an easy-going adult sentimentalist.

If interviews are to be really profitable so far as the pupils' growth toward maturity and sensitivity to the community are concerned, they must be carefully developed on an individual basis by a teacher who is alert to the personality characteristics of both interviewers and interviewee, and who can therefore sensibly match the personalities involved.

It is taken for granted that no student should be sent out for very many interviews of a formal character, and that no adult will have his time and energy exhausted by the arrival of too many interviewers. As with all educational techniques, the program of interviews must be administered guardedly.

Preparing for the Interview

When definite need for expert outside aid is felt and the resolve taken to seek it through interview, the class should cooperatively:

1. DETERMINE THE OBJECTIVE

This may be done through general group discussion, and will involve clear relating of past academic experience to present questions and future activities.

2. DECIDE WHOM TO INTERVIEW

Any of the resource persons suggested in the previous chapter may be helpful. For other possibilities, consult the card file of community resources. If the problem in question is a controversial one, be sure that all viewpoints are represented in the interview program; do not permit a situation to develop in which a minority opinion goes unheard.

3. LEARN ALL YOU CAN ABOUT HIM

If pertinent, worth-while questions are to be framed for him, the interviewing committee must be aware in advance of his general experience and specific responsibilities. Such information is essential for a second reason also: it provides a basis for knowing what is "common ground" and hence enables the interview itself to get off to a good start.

4. ANALYZE THE QUALITIES OF A GOOD INTERVIEW

The student goes not merely to listen, but to converse; he must therefore have in mind the questions he wants answered—including questions or comments which are intended to bridge awkward gaps and halts in the interview—and should, if possible, have something definite to contribute to the conversation from the school itself. There should be tentative decision as to how many students shall participate in the interview; the form in which it is to be recorded; whether notes are to be taken during the interview or subsequent to it; how the interview is to be terminated.

5. DECIDE WHAT QUESTIONS TO ASK

All questions should reflect sober thought. They should relate to significant aspects of the work or experience of the person to be interviewed, and must never be superficial or malicious. When decided upon in final form, the questions should be typed in triplicate, the original copy for the interviewee, and carbon copies for the committee chairman and the class librarian, respectively.

6. DESIGNATE AN INTERVIEW COMMITTEE

This committee should be composed of three or four class members, and should include a chairman and a reporter. The latter's function is to write up the interview after it has been held; he should do this as an objective reporter of questions asked and answers returned. No part of his responsibility in writing will have to do with interpretation; his job is that of recording what happened.

7. MAKE INITIAL CONTACT WITH THE INTERVIEWEE

Unless the students are quite mature, it is wise for the teacher to make first contact with the citizen to be interviewed. This contact will preferably be through personal interview by appointment, although a telephone call or letter may be sufficient in some cases. The purpose of this teacher's initial contact is to acquaint the interviewee with the objectives of the project, and to be sure that he is willing to cooperate with it.

8. PLAN DETAILS WITH HIM

Now the chairman and one other member of the committee should call upon the interviewee in person. They should outline the general purpose of the interview, and then explain what the full committee would like to talk about when they come. A copy of the questions listed by the class should be given to him, and a time for the full committee interview arranged.

9. MAKE TRAVEL ARRANGEMENTS

A public conveyance is preferable for travel because of the safety hazard involved in the use of private machines (see Chapter 15). Determine the time needed for the committee to get to the interview location, and then add fifteen minutes to allow for those unforeseen delays which are always probable.

10. EMPHASIZE GOOD BEHAVIOR

The group should anticipate that people will ask what school they represent—either because the committee members are crude, loud, and boisterous, or because they appear to be well-mannered and quiet. Of such impressions is a school's public reputation made, and of this fact the class as a whole should be fully aware.

These ten steps should all be taken well in advance of the day set for the interview proper. Although casual and unplanned interviews may occasionally be highly successful, continuously good results require conscious and careful planning of every predictable detail.

Conducting the Interview

When the committee arrives at the interview point, the chairman should be the spokesman stating the business of the group. Good social sense on the part of the other committee members is also important. The group should stay together, and not monopolize an outer office while waiting for the interviewee. Boys' hats should be removed. Voices should be softened. Members should be seated, if possible. Gum should not be in evidence.

When the committee is invited in to begin the interview, it should carry out these activities:

11. INTRODUCE THE VISITORS

The chairman of the committee is responsible for introductions, which should be individual and personal.

12. GET THE INTERVIEWEE TO TALK FREELY

Here is where adequate understanding of his background, responsibilities, and interests bear fruit. Tactful mention and brief discussion of interests held in common helps to clear the psychological atmosphere and stimulates good will.

13. GIVE HIM YOUR FULL ATTENTION

Busy persons have no wish to talk with students who exhibit slight interest in their conversation. This is not to suggest that committee members should react in starry-eyed amazement to everything that is said, but only that outward signs of interest, sympathy, and understanding should always be shown.

14. MAKE NO ATTEMPT TO DOMINATE THE SITUATION

Let the interviewee talk as he wishes without interruption and without disagreement. Don't argue, and don't become clever, impertinent, or angry. Pass no moral judgments at this stage; just seek to understand *his* view, whatever it may be, and to draw him out in exposition of it. Listen as much for what he does not say as for what he does.

15. TAKE NOTES ONLY AS NEEDED

The mechanics of note-taking during an interview should be of such nature as not to hamper the psychological freedom of the person being interviewed. Two or three words jotted down for each major point may be enough at the moment; these reminders can be expanded in detail as soon as the interview is over.

16. ASK QUESTIONS INTELLIGENTLY

The person being interviewed may or may not use the set of questions previously given him. The committee will have to adjust its interview to his decision in this matter. In any case, the chairman should have his list of questions before him in order to be sure that the ground covered by those questions is not ignored. All committee members should be certain they do not ask questions that have already been answered; for to do so wastes time and clearly indicates a discourteous lack of attention. If questions come to mind which do not appear on the prepared list, they should be interjected at transition points in the interview, not simply thrown out in a hit-or-miss fashion.

17. REQUEST READING REFERENCES AND FURTHER SUGGESTIONS

During the interview, or at its conclusion, or both, the committee members should solicit from the interviewee whatever suggestions he may have concerning useful reading references or other experts whom they might also consult.

18. CONCLUDE THE INTERVIEW

The committee should be very careful not to outstay its welcome. When the chairman feels that the ground has been covered, or when the interviewee indicates by some sign or mannerism that he has finished, the chairman should express appreciation in behalf of the committee and the whole class, and then lead the group out of the room.

19. Expand the Notes Taken

As quickly as possible after the interview, each committee member should expand his brief notes into full form. The sooner this documentary record is made the better, for notes rapidly become "cold" and even unintelligible as the vivid memory of the immediate experience begins to fade.

Interpreting the Interview Experience

Although the interview has been concluded, the committee now has the further responsibility of organizing its findings and reporting them to the class as a whole. It should therefore, as soon as possible, engage in several significant follow-up activities, as follows:

20. Reconstruct the Interview

The committee should meet as a group to decide just what was said in the interview. The official reporter might well summarize aloud the substance of the interview, thus permitting other members to check him and each other upon such items as figures and dates, as well as upon less specific factors noted.

21. Analyze the Findings

Having reached a measure of agreement as to what the interviewee actually said, the committee is now ready for analysis and interpretation. What is the real significance of the remarks made? Were the ideas of the interviewee guarded in their expression? Was he holding anything back? Was he on the defensive? Was he seeking converts to his point of view? Was there anything peculiar about his situation which may minimize the worth of his opinion? Such are the types of queries to be asked within the group. Before beginning analysis of this nature, however, students should be warned that usually there are several sides to any question, with consequent possibility that even varied interpretations of it may be equally correct. Dogmatism and pat definitions are both unscientific and dangerous.

22. RECORD THE DATA

After the committee has thus summarized and interpreted the interview, it should proceed to make a written record of its findings. The reporter may be expected to write out a summary statement; when completed this should be submitted to the committee as a whole for checking of questions asked, answers given, and figures included. Committee members should not hesitate to suggest needed improvements in grammar, sequence, or construction. After the report has thus been corrected and approved, it should be put in permanent form.

23. REPORT TO THE CLASS

At the appointed time, a formal, oral report should be given by the committee to the class it represents. All committee members should share in making this report. Attention should be focused upon specific purpose of the interview, questions asked, answers returned, general findings, conclusions, and interpretations. If the committee's opinion upon any of these areas is not unanimous, both majority and minority reports should be presented for further analysis by the entire class. In any event, full class discussion of the committee report should be encouraged.

24. FILE A WRITTEN REPORT FOR FUTURE USE

This final report may be deposited in the class or school library, museum, or social studies' laboratory. Such reports, if properly annotated and permanently filed, may add richly to a school collection suitable for laboratory study and comparison in subsequent years.

Through such procedures, the essential contributions of the interview will best be defined, clarified, and perpetuated for the class and the school. The interview technique thus takes its place as another significant avenue of realistic, life-centered education.

What Are the Limitations of the Interview?

Although interviews are realistic and worthwhile techniques of community study, they do have two real limitations which should not be overlooked. These are:

1. **Restriction to a few students.** A personal conference of this nature must necessarily be limited to a very small committee of students. Other

members of the class are thus barred from sharing the superior educational values of the interview experience itself.

2. Secondhand nature of the experience. Listening and talking are the chief activities of the interview; there is little opportunity for directed observation of the processes or problems being discussed. In a sense, therefore, and apart from the socializing values involved, the interview is still a mediated experience rather than a firsthand observation.

How fine it would be if the entire class could hear expert opinion, and at the same time, observe actual field conditions for themselves! How might that be done? The answer is obvious and is presented in the next chapter.

SELECTED REFERENCES

Bingham, W. V., and B. V. Moore, *How to Interview*. New York: Harper, 1941. The uses, techniques, and dependability of the interview. Being designed for social workers, vocational counselors, physicians, etc., this book will be of most value to adults.

Hulett, J. E. Jr., "Interviewing in Social Research: Basic Problems of the First Field Trip." *Social Forces* 16:358–66 (March 1938). Practical suggestions, especially designed for the social surveyor going into a new community, concerning the planning, arranging and conducting of interviews with local residents.

Symonds, Percival M., "Securing Rapport in Interviewing." *Teachers College Record* 39:707–22 (May 1938). Working techniques for interviewing students, but adaptable for student interviews with adults.

Young, P. V., *Interviewing in Social Work*. New York: McGraw-Hill, 1935. Offers many suggestions of value for interviewing in other fields as well as in that of social work.

CHAPTER 8

Field Trips

Teachers Investigate Housing Conditions

"He's funny!" shrieked a small boy as the smiling, hatless, gray-haired man strode down the littered street, blowing melodiously upon a golden hunting horn. "They're slumming," remarked one interested spectator to another, as they watched a crowd of young men and women follow the man with the horn into a ramshackle tenement house on the East Side of New York City. But he was not funny, and they were not slumming, for this was a serious field study of housing contrasts being made by a teachers' college class under the personal direction of Clarence V. Howell, founder and director of a most unique educational agency called *Reconciliation Trips, Incorporated*.

Following the clarion call of that little Swedish hunting horn, these future teachers had begun their housing tour with a visit to luxurious uptown apartment penthouses, which rent unfurnished for twenty-five thousand dollars a year. Wide-eyed, they learned that many tenants in such apartments would spend twenty or thirty thousand dollars for redecoration before they moved in. Then they continued through the famous Waldorf-Astoria Hotel with its spacious facilities, great dining rooms, costly furnishings, and its suites of rooms renting for thirty-five dollars a day and more. Thrilled, yet sobered too, were these young people as they contemplated all this material magnificence.

An hour later, the group had entered a dark and crowded "flop house" on the Bowery where tiny, cubicle-like rooms may be occupied by migrant workers for twenty cents a night. What a contrast with the great Waldorf-Astoria, whose majestic appointments were still fresh in mind! Yet the realization came that both are New York hotels, each catering to its own particular clientele.

Now the golden hunting horn is piping the group into dilapidated East Side tenement houses where railroad apartments, box apartments, and dumbbell apartments may be rented for eight to twenty-three dollars a month. Fire hazards, inadequate ventilation, unhealthful conditions generally are pointed out and explained by Director Howell. With mounting indignation, these students learn that nearly two million New Yorkers live in apartments like these, and that forty years ago an official Housing Com-

147

mission condemned as unfit for human habitation these and sixty-seven thousand other such "old-law" tenements. "Oh!" cries a social studies teacher from a suburban school, "I've read about slum housing! I've seen pictures of these tenements. But I never dreamed it was as bad as this! Why doesn't somebody *do* something about it?"

"Somebody *is* trying to do something about it," answers Mr. Howell, a kindly gleam in his keen eyes. "That's where we're going next!" And once again the golden horn trills its guiding music as the group proceeds to a nearby Federal Housing project. Here are safe, sanitary, well-lighted rooms with steam heat and electric refrigeration, renting to a fortunate few at eighteen dollars and fifty cents a month, and up. "How lovely!" exclaims a girl in the student group. "Isn't it wonderful what the government can do?" she remarks to her momentary companion. "Yes," he retorts, "but it's socialism, isn't it?" "I don't know about that, but if it is, I'm for it!" "Look here," he objects, "I don't agree at all! You see . . ." Mr. Howell grins delightedly, for his purpose is being achieved. Critical thinking about important social issues is beginning to emerge.

Before this day of wondrous new experience is ended, these students will have eaten a fifteen-cent dinner on the Bowery, attended an all-night rescue mission where crowds of men sleep sitting up to keep out of the cold, talked with inhabitants of a waterfront "jungle" or shantytown, and discussed the meaning of it all with a philosophic professor from Hobo College. How better could these future teachers of American youth orient themselves to the whole human problem of urban housing than through this vital field experience? For this is no abstract discourse pontifically delivered in some secluded academic hall of learning; rather it is a realistic, challenging introduction to one throbbing aspect of a city's very soul! . . .[1]

What Are Field Trips?

The term "field trip" is used to designate any organized excursion which is taken by school pupils as an integral part of their academic work, and primarily for educational purposes. Although field trips have many nonacademic values, their major purpose is instructional, and as such, they are not to be identified with school trips taken to participate in athletic, musical or forensic contests, with hikes or picnics organized for pleasure purposes, or with sight-seeing journeys taken by graduating classes. None of these activities should properly be called a field trip.

---

[1] From Edward G. Olsen, "Pioneering in Community Study." *Educational Method,* February 1941, pp. 236–43.

How Does the Field Trip Prove Its Worth?

Firsthand acquaintance with varied natural and social phenomena is an essential aspect of realistic school instruction. As one means to this end, the field trip technique possesses certain specific values of great significance. Excursions:

1. Facilitate opportunity for personal experiences which are real, concrete, dramatic, and hence, highly educative.

2. Provide sensory perceptions which cannot otherwise be experienced—the taste of fresh milk, the odor of wild flowers, the roar of machinery, the heat of a steel mill, the sight of real things in the real world of adults.

3. Deepen insight into even familiar phenomena in the environment, for as these matters are freshly interpreted, they take on new meaning.

4. Motivate school work by utilizing natural curiosity, and thus make possible those deep satisfactions which arise out of personal exploration and discovery.

5. Arouse student interest in new areas of thought and activity, thereby often leading to further individual reading and field explorations outside of school hours.

6. Integrate classroom instruction by exposing conventional subject matter divisions as artificial, and by enabling pupils to view facts and forces as they exist in their everyday relationships.

7. Enrich the instructional process for both pupils and teacher, since the very activity of jointly planning, executing, and evaluating an excursion provides a common experience of considerable educational significance.

8. Build character through the practical necessity of developing such traits as courtesy, patience, sportsmanship, cooperativeness, and the like.

Every community, however small or isolated, is a veritable microcosm of civilization, since within its own borders, the essential processes of living go on. That is why every school can richly extend its curriculum by utilizing local resources through excursion experiences.

What Types of Field Trips Are There?

Excursions are not limited in value to any specific curricular area, particular purpose, academic level, or length of time required. Yet it is sometimes worthwhile to classify them in terms of this fourfold division. Let us therefore note that any trip can be classified in accordance with each of four factors, which we shall describe.

1. Curricular area involved. Excursions may relate directly to a conventional academic subject field such as art, foreign language, geography, history, literature, mathematics, music, nature study, science, sociology, vocational guidance, etc. Excursions may prove just as useful in the study of social processes such as making a living, sharing in citizenship, maintaining health, enjoying beauty, and the like. In precisely the same way, the excursion technique may be applied to the study of social problems within the local community.

2. Primary purpose sought. The motivating reasons behind a given field trip may be varied, but it is probable that among them one or two of the following are predominant: securing information, changing attitudes, awakening interests, developing appreciations, promoting ideals, enjoying new experiences.

3. Academic level embraced. In their specific purposes, planning arrangements, disciplinary problems, and follow-up activities the excursions taken will differ somewhat according to whether they are utilized by young children in the primary grades, older children in the middle grades, adolescents in high school, or young adults in the college or university.

4. Amount of time required. Some satisfactory trips may require only a few minutes of time, as when a class goes into the school yard after a heavy rain to observe the effects of small-scale erosion. Other trips will need a full class period, several hours, or perhaps an entire day. Longer trips, involving overnight arrangements, are sometimes called excursions, but it is better to classify them instead as extended field studies. (See Chapter 10.)

Field trips, it now appears, are of multiple type, depending upon the particular interrelationship of these four factors. A given field trip may thus be classified as a brief fact-finding excursion in elementary school science, as a two-hour high school trip to develop student interest in problems of public health, as an all-day college excursion to promote sympathetic appreciation of other religions, or by any other combination of the four basic factors described above. The important thing is not a meticulous classifying of types, but rather a clear awareness that different types of trips do require varied organization if they are to be used with maximum success by the school.

How Can the Field Trip Best Be Used?

"Going places and seeing things" is an educational technique of prime significance—providing always that it is used with care, discrimination, and intelligent foresight. If it is not so used, then the excursion will likely become a mere lark and hence quite unwarranted in the schools. No excursion can be justified unless the total learning values achieved thereby are genuinely superior to those possible through other instructional procedures.

Worthwhile trips require very careful planning, not only of each particular trip to be taken, but equally in terms of the school's general excursion policy and program. Let us therefore examine vital aspects of both these areas in some detail.

Develop a General Field Study Program

Behind every successful excursion there lies a vast amount of preliminary and essential "spade work." We shall note, in passing, five important steps to be followed in organizing the general excursion program of the school.

1. DISCOVER THE RESOURCES OF YOUR COMMUNITY

A thorough community survey should be made according to the pattern of analysis already outlined in Chapter 3, and through procedures to be explained in Chapter 9. This survey will produce an annotated list of available points of educational significance in the community—resource people, art exhibits, parks, lighthouses, historic buildings, radio stations, markets, factories, racial and national neighborhoods, welfare centers, churches, government offices, intercultural agencies, and numerous others.

2. EVALUATE THE SUITABILITY OF THESE RESOURCES

Each discovered resource center should be approached, through a personal interview if possible, in order to discover whether it is willing to cooperate with a program of school visits, what facilities it has and what provisions may be made for such excursions, and the extent to which students' observations there would probably correlate with their school program. Such specific factors as the following should be considered: the general attitude of the officials concerned; the number of students who would be welcomed on any one occasion, day, week, month, or year; the exact dates, days, and hours during which school visits might be made; whether guides, exhibits, visual aids, auditoriums, and the like are available; the exact location of the center and how to get there by available forms of transportation; the possible safety hazards such as necessary traffic crossings, unguarded machinery, dangerous streams, cliffs, wildlife, and others.

3. ANALYZE THESE RESOURCES EDUCATIONALLY

Curriculum committees—preferably including students and parents as well as teachers and administrators—should now make detailed analysis of each suitable resource center. This analysis should seek to determine:

The areas of instruction, or subject matter divisions, within which each resource may be fruitfully used.

The general grade level whereon each resource may be well used.

The correlations possible between each resource and the specified academic program of the grade levels and areas of instruction already noted.

Other significant features such as the history of the resource center, its architectural characteristics, attitude of its personnel toward the school, and so on.

4. RECORD THE INFORMATION GATHERED

Data thus secured can now be written up in some detail by the curriculum committee or by the individual teachers most concerned. A standard card form such as that described and illustrated on pages 350–53 is excellent for this purpose. The need for obtaining and recording primary information about interesting community resources is surely obvious; science classes in New York City, for example, could have no sound purpose in visiting the Museum of Science and Industry unless they knew in advance that this museum offers active educational experiences in the fields of communication, electrotechnology, foods, health, housing, textiles, tools, machines, and transportation.

5. CORRELATE RESOURCES WITH THE SCHOOL CURRICULUM

Some correlation, in written form, is essential in order that the classroom teacher may perceive precisely which available excursions are directly related to the grade and subject matter he teaches. Two sample worksheets showing such correlation are reproduced here. The first is for a curriculum organized along conventional academic subject lines, while the second is useful where activity principles operate. Both were devised for use in New York City elementary schools.

A CONVENTIONAL PROGRAM

AMERICAN HISTORY
GRADE: 5A

Syllabus Unit	Syllabus Topics	Suggested Excursions
American History	1. *Spanish Explorers*	
	a. Cortez	Hispanic Museum
from the beginning	b. Balboa	American Museum of Natural
	c. Pizarro	History (Aztec, Mayan,
	d. Coronado	Peruvian Halls)
of the Period of	2. *French Explorers*	
Discovery and	a. Champlain	Metropolitan Museum of Art
	b. Marquette	Museum of American Indian
	c. LaSalle	French Embassy
Exploration	d. Cartier	
	3. *Colonization*	
through the	a. Pilgrims	Dyckman House
	b. Puritans	Lefferts House
	c. William Penn	Jumel Mansion
Period of	d. Roger Williams	Billopp House
	e. John Smith	Inwood Park
	f. Dutch in America	Van Cortlandt Park
Colonization	g. Homes and Industries	Museum of the City of New York

AN ACTIVITY PROGRAM

TRANSPORTATION
AGE–GROUP: 10 YEARS

Aims: To trace the development of methods of travel from primitive times to the present

To understand man's conquest of nature by invention

Leading Themes:

1. *Primitive Travel:* travel by foot; the earliest boats; discovery of wheel, how heavy loads were carried before the wheel; pyramids in Egypt; use of man power; domestication of the horse, the dog, the reindeer; military importance of roads to Romans; methods of travel in different lands: sled, camel, junk, wagon, jinrikisha, sedan chair, elephant, etc.

2. *Travel by Land:* travel by foot; wheel; domestication of animals; power plus wheel; street cars; the automobile; railroad: steam locomotive, streamliners; railroad lines, terminals; subway, elevated.

3. *Travel by Water:* swimming; log; raft; dugout; canoe; rowboat; sailboat of ancient times; historic boats—*Halfmoon, Mayflower,* Viking ships, the *Clermont,* the *Savannah,* the *Normandie*—use of steel; screw propeller; diesel engine; nautical instruments.

4. *The Harbor:* New York City; the bays, the ocean; steamships, tugboats, barges; Statue of Liberty; Ellis Island; the Customs; docks,

waterfront, piers; buoys; lighthouses; dredges; skyline; sea gulls; stevedores, pilots, coastguard; ferries; Battery Park; Ernest Poole's conception of the Harbor; local geography; bridges, tunnels, tubes.

5. *Travel by Air:* study of birds; Da Vinci's flying machines; parachute; balloons; dirigibles; famous dirigibles—*Norge, Los Angeles, Hindenburg*—gliders; airplanes; rockets; imaginary and possible flights to the moon.

Activities:

1. Trace the development of travel by land with the use of clay. Include travel by foot, wheel, wagon, animal, street car, auto, railroad, and so forth.

2. Make a sandtable exhibit showing the development of travel by water. Include log, raft, dugout, canoe, sailboat, steamboat, modern ocean liner.

3. Trace the development of travel by air. Include balloon, glider, dirigible, airplane.

4. Prepare a sandtable exhibit of New York Harbor. Include tall buildings, docks, ferry, Statue of Liberty, tugboats, barges, bridges, lighthouses, and the like.

5. Make posters showing how people travel in various lands—the camel, the sled, the jinrikisha, and others.

6. Make models of famous ships such as the *Maine*, the *Lusitania*, the *Santa Maria*, and the like.

7. Have a "Transportation" bulletin and scrapbooks.

Related Excursions:

1. Grand Central Railroad Terminal
2. An ocean liner
3. Floyd Bennett Airport
4. The Holland Tunnel
5. New York Harbor by ferry
6. U. S. Government Lighthouse
7. Brooklyn Navy Yard
8. Cooper Union Museum (first locomotive)
9. Museum of the City of New York (marine gallery)
10. Museum of Science and Industry (highway transportation, marine and railroad halls)

Such are some basic suggestions for the development of a general excursion program in any school. Now let us consider the related problem of successfully organizing any particular excursion.

Organize Each Field Trip with Care

Any excursion divides into three sequential phases or steps: (1) planning, (2) conducting, and (3) interpreting the experience. Let us therefore examine each of these phases in turn.

Planning the Trip

Certain general considerations are fundamental in the planning of all successful school excursions. These may be summarized quickly by noting that every excursion should:

1. **Arise out of class or school activities,** and be intimately related to those activities.

2. **Maintain a definite purpose:** to meet a specific need or to solve a particular problem.

3. **Be limited in scope.** It is foolish to attempt too much on any one trip. Several excursions, each with a limited and definite objective, are always preferable to a single hurried and superficial experience.

4. **Utilize all opportunities for character training.** Especially on the elementary school level the teacher and pupils together should discuss the importance of courtesy, cooperation, and good citizenship. While en route, watch should be kept for any especially desirable or negative behavior, and these findings might well be later discussed and appraised by the class.

5. **Be planned with care,** so as to avoid waste of time and effort. This requires preliminary as well as later attention to such questions as these: Are the projected experiences likely to be the most fruitful possible at this time? Is there proper reading material for advance preparation as well as for the follow-up? How much time will be required for the total trip? Just what arrangements need to be made? What kinds of related or culminating activities may be expected to follow the excursion experience?

With these general considerations in mind, let us now proceed to analyze various specific steps within the planning process itself.

1. DETERMINE THE PURPOSE

School journeys may be undertaken for many specific reasons, among which might be any or several of these:

a. **To serve as a preview** of a lesson and for gathering instructional materials.

b. **To create teaching situations** for cultivating observation, keenness, discovery—to encourage children to see and know the things about them.

c. **To serve as a means of arousing specific interests**—as in birds, trees, art productions, historical settings.

d. **To supplement classroom instruction;** to secure definite information for a specific lesson—as in arithmetic, civics, geography, literature.

e. **To verify previous information,** class discussions and conclusions, or individual experiments.[2]

---

[2] From *Visual Education and the School Journey*, p. 16. Pennsylvania Department of Public Instruction, 1930.

Such a list might be continued at length. It is apparent that there may be as many objectives for school excursions as there are learning problems. The important thing is that every pupil, as well as the teacher, become fully aware of just *why* this particular trip is being planned, and of *how* it relates to his own classroom experiences and activities. General group discussion is excellent in this connection.

2. STUDY THE PROBLEM

Intellectual preparation is essential before any excursion is actually undertaken. Teacher and students alike need to study the problem at hand in order that they may possess sufficient background to make the excursion itself really meaningful. Relevant documentary materials should be utilized by the teacher, by individual pupils, by committees, or by the class as a whole, and all worthwhile information found may be shared with the group through reports, panel analyses, or in general discussion. Appropriate audio-visual aids may also be used, both for initial motivation and for general orientation to what will be seen on the trip itself. In these and other similar ways central issues should be identified, basic problems recognized, and major purposes further clarified and made specific.

While careful advance preparation of this nature is essential, it should not be made in too great detail; room should always be left for some surprises and for the thrill of personal exploration and discovery on the field.

3. FORMULATE QUESTIONS TO BE ASKED

Once the basic purpose of the trip has been determined and a background of understanding attained, the next step in planning can be taken. This step consists in preparing fairly definite questions and problems for which specific answers will be sought at the resource center itself. In the case of an elementary school class planning to visit a dairy, for example, such queries as these should be formulated through advance class discussion, and then perhaps divided among various pupils or committees for further investigation, both in books and in the field:

> How does grass in a cow change to milk?
> What is a cow's cud?
> How much milk does a cow give?
> Why should there be many windows in a cow barn?
> Why should cows be kept clean?

What is pasteurization?
Why does cream come to the top of the milk?
What makes milk sour?
Why is milk good for people?
How do we know what milk contains?

In cases where the excursion is to be one of purely observational character, no advance questions such as these are required. Instead, as in the case of a trip made to ascertain signs of spring, a simple work sheet, such as the one reproduced below, may be given each child. The data thus recorded are afterward made the subject of discussion by the class.

LIST ALL SIGNS OF SPRING YOU CAN SEE

What I Saw (describe it)	Where (describe place)	When (date and time)

4. Make Necessary Arrangements

Cooperative planning of the trip itself is now in order. Class committees or the whole group should work with the teacher to arrange as many of the following details as are relevant in the particular situation:

a. **Invite a few helpful parents.** Be sure they understand what is planned and how they can best assist the project. Let them be present at the preparatory class sessions.

b. **Secure permission to visit** the chosen centers of interest. How approach their officials? A telephoned request is easy to make, and equally easy to refuse. A letter is somewhat better, but it, too, may easily be refused or neglected. A personal visit will accomplish more, yet it is costly in time and effort. Best of all approaches is a personal introduction by an interested third party—an influential parent, business executive, civic organization secretary, or the like.

c. **Complete all necessary business arrangements** with the proper officials involved—with executives, speakers, auditorium managers, transportation companies, and so forth.

d. Arrange with hosts and speakers for a definite schedule and sequence of events, and for specific time limits on their talks and instructions. And be sure that they include within these time limits, adequate opportunity for questions from the group.

e. Send written reminders to all these persons a day or two in advance of the trip itself. In case of any doubt, also telephone them.

f. Make adequate provision for meeting the necessary expenses involved in the trip (see Chapter 15 in this connection).

g. Decide what wearing apparel is appropriate, what materials such as pencils, note pads, maps, cameras, baskets, measuring tapes, knives, hammers, magnifying glasses, flashlights, etc., should be taken along, and by whom; what kind of lunch to bring if one is required, and so on.

h. Be sure that the teacher goes over the entire itinerary in advance. This is essential so that he may be thoroughly familiar with the best route, bus stops, parking facilities, provisions for guide service, things to be seen and done by the group, aspects or phases of the resource center to be stressed or ignored, eating and toilet arrangements, time needed at each stage of the trip, special safety hazards, and similar factors. Through such preliminary observations, the teacher can also determine the best sequence in which various centers may be visited on a single trip.

i. Develop a printed guide sheet to be given to each excursion member. This sheet should list at least the itinerary, traveling directions, and names of speakers with their topics. It may well also include some significant problems for thought, questions to be answered, and reading references for further investigation.

5. Secure Consent Slips from Parents

No elementary school pupil or high school student should be taken on an excursion unless an official consent slip, signed by the pupil's parents and properly dated, has been filed in the Principal's office. The legal importance of the consent slip is a topic to be treated in Chapter 15; it is sufficient at this point to say that teachers cannot generally be held liable in the event of accident to a pupil providing the teacher can demonstrate that reasonable care had been exercised. One evidence of such reasonable care is the procurement of parental consent slips before children are taken on scheduled trips.

6. Make a Travel List

No class should leave a school or college unless a travel list for that trip has been prepared. Such a list, which might well be done in duplicate, protects the school by enabling the responsible administrator to know who went where, and when; it may also serve as the teacher's attendance sheet for the trip. Below is one possible

OUTLINE OF TRIP

2:25 P.M. - MEET AT TEMPLE EMANU-EL, 4 E. 65th St.   TO REACH THERE: - 5th Ave.
Bus, off 64th St. B. M. T. subway, off 5th Ave. station.   Lex. Ave.
subway, off 59th St., north, west.

2:30 P.M. - TEMPLE EMANU-EL, 65th St. & 5th Ave.   Vistors from all parts of
world. Most costly Jewish temple in U.S.A. --delicate and rich imported
marbles - the Great Temple with mighty span and cathedral eloquence.
The small Temple Beth-El - a beautiful synagogue.

3:00 P.M. - FIFTH AVE. BUS #4, uptown, off 122d St., east to Broadway to
Jewish Theological Seminary, for:

3:30 P.M. - JEWISH MUSEUM -- ancient Torah scrolls, the famous Bologna Bible
printed 1482, other objects 3300 years old - coins, amulets, Chanukah
lamps, Passover plate, the only one of its kind; etchings, originals
by Rembrandt; Ketubah (marriage contract); Tifilim, ark -- interpreted by
Dr. M. Romanoff, in charge. Answers to questions. Usually closed on
Jewish holiday. Opened especially for us.

4:15 P.M. - BROADWAY SURFACE CAR, downtown, off 89th St., north, west to
270 W. 89th St., for:

4:40 P.M. - HARVEST FESTIVAL BOOTHS, especially constructed frame, richly
laden with leafy boughs, from which hang rich ripe fruits: grapes, pears,
apples, peaches - even vegetables and grains.   All symbolic of
Thanksgiving, reminiscent of leafy tents in the wilderness. "The Feast
of Tabernacles is always observed with great rejoicing and gladness."

4:50 P.M. - "WHAT IS THE FEAST OF TABERNACLES?" - by Dr. Israel Goldstein,
Rabbi, Temple B'Nai Jeshurun. No one is better able to make the fruits,
the vines, the leafy boughs talk joyfully and deeply than Dr. Israel
Goldstein. He will tell us what is the Feast of Tabernacles and why
this joyful festival. Then he will usher us into the richly beautiful
Temple B'Nai Jeshurun of second oldest congregation in U. S.A. He will
tell us about the ark, showing in detail how they worship, the singing
of the Cantor and tell us how the Orthodox, the Conservative and Reformed
differ and wherein they agree.

5:45 P.M. - 86TH ST. CROSSTOWN BUS to 92d St. and Lex. Ave., for:

6:15 P.M. - KOSHER CAFETERIA DINNER - most delicious, savory, wholesome food -
no butter, no milk products with meat. Why? What is Kosher? We shall be
told. Following supper we expect to visit another harvest festival booth
hanging rich with foliage and fruits.

7:45 P.M. - "JEWISH PEOPLE IN THE MODERN WORLD" - by Morton M. Berman, Director,
Religious Education, Free Synagogue. Answers to questions. One of
the best youthful Jewish speakers in Greater New York.

EXPENSES:- 50¢ each for trip or fraction. Add cafeteria dinner, fares.

DIRECTORS THIS TRIP:- Edward G. Olsen, Clarence V. Howell.

RECONCILIATION TRIPS - 89 Bedford Street, New York City.
Phone: CUmberland 6-0544.

TYPICAL GUIDE SHEET FOR A COLLEGE CLASS. Reconciliation trips,
New York City

form for such a travel list, including space for notation of any students who do not attend the trip.

FIELD TRIP RECORD

Class _____ Teacher _____ Date _____

Destination _____

Transportation Used _____

Time Leave School _____ Arrive Destination _____

Time Leave Destination _____ Arrive at School _____

Comments _____

Students Attending

1.   3.
2.   etc.

Students Not Attending

	Names	Reason	Provision Made
1.			
2.	etc.		

7. PROVIDE FOR ADEQUATE ADULT SUPERVISION

The safety of the students must be a prime consideration at all times. Every precaution must be taken, and the younger the children, the more important this becomes. Before leaving the school (in a large city), each elementary school child should be given an identifying tag bearing his name, address, and school name. Such tags, which should be worn on the clothing of smaller children rather than carried in their pockets, serve well in the event that a child becomes separated from the group. It is desirable to have people of any age display their identifying tags before entering buses, buildings, and the like; this precaution will prevent unauthorized persons from joining the party en route.

Conducting the Trip

The day of the excursion has arrived. Before the class actually departs upon it, there are several important details which the teacher should check upon. These may seem like trivialities, but the experienced educator knows only too well how an apparent triviality, if overlooked, may destroy the best-laid plans.

8. Make Last-Minute Check

Before the trip begins the teacher in charge of small children should do as many of these things as seem desirable:

a. Check on physical condition of the pupils. Those with symptoms of illness should be left behind in care of the school nurse.

b. Note the appearance and dress of the students; see that each is appropriately attired and that no one wears a flowing scarf or other article of clothing which might become entangled in machinery.

c. Determine whether each pupil has brought his correct carfare, lunch, equipment, and so forth.

d. Consult the school secretary to be certain that consent slips for each child have been received.

e. Check the travel list to be sure that it is correct as of the moment.

f. Summarize and clarify, for the class, the purpose of the excursion.

g. Ascertain whether those pupils with special assignments understand their responsibilities.

h. Emphasize again the importance of safety first, and indicate the nature of special hazards, if any, to be avoided on the trip.

i. Review the essentials of good behavior, stressing the fact that all will be guests at the centers of interest and will wish to act as such.

j. Permit the class to get drinks and go to the toilet.

If the class has already been organized by small groups for travel, the teacher can easily utilize the services of group captains for checking on points b, c, and g and reporting their findings to the teacher. He, meanwhile, can take care of points a, d, and e, and also be ready to examine doubtful cases brought to him by group captains. After these matters have been managed, the teacher can quickly take care of points f, h, and i. For point j, it is well to dismiss the class for perhaps five minutes, with the announcement that at the end of that time, the excursion will begin.

9. Provide for Children Left Behind

When it is necessary to leave someone behind because he did not bring a consent slip, or for other non-medical reasons, the teacher should send the pupil in question to another teacher's room. So far as feasible, he should go there with some special assignment directly related to the class trip underway; thus he can maintain some feeling of sharing in the enterprise and contribute his bit to it in succeeding group discussions. The names of all pupils left behind, together with their temporary room numbers, should be sent to the administrator's office on the travel list.

10. FORMALLY CANCEL THE TRIP, IF NECESSARY

If for any reason a scheduled excursion cannot be taken, all persons concerned in its operation should be notified as quickly as possible, including the school or college officials who had recorded it. Appropriate explanations may be made at the time of cancellation, or may be offered within a short time by letter if the former course is impracticable.

11. ORGANIZE THE GROUP FOR TRAVEL

Public relations, as well as physical safety, require that the teacher have some definite procedure for insuring discipline during the trip, and also for making routine checkup upon pupil attendance at various points along the way. These needs are especially important on the elementary school level, but are by no means to be neglected with even college students.

What can be done? One suggestion, particularly appropriate for younger pupils, is to organize them into squads of four, with every odd-numbered child on the curb side of the route acting as captain of the child on his right as well as of the two children immediately behind him, thus:

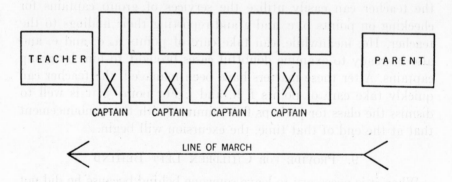

With such younger groups, it is well to give the squad captain some special badge of distinction, have him realize the nature of his responsibilities, and see that he lives up to them throughout the trip.

Under this arrangement, when the teacher orders "Check squads!", the captains immediately check upon their respective squads and, having accounted for these members, proceed to raise their right hands. The teacher then has merely to count the number of hands and multiply by four to complete the physical check. Older pupils, of course, need not be organized so thoroughly, but they too must be carefully checked at frequent intervals, and to that end, the use of small groups with chosen captains is strongly recommended even though no formal order of march need be maintained.

12. Proceed En Route

As the class files out of the building, the teacher takes his position at the head of the line, while a parent or other responsible adult brings up the rear (see diagram). The teacher, knowing the way, leads the group while the assistant follows to prevent straggling and falling behind. Certain general considerations for the happy and orderly conduct of the trip itself should now be observed:

a. Encourage marching songs, school songs, and group cheers if the class is on foot or in a private bus. Such vocal expression of student enthusiasm is desirable, since it develops a desired esprit de corps and also drains off a certain amount of youthful exuberance before the more serious part of the trip begins.

b. Halt approaching traffic, if necessary, before the group attempts to cross a street. If no traffic officer is on duty where a crossing must be made, the teacher should stand in the middle of the street and stop the traffic by raising his hand. The assistant, meanwhile, should hurry to the head of the line and lead the group across the street, the teacher then bringing up the rear onto the opposite sidewalk.

c. Point out and interpret interesting items to be seen along the way. Ability to do this successfully will obviously require careful advance preparation by the teacher in charge. If a private bus is being used, the telling of relevant anecdotes en route may heighten general interest in the trip itself while also relieving the tedium of a lengthy ride.

d. Keep the group together. In wooded sections and in cities some audible signal such as a whistle or horn is essential for the teacher's use. In noisy situations such as a busy station, a raised handkerchief or similar visual signal is necessary unless the class is very small.

e. Avoid side-interests or stops not directly related to the major purposes of the excursion. Too many sensations will diminish interest, confuse comprehension, and induce emotional as well as physical fatigue.

f. Watch constantly for signs of fatigue and lagging behind. Keep stragglers up with the party through friendly encouragement; hold back the more impetuous by appealing to their group loyalty.

g. Stay on schedule. Always endeavor to be just a little ahead of time at the next point, so as to allow for unforeseen delays. Be sure not to overstay your allotted time in any one place.

h. Approach the city destination from the opposite side of the

street. This approach enables the group to see their goal to best advantage before they reach it, thereby heightening their sense of expectancy.

i. **Halt the group outside the resource center** while the teacher enters to announce its presence. When the guide or other host has been located, the students may enter at his invitation. Introductions should now be made. These may be personal if the group is small and composed of relatively mature people; otherwise a general presentation as a class will be sufficient.

j. **Arrange for the speaker, guide, or host to talk with the students most of the time,** rather than with the teacher or his assistant. While en route or during a meal together, have him walk or sit in the midst of the group in order that they may benefit to the full from his presence. If a meal is to be served before his address, see that he starts eating first so he can be finished before his hearers. This can be arranged by having the waiter serve him first, or by putting him at the head of your line in a cafeteria.

Thus, the traveling and waiting time passes easily, and the pupils come to their destination psychologically ready to begin their active learning at that point.

13. STIMULATE LEARNING AT THE CENTER

Although the resource center has assumedly now been reached, the teacher's vigilance must not be relaxed. Even if professional guides have taken charge of the student group, the teacher has a number of new responsibilities which should not be overlooked. To illustrate, he should now:

a. **Arrange opportunity for the pupils to carry on their previously chosen learning activities** such as questioning, taking notes, sketching, photographing, collecting specimens, making maps, conversing with workers, and so on.

b. **Keep authorized groups together;** do not allow aimless wandering about or undue attention to irrelevant exhibits, however interesting they may be.

c. **Be sure that insofar as possible every pupil is able to see and hear** what is occurring for his benefit.

d. **Remain constantly sensitive to background factors** such as weather conditions, traffic movements, seating arrangements, ventilation, emotional atmospheres, amorous interests, and similar influences of present or potential significance.

e. **Watch the time carefully.** If speakers or hosts take more time than was previously arranged, the teacher should be tactfully insistent upon moving on at the appointed time. Failure to do so at one center will invalidate schedules planned with others, or will end the trip at a later hour than announced.

Promptly at the designated time, therefore, the group should leave the resource center. The teacher will then thank the guide or host at an appropriate moment; the pupils should be encouraged to express their appreciation also as they go out. Everyone who has served the group should personally be thanked for his efforts if that can be done without disrupting the excursion schedule.

14. Dismiss Pupils from the School

If the class departed from the school for its excursion, then the class must be returned to the school upon completion of the trip. Under no circumstances should a teacher take it upon himself to dismiss an elementary or secondary school class from any other place, such as a bus or railroad station. Such action in the case of immature pupils would be evidence of the teacher's failure to exercise reasonable care. (See pp. 313–314.)

At the school, and before final dismissal, the teacher should check quickly to see that every one is present and everything is all right. Not until then should the pupils be released from the jurisdiction of the school.

Interpreting the Field Experience

Completion of the excursion proper does not terminate it as a project. On the contrary, much still needs to be done before the trip's full educational value can be realized. Definite follow-up activities form an integral part of any well-managed excursion project. Such activities, if properly planned and carried out, will result in more vitalized education—not only from the curricular point of view, but also in improved pupil-teacher relationships. Since the excursion has enabled teacher and students to share interesting common experiences, it provides excellent intrinsic motivation for further study. The wise teacher will be well aware of this fact, and will take immediate steps to capitalize upon it.

Follow-up activities are of two chief kinds: (1) those which analyze and appraise the trip itself, and (2) those which grow out of information, appreciation, or interests developed on or as a result of the trip. Suppose we notice each type in turn.

15. Appraise the Trip

As soon as possible—else interest and enthusiasm will cool—the field experience should be analyzed by the group in general free discussion. Information gathered and incidents remembered should be discussed and evaluated. Often, the emotional experiences of a trip are of more permanent educational value than is the factual information received. Yet such experiences must be analyzed in retrospect if they are to be of most value. More specifically, therefore, the group should:

   a. **Evaluate the trip in terms of the purposes** originally established for it.
   b. **Diagnose mistakes, difficulties,** and other lost opportunities from the standpoint of how to improve future excursions.
   c. **Discuss the conduct of the group and appraise it,** in specific but impersonal terms.
   d. **Write letters of thanks** to officials, speakers, guides, bus drivers, parents, and all others who helped to make the excursion possible.
   e. **Record the highlights of the trip** in some permanent form for future use.

Honest evaluation of this nature will do much to mature the thinking of pupils, for it will force them to appraise their own educative process in concrete terms. A further excellent outcome will be that of improved pupil-teacher and pupil-pupil relationships for the future.

16. EXPRESS EMERGENT INTERESTS

Every really successful excursion will arouse new interests which, properly stimulated, may be of great educational significance. Every opportunity should therefore be provided for appropriate mental, motor, and emotional activities as personalized outgrowths of the excursion experience. Individual projects, committee work, class activities of many sorts should now develop as a definite part of the total excursion project. Such activities as these are eminently suitable as follow-up procedures of this second type:

   a. **Discuss the significance of things learned** as they relate to the subject, unit, or problem which originally inspired the excursion itself.
   b. **Express ideas and feelings** through oral reports, written compositions, scrapbooks, photographic exhibits, graphs, maps, sketches, drawings, murals, scaled models, dramatic productions, public addresses, and the like.
   c. **Relate important findings, wherever possible, to other subject fields** or areas of experience. By so doing, the student becomes more aware of the essential unity of all knowledge.
   d. **Test for increased information, deeper insights, changed attitudes.**

e. Share the experience with others. Committee visits, classroom displays and exhibits, dramatic skits, class newspaper, special assembly programs, and the like, are all excellent means whereby other pupils may share the excursion experience.

Carefully planned, conducted, and followed-up excursions provide for students and teachers alike both realistic and vital educational experiences. Out of them will come enriched knowledge, increased maturity, sustained interests, and personal satisfaction of a high order. The alert teacher, knowing these results and appreciating their lasting value, will make wide use of the excursion technique.

What Are the Limitations of the Field Trip?

Despite its evident advantages, the school excursion as a technique of community study has several definite limitations. Among these are three which merit recognition:

1. **Disruption of the school program.** Most secondary schools and colleges operate on the traditional plan of fixed periods for different subjects. A single class period is inadequate for most excursions; this generally means that when trips are taken it is at the expense of succeeding classes to which these students have equal academic responsibilities.

2. **Expense is inevitable,** and often constitutes a real problem in the democratic school. Most school budgets do not provide for class excursions as they do for other learning aids—documentary materials and audio-visual aids, for example. Yet if pupils are required to pay their own expenses, it is difficult to make the excursion a required activity.

3. **Restriction of field study to occasional trips.** Despite many students' wider interests, they cannot be allowed to pursue them in sustained and directed fashion on the field itself. The classroom is still their chief center of learning activity, and within its walls they must confine most of their school-directed experience. For excursions, by their very nature, are exceptions to standard procedure, rather than the essence of everyday practice.

Might it be possible, however, to use the basic school journey technique—first-hand investigation in the field—without disrupting the school schedule, embarrassing those pupils who lack financial means to participate, or restricting students with enduring field study interests to occasional periods of brief observation? Yes, it might be possible! We shall find some suggestions for doing it in the chapter to follow.

SELECTED REFERENCES

Ade, Lester K., "Expanding the Classroom." Harrisburg: Pennsylvania Department of Public Instruction, 1938. Practical suggestions for developing an excursion program in the public schools, with examples of field trips.

Atyeo, Henry C., *The Excursion as a Teaching Technique.* Teachers College Contributions to Education, No. 761. New York: Bureau of Publications, Teachers College, Columbia University, 1939. Origins and development of the school excursion abroad and in the United States, administrative problems involved, suggested excursion procedures, and the report of an experimental comparison of the discussion and excursion techniques in the teaching of history.

Bowen, Ward C., "The School Journey." *Educational Screen* 19:185–86, 203 (May 1940). Successful excursions need not be highly organized or taken to distant points; there are real educational values in studying soil erosion in one's own schoolyard after a heavy rain, or in speculating intelligently about the concrete highway.

Brink, I. K., "Science Excursions in Winter." *Instructor* 49:25 plus (Jan. 1940). Suggestions for brief trips to see what birds are doing, where animals stay in winter, follow rabbit's tracks to see where they go, etc.

Crewson, Walter S., "Field Work in Secondary School Geography." *Journal of Geography* 40:153–56 (April 1941). Warns that field work may be either busy-work or vital education, depending upon the care in planning, executing, and following it up. The geographic relationships underlying the manufacturing activities of a city are explained as illustration.

Ewald, Hattie, and W. W. Ludeman, "The Excursion Method in Primary Reading." *Educational Administration and Supervision* 24:172–76 (March 1938). A farm excursion was used as a means of motivating reading and providing content for it.

Hoban, Charles F., Charles F. Hoban, Jr., and Samuel B. Zisman, *Visualizing the Curriculum,* Ch. II. New York: Cordon Company, 1937. History and analysis of the school journey, with specific examples of its use.

Horsman, Ralph D., "Visiting and Studying Local Community Institutions." *National Elementary Principal* 18:465–71 (July 1939). Presents a working outline as a guide to excursion planning, and then describes some typical excursions taken to a greenhouse, a farm, a museum, and an observatory. The initial preparation, forms of motivation, activities and integrating procedures are mentioned for each.

Hubbard, Elizabeth V., *Your Children at School,* Chs. VI and VII. New York: John Day, 1942. Describes in detail the enthusiastic activities and reactions of primary school children as they enjoy excursions to a farm, grocery store, filling station, garage, railroad station, house being built, and the school buildings and grounds.

Kruglak, Haym, "The Specialized Field Trip." *Educational Screen* 20:341, 355 (Oct. 1941). Essential steps in the organization of an excursion which concentrates attention upon a single process or principle, rather than upon general observation.

Miller, L. Paul, "School Journeys and School Journalism." *Clearing House* 5:229–31 (Dec. 1930). Emphasizes the possibilities of following up an excursion through journalistic accounts written by pupils and published in school paper of local newspapers. Sample stories illustrate.

Nelson, J., "Organizing a Biology Field Trip." *University High School Journal* 11:253–93 (March 1932). Extended directions for planning, meeting school requirements, preparing the students, making worksheets, providing for students who will not take the trip, the teacher's work, the follow-up, etc.

Pitluga, George E., *Science Excursions into the Community.* New York: Bureau of Publications, Teachers College, Columbia University, 1943. A Handbook for teachers, presenting ideas and suggestions for fourteen science trips and related activities. Techniques and administration as well as content are stressed.

Rife, Marvin, "Tours in Dynamic Education." *Educational Method* 20:223–25 (Feb. 1941). Poses many basic questions about the technique and status of excursions.

Snedaker, Mabel, "Using Community Resources in the Primary Grades." *Social Education* 4:188–93 (March 1940). How the third grade made history vivid by field trips, the fifth grade found geology thrilling when studied on the field, and another grade spent a year on a Farm Unit.

Spacht, Charles A., and Allie L. Harman, "Trips, Excursions, and Lectures." *Educational Method* 14:144–46 (Dec. 1934). Detailed suggestions for cooperative planning of excursions, for interesting parents in the project, for making necessary arrangements, and for correlating subject field activities.

United States Office of Education, "Conservation Excursions." Bulletin 1939, No. 13. Washington: Government Printing Office, 1940. A hundred page pamphlet of detailed suggestions for planning, conducting, and following up school excursions concerned with the problem of conservation.

White, Kenneth B., "Field Trips and the Education of College Students." *Journal of Higher Education* 11:157–59 (March 1940). Describes the program of excursions carried on at a New Jersey State Teachers College, and lists the principles of procedure followed.

Wood, Dora, "Planned Field Trips—An Integral Part of Science Units." *School Science and Mathematics* 41:28–35 (Jan. 1941). Suggestions and warnings for general procedure, illustrated by description of one trip taken to study rock layer formations. The guide sheet used is reproduced.

Zachari, E. D., "Field Trip Experiences in the Intermediate Grades." *Journal of Geography* 33:49–60 (Feb. 1934). Examples of geographic excursions, how they are planned, integrated with classroom work, and followed up afterward.

CHAPTER 9

Surveys[1]

THE COP ON THE CORNER

What does a policeman do, anyway? How did our modern police system develop? What kind of a society would we have without a police force? What are some of the outstanding police systems in America, and why are they considered superior? What are the qualifications of the policemen in our town? Are these standards as high as they should be? Why do we disparage many policemen? What would our town have to do to secure the best possible police force?

Together with her pupils, a teacher of social problems studied these and other questions. One of the class members was the daughter of a policeman. This father, as a resource person, outlined for the group the responsibilities of his occupation, and answered their questions concerning requirements for entrance into the service, training while in service, salary, promotion, tenure, politics and the police force, and retirement provisions. A substantial reading program was then launched to provide further background for class discussions, and to aid in the preparation of questions for interviews with other police officials. Excursions were taken to nearby towns and cities to enable the pupils to talk with police officers in systems of varying merit. Members of the County Attorney's staff were interviewed concerning their work and their relationships to the local police department. An F.B.I. officer described what he felt to be good police conditions generally. Newspaper reporters on the "police beat" were questioned for their frank appraisal of local police service.

When the survey was completed, these students had an excellent conception of what constitutes a good police department, how closely their own local department approximated that standard, and some idea of what it is worth to a community to have a competent police force. To many of these pupils, the policeman was no longer merely "a cop on the corner"; he was, at his best, a friend and an ally in maintaining genuine community welfare.

What Are Surveys?

The term "survey" is almost as broad and elusive as "community" itself; for a survey may deal with a single feature, as

---

[1] Some material in this chapter was prepared by Howard E. Wilson and at his request is used without specific acknowledgment but with many thanks.

the provision of recreation for a given neighborhood, or it may involve a general overview or cross section of the entire locality, as in a professional analysis of a community. Yet in either case, the survey may be defined as an accurate determination, through organized study, of social or physical data, particularly with reference to its spatial patterning and causal relationships. The survey concept should probably also include the recording of discovered data upon some form of spot or base map.

What Makes Surveys Valuable?

From their earliest childhood, pupils are engaged in exploring the world about them. Much of this activity is both unconscious and unsystematic in character, yet it is clearly purposive for all of that. Through such activity, the growing child is seeking to develop improved personal controls over his own physical and social environment. The community survey thus functions as an organized and systematic procedure whereby the random explorations of childhood may be transmuted into conscious adult capacity for intelligent local, regional, national, and international planning. If the survey is properly adjusted to the maturity of pupils, the making of it may be an excellent educational experience —not alone for the data it reveals, but also for the cooperative planning and activity it entails. A survey is likely to involve field trips and interviews, and to combine them with library research and all the activities of a classroom laboratory. Under good conditions, the making of a survey is a project with all the merits which were attached to project teaching in its original sense. The survey technique:

1. **Fosters comprehensive understanding of community structure and processes** in their everyday operation, interaction, and complexity.
2. **Stimulates depth of insight into vital community problems and trends** as these have been influenced by past conditions, present developments, and future prospects.
3. **Discloses problems which should be met**—not because teacher or textbook loftily says so, but because the evidence itself inescapably reveals the need.
4. **Suggests possibilities for student participation** in the ongoing processes of the community. Such constructive participation, cooperatively carried on, provides fine personal satisfactions, as well as essential training in democratic citizenship.
5. **Develops awareness of human interdependence** and of the prac-

tical necessity for general civic cooperation in carrying on successful individual and group living.

6. Promotes superior citizenship by providing extended experience in the making of critical judgments concerning existing conditions. Students learn, through personal actions, to base conclusions and recommendations upon factual data carefully assembled, objectively interpreted, and meticulously verified.

Every community carries on the fundamental social processes and experiences some of their related social problems. Every school can vitalize its students' education by encouraging them to make selected local surveys part of their academic experience.

What Are the Types of Surveys?

Surveys may well be classified according to the types of community phenomena which they examine. It will be remembered that Chapter 3 presented a pattern for analyzing any community in terms of four major factors, and that these factors were further divided and even subdivided as follows:

COMMUNITY STRUCTURE

AREAS	LEVELS
Local	*Material*
Regional	*Institutional*
National	*Psychological*
International	

COMMUNITY SETTING

GEOGRAPHY	POPULATION

COMMUNITY PROCESSES

UTILIZING ENVIRONMENT	MAINTAINING HEALTH AND SAFETY
APPRECIATING THE PAST	IMPROVING FAMILY LIFE
ADJUSTING TO PEOPLE	SECURING EDUCATION
EXCHANGING IDEAS	MEETING RELIGIOUS NEEDS
MAKING A LIVING	ENJOYING BEAUTY
SHARING IN CITIZENSHIP	ENGAGING IN RECREATION

COMMUNITY TIME PERIOD

HISTORIC	CONTEMPORARY	FUTURE

COMMUNITY AGENCIES

GOVERNMENTAL	COMMERCIAL	PRIVATE NONCOMMERCIAL

Now it is apparent that a survey might well be undertaken to discover how (all, some, one) of the *social processes* operate through (governmental, commercial, private noncommercial) *agencies,* in the (local, regional, national, international) *area,* on the (material, institutional, psychological) *level,* as influenced by the (geographic, population) *setting,* during the (historic, contemporary, future) *period of time.* Mathematically and practically considered, there are hundreds of possible combinations among these significant variables. Actually, however, most useful community surveys emphasize some variation of the two following fundamental patterns:

1. **Extensive, general overview of a community setting or of many processes** as they operate contemporaneously in the local or regional area and upon one or more of the three levels.

2. **Intensive, detailed analysis of one process or problem** as it operates contemporaneously in the local or regional area upon all three levels.

A few illustrations centering in typical social processes may serve to point up and clarify these basic survey patterns in some of their many possible variations.

COMMUNITY OVERVIEW

The "School Correspondence" program of the Junior Red Cross offers excellent survey possibilities. In this program, two pupil groups, situated some distance apart, arrange to tell each other the story of their own communities. For instance, a class in Minnesota and another in Arizona may be cooperating, or a group in an Oregon town may work with one in Mexico City. (Where different languages are involved, the Red Cross arranges for translation.) Such correspondence may be widely international as well as intersectional.

Each group sets itself the task of surveying its own community to discover what it can about local history, cultural resources, social organization, economic background, and political organization. A reading program is set up, following which the pupils interview local leaders in the various areas.

The data collected may be presented in various forms: through personal letters, essays, photographs, and sketches; collections of rocks, leaves, pressed flowers, bird pictures, etc. with brief descriptions of each item; small costumed dolls; and directions for playing games peculiar to each locality. The chosen items are then brought together in portfolio form, and sent to the cooperating group.

In this kind of general survey, each student group discovers much about its own local community through personal research, and also learns something of life in the distant community through the study of materials received. Pupil motivation is excellent, for in making the survey, each group is stimulated to do its best through the knowledge that the distant children will get an inaccurate or incomplete conception unless the portfolios sent them are true and well-done.[2]

---

[2] Suggestions and aids for making such survey-exchanges may be secured through any county Junior Red Cross chairman.

CONTROLLING ENVIRONMENT

A science teacher suggested that her class delve into the history of man's efforts to provide pure water, and that this be followed by a survey of water purification methods used in cities of the immediate region. This was done; as time and means permitted, various class members went to these cities for first-hand observations and then reported their findings to the entire group. Since the survey emphasized the local situation, the pupils became familiar with an important governmental service, as well as with basic techniques for purifying water today.

MAKING A LIVING

What are the job possibilities in our community? This question carries deep significance for most students nearing the close of their high school careers. To answer it for themselves, one high school class made a survey of local occupations. First, they inventoried all the business enterprises in the town. Next, they interviewed the head of each establishment, inquiring about employment possibilities, types of jobs, compensation, promotion policy, security, total training required, aspects of necessary training already available through the school program, and the general future prospects of that enterprise in their community. Finally, the students constructed charts and graphs comparing data received, and with these as a basis, engaged in serious individual thinking and group discussions of the whole employment problem.

SHARING IN CITIZENSHIP

For years students of government have been concerned about the failure of many voters to make use of the franchise, especially in cases when charter amendments are placed upon the ballot. Such amendments, however worthy and non-partisan, often fail of adoption, not because the citizens do not approve their proposals, but simply because many voters, uninterested in "dusty" amendments, fail to vote upon them at all. These voters usually do not realize that adoption requires affirmative votes from a stipulated percentage of all voters registered.

The public school must not take sides in partisan election contests, but it can freely urge qualified citizens to accept their franchise right and responsibility. In this spirit, a civics teacher proposed to his students that they make a house-to-house canvas in a number of election precincts near the school. The class favored the suggestion, and proceeded to the task. Each voter was given a copy of the amendments to be voted upon at the coming election, was urged to read them carefully, and was reminded that failure to vote upon the amendments would constitute a vote against them.

After the election, a check was made. Although two praiseworthy amendments failed of passage by close margins, it was found that in the precincts canvassed by the pupils, a far greater percentage of voters had expressed themselves upon the amendments than did citizens in precincts of comparable population not covered by the pupils. Thus, the students vividly discovered that voters often defeat their own best interests through sheer indifference.

Maintaining Health and Safety

Using the Junior Red Cross "Check List for Common Hazards In and About the Home," a seventh-grade class made a safety survey of their local community. Each pupil in the school was given a copy of the check sheet; against this he checked his own home for such hazards as might lead to falls and broken bones, electric shock, burns and scalds, asphyxiation and suffocation, cuts and infection, poisoning, and gunshot wounds. Homes not represented in the school population were assigned to class members in order to make the survey complete for that community. Such residents were called upon by student teams and asked to check their houses against the check sheet furnished them.

The data thus gathered provided a clear picture of local home conditions so far as accident hazards were concerned. As a result, a majority of the pupils and many adults became conscious of home hazards to safety, and a considerable number of home repairs followed.

Improving Family Living

Where does our Community Chest money go? What services are thus rendered? To whom? By whom? Under what conditions? A high school social problems class became concerned with this aspect of community living. Following a reading program, the group divided itself into small committees which sought out heads of the various social agencies sharing the Community Chest funds. Previously prepared questions were posed by the pupils in these interviews. Then arrangements were made whereby committee members might spend some time in the agency offices, and sometimes participate in their welfare programs and activities. Some girls, for instance, had been observing settlement houses; during the following summer they acted as cottage leaders in summer camps provided for underprivileged children. Other students helped care for the children of working mothers on Saturdays; still others attended sessions of the Juvenile Court where they observed the part played by some of the agencies in providing desirable home conditions for predelinquent children.

Engaging in Recreation

What do we do with our own leisure time? An English class pondered that query, and decided to make an investigation. After quizzing the members of their own group, they broadened the scope of the survey to include the whole high school. Among other questions the class asked of all school students:

To what radio programs do you listen?
How much time do you devote each day to the radio?
Do you study with the radio on?
How many movies do you see each week?

Do you go to the movies on certain nights, or do you select the films
you wish to see?

What movies have you seen in the past two weeks?

How many afternoons a week do you spend in drug stores, confec-
tionery stores, or in similar places?

How many evenings a week do you spend in such places?

What unassigned reading have you done in the past two weeks?

Which magazines do you read?

What out-of-school exercise have you had in the past two weeks?

Other questions bearing on the use of leisure time were included. Class
members summarized the check sheet findings, and the results were made
generally available. In the light of these findings and their background
reading about recreation, the students with the teacher then considered
soberly the elements of a commendable leisure-time program. The school
newspaper ran a feature story on the survey, and this provided further
stimulation and discussion in other classes.

It is evident that any aspect of the community which has meaning for young people, either now or in the future, may properly be
considered an appropriate field for school surveys. The scope and
depth of each such survey will depend upon the time available for
the study as well as upon the maturity of the pupils involved.

How Can the Survey Best Be Used?

In many instances, a survey is a mere mechanical piece of busy-
work, an arid accumulation of knowledge for its own sake. One
school proudly reports a survey, participated in by almost three
hundred pupils and covering an area of many city blocks, in which
the outcome was apparently the preparation of thirty statistical
tables summarizing such varied items as number of houses in each
block, number of persons in each family, number of college graduates, number of illiterates, number of homes with gardens, amount
of home ownership, amount of sickness, the number regularly attending church, and the number of books in each house. While
these are potentially interesting data in some respects, they are unrelated in their own parts or to any general purpose. Such rudi-
mentary counting might well be the beginning of a survey, but
hardly its outcome. It needs to be followed by an analysis of relationships or of problems or of social changes. Any survey of educational significance is not merely an experience in tabulation, but
is in tabulation for the definite purpose of interpretation and social
action. The means ought not to be confused with the ends, yet many

surveys made by pupils or by adults do not go beyond the accumulation of undigested data. At its best, the survey is a creative rather than a routine procedure. Anything less than enlightening interpretation of accumulated data is to be avoided by the school. Let us therefore examine the characteristics of a truly constructive survey, noting these according to our threefold pattern of (1) preparing for the survey, (2) making the survey, and (3) interpreting the survey experience.

Preparing for the Survey

A number of significant procedures are in order in this initial planning stage. These procedures may well be outlined as follows:

1. LET THE TEACHER PREPARE IN ADVANCE

If a teacher is to be effective in stimulating pupil interest, he must orient himself to survey possibilities well in advance. Inadequate preparation will quickly be sensed by the pupils; they do not readily follow a leader in whom they detect signs of uncertainty, indecision, or lack of confidence. While the teacher should always work with students in a spirit of mutual adventuring and should not appear to know all the answers in advance, it is equally important that he possess some definite awareness of directions and possibilities before such explorations are undertaken by the group.

Perhaps the best single outline of community survey possibilities is that presented in Colcord's *Your Community*.[3] Here are easily understood directions for undertaking and reporting a simple survey, together with detailed suggestions as to sources of data under each of the following major categories:

Community setting, founding, and development
Local government
Provision for dealing with crime
Provision for public safety
Workers, wages, and conditions of employment
Housing, planning, and zoning
Provision for health care
Distribution of health care
Provision for the handicapped
Educational resources
Opportunities for recreation
Religious agencies
Public assistance

---

[3] New York: Russell Sage Foundation, 1939.

Special provisions for family welfare
Special provisions for child care
Foreign-born and racial groups
Clubs and Associations
Agencies for community planning and coordination

"Know Your Community" by Bess Goodykoontz is an excellent bulletin of similar though restricted scope. This pamphlet summarizes the practical significance of understanding ten aspects of the community, and presents basic questions with suggestions for investigation and discussion of each. The ten areas covered are these:

Size of the community	Community organization and government
Location	The community's health
History	Recreational and cultural opportunities
The People	Housing
Making a living	Welfare services

The National League of Women Voters has published two similar pamphlets which are of considerable value even though they merely list questions and problems for investigation. Major topics outlined in these bulletins are as follows:

"Know Your Town"	"Know Your County"
History and population	County government in your state
Industry and workers	Overhead functions
Public welfare	Administration of justice
Education	Public welfare
Health	Public health and sanitation
Recreation	Education
Courts and juries	Public works
Streets, transportation, and public utilities	Other important functions
Housing and living costs	
Local government	

All four of these publications are devoted to the problem of analyzing various aspects of the community; they do not present survey findings as such. Yet the teacher's preliminary orientation requires also some awareness of what a finished professional study is like—not that he will duplicate its excellence, but that he may at least adopt high standards of criteria. The teacher should therefore familiarize himself with one or two complete survey studies such as the Lynds' *Middletown* and *Middletown in Transition*, Klein's *Pittsburgh Survey*, or Harrison's *Springfield Survey*. For rural regions, the teacher may seek advice and assistance from local or nearby university departments of rural sociology.

In addition to his reading, the alert teacher will spend as much time as possible in personal observations of the community in order to get the "feel" of it for himself. The aridity of the printed page often springs into life as the teacher supplements it by immersing himself in related community activities.

2. AROUSE STUDENT INTEREST

Little of lasting value will result from a survey if pupils look upon it as just another assignment. Assuming that the area, process, or problem to be examined has genuine social significance, the teacher's task is to translate that significance into terms which will motivate his students to personal interest and group action. If the teacher cannot relate the proposal for a survey with factors that already touch the lives of his pupils, it would be better not to proceed any further.

In this world "aching with vividness," there are innumerable areas of activity which carry deep and personal significance for youth. The resourceful teacher will seek, wherever possible and within reasonable limits, to let the survey have its basis in the achievements, good and bad, of people. A survey of juvenile delinquency, for instance, will be much more eagerly approached by pupils if they are not initially frightened by too many statistics. Let them come to know something of the human factors first, and then go on to statistical summaries and generalizations. *Start with people* and the survey will come alive.

Is it to be a survey of public health agencies? There is romance, heroism, defeat, victory in the lives of people engaged in this field. Lift the cold statistics from the printed page and blow life into them through some revelation of what men and women have done to throw safeguards around human life. What has happened to American life expectancy in the past hundred years makes only indifferent statistical reading. But dramatized in personal, human terms, it becomes a thrilling story.

Genuine student interest will depend, to a marked degree, upon what answers can honestly be given to these two basic questions, both of which are useful criteria for appraising the choice of survey:

a. **What difference does it make?** If there is to be an adequate development of pupil interest in the survey, the teacher must be sure that a positive answer is returned to this query. Unless students can see a functional value in the making of a survey, they will properly remain uninterested in it.

b. **What can we do about it?** Besides recognizing the real value of a survey, students need to feel that they themselves can actually help to improve conditions disclosed. If they cannot actively contribute, either now or in the future, they will often develop feelings of frustration and eventual indifference or cynicism.

It is of crucial importance that the teacher does not assume the position of taskmaster, but rather that of a colleague engaged in mutual research. Beware of that I've-been-through-all-this-before attitude, and be sure never to reflect boredom. Positively stated, let teacher and students work cooperatively together in a spirit of shared research, seeking information which is of genuine significance. To the extent that this is done, the survey will not be just another assignment; it will possess the breath of life itself.

3. IDENTIFY THE PURPOSE

The basic necessity in planning a survey is the thoughtful, precise formulation of the major purpose or end toward which it is directed. The first step in reflective thinking upon any problem is always a clear definition of the question involved. One of the paramount values for pupils making a survey is the exercise it may afford in clear thinking—and that thinking must be initiated in the question: *just what are we trying to accomplish?* It is relatively easy to accumulate data, but there is little value in collecting them in random fashion or in the vague hope that they will turn out to be interesting or illuminating. Only when the purposes for which data are wanted are precisely known, can they be assembled efficiently. There can be no efficiency in any survey until its purpose has been stated and all its aspects related to the achievement of that purpose. The more thorough the planning, the less lost motion there will be.

Michener suggests that the survey problem be formulated as a question, and that this question be checked against five criteria as a means of appraising its educational validity. The central survey question should thus:

a. *Contain one idea*
b. *Be comprehensive, but not involved*
c. *Not be answerable by a simple "yes" or "no" reply*
d. *Be unambiguous and pertinent*
e. *Possess social significance* [4]

---

[4] James A. Michener, "Participation in Community Surveys as Social Education." In Ruth West (ed.), *Utilization of Community Resources in the Social Studies,* pp. 144–63 (153). Ninth Yearbook, National Council for the Social Studies, 1938.

"How Can Traffic Accidents Be Controlled?" and "Can We Believe What We Read in the Newspapers?" are examples of survey problems which satisfactorily meet these five criteria.

Persons active in the field to be surveyed should be consulted as the survey problem is being defined. Some of these people, together with the teacher and a committee of students, should meet once or twice at the outset to define the limits of the field, and should also meet as often as necessary during the whole period of the survey in order to check both direction and progress.

4. GAIN PERSPECTIVE UPON THE PROBLEM

Students should now be immersed in a reading program as the springboard for direct contact with the field. It would be a grave mistake to start field contacts if the students have no background of general understanding in the area chosen for survey. Only as they come to know a given field in terms of its literature, as well as its immediate phenomena, will they secure an intelligent understanding of it.

Documentary sources must be chosen with care, and must always be appropriate to the mental level of the students using them. These materials should first deal with general aspects of the problem, and thus provide an initial overview for all of the students concerned. With that background in common, the reading program may then be diversified for detailed treatment of specific sub-problems by various committees or individuals.

Such general and specialized reading, accompanied by adequate classroom discussions and interpretations, should enable the students to sense the "topography" of the problem and thus be in position to break it down into its component elements.

5. ANALYZE THE PROBLEM

The chosen problem should next be divided into several constituent sub-problems. This should be done by the students and teacher in free discussion. *What are the essential and detailed features of this problem?* To stimulate thinking it is well to develop an outline on the blackboard; each student making his own notebook copy after it is completed. A sample breakdown of one fundamental question might thus be outlined somewhat as follows:

"Can We Believe What We Read in the Newspapers?"

(a) *What is a newspaper?*
(b) *How is news gathered?*

(c) *How is news edited?*

(d) *How is a newspaper financed?*

(e) *What connections may exist between editorial policy and advertising revenues?*

(f) *How do publishers decide what political issues or candidates to support?*

(g) *Is the news censored in any way?*

(h) *What ethical standards are expected and maintained in journalism?*

In developing such a breakdown, the subtle skill of the teacher will be of paramount importance. Much time can be saved if students are prevented from getting too far afield in pursuit of relatively unimportant features. The incidental and inconsequential must not be allowed to obscure the fundamental issues; neither must any really significant aspects of the problem be ignored. A good analysis always simplifies the general problem, stimulates insight into its interrelated elements, and facilitates division of labor among several committee groups.

6. Discover the Practical Limits of the Survey

Having identified and analyzed the problem, the teacher and pupils are next confronted with three basic questions concerning the desirable range of the survey being planned. Those three questions are these:

a. Are the pupils mature enough? In a survey of housing, for example, it is obvious that the approach made by a class of seventh-graders would have to be different from that employed by a group of college seniors. The mental maturity of the students must always determine the *depth* of the survey they undertake; that is, the degree to which they probe beyond the material level and into the institutional and psychological levels of the housing problem. Furthermore, their mental development should always condition the *extent* of the survey: their study of regional, national, and international housing trends and policies as related to the local housing situation. Both depth and extent of student interest and ability will depend in large measure upon their general grade level.

b. Will community mores permit? Pupils must not be sheltered from reality, but at the same time the school cannot usually go much beyond dominant community attitudes in its teaching program. In some sections, for example, a survey of the cultural contributions of minority groups may be charged with social dynamite. The teacher who really knows his community should be able to avoid areas of investigation about which local feelings run high. This is not to suggest that all controversial issues be avoided, but only that the teacher's good judgment must be exercised to avoid those areas which are practically "untouchable" in that community.

c. Is the survey over-ambitious? It is better to do an adequate survey in a limited field than to spread efforts so thin that results are necessarily sketchy and unsatisfactory. Teachers are reminded that pupils should learn something of the technique and spirit of the survey, as well as finding genuine personal satisfaction in its results. If too pretentious a survey is attempted, both these values will be lost. Time is a real factor here. Such matters as distance between the school and the survey-field, post-school availability of pupils, and means of transportation must also all be taken into careful account.

7. Determine What Data Are Needed

The obvious next step is to decide what types of information may be secured to throw most light upon the problem chosen. To illustrate, the class may conceive its purpose as that of finding out how public opinion in the local community is formed. With this objective in mind, the pupils may then consider the availability and relative usefulness of data on citizens' reading habits, on the use of commercial advertising, on the extent to which people use the radio and the types of programs they select, on the influence of movie newsreels or public forums. Probably it would not be feasible to tap all these sources of information, but within practical limitations the sources chosen must be selected in terms of their pertinency to the general purpose of the survey.

8. Decide upon Techniques to Be Used

Now comes the problem of determining what survey techniques to use—source documents, audio-visual aids, resource people, field interviews, excursions, questionnaires, public opinion polls, and the like. Detailed suggestions have already been given for using most of these approaches, so attention here will be confined to brief descriptions of questionnaires and polls.

a. The questionnaire. Questionnaires should be relatively simple and brief, and should deal with materials fairly easily recorded and tabulated. Since comparable replies to the questionnaire are desired, as extensive use as possible should be made of check lists and mechanical markings on the form devised. A questionnaire, once prepared, should be tried out on a small group and then revised before final and extensive use of it is made. The persons to whom it is taken or sent should be carefully selected. An accompanying letter; perhaps signed by the school administrator, should explain the purpose the school seeks in allowing pupils to circulate their questionnaire.

b. The opinion poll. In many respects this is similar to an interview.

The techniques developed by professional analysts of public opinion, such as the Gallup Poll, are useful; they involve especially critical care in two areas: the selection of subjects in the sampling used, and the careful formulation of the questions asked. The sampling need not be large but should be representative. The questions chosen should be direct, unequivocal, and simply phrased.

Some schools have found it useful to secure generalized data through reports made by the pupils of themselves, or of their families. Records of reading done, recreations enjoyed, purchasing habits, church interests, and the like may serve many educational purposes. Care must always be taken that items to be reported by pupils be very clearly understood by them in advance, or the reports may not be accurate or even be returned. And every precaution should be taken to avoid the appearance of prying into personal affairs. Data must be generalized and impersonalized if their educative use is to be possible.

Obviously the variety of techniques to be used is as great as the variety of possible purposes or the number of areas to be surveyed. The choice of each is dependent upon the local situation and upon the alertness and ingenuity with which the teacher approaches the project.

9. ORGANIZE CLASS COMMITTEES

Having general plans well in mind, the students and teacher now turn to the matter of committee organization. The committee approach is recommended because it makes for economy of effort, and it provides a situation where students may work intimately together, where group responsibility may be readily shared, and where observation of individual efforts is expedited.

Committees should be established on the basis of student interests. Teachers should urge that each class member select for study that aspect of the problem which most appeals to him. John should be discouraged from joining a committee just because his friend, Bill, is already on it, or because he has amorous inclinations toward one of its feminine members.

a. **Decide committee numbers.** The number of interest committees will depend upon the number of significant areas or sub-problems requiring attention. The personnel of each committee should number between three and seven. Fewer than three members fails to provide sufficient opportunities for intra-committee discussions, and bears the further hazard of not providing sufficient numbers to cover the field adequately.

More than seven may result in non-participation by some members, with consequent loss of interest by all of them.

b. Elect officers. Each interest committee should have the following officers: chairman, vice-chairman, recording secretary, corresponding secretary, and librarian. These are all traditional officials with the exception of the librarian. His function is to keep a master list of sources in the special field to be surveyed, adding to it references brought to his attention by committee members. He keeps a file of newspaper clippings relating to the field, and acts also as custodian of all audio-visual aids utilized by the group. All this material should be kept in a classroom filing cabinet where it will be available to committee members and the teacher. The vice-chairman's function is to assist the chairman in checking over the reading program of individual committee members, to aid the librarian in special phases of his work, and to sit in at general conferences between the committee chairman and the teacher.

c. Learn note-taking. Some students are readily able to catch the thought of a printed paragraph and put its substance into a few words; many others cannot. Before the committees go into their reading programs, the teacher should therefore give the class some practical suggestions about efficient taking of notes. This is important, for if students are allowed to make a laborious task of recording notes on reading and observations, they will lose interest in the project itself. There are many excellent short-cuts in note-taking which the teacher should demonstrate for the class. From time to time, he should also sit down with individual committee members and check their notes, asking them to make oral reconstruction of information summarized in their notebooks.

d. Follow parliamentary procedure. Nothing so dulls the ardor of committee members as fumbling conduct of meetings. To forestall this possibility, the teacher should explain and demonstrate simple rules of parliamentary procedure before the committees hold their first sessions.

10. Comprehend the Committee's Function

Emphasis has already been placed upon the importance of breaking down the field or problem into its constituent elements, and upon the desirability of allocating each such sub-problem to one of the interest committees. Within each committee, the same process should now be repeated; each subquestion should in turn be analyzed into *its* logical aspects. Continuing the newspaper illustration offered on pages 181–82, let us suppose that Committee F is composed of pupils who are especially interested in subquestion (f). This committee might therefore break down its problem somewhat as follows:

(f) "How Do Publishers Decide What Political Issues or Candidates to Support?"

(1) *How does the editorial page differ from the rest of the newspaper?*
(2) *What general training do editorial writers have?*
(3) *How much do editorials influence readers' opinions?*
(4) *What is the relationship between the news and the editorials?*
(5) *What is the relationship between editorial opinion and the news presented?*
(6) *What is the. relationship between the publisher and the editor?*
(7) *How does the business office influence both publisher and editor?*

These specific subquestions will now be divided among the members of Committee F on the basis of their individual interests in these topics. Members will then pursue reading programs and accept field responsibilities centering in their chosen subareas; they will also stand ready to report their findings to the whole committee or to the entire class at stated times. All members should be responsible for covering (1) all subquestions included in the committee's field, and (2) all available sources of information such as newspapers, periodicals, government reports, radio programs, visual aids, and so forth. Such coverage for questions specifically assigned to others will consist in making brief written memoranda for the fellow workers most concerned.

11. Hold Teacher-Chairmen Conferences

A definite schedule of conferences between the teacher and all the committee chairmen should be worked out. These meetings will provide opportunity for the teacher to check upon the general program and progress, to inject a sense of direction as needed, and to stimulate rapport between the various chairmen. If at all possible, most of these conferences should be held out of school. Experience suggests that more can often be accomplished around a campfire or over a cup of cocoa than within the familiar classroom itself. The student chairmen are the key people of the class, and the success or failure of the whole survey will usually hinge upon their attitude and sense of responsibility toward it.

12. Seek Lay Advisors

"Lay advisors" are persons active in the problem-field who may be induced to associate themselves with the survey of that field. Even busy people will cooperate in this manner if they can be convinced that the students are serious in their purpose and intelligent in their planning. It should be remembered that nearly everyone is trying to *sell something*—perhaps an idea, a service, or a commodity. This being true, nearly everyone will respond to a request for counsel in the area of his interest. It is therefore well to use appropriate lay leaders as general advisors, both in the planning stage and in evaluation of the findings. Since these lay advisors are actually "resource people," they should be utilized according to the techniques outlined in Chapters 6 and 7.

At suitable times, the interest committees most concerned, the teacher, and the lay advisor should meet together. The latter's function is chiefly that of interpretation, direction-pointing, and stimulation of student interest. Being human, he has his own prejudices and predispositions, all of which must tactfully be taken into account as the survey progresses.

Assuming now that these twelve steps of survey-planning have been successfully completed, the class is ready to start the actual field survey. Let us therefore see how this second general stage may best proceed.

Making the Survey

All preparations have now been completed, and the stage of active investigations in the field has been reached. Five major steps now become necessary: gather the data, report findings within the committees, present committee reports to the entire class, synthesize committee findings, and verify conclusions. Let us analyze each of these steps in turn.

13. GATHER THE DATA

Keeping foremost in mind the central and subsidiary purposes of the survey, the interest committees now proceed to gather the data previously determined upon as necessary and desirable. This they will do by utilizing those varied techniques of investigation already chosen as appropriate. Before any of these techniques are actually attempted by the students, however, all the suggestions previously offered for their effective use should be carefully reviewed. As a final safeguard, the teacher should once more stress the vital importance of cultivating public goodwill in all the field investigations about to be made.

14. REPORT FINDINGS WITHIN THE COMMITTEES

Some definite plan for reporting individual and sub-committee findings is essential to sustained interest and group efficiency. Such a plan must include at least seven significant aspects, as follows:

a. **Schedule report meetings.** Each committee secretary should prepare a report schedule after teacher-committee discussion of progress and needs. A copy of this schedule should be given to the teacher, who thus knows where responsibility lies in each committee all of the time. Committee members likewise know definitely on what days they are to make their reports. Thus, there is no necessity for frenzied, last-minute activity on the part of those presenting reports. If the chairman or the vice-chairman constantly checks upon the reading and field research programs of all committee members, much "cramming" for report days will be avoided.

b. **Maintain a balanced program.** No fixed rule for the frequency of reports can be suggested here. That will depend upon the age of the students, the volume of material available, the abilities of individual pupils, the number of class periods devoted to the survey, the amount of time that committee members can work upon their assignments, and similar factors. At all times, the teacher must seek to maintain a nice balance between the requirements of a thorough investigation and the limitations of committee members.

c. **Require adequate notes.** If the teacher has helped students with the mechanics of note-taking, the presentation of reports will be much more meaningful than is likely if pupils have little idea of what is important or trivial, significant or irrelevant. Adequate notes will do much to foster such discrimination. These notes will be carefully taken and organized, and preserved together in a notebook of reasonable size. Taking notes on scraps of paper of varying size is apt to be disastrous if the hope is to assemble information of lasting value. If possible, all notes should be taken in ink.

d. **Present formal oral reports.** According to the committee schedule, individual members make oral reports of findings to the committee as a whole. It is important that the notes from which these talks are made be prepared upon cards in basic outline form. The student's original notes, whether of reading done or of conditions observed in the field, should not be used directly. The reason for this is that the student will have taken notes about many items which will not be of paramount significance in a summary talk to the entire committee. For them, he must present only that material which all should remember; every other item is extraneous and should be omitted. If he speaks directly from his original notes, the fumbling which ensues injures effective presentation. The talk should be made in such a manner that the other members readily discern its outline, and should be concluded with a brief summary which says in effect, "Now, out of all I have told you, here are the highpoints."

e. **Make occasional reports to the entire class.** During the course of the survey, one individual report from each committee should be made before the entire class. This procedure provides excellent general motivation since it introduces an element of desirable group competition, and it also enables the teacher to comment profitably upon good and bad techniques of presentation. Students who are to make these reports should be selected by the respective committee chairmen.

f. File written reports. After each member has reported to his own committee, he gives the committee librarian a written summary of his talk. This summary is based upon his speech notes, but is written out in full and includes a bibliography. The length of this statement is determined by the importance and volume of the material covered; its adequacy as to form and content is ascertained by the chairman, vice-chairman, librarian, and teacher. After approval, this report is type-written by a committee member, or by someone else who does type, and is then filed by the librarian in the teacher's room or office. Thus, a library of information is currently developed for the use of all, but with individual authorship properly credited.

g. Summarize committee findings. The final step within this purely committee procedure is to bring all the individual's findings together for organization, summary, and interpretation. This can best be done in a discussion group composed of the entire committee, the lay advisor, and the teacher. The blackboard should be freely used as an aid in visualizing ideas, relationships, and relative significance of findings. When the group has agreed upon its completed summary, the recording secretary should write out that summary in full and have it typewritten in triplicate—one copy for the class or school library, one for the committee chairman, and one for the teacher.

If all the committees flexibly follow this general procedure, they will be ready at the appropriate time for the third step in active survey-making: that of exchanging findings through general class presentations.

15. Present Committee Reports to the Entire Class

When a survey is thus undertaken on a committee basis, it is as though a structure, let us say a house, is to be built in sections and later assembled. Each committee is given responsibility for a part of the whole; each "crew" must contribute its share to the total project. Not to do so adequately would produce something less than a finished structure. The reading and the field research programs are the materials out of which each committee constructs its allotted portion of the common dwelling.

With this accomplished, however, the next problem is that of combining findings through committee presentations before the entire class. This requires consideration of five major factors, as follows:

a. Schedule each report. The committee chairman, with the teacher's advice and approval, should establish a definite schedule according to which the various committees will present their findings to the entire class. The amount of time allowed each committee will depend upon (1) the significance of the total problem, (2) the importance and proportionate value of each committee's findings, and (3) the time which the teacher feels can be devoted to presentation. In a survey of newspapers, for example, the time allotted to the committee on censorship might be greater than that assigned to a committee on newspaper finance.

b. Decide what to present. In preparing its class presentation, each committee should bear constantly in mind this essential query: "What should the intelligent member of this community know about this problem-field?" Every committee will have uncovered numerous details which it would be pointless to present to the entire class group. What should be known and remembered? What is genuinely significant? What information does our committee have which will help to make its other classmates more effective citizens both now and later?

c. Determine the form of presentation. Each committee must next decide how and by whom its report is to be presented. The nature of the material will naturally determine whether panel discussions, motion pictures, dramatizations, charts, drawings and sketches, or direct talks are most appropriate. A single committee may utilize one, several, or possibly all of these devices. In any event, presentation should not be restricted to the "star" members of the committee. In the interests of general pupil growth, it is always desirable that every committee member participate. Members who lack oral facility should be required to contribute directly in some other capacity.

d. Hold a "dress rehearsal." Whatever the form chosen, the committee should practice the technique of presentation. At this point it is often desirable to enlist the aid of other teachers, such as those of speech, dramatics, or art. Committee members engaged in presenting the group's findings should know their material well enough so they will not be too dependent upon notes or other props. This is not merely "making a report"; it is telling a story of vital import to those in the audience.

e. Stimulate audience questions. When the committee has completed its presentation before the class, all students should have a clear understanding of the facts uncovered by that committee, and of the significance of those findings for the entire survey problem. Such understanding is not likely to be complete upon the basis of the committee's presentation alone; it requires questions by the audience and replies from committee members. If students are not thus stimulated to ask questions, it may be taken for granted that the committee presentation was either perfect or most inadequate.

In such manner, the entire class is made aware of the major findings, conclusions, and generalizations reached by its respective committees. The obvious next need is for the class as a whole to organize these separate findings into a coherent general picture.

16. SYNTHESIZE COMMITTEE FINDINGS

After all committees have reported, general class discussion of their findings is in order. The fundamental purpose of this discussion should be to synthesize the data presented—to organize all of it into some consistent amalgam out of which may be refined several significant generalizations. The teacher should serve as chairman of this class discussion, since he alone has been constantly in touch with all committees throughout the survey, and since he is presumably more skilled in organizing data and in detecting relationships. Yet he must avoid dominating the group since students need real experience in analyzing, relating, and interpreting discrete data. If the teacher acts in a residual capacity, the students will enjoy that experience and yet will be safeguarded against serious error in their interpretations of data.

Conscious effort should thus be made to crystallize all reported data into three or four major generalizations, each concisely stated and subject to verification in the future. Meanwhile, however, one further step should be taken; this is to refine these several generalizations into one inclusive statement. In other words, an hypothesis is formed as the intellectual basis for appropriate social action in the future.

17. VERIFY CONCLUSIONS

Every effort must now be made to verify the data, the generalizations based upon the data, and the hypothesis crystallized from the generalizations. Verification may be sought by submitting findings to the best available experts for review and criticism. Lay advisors and other resource persons should be invited to evaluate the validity of the data and the logic of interpretations made from it. In the light of their criticisms, objectively considered, necessary changes should be made in the generalizations and hypothesis itself. Only after both facts and logic have been verified, is the class justified in assuming the truth of its findings.

Thus, it is apparent that the whole process of planning and conducting a survey is properly a directed exercise in reflective thinking: identifying and analyzing the problem, gathering and synthesizing data, formulating and verifying hypotheses. But thinking unrelated to action is sterile, and so is a survey which fails to eventuate in some form of social activity. Thus, we pass into the third basic stage of the survey project: acting upon the findings.

Interpreting the Survey Experience

Community study should not "evaporate into thin air." Data are to be accumulated and recorded, not merely to fill up files, but to be *used*. One test of the value of a survey is the extent to which it is the basis for further study and for wider activity in the community itself.

The data of a survey, however reported and recorded, are finally to be closely related to the basic purpose for which the survey was made. Until the data are used to answer the question with which its accumulation began, the project has not been consummated. All that has been said about follow-up teaching of an excursion is equally pertinent to the final phase of teaching through the making of surveys. "What do these data mean for us and for our community?" ought to concern pupils and teacher jointly. In addition to the careful interpretation they demand, the survey data should be made the basis of any possible social action on the part of the students. Such action should consist in the application of data to problems within the framework of the basic community processes (see Chapter 3). Such follow-up of the survey proper commonly requires three further steps: prepare visual aids, publicize the findings, and take community action. We shall briefly examine each in turn.

18. Prepare Visual Aids

Having tabulated and interpreted its data, the class ought now to exercise all possible skill in planning how to present its findings to wider audiences. While the exact devices to be used are dependent upon the nature of the data and the audience to which they are to be presented, it may be generally urged that as many pictorial and graphic means of summarization and presentation as possible be utilized.

The language of graphs, diagrams, charts, and pictograms is becoming a language of the common man in an age where quantitative analyses were never so important as now. It is therefore imperative that students be trained in the making, use, and interpretation of such aids to learning. Visual expressions of data should not, of course, displace written and oral reports, but they ought to be extensively used, at least for their supplementary value.

The class should therefore now proceed to construct whatever "visual aids" are appropriate and feasible as media for presentation of survey data to wider audiences. Among such aids frequently utilized are these:

photographs	land use maps	charts
relief maps	social base maps	graphs
scale models	pictorial charts	diagrams

Suggestions for construction of these and other visual aids were given in Chapter 5. At this stage those suggestions should be again consulted.

In developing these visual summaries, it is economical for the students to work as small committees. These committees may be either those which originally gathered the data, or new committees formed on the basis of individual interest in the construction of different visual media. The latter alternative is generally preferable since it provides better for personal creative interests, and serves also to promote wider cooperation between class members. Thus the survey, beginning as a class project, proceeding through committee endeavors, again becomes a class interest as it moves along in this third major stage.

19. PUBLICIZE THE FINDINGS

Teachers and students should constantly be alert to ways in which the survey findings may be related to life concerns within the school and the local community. What, then, might be done to bring findings to the attention of a larger audience? Among many vital possibilities such projects as these suggest themselves:

    a. Prepare an exhibit of material for school, library, or museum display.

    b. Write news and feature stories for school and community newspapers or magazines.

    c. Speak before school classes, one member representing each interest committee.

    d. Conduct a colorful school assembly program, using visual aids, panel discussions, or dramatic productions.

    e. Mimeograph a summary report for distribution to parents, lay advisors, other resource persons, local newspapers, etc.

    f. Address business, professional, and service clubs, utilizing all avenues of publicity before and after the event.

    g. Hold a public meeting to present findings, and send special invitations to all people who were interviewed, all lay advisors, all teachers and parents intimately concerned, and all local newspaper editors.

    h. Broadcast by radio, and offer to send mimeographed summaries to all listeners who request them.

Through scores of such approaches, the school and community publics may be reached. And in reaching these publics, students gain invaluable personal experience in speaking, writing, organizing, interpreting, as well as in the more fundamental processes of scientific thinking.

20. TAKE COMMUNITY ACTION

At its best, the survey will achieve the triple aim of community study generally; that is, it will (a) deepen participants' *understanding* of community structure, processes, and problems, (b) develop positive *attitudes* leading to group attack upon revealed problems, and (c) provide extensive practice in applying social *skills*. Any survey which ends in cold understanding, untouched by enthusiasms and skills directed toward the making of needed community improvements, is hardly justifiable in the genuinely democratic school.

The ultimate value of the survey project thus appears as it leads into constructive, cooperative, and civic activity within the community itself. Specific suggestions for planning, executing, and evaluating such *service projects* are offered in the following chapter and need not be previewed here. At this point, let us simply emphasize again that the purpose of the survey is not to *be* an activity complete in itself; rather it is to *result in* further social action.

What Are the Limitations of the Survey?

Despite its obvious values, the survey as a technique of community study is limited by two major factors, neither of which is inherent in it, but only in the viewpoints of the typical school's administration and instructional staff:

1. **Opposition to students "scurrying around" in the community.** Many administrators and teachers eagerly utilize documentary materials and audio-visual aids, welcome resource people into the classroom, and even tolerate field interviews and excursions. Yet these same persons fail to envision sufficient educational value in student-made surveys to justify the necessary field activity.

2. **Teacher domination is habitual in many classrooms.** Even when a survey is approved, the teacher in charge is likely to do all the real planning and evaluating, leaving it to his students to carry out his directions. Such domination, however kindly it is exercised, will defeat some of the central values of the survey experience. Unless the teacher is willing to consider courteously the ideas, opinions, reactions and prejudices of his students, and to engage in genuinely cooperative planning and evaluation with them, the survey will fail in its essential educative purposes.

Both surveys and excursions are in one sense still classroom projects; that is, the school remains the essential center of operations from which students sally forth for short periods and then quickly return to the ever-familiar home environment. But how much more vital this technique would be if the mature students could *live in* as well as study about an unfamiliar environment for a longer period of time! In short, why not combine the basic features of the excursion as social travel with those of the survey as systematic exploration? Would that be feasible? Certainly! Suggestions for effectively organizing such a combined program are therefore now in order, and appear in the following chapter.

SELECTED REFERENCES

(See also references following Chapter 3: Community Analysis)

Alabama State Department of Education, "Survey Work-Book for Community Analysis." Montgomery: Alabama Education Association, 1939. Work sheets and directions for surveying a community's history, setting, population, industries, transportation, government, etc.

Baumgarter, Joseph C., "A Housing Study—Correlating a National Problem with a Community Project." *Social Education* 4:470–73 (Nov. 1940). A housing unit in which field study of local conditions led into a larger study of housing as a national problem. The topic outline is presented, with class activities.

Bush, Ada L., "Suggestions for Use in Making a City Survey (Industrial and Commercial)." Washington: U. S. Department of Commerce (order from Superintendent of Documents). Outlines the purposes and procedures of such a survey, and lists in detail many community features to be noted.

Chambers, M. M., and Howard M. Bell, "How to Make a Community Youth Survey." American Council on Education Studies, Series IV, Vol. III, No. 2. Washington: The Council, 1938. Useful suggestions for preparing, conducting, and reporting a survey.

Davis, L. C., "Field Work in Geography." *Educational Method* 17:293–96 (March 1938). How pupils from fourth grade through tenth vitalize geography by local field surveys, and how a state teachers college builds its own similar course.

Ellis, Mildred P., "Framingham Facts: Our Pupils Investigate Local Standards of Living." *Clearing House* 16:140–42 (Nov. 1941). An annual survey of living conditions by a high school sociology class.

Fitzpatrick, Frederick L., "A Method of Field Study in Biology." *Teachers College Record* 34:481–89 (March 1933). Recommends intensive study of interrelationships of species within a given limited area, and of ways in which these species adjust to their environments. Shows how valuable field study can be carried on in any city park.

Frederick, O. I., and E. C. Geyer, "Study of Battle Creek Community." *Curriculum Journal* 10:325–27 (Nov. 1939). Outlines a practical plan whereby large classes can survey a community cooperatively. Committees for various aspects were formed; their general procedures and responsibilities are suggested.

Gordon, Laurin P., "Surveying the School Community." *School Executive* 61:1–11, 52 (July 1942). A socio-economic survey by high school freshmen produced useful guidance and curriculum material and also better understanding among community groups.

Gossard, A. P., "High-School Pupils Study Their Community." *School Review*

43:268–72 (April 1935). How a class surveyed its town to discover homes, occupational distribution, religious preferences, ages of pre-school children, amount of home ownership. The class was organized as census-takers, clerks, and inspectors, with a business manager over all.

Grim, Paul R., "Housing Study: Our Pupils Investigate." *Clearing House* 16: 402–04 (March 1942). A junior high school housing study in the local community.

Hallenbeck, Wilbur C., "Surveying the Community." Chapter XIX in Florence E. Bingham (ed.), *Community Life in a Democracy*. Chicago: National Congress of Parents and Teachers, 1942. Practical outline for making community surveys. Step-by-step suggestions are given.

Harper, Florence S., "Students Make a Recreational Survey." *Educational Method* 18:279–83 (March 1939). A form inquiry was used by high school seniors in canvassing the city. Students summarized findings and a handbook of recreational facilities was later issued.

Malan, Clement T., "Social Survey of a School District." *Social Education* 3: 409–12 (Sept. 1939). The story of how a local survey was initiated and carried through by student-teachers. Motivating and procedural methods are described, findings are stated, and results are outlined and approved.

Michiner, James A., "Participation in Community Surveys as Social Education." In Ruth West (ed.), *Utilization of Community Resources in the Social Studies:* Ninth Yearbook, National Council for the Social Studies, pp. 144–63. Cambridge, Mass.: The Council, 1938. The survey as a civic education technique, criteria for selecting problems to survey, analysis of 13 typical surveys, survey procedures and costs, detailed analysis of one survey.

Murphy, J. Fred, "A Student Survey of Local Occupations." *Social Studies* 27: 474–76 (Nov. 1936). Three civics classes in senior high school made an occupational survey of a city of 18,000 population. The purposes of the survey, the techniques followed, the limitations felt, the facts obtained, and the uses made of the data are all described briefly.

Newell, Bernice, "Trends in Community Surveys." *Educational Method* 18:7–13 (Oct. 1938). Historical analysis of the community survey movement during the past thirty years. General trends, purposes, techniques, organization of data, and use of data are all discussed.

Repke, Arthur, "Society Is Our Laboratory." *Social Education* 3:620–22 (Dec. 1939). Reports student-teacher experiences in making local surveys of families on relief, occupational possibilities, housing, health and recreational facilities. Describes the committee planning, individual investigations, correlative reading program, class procedures, and the student forum to which findings were reported.

Sammartino, Peter, "School and Business Plan Together." *School Executive* 63: 44–45 (May 1944). Junior college students make a local survey of consumer statistics to help merchants plan postwar development.

Sears, J. B., "School and Community Surveys." *Review of Educational Research* 9:508–13 (Dec. 1939). The literature on school and community surveys as procedures is cited in detail under these headings: Social Surveys, Recent Methods of Social Surveys, School Survey Trends, History and Development of Surveys, Methods and Techniques Used in Surveys.

Skeen, Roy L., "Community Study and Educational Administration." *Journal of Educational Sociology* 13:403–10 (March 1940). The alert school administrator must act on the basis of facts, not guesses. To gain such facts, he should survey the various aspects of the community which have implications for education. Several such aspects with their implications are outlined.

Spears, Harold, *Experiences in Building a Curriculum*, Ch. V. New York: Macmillan, 1937. Reproduces a complete report on a job-opportunity survey of the community, made by commercial teachers with the help of high school seniors. Purposes, procedures, personnel, publicity, findings and conclusions are stressed.

Stowell, Margaret, "A High-School Class Surveys Its Town." *Journal of Geography* 41:179–85 (May 1942). Students in economic geography made a land-use map of their city as a two-week project. Steps taken are detailed and the final map is illustrated.

Sutherland, Miriam, "The Children Survey the Community." *Curriculum Journal* 10:317–19 (Nov. 1939). How seventh- and eighth-grade children planned and carried through an extensive survey of their community, in order to provide civic information needed by the town.

Ward, Douglas S., "Community Surveys for Junior High Schools?" *Social Education* 4:553–56 (Dec. 1940). Warns against perfunctory surveys, and stresses importance of basing surveys on children's real interests. An accident survey and a housing survey are described as illustration.

Zapoleon, Marguerite W., "Community Occupational Surveys." Washington: U. S. Office of Education (order from Superintendent of Documents), 1942. Reports on 96 different occupational surveys, and suggests specific steps to be taken in making a good survey.

SCIENTIFIC SURVEY TECHNIQUES

For adults making thorough sociological surveys the following books are recommended:

Brunner, Edmund deS., *Surveying Your Community*. New York: Doubleday, Doran, 1923.

Chapin, F. Stuart, *Field Work and Social Research*. New York: The Century Company, 1920.

Elmer, Manuel C., *Techniques of Social Surveys*. Los Angeles: Jesse Ray Miller, 1927.

Fagg, C. C., and G. E. Hutchings, *An Introduction to Regional Surveying*. Cambridge, England: The University Press, 1930.

Fry, C. Luther, *The Technique of Social Investigation*. New York: Harper, 1934.

Walters, R. G., "The Community Survey." Monograph 58, South-Western Publishing Company. Cincinnati: The Company, 1942.

Young, Pauline V., *Scientific Social Surveys and Research*. New York: Prentice-Hall, 1939.

CHAPTER 10

Extended Field Studies

TEACHERS EDUCATE THEMSELVES IN EUROPE

European Field Course in Nursery School, Kindergarten and First Grade Education was the title of a summer travel course offered by Teachers College of Columbia University and arranged by the Open Road, Inc. Twenty-eight students enrolled. The instructor had been abroad a number of times and had studied European educational systems, but she did not speak any foreign language. The course lasted two months from departure to arrival back in New York. The group studied elementary education in four countries, traveled by train, and lived in student hostels, boarding schools and simple hotels.

The stay in each country was organized by student or cultural organizations, with the collaboration of leading educators. A native guide-interpreter, interested in education, accompanied the group in each country. There were visits to schools, meetings with educators, and much fraternization with European teachers who accompanied the group on its visits to historic landmarks, museums, and other similar centers, and on occasions entertained the Americans in their homes.

What Are Extended Field Studies?

"Extended field studies" combine the essential elements of a long excursion and a survey; that is, they take the group out of its home environment and into a new one for purposes of serious field analysis over an extended period of time. Such a field study may last from several days to several months; its geographic area may be the local, regional, national, or even international community; it may be confined to one small community, or it may require travel over thousands of miles. Yet the members of the group engaged in extended field study always work, learn, and live together during the course of the project.

Although educational field study may properly include opportunity to "see the sights," it should never be confused with mere sight-seeing. Whereas genuine field study measures up to academic standards in the definition of its subject matter and the rigor of its methods, the sight-seeing trip rushes from place to place, its members absorbing sensory impressions largely devoid of intellectual or emotional substance. Too often, the purely sight-seeing trip masquerades as "education," and too often teachers are accessory to that deception.

Why Is Extended Field Study Profitable?

Most of the values of making surveys and excursions are implicit in extended field studies, just as are many of the advantages resident in community-centered education generally. In addition, the extended field experience affords some other opportunities peculiar to itself. For extended field studies:

1. **Stimulate imagination and learning interests** as they introduce us to new and different environments.

2. **Expand horizons** by making us acquainted with people whose manners, customs, living standards, outlooks, and interests may be quite different from our own.

3. **Facilitate objectivity in studying controversial issues.** The tax-supported public schools, and even the parent-supported private schools, have to approach many local situations with caution. Often, the most acute problems cannot be touched because of the adult emotions involved. But these very problems may often be studied with complete candor in another community removed from one's own.

4. **Provide perspective upon the home situation.** No one really knows his own environment and his own neighbors until he has compared them with something different.

5. **Teach the art of living with others.** The day-in-and-day-out association—traveling in the same conveyances, sharing rooms, sitting at the same table, participating in the same experiences, getting deadly tired together—is not without strains and stresses. Idiosyncrasies and character defects come to the surface; so also do traits of nobility. The purpose of the field study is to focus attention upon the outside world, but in the business of living and working intensively with others, the student also gets under his own social microscope.

6. **Treat students and teacher as complete personalities.** The limited and somewhat hierarchical relations of the classroom are discarded. The teacher is no longer merely an instructor; he is now also parent, companion, arbiter. Students are no longer detached from their backgrounds; it is now as though they have moved into the classroom, bag and baggage.

Extended field study is a highly dramatic and satisfying experience. Above all, it motivates participants to engage in new activities and assume new responsibilities.

What Are the Types of Extended Field Study?

Extended field studies, which are essentially surveys carried on outside one's accustomed environment, are therefore properly classified according to their primary purpose, basic curricular program, major locale in which they are carried on, and the community area they survey. These four factors may easily be charted as follows:

CLASSIFICATION OF EXTENDED FIELD STUDIES

PRIMARY PURPOSE	CURRICULAR PROGRAM	MAJOR LOCALE	COMMUNITY AREA
I. *Organized education* with a curricular program	A. *Specific study* of some broad topic, theme, process, or problem with only incidental reference to its community context. Samples: geological formations, race relations, the T.V.A., European housing or music festivals	1. *Within the United States*	a. *Within a local community*
			OR
			b. *In several contrasted local communities*
OR	*OR*	*OR*	*OR*
	B. *General overview* of a community's setting or of many social processes or problems as they conjointly operate. Examples: life in a coal mining town, study of Southern economic conditions, cultural survey of Europe		c. *Within a region or nation*
			OR
II. *General culture* based on social contacts and acquaintance with customs		2. *In another nation or in several other nations*	d. *In several contrasted regions or nations*

Any particular field study of extended nature may easily be classified as to fundamental type by reference to this chart. By way of illustration, consider several varied field studies carried on before World War II and listed on page 201.

The most fruitful field trips in the United States are those which concentrate on a specific topic or focus on a local community. But since the concentration of interest which is possible at home can hardly be expected abroad, it is obvious that the general cultural tour and the general overview curriculum are both more popular and usually more desirable for the foreign locale—especially for those taking their first trip outside the United States. Such generalized field studies offer valuable learning experiences, providing

TYPE SYMBOL	TITLE OF FIELD STUDY	SPONSORING AGENCY
I A 1 a	*Field Geography*	Pennsylvania State Teachers College, at Indiana
I A 1 c	*Indian Culture of the Pacific Northwest*	University of Washington
I A 2 d	*Traveling Inquiry into Public Housing in Europe and the Soviet Union*	The Open Road, Inc.
I B 1 a	*Sociological Field Course in Southern Conditions*	Teachers College of Columbia University and the Open Road
I B 2 c	*Mexican Seminar*	Committee on Cultural Relations with Latin America
II B 2 c	*Experiment in International Living*	Donald Watt
II B 2 d	*Civilizations of Central and Southeastern Europe*	New York State Teachers College, at Oneonta

they do not cover too much ground, are built on contacts with people, and penetrate below the sight-seeing level on which most tourists pursue their way smoothly, comfortably, and in almost perfect isolation from the life around them.

The specific study, on the other hand, offers superior advantages to those who already possess a general background derived from previous travel, and to those whose special interests are already sharply defined, whether or not they have already been abroad.

What Are the Human Prerequisites for Extended Field Study?

Extended field study should come at a later stage in education than does the making of local surveys or participation in local excursions. It is essentially an activity for the maturing mind. Graduate students and people already practicing their professions get more from extended study trips than do college undergraduates. The latter, in turn, benefit more than high school students. It is questionable whether educational returns commensurate with the effort and expense can be obtained at a lower level than the senior or junior years of high school.

When a group of adolescents travel together, their administration presents obvious problems. First of all, is the feasibility of combining the sexes. This will depend upon the social pattern which has governed their previous relation in school life and in the community, on the intellectual intensity of the experience being offered, and on the teacher's character and personality. These are factors which each school's administrators must weigh for themselves. There is one rule, however, which it is perilous to violate: no one should be admitted to the group who might present behavior problems or be a social misfit. Living with difficult personalities is in its way educational, but is nevertheless certain to hamper the group in achieving the objectives of the course.

The group engaged in field study should never be too large. Fifteen is the maximum number that any teacher should try to supervise singlehanded. Larger groups, even if the teacher in charge has adult assistance, tend to become unwieldy. The larger the group, the more formal its program must be and the less opportunity there will be for intimate relations with hosts and informants, and for that casual observation which is so often the most revealing.

Great care must be exercised in admitting outsiders to the course. Brothers, sisters, and friends of the same age level should be taken only if they are otherwise qualified for the experience that is planned. The inclusion of qualified students who are native to the locality to be studied, however, can greatly enrich the group's experience. Parents and other adult relatives should generally be excluded. It must always be borne in mind that to succeed in their work the students have to develop a group life; the mere presence of nonfunctional adults, especially those with ties to particular students, is invariably disruptive.

Everything depends upon the teacher. The better he gets along with others and the more he knows about the subject to be investigated, the greater is the likelihood of success for the project. Ideally, the teacher should be thoroughly familiar with the locale of the study. Yet successful European field courses have very often been conducted by teachers who had never been abroad, and even by those who did not speak any foreign language. Similarly, successful field courses have been given in the United States by teachers who had never previously visited the community to be studied. Character and temperament are far more important than specific knowledge or experience. Generally speaking, the teacher best qualified to conduct a field course is the teacher who is student-centered in his thinking, who is successful in human relationships outside the classroom, and who has administrative ability. It is frequently the case that a stimulating and popular classroom teacher is educationally lost outside school walls.

How Can Extended Field Studies Be Carried on Successfully?

In the planning of an extended field trip, there is the closest interrelation between technical preparation on the one hand and curricular and social preparation on the other. One does not first do the technical planning and then the program and the social planning, or vice versa. The planning must be one indivisible process: technical arrangements are naturally shaped to the purposes of the trip and the curricular and social programs by which those purposes are to be achieved; on the other hand, curricular and social arrangements may be modified by exigencies of a technical nature, and often plans of either a technical or nontechnical nature have to be revised more than once before the preparations for the trip are completed. Following are the principal things to be considered in preparing for an extended field study trip.

1. PLAN DEMOCRATICALLY

The teacher in charge must be the acknowledged head of the group, with all that this implies as to responsibility and authority. It is not necessary, and certainly never desirable, that he be authoritarian; experience shows that the best field courses are those in which students assume most responsibility for their daily lives, as well as for their academic work. The extent to which group democracy can be practiced depends primarily upon the teacher's philosophy and proficiency in democratic techniques. But the nature of the course is itself an important factor. One which travels far and fast, or one which has a crowded and rigid program, requires more authoritarian direction than one which is stationary or seldom changes its locale and which can therefore have a more flexible program. The authoritarian approach is typified by a recent summer school course which studied the Tennessee Valley Authority and its social effects. The instructor was autocratic; the subject was tremendous in scope; there were 2,500 miles of travel with a good many one-night stops; such an intensive and detailed program was laid out in advance that there was little time for any unscheduled events. In contrast was a course of the democratic type which was given by a different institution. The students in it spent six weeks studying a Maine textile town. A program was elaborated in advance which filled the first three weeks; the program of the last three weeks was developed by the group itself on the basis of what it had already seen and done. The instructor was a man of philosophic depth and great human insight; he was a passionate practitioner of democracy; nothing happened in the group which escaped his notice or to which he was indifferent, but he knew how to stay his hand while his students worked at the problem of group living and personal relations; conflicts developed, came to crisis, and were resolved. His students learned a lot of sociology. They also learned a lot about human relations.

Student participation in planning is the first step in making the trip democratic. It may be simpler for the teacher by himself to define the objectives, formulate the program, and make the technical arrangements. But a trip which in its inception is authoritarian will not be truly democratic in execution. If students share responsibility for all decisions, they can also be expected to share responsibility for carrying them out.

Democratic planning does not imply an unrealistic division of labor between teacher and students. There are some things which the teacher can do best, and these he should do. Example: It would be desirable that someone visit the various locations of the field course in order to learn essential facts and make necessary arrangements. Obviously, the teacher is the one to do this. In such cases, the democratic principle will be served if the problem has been thoroughly discussed in class and the teacher goes as the representative of the group.

2. DETERMINE PURPOSES AND LOCALE

The next need is to determine the essential type of field study to be made. Will its purpose be organized education or general culture? Should it concentrate upon some specific topic or problem, or seek a more generalized comprehension? Is it to be carried on in the United States, or is the major locale elsewhere? What is the basic community area to be surveyed? Each of these fundamental queries must be answered in terms of many factors inherent in the needs, interests, and purposes of the particular group.

Sometimes the project presents itself complete. The planners know what they want to investigate and where it is to be found. But often there are missing links. For example, the field course which studied the textile town in Maine started with the idea that it would be worthwhile to spend some weeks getting to know a typical textile community. Maine was chosen because the instructor hailed from Maine and it was felt that his background should be used. It was also decided that the town to be studied ought to be an independent community, not the satellite of a large city. After these decisions had been made, a representative of the college spent several weeks studying possibilities. He gathered preliminary data about the textile towns of Maine and consulted both trade associations and union organizations. A certain town was selected, but it was discovered that the dominant textile interest would not welcome "professors and students poking their noses in." The emissary of the college thereupon tried another town and, guided by his previous experience, approached the powers in a way which enlisted their enthusiastic support.

The determination of locale can be made with relative ease if the field trip is to be made in the United States where needed data is readily obtainable. But deciding where to go abroad is much more difficult. A group planning a public housing study in Europe, for instance, will probably be unable to gather the requisite preliminary information from American sources. The best plan would be to establish connections with some competent European organization. But doing that is not easy, and consultation at such long range takes considerable time. In such cases, the services of an educational travel agency may become essential.

3. STUDY THE FIELD IN ADVANCE

We have already said that the teacher's temperament, character, and skills are more important than his specific information. Every teacher, however, will want to approach the field with the fullest possible knowledge. He should first familiarize himself with all available documentary sources, and consult with everyone he can find who has knowledge of the area to be visited. Where he has adequate prior acquaintance with the subject and the locale, or where an expert organization is employed, program planning may be done at long range. But if the trip is within the United States, best results will be obtained if the teacher can visit the locations of the course and make arrangements on the spot. This does not mean that the teacher ought to interview everyone who is to participate in the program. The purpose of such a reconnaissance is achieved if it enables the teacher to survey the resources and to find competent local confederates, to work out the general plan with them, and to convey to them his point of view and its requirements. The detailed planning can be carried forward from that point by correspondence between the teacher and those whom he has chosen to represent him locally.

4. Plan the Curricular Program

A good field study has clarity of purpose, deals with live material, and is arranged with an eye to dramatic development and effect. Planning the program involves knowing the needs, resources, and capacities of the group. And the more the students know about the study subject in advance, the greater will be their zeal and achievement in the field. Students should therefore be given background and an overview by means of orientation talks and through assigned reading. It may be worthwhile to get them to do preparatory individual or group research, and to share their findings with the rest of the group. In any event, maps showing political, economic, cultural, demographic and other relevant factors should be fully utilized.

It is of utmost importance that when it has been completed, the program be communicated to all concerned, including the students, and that they be informed of any subsequent changes. At all times, those concerned should know in advance the principal things that are going to happen. But be sure to plan a few surprises to add zest for the group!

5. Establish Standards of Travel

Uniformity of standards is more important than quality. A group which accustoms itself to simple standards will be happy as long as it does not spend a night in a first-class hotel. On the other hand, a group which alternately stays in cheap and de luxe hotels is likely to be continually discontented. However, fluctuations in standards which are due to lack of facilities, or which have educational reasons, will always be understood and accepted. Groups accustomed to staying in comfortable inns, have thoroughly enjoyed being billeted in farmhouses without modern conveniences.

6. Decide Whether to Use a Travel Agency

An obvious first thought in planning an extended trip is to turn the business management over to some travel agency. Unfortunately, however, there are few agencies which are competent. Most travel agents know only how to sell transportation and to retail the standard tours which they purchase from wholesalers such as Thos. Cook & Son or the American Express Company. Furthermore, the services which they sell—excepting transportation, for which there are standard rates—are designed for middle class and wealthy tour-

STANDARDS IN THE UNITED STATES

STANDARDS ABROAD

TRANSPORTATION

The ideal arrangement is for the group to have its own automobiles. This facilitates mobility in carrying out the program, and makes possible diversification of activities. The problem is to recruit, cars with safe drivers. The cost of such transportation, when prorated among the group members, is very low. Where the use of private cars is not feasible, a school bus may be used. This, however, has the great disadvantage that all must do the same things at the same time, and that the group is conspicuous wherever it goes. Train travel is generally inadequate because it leaves the problem of local transportation unsolved. Over long distances, however, railroad or air travel may prove most feasible.

Before World War II, there were three standards of ocean travel: first class, tourist class, and third class. Students and professional people generally traveled third class. Presumably, there will be several classes of steamer travel after the war, and without doubt, the cheapest will again be adequate unless the group is impatient of travel time and prefers the more expensive air line transportation.

The use of private automobiles is not feasible abroad. Transporting cars from this country is exceedingly expensive, and renting them abroad is likewise prohibitive from the point of view of cost. A foreign field trip must therefore rely on common carriers for all transportation. In Europe, there are several classes of train travel; students and intellectuals generally use the cheapest, except for very long journeys.

LODGINGS

Group rates can often be secured at a standard hotel which compares favorably with the rates of an inferior hotel. It is frequently feasible to use the Y.M.C.A. and tourist homes, the one disadvantage of the latter being that it is likely to necessitate scattering the group. Where a field trip spends considerable time in one place, it may be advisable to rent a house. This was done by the field course which studied the Maine textile town; the group lived in several cottages on a lake five miles from the town center and did its own cooking, with the result that the charge to each student for living and travel during six weeks was well under a hundred dollars.

There are various distinct grades of hotels in Europe, with corresponding price differences. It is a good rule to patronize small hotels and pensions (a combination boarding house and hotel, and generally a family institution); these are often very comfortable and the food excellent. Such places are overlooked by the commercial travel trade, but agencies catering to students will know them. There are also student hostels, clubs, and, in a few instances, International Houses connected with universities. These facilities should be available through the special type of travel agency recommended in these pages.

BOARD

In rapid movement, hotel dining rooms, restaurants, and cafeterias must be used. But when the group settles down for an extended period, it may be possible to utilize boarding houses or even to establish cooperative housekeeping arrangements as was suggested above.

It is usually cheapest to take all meals in lodgings. This arrangement is known as "full pension." However, such an arrangement necessitates return to lodgings in the middle of the day and hampers the educational program. It is therefore best to take breakfast and dinner, or only breakfast, in lodgings.

ists; these services are basically expensive and the surcharges of the wholesaler and the retailer are excessive.

As a general rule, the school which plans a field trip in the United States does not need the technical assistance of a travel agency. The business of arranging transportation, lodgings, and meals in home country is not difficult and goes hand in hand with the elaboration of the program. To illustrate: the local citizens who help to arrange an educational program in their community can also be relied upon to find lodgings at minimum cost. But the technical planning of a trip abroad requires organization and experience which no school is likely to possess. The intricacies of foreign time-tables, connections, standards of travel and rates, the procedure of getting reservations, payment in foreign currencies, and the securing of visas are the functions of specialists. Before World War II, there were several educational travel organizations which existed to serve students and which could be relied upon to give competent service at reasonable cost. Following the end of hostilities, some of these may resume operation, and others will doubtless come into existence. Any school which then contemplates a foreign field trip would do well to consult the Institute of International Education, 2 West 45th Street, New York 20, N. Y., for full information regarding reliable educational travel agencies.

7. CONSTRUCT A TIME SCHEDULE

Perhaps the next important step in planning any successful field trip is to build a calendar. This calendar or schedule must show the dates planned for each place, the exact times of arrival and departure, and the details of routings and connections between points. Such a schedule outlines the technical structure of the trip. On it are based cost estimates, reservations, and the timing of the study program.

When the calendar has been provisionally drawn, many details will emerge for consideration. One knows how many nights of lodging must be reserved in each place; how many meals there will be at each center, and what meals have to be provided for en route between points; exactly how much working time the group will have in each place, and so on.

With the skeleton calendar in hand, it is possible to start organizing the study program. As engagements are made and events are scheduled, they should be entered in the calendar so that upon completion of preparations, there will be a day-by-day, hour-by-

```
                        AMSTERDAM 2½ DAYS
                 July 22 Evening through July 25 Morning

Organizer                                        Accommodations
Miss Olga van Delden                             Hotel Polen
ISHA-in-Holland                                  Kalverstraat
105, Statenlaan                                  Amsterdam
Telegrams: VANDELDEN STATENLAAN HAGUE
Telephone: 553115
Der Haag
```

July 22	On arrival the group went to the hotel where dinner was served.
Evening:	Free

July 23

9:30	The group was shown through the new open air school for healthy children of Amsterdam. This school has now been in operation for about 7 years and Mr. Janssen, who has taught there during this entire period, led the group.
11:00	Visited Miss Bienfait's private Montessori school, where Miss Bienfait herself gave detailed information about her methods of teaching and theories.
12:00	Visit to the Rijksmuseum. Lunch at the Hotel Polen.

Afternoon:	
14:30	Boat trip through the canals and harbor of Amsterdam. Rest of afternoon free. Dinner at the Hotel Polen.
Evening:	
20:00	Lecture on Dutch nursery schools, kindergartens, etc. by a young student in this branch: Miss T. van Poelje of The Hague.

July 24

8:30	Left for The Hague by bus.
10:00	Visit to a municipal nursery and Montessori school in the Delagoastraat. The group watched the children at work and at play and special demonstrations were given for the benefit of the group. The principals, Miss Smit and Miss de Haan, showed the group around.
11:30	Visit to the Municipal open air school for children with noncontagious cases of tuberculosis at the Doorniksche straat in Scheveningen. The gardens of this school are right in the dunes. The group was shown around by the principal, Mr. Wagner.

Afternoon:	
13:00	Lunch at "Seinpost" in Scheveningen overlooking sea. Short walk on beach.
15:00	Visit to the municipal school museum of The Hague. Short lecture by the Director of this museum, Dr. W. E. van Wijk. Tea at the museum. Free for shopping.
Evening:	
18:30	Dinner at historical Witte de Witt mansion, where national Javanese food "Rijsttafel" was served. Through The Hague visit the group was also accompanied by Mr. Wimmers of the municipal school inspection.

July 25	Lv. Amsterdam. 10:15	MISS VAN HOYTEMA LEAVES
	Ar. Vlissingen 13:37	(Dutch Guide)
	Lv. Vlissingen by boat . . .13:50	
	Ar. Harwich. 19:10	MRS. MUNRO JCINS
	Lv. Harwich by train 19:55	(English Guide)
	Ar. London Liv. Str. St. . .21:30	

TYPICAL PAGE FROM A FIELD STUDY SCHEDULE. European Field course in nursery school, kindergarten and first-grade education.

hour record of all that is planned. Such a calendar will be found indispensable in operating the trip later on, as well as in planning it.

A common defect of field trips is the overcrowded schedule. Adequate time must be allowed for each event, and there must be enough time, between events, for getting from one place to another. Furthermore, the day must not be too full. It is a good general rule to leave a third of each day—morning, afternoon, or evening—free from prescribed activities. Students need time to digest their experiences, to do things on their own, and to attend to personal affairs and interests. This is the best insurance against jangled nerves and jaded sensibilities. Those who construct field trips, like those who arrange public meetings, often overestimate human capacities. A program which looks meager on paper often overtaxes its participants.

8. ESTIMATE COSTS

In establishing a cost estimate, calculation should first be made for the group as a whole; this figure may later be divided by the number of participants to determine what each individual should pay. Some items can be estimated with precision; others can only be approximated in advance. It is well to add a small sum or percentage to the total of any estimate as a safety margin. Students can be assured that any savings will be returned to them at the conclusion of the trip. Complete cost estimation on a day-to-day basis is the only safe course to take. Such an estimate is reproduced on pages 212–214 to illustrate both the importance and the technique of this step.

COSTS WHICH CAN BE DETERMINED IN ADVANCE

Extended transportation: Money can often be saved by buying all transportation as a single unit. Round-trip rail, bus, or airplane tickets can be purchased from any point in the United States at a saving; a round-trip steamship ticket is cheaper than two one-way tickets; remarkable economies can often be achieved by purchasing part, at least, of the European rail travel in conjunction with the round-trip steamship ticket. Discounts for students and small groups are not obtainable on American railways, but prior to World War II, the government-controlled railroads of Europe generally gave discounts to students and to travel groups.

Lodgings: Many standard hotels, here and abroad, give group rates which are lower than their ordinary tariffs; many of them also give the person in charge of the group free lodging. These concessions, however, are not always granted by small hotels, boarding houses, and pensions.

Board: Meals in lodgings can be precisely estimated. The cost of meals taken outside is more difficult to calculate and a certain amount of guesswork may be unavoidable in this instance.

Guides' fees: These can generally be known in advance.

Passport and visas: Rates are established by law and can readily be ascertained.

COSTS WHICH MAY BE ONLY APPROXIMATED IN ADVANCE

Local transportation: Where common carriers are used for local transportation, one can either allocate a lump sum by guesswork or ascertain the transit rates and work out a budget accordingly.

Entrance fees: Many museums and historic places, local sight-seeing trips, theaters, movies, etc. involve entrance fees. Some information may be obtained in advance, but an arbitrary allowance will probably have to be made.

Instructor's administrative fund: The teacher in charge should have at his disposal funds to defray such incidental expenses as telephone, telegraph, cable or radio charges, tips, porterage of luggage, reciprocal hospitality to hosts and informants, occasional treats for the group, and minor expenses which cannot be foreseen. These contingency funds should be sufficient so that it will not be necessary to take up collections from the group members. "Treats for the group" may mean an ice cream soda at the psychological moment on a hot day, or a snack to eat when the next meal is too far off.

Organization expenses: It is best if the school meets the expenses of organizing the trip. Such expenses may include guide books, source materials, stenography, telephone, telegraph, and cable charges, and travel expenses incurred when arranging the program. To the extent that such items are not met by the school, they must be prorated among the group members.

9. SECURE REGISTRATION

When the plans are sufficiently definite, a prospectus should be prepared for the information of all concerned. It may be necessary to issue a preliminary prospectus along general lines, to be followed by a final prospectus when the plans are in final form and the price which each participant must pay has been established. Pages 212–214 show the first three pages of such a prospectus.

It will be noted from these figures that the prospectus should include the following data, together with anything else which the school considers pertinent:

General statement regarding the aims of the field study project, the way it has been conceived and is to be carried out, who is eligible to join, etc.

Summary of the program planned. This may, but need not necessarily, include a calendar in detail.

Description of standards of travel, and of living accommodations to be used.

The services provided for the stated price, with a statement of possible services or extras which are not covered by the inclusive price.

Price to the student. This figure may be merely a total, or it may include a breakdown of that price in some detail.

Good management requires that business relations between the school and the parents should be clearly defined and stated from the outset. This is best accomplished by means of a registration

FIELD SEMINAR IN THE SOCIOLOGY OF THE TENNESSEE VALLEY

offered by

The Department of Educational Sociology of the School of Education

NEW YORK UNIVERSITY

and

THE OPEN ROAD

C O S T   E S T I M A T E

Beginning in Norris July 5 morning and ending in Norris August 9 afternoon--
based on 15 students, instructor, instructor's wife, Commission on Teacher
Education evaluator, and Open Road representative. Total: 19 persons.

1. TRANSPORTATION (by 5 private automobiles):   Per Person

   Total mileage 2,500
   Gas: 2,500 miles at 15 miles to a gallon: 167 gallons
        at average of 21¢ a gallon $ 35.07
   Oil: Two changes at 8 quarts a change: 16 quarts at 25¢
        a quart average   4.00
   Greasing: Once   1.50
   Repairs: 10.00
   Payment to Car Loaner: 50¢ a day for duration of course
   --35 days   17.50
                                                            _____
                        Total cost per car   68.07
                                                            x 5 cars
                                                            $340.35
                        Divided by 19 persons   cost per person $17.92

2. ACCOMMODATIONS (including American plan meals in Gatlinburg):

   Norris Park: 14 nights -- July 5-18 inclusive -- 9
                    double cabins plus 1 single -- total cost
                    $414 divided by 19 persons $ 21.79

   Dayton: 3 nights -- July 19, 20, 21 -- all singles
                    with bath, at $1.50 per night (Hotel Aqua)   4.50

   Chattanooga: 1 night -- July 22. Patten Hotel or Look
                    Out Mountain Hotel. 9 double rooms with
                    twin beds and private bath at $4 and 1
                    double at $3 -- $39 divided by 19 persons   2.05

   Monte Sano Park: 9 nights -- July 23-31 inclusive -- 10
                    cabins for two each at $19 per cabin for
                    entire period -- $190 divided by 19 persons   10.00

   Choe Stoe Watershed (Near Blairsville): 1 night in farm homes
                    -- Aug. 1 -- no charge   -----

Gatlinburg:	3 nights -- Aug. 2, 3, and 4 -- Mountain View Hotel, American plan, at average of $4.50 for single rooms (group misses one lunch)	$13.50	
Kingsport:	1 night -- Aug. 5 -- Kingsport Inn. 9 double rooms with twin beds and private bath at $2.50 per person, and 1 single with bath at $2.50	2.50	
Norris Park:	3 nights -- Aug. 6, 7, and 8 -- $103.50 divided by 19 persons	-----	$59.79

3. MEALS

Norris Park:	14 days, 3 meals daily at $1.50. (Begins with lunch July 5 and ends with breakfast July 19)	21.00	
	July 19: lunch en route to Dayton	.60	
Dayton:	July 19, 20, 21 -- 3 dinners at 50¢ $1.50 July 20 and 21 -- 2 lunches at 50¢ 1.00 July 21, 21, 22 -- 3 breakfasts at 35¢ 1.05	3.55	
	July 22: lunch en route to Soddy	.50	
Chattanooga:	July 22 dinner .85 July 23 breakfast .35 July 23 lunch .60	1.80	
Monte Sano:	Beginning with dinner July 23, ending with breakfast Aug. 1: 8 full days at $1.60 a day plus 1 dinner at 75¢ and 1 breakfast at 35¢	13.90	
Florence:	Lunch at Negley Hotel July 26	.75	
	Aug. 1: lunch en route to Blairsville	.60	
	Aug. 1: dinner 60¢) at Farm Home near Aug. 2: breakf. 35¢) Blairsville or restaurant	.95	
	Aug. 2: lunch en route to Gatlinburg	.75	
Gatlinburg:	Beginning with dinner Aug. 2 and ending with breakfast Aug. 5 -- included in American Plan hotel rate	---	
	Lunch on trip to Smokies	.50	
	Aug. 5: lunch en route to Kingsport	.75	
Kingsport:	Dinner at $1 Aug. 5 and breakfast at 50¢ Aug. 6	1.50	
Norris Park	Beginning with dinner Aug. 6 and ending with lunch Aug. 9: 3 full days at $1.50	4.50	52.40

4. **TIPS**

Meal tips:	15% of $52.40		$7.86

Chambermaids: Norris, first visit $1.00
Norris, second " .25
Dayton, 3 nights .25
Monte Sano, 9 nights 1.00
Gatlinburg, 3 nights .25   2.75

Bellhops: 2 bags per person, 20¢ up to rooms and
20¢ down:
Dayton .40
Chattanooga .40
Gatlinburg .40
.40   1.60 $12.21

5. **GARAGING OF CARS** - including tips at garages:

Norris: none ----
Dayton: 3 nights @ 75¢ 2.25
Chattanooga: 1 night @ 75¢ .75
Monte Sano: none ----
Farm: none ----
Gatlinburg: 3 nights @ 75¢ 2.25
Kingsport: 1 night @ 75¢ .75
Norris: none ----
Per car 6.00
$6 x 5 cars = $30. $30 divided by 19 persons   1.58

6. **INSURANCE**

Accident $6.90
Liability 1.00
Supplementary automobile insurance 2.00   9.90
$153.80

7. **INSTRUCTOR'S TRAVEL AND LIVING EXPENSES DURING COURSE**

    $153.80 divided by 15 (paying) members   10.25

8. **INSTRUCTOR'S TRAVEL AND LIVING EXPENSES TO NORRIS AND RETURN**

    $51.70 divided by 15 (paying) members   3.45

9. **INSTRUCTOR'S FUND FOR ADMINISTRATION AND INCIDENTALS**   15.00

10. **NEW YORK UNIVERSITY TUITION FEE**   102.00

11. **OPEN ROAD FEE**   none   ------

             TOTAL COST PER STUDENT $284.50

A COST ESTIMATE FOR EXTENDED STUDY made by the Open Road.

blank to be signed by the parent or guardian at the time when he enrolls his child in the trip. The following represents a typical form which has been drawn up on the basis of experience and legal counsel.

10. PLAN FOR PAYMENT

It is advisable to collect a deposit at the time of registration. This is usually ten per cent of the total price. Payment of the balance should then be required before the start of the trip. It is common practice to collect in full thirty days before departure. Payment of an initial deposit is the best evidence that the parent really intends to send his child, while collection of the balance a month in advance is the final test. This allows time to enroll another group member in the event of a cancellation.

11. PROVIDE INSURANCE

Insurance is a form of financial protection which should be utilized to the full for all off-campus travel. Four types of insurance are applicable to extended field trips:

Public Liability: The school should protect itself against claims by parents in the event of accident.

Individual Accident Insurance: It is recommended that students be required to buy individual accident insurance policies. Premiums should be included in the price of the trip.

Baggage Insurance: This form of protection is desirable unless the effects of the student are already covered by a family floater or by provisions in family fire and theft policies.

Automobile Insurance: If private cars are recruited for group travel, the school should see to it that each car owner carries adequate public liability insurance on his car. Any automobile utilized on a field trip should carry public liability insurance in the sum of $100,000/$300,000. If the owner is insured for less, the school should request the above figure and itself pay the difference, which is negligible. The insurance company should be notified of the use to which the car is being put, lest policies be invalidated.

All insurance problems should be taken up with a *first-rate* insurance agent for the following reasons: it may be impossible to obtain a standard public liability policy which protects the school, in which case the agent must be capable of securing a special policy; a number of companies write individual accident policies, few of which are adequate; and the general assistance of a good agent may be most helpful, not only in writing insurance, but also in the event of claims.

TO THE RICHARD ROE SCHOOL:

Having read and accepted the terms and conditions contained herein,

I herewith enroll my son
daughter

in the _____
(name by which trip is known in prospectus)

I make payment herewith of $_____ deposit, it being understood by me that

the balance of $_____ is due _____ days before the trip begins.

Date_____   Signature_____

Terms and Conditions

The engagement of services is secured by payment of a deposit of _____ per cent of the total price of the trip. The balance is payable _____ days before service begins.

On cancellation made _____ days before services begin, the full amount received will be refunded. In case of later cancellation but prior to the date when services begin, the school may retain up to _____ per cent of the price of the trip as compensation for losses sustained.

Students who find it necessary to absent themselves from the trip while in progress are requested to notify the teacher well in advance. Where this is done, the school will use its best efforts to effect cancellation of those travel facilities which are not' to be used. Such amounts will be refunded as the cancellations enable the school to save on the total expenses of the party. The decision of the school as to the amount refundable shall be final and shall bind all parties. Should the conduct of a student oblige his elimination from the party, refund will be made in accordance with the above.

In view of the character of the trip, the school reserves the right to decline to accept or retain any person as a member at any time. It also reserves the right to withdraw the trip and to make such alterations in plans as may be found desirable for the convenience of the party and the proper carrying out of the program.

Prices are subject to marked fluctuation in rates of international exchange. (To be included of course only in a trip outside the United States.)

All expenses due to delay, deviation or alteration of plans, arising from causes, or as a result of causes, beyond the control of the school shall be borne by the student.

The school, except for the wilful negligence of itself or employees, disclaims all liability of whatsoever nature for loss or damage to property or injury to the person of a student.

The exercise of judgment granted herein to the school may be delegated by it to such agencies or persons as may have immediate local control or charge of the trip, with full power to them or any of them to act in the premises as the exigencies of the case at the time being may warrant.

REGISTRATION BLANK FOR FIELD STUDY used by the Open Road, Inc.

12. Make Reservations

After the calendar has been established, and at the earliest possible date, tentative reservations should be made for steamer or plane accommodations, for lodgings, and for any other form of transportation or accommodation for which there is heavy demand. It is often necessary to make deposits for such reservations, which is another reason for requiring them from parents at the time of registration. Care should be taken to assure that deposits on tentative reservations are refundable in case the contemplated number is reduced or the trip cancelled.

As the contemplated numbers in the trip increase or shrink, the tentative reservations should be increased or reduced accordingly, so that good relations are maintained with carriers, hotels, and the like. When the exact number of participants is finally known, the tentative reservations should immediately be made definite.

13. Develop a "Who's Who" of the Group

Those who are to receive the group must know with whom they will be dealing. Care must be taken to see that every participant in the program knows the size of the group, the average age, the balance of the sexes, and the stage of intellectual development of the group as a whole. Sometimes it is a good idea to prepare a *Who's Who* of the membership which indicates for each individual his name, residence, major field of study, special interests, etc., and to circulate this memorandum among those who will meet the group.

14. Arrange Passports and Visas

These credentials are required for foreign travel, and must be secured before leaving the United States. A travel agency or steamship line will advise and assist in obtaining them. Loss of a passport is attended with great inconvenience, and it is advisable for the leader to carry them for the group. Each individual, however, should have on his person, at all times, a memorandum of identification which includes the number of his passport.

15. Advise on Clothing and Other Equipment

The less one takes, the better. Neatness and suitability are the essentials. Students are advised to consider the packing qualities of clothes and to avoid things that must be freshly laundered or pressed to look well. Shun objects that make bags heavy—like weighty cold cream jars. Valuable jewelry should be left at home, also electrical appliances unless the group is to spend a period of weeks in one spot. American appliances are useless abroad. Room should be left in suitcases for the things one will want to buy en route. It is suggested that before the trip starts the group come together to decide what type of clothing will be needed and how it can be kept at a feasible minimum.

16. SPECIFY BAGGAGE LIMITATIONS

It is desirable to keep baggage to the minimum. This means that clothing and other personal effects must be chosen with great care. Group members should be furnished with a maximum list of needed items and be obliged to adhere to it. In the case of a trip abroad, several group suitcases should be taken on the voyage; heavy clothing needed only on shipboard can then be packed in the group suitcases when port is reached. Arrangements can be made with the steamship line to store the cases and to deliver them on board the return vessel.

Each student should be allowed to take one suitcase measuring $29 \times 17 \times 9$ inches maximum size, and one handbag not exceeding $18 \times 12\frac{1}{2} \times 6$ inches in size. There are good reasons for these specific limitations: the larger case is the biggest that can conveniently be packed in the luggage compartments of automobiles or fitted into luggage racks of trains; the smaller case is of a size which the individual himself can carry at all times and for some distance if necessary. If the large bag exceeds the recommended limits, it will be a continuous annoyance; if the small one is larger than suggested, it may involve extra charges for porterage. If automobiles are to be used, it will be necessary to make an exact study of the luggage capacity of each before issuing baggage instructions, for it will frequently be found that the limits outlined above are too generous. Luggage can satisfactorily be shipped from point to point in the United States by common carrier. Doing so abroad is more troublesome and delivery is less certain.

17. LEAVE MAILING ADDRESS

Nothing is more essential to group morale than hearing from home and friends. Arrangements for the reception of mail must be carefully worked out. A memorandum should be prepared and each student given enough copies to cover his correspondents' list. The memorandum should contain this information: A list of addresses, with the dates of each, and instructions always to address the student as

> Mr. John Doe
> Member, _____ School Group,
> Address

By identifying the student with the school or the name of the trip, the problem of forwarding mail is greatly simplified. It saves the teacher the trouble of including all names in his forwarding instructions to a hotel when the group leaves it.

The foregoing system applies if the trip is within the United States. If the group goes abroad, it is advisable to have all mail addressed in care of the central foreign office of the travel agency, for these reasons: it is almost impossible for friends at home to gauge the time a letter will take to reach its destination and mail is likely to arrive after the group has left; time tables and hotels often have to be changed in the course of the trip; only the central foreign office of the agency will know where the group is going to be at all times, and so be able to send mail to the right place at the right time; the slight delay occasioned by the re-directing of mail from a central foreign office is overbalanced by the greater certainty of delivery.

18. CARRY FUNDS SAFELY

It is recommended that individuals put their personal funds into traveler's cheques. The teacher should also carry group funds in traveler's cheques unless the sum exceeds a thousand dollars, in which case a letter of credit may be advisable.

19. AGREE UPON A CODE OF BEHAVIOR

The success of an extended field trip depends in part on the code of behavior which governs its participants. There has to be agreement regarding the function, responsibility, and authority of the teacher, the relations of students to each other, and the relation of the group to those it meets along the way (hosts, informants, guides, servants, etc.). It will not be difficult to define the position of the teacher or to develop rules of conduct within the group. But the formulation of attitudes toward outsiders requires imagination.

There are a few fundamentals of "public relations" which must not be overlooked. People in all walks of life are glad to talk about their jobs, their interests, and their problems—*provided the inquiry is friendly, intelligent, and not condescending.* The secret is to establish a degree of identification with all whom one meets. Once this has been done, it is possible to be searching in one's queries without giving offense. There are situations of conflict and tension in which great tact is required, but it is generally possible to meet all factions and get all points of view, provided partisanship is avoided. The right of students to learn facts for their own enlightenment is conceded, so long as there is no feeling that the students are "slumming," or that they are going to take sides or "expose" anyone. The watchwords of any field study which seeks social understanding must be humility, friendliness, and sincerity.

The character of the group and its purposes should be made publicly known wherever it goes. Statements regarding the group should be made to the press on arrival in any center. No member of the group should ever give an unauthorized statement to the press.

Punctuality is a group obligation which must be impressed on everyone. Nothing is more destructive of group morale and good public relations than the thoughtlessness of laggards.

20. DIVIDE THE LABOR

The teacher carries the general responsibility, but he cannot attend to every detail of execution and also perform his essential intellectual, social, and guidance functions. It is therefore advisable that as many jobs as possible be assumed by students, perhaps in rotation. Some of these student assignments might be:

Laundry: Immediately upon arrival in a place where there is to be a sufficiently long stay, arrangements should be made to get laundry done.

Mail: Inquiry must be made concerning mail which has already arrived; it must be distributed; and, in departing, a group forwarding address must be left.

Room assignments: Accommodations reserved in advance must be checked; if not reserved, suitable quarters must be located without delay.

Accounting: Someone should check bills before they are paid, and also collect from individuals for items which they personally owe.

Recording secretary: It may be desirable to have someone keep a record of the names and addresses of persons with whom the group has contact, and of all the important events which occur.

Social secretary: Perhaps some individual should see that everyone who extends hospitality or assistance to the group receives a suitable acknowledgment.

Confirming technical arrangements: Some member might arrange for meals to be taken outside of lodgings; check time of plane, train, or bus departure and reservations, if any; time and place of meeting with guides, etc.

Confirming curricular arrangements: There may be someone in the group sufficiently mature and adroit socially to check the engagements with institutions, speakers, etc., in so far as this may be necessary.

21. PLAN LEARNING ACTIVITIES

A field trip affords only limited opportunity for reading. It is well, however, to carry a small carefully selected library of books, periodicals, and reports to which students can refer. But in the main the learning activities are the gathering of impressions from life, their organization, interpretation, and evaluation.

Students must be taught how to conduct interviews, both as a member of a group and individually. This calls for thought and experimentation on the part of the teacher. But the gathering of data is a much simpler business than the reflective process by which meaning is derived from impressions. Obvious devices for this are group discussions and the preparation by individuals or committees of reports to form a basis for such discussion. It may also be desirable to have each student keep a notebook or "log" in which he summarizes those facts which he has learned and which seem to him important, and in which he records reactions to experiences of the trip, etc. Such an intellectual diary induces reflection, thereby carrying the learning process to a higher level than is usual with young students. A further value of such notebooks is that they furnish a basis for discussion between teacher and student regarding the latter's habits of observation, sense of the significant, clarity of thought, imaginative freedom, and the like.

Other forms of recording and expression are photography, sketching, and the making of collections. While very interesting and useful, these media are not as fruitful for intellectual development as is the reflective diary, and should therefore be regarded as of secondary value.

What Are the Limitations of Extended Field Study?

Extended field study is characterized by certain manifest limitations as well as by the demonstrable values we have already analyzed. Some of these limitations, such as those of finance and scheduling, are essentially administrative in nature and therefore of secondary importance. Others among these handicaps, however are directly inherent in the technique itself. We shall take notice of both types, as follows:

1. **Expense is often prohibitive.** The added financial cost of travel and of living away from home puts extended field study beyond the reach of most students.

2. **Scheduling difficulties may be great.** The period of time which must be taken from the classroom generally makes extended field work a vacation activity, except in those progressive schools who plan their programs to permit such field study.

3. **The number of participants is necessarily restricted.** This is hardly a technique of mass education, for unless the number of students in each field group is kept small, effective work cannot be done.

4. **It is difficult to be academically precise.** The richness of the experience, the time it takes to gather materials, the business of daily living, and the distractions of strange environments limit the use of books and the production of written responses. This is as it should be, for the extensive employment of classroom techniques in the field would be a real waste of valuable opportunities. For the most part, reading and writing should be done before and after the field experience itself. Meanwhile, it is of utmost importance that students be constantly reminded that observation and immediate impressions do not exhaust a subject, and that they should continually evaluate the information and impressions which they gather. Academic procedures more precise than this can hardly be expected.

5. **There may be language and class barriers.** When field study is extended to non-English speaking countries, these two factors become significant. A student group is then largely confined to association with English-speaking people, who generally belong to professional circles or are in the upper economic strata. Thus, the fundamental characteristics of the country and its people are likely to be somewhat distorted in the students' minds.

6. **Romantic impressions are hard to avoid.** This is true, whether the locale of the field study be another local community in the United States, or another nation abroad. Low living standards and back-breaking toil often appear in the guise of picturesqueness. A traveler who spent two weeks in a Swiss Alpine valley was charmed, until he discovered the dirt and discomfort of the peasants' homes, the labor which they expended on their small fields, the meager return which it brought them, and the inbreeding which was the result of isolation. Had he stayed only one week, he would have gone away thinking of that little valley as a veritable Shangri-La.

Extended field studies, like surveys and excursions, are largely observational in nature. A survey in the local community should lead to constructive social action, but students engaged in extended field study are foreigners and guests wherever they go, and must observe the amenities which such status requires. They will be welcome as visitors only so long as they are learners. While it is true that extended field study may lead to individual or group action later on in the home community, this should not be expected nor regarded as a necessary outcome.

Extended studies of the kind indicated nearly always seek to observe people, and hence concentrate upon the study of social processes and problems in the community. But what of the physical and biological realms, the whole world of Nature in the great outdoors? Is this to be neglected as we seek more effective means of relating school and community? Surely not! Young people deeply need the wholesome experience of cooperative group living close to Nature, particularly during their childhood and adolescent days. How can this outdoor living experience be given them? Some suggestions toward that end are offered in the succeeding chapter.

SELECTED REFERENCES

Blackwell, Gordon W., "Sociological Analysis Through Field Course Procedure." *Social Forces* 19:356–65 (March, 1941). Descriptive evaluation of a summer field course in Southern Conditions, sponsored by Teachers College of Columbia University in cooperation with The Open Road, Inc.

Carley, Verna A., "Teacher Education in the Study of a Region." *Educational Method* 20:226–35 (Feb. 1941). Experiences and itinerary of 24 supervisors of student teachers who developed a Traveling Seminar to study the Tennessee River Valley at first hand.

Emmert, Wilber, "History and Geography Integrated Through a Study Travel Workshop Course." *Educational Screen* 20:386, 405 (Nov. 1941). Procedures and route followed by a teachers college field study class during a three-week special course.

Fitzgerald, J. C., "Rural School Sponsors Long Summer Journey." *Curriculum Journal* 12:213–15 (May 1941). An elementary school Travel Club took a school bus trip from Oklahoma to New York, at a total cost of $14 per pupil.

Godfrey, George H., "University Summer Cruises." *School & Society* 32:562–63 (Oct. 25, 1930). Describes the University of Oregon's summer school credit cruises to Hawaii and to Alaska.

Grodman, Edna V., "American Youth Hosteling." *Progressive Education* 17:262–69 (April 1940). A balanced account of the youth hostel movement in this country, with emphasis upon its significance for youth education and for the schools.

Jacobsen, Paul S., "Viewing Government at Work." *Journal of Higher Education* 8:7–13 (Jan. 1937). Evaluative description of Colgate University's Washington Seminar, wherein honor juniors in political science may have a semester's study-internship in a federal government bureau.

Lucke, Elmina R., "Travel Toward Economic Realities." *Progressive Education* 15:617–28 (Dec. 1938). General description of three long field trips financed by the Sloan Foundation in 1937–38, with emphasis upon the student evaluations of such study.

Michener, James A., "Teachers in the Community." *Social Studies* 32:219–21 (May 1941). Brief description of a summer school course in which secondary school teachers did field studies in three New England communities. Conclusions reached are given.

Ohio State University, College of Education, *Educational Research Bulletin* Vol. 20, No. 3 (March 12, 1941). Careful analysis of Antioch College's eight-week field course in the comparative study of two textile towns.

Olsen, Edward G., "Tours and Travel Courses for Social Studies Teachers." In Burr W. Phillips (ed.), *In-Service Growth of Social Studies Teachers:* Tenth Yearbook of the National Council for the Social Studies, Ch. VII. Cambridge, Mass.: The Council, 1939. Advantages of conducted travel, criteria for evaluating tours, major sightseeing tourist agencies, educational travel organizations, and professionally sponsored tours.

Payne, V. F., "Travel Study in Transylvania College." *School & Society* 43:265–67 (Feb. 22, 1936). Describes in some detail the physical management, faculty, institutional contacts, registrations, and credit requirements of the college's extended study tours.

Waldron, Webb, "Internes in Government." *Survey Graphic* 27:475–78 (Sept. 1938); condensed in *Reader's Digest*, September 1938. Origin, development, and program of the National Institute of Public Affairs which relates college and government through a system of federal internships for college students.

White, Langdon, "Value of Educational Travel for Students and Teachers." *Education* 52:300–03 (Jan. 1932). Informal and enthusiastic account of the Clark University Transcontinental Field Trips, describing major techniques of study and stressing intellectual and emotional values felt by a member of the group.

CHAPTER 11

School Camping

LET'S VISIT A SCHOOL CAMP

As we walk into Life Camp Raritan we see no one, and are told that the buildings before us do not house campers. Instead they are the village where campers get their daily supply of food from the camp store, deposit their pennies in the bank, get books from the library, receive tools and supplies from the repair shop, make their bed-rolls, check equipment for short camping trips, and visit the clinic for any treatment that demands the attention of the camp doctor.

Campers and counselors live together in the woods. One small group lives in three long houses that look like wind tunnels. The boys have built these themselves out of saplings. A canvas shelter provides a dining room and kitchen. Two boys are busily engaged in repairing an oven and fireplace made from rocks, clay, an old five-gallon metal ice cream freezer, and a few iron bars. We are told this task must be completed today because their tomorrow's menu calls for a meat loaf and two berry pies. Another camper, while building a small wash water dam, becomes more interested in catching salamanders and crayfish, which he has never seen before. We suspect that the wash water dam will soon turn into an aquarium.

Another group of boys is following a team of horses that is dragging a ten-foot log. We are told that the horses belong to the covered wagon group who travel about the country camping in the pastures of friendly farmers. They are back at camp now, however, and a neighboring group of campers have borrowed the horses to pull this log to their camp, where it will be sawed up and used for seats at their dining table.

Here is another group composed of boys thirteen and fourteen years old who have been at camp two weeks and are establishing a new camp site. Under the direction of their counselors they have cleared a place in the woods, erected three tepees, a dining room shelter and a temporary kitchen. A fireplace and oven have been completed and a play area cleared. A hole dug in the side of a bank near the small stream is the first step toward a refrigerator.

After a supper the boys themselves have prepared, the campers have a pow-wow around their fire. Stories are told and songs sung, but more important to this group is a discussion of what to do next day. A hike is suggested, a game, a visit to another camp, a swim in the river, a raking and cleaning up of their camp site. Finally, the group decides to do things around their camp in the morning, hike in the afternoon, visiting the other camp on the way, and to end the day with a swim in the river.

. . . As darkness overtakes the group, songs around the campfire end a day filled with new experiences—experiences these underprivileged children couldn't even dream about before, because the U.S.A. had meant a city street to them.

They won't forget the way they lived, the fun they had. They won't forget the real America.[1]

What Is "Camping"?

Camping is defined as group living close to Nature. Although the term originally assumed military significance—referring as it did to the crude, regimented living arrangements of an army in the field—it has since been broadened to denote an informal yet organized rural living experience particularly designed for city youth. For it was the growth of great cities, separating urban children from the "elementary experiences of humanity," which forced educators to find in creative outdoor camping another vital bridge to link city school instruction with country community living. Meanwhile, rural camping developed also, particularly among boy and girl scouts and members of 4–H Clubs, Future Farmers of America, and similar organizations.

How Is Camping Beneficial?

Paradoxical, indeed, is the learning situation conventionally represented by our city schools. We spend thousands or millions of dollars to build and equip large school plants which become, in primary effect, temples of vicarious learning. How constantly we continue to ignore the real world of Nature beyond and above the city—that world so pregnant with fundamental meaning, with concrete learning opportunities, with direct educational experience! Sometimes, to be sure, we have arranged Nature and Science excursions into the countryside; most of the time, however, we have merely smuggled Nature into our schools in the forms of classroom plants, aquaria, zoological exhibits, flat pictures, slides, movies, and the like—all too frequently, unrelated to our highly-graded and compartmentalized curricula, usually devoid of their normal habitat relationships, and always meager substitutes for living reality.

Furthermore, our city schools have typically remained indifferent to the non-academic purposes of education—among which is the

---

[1] W. L. Gunn, "A Weekend at Life Camp Raritan For Younger Boys." *Life Camps Memorandum,* January 15, 1942.

development of each pupil as a well-integrated personality, psychologically adjusted within his group and socially sensitive to his citizenship responsibilities in the local, regional, national, and international community areas. How can teachers exemplify for their students those essential qualities of genuine loyalty, initiative, cooperation, and the like when the environment within which they work offers minimum opportunity for vital give-and-take? Even school excursions and surveys, advantageous as they surely are, do not provide the *real* social experience of students and teachers living and working together not six hours each day, but rather twenty-four! Only extended field study and full-time camping offer this maximum experience in group living.

We talk much, these days, about the importance of teaching democracy in our schools. Yet democracy, like religion, must be lived to be understood. And it must be vividly lived and concretely experienced if it is to take definite shape and assume a depth of meaning in the lives of youth. Our students must therefore be given every possible opportunity to live, plan, and work together in a simple, dynamic, democratic environment. For this diagnosis there is no better prescription than that of the well-organized camp experience.

Camping is thus a superb bridge between school and community. Perhaps it comes closest of all our ten approaches to being a continuous, direct, and responsible personal experience with the realities of our natural environment. Camping:

1. **Provides sustained experience in democratic living and community service.** The exigencies as well as the programs of organized camping require that each camper live and work as a participating member of a democratic social group. As such, he must respect the origins, actions, and opinions of his fellows. He must share with them in responsibly deciding group policy and in executing the chosen course of action. He has every chance and stimulus to exercise personal leadership, loyal followership, initiative, self-control, good sportsmanship. He can enjoy the deep satisfaction of working with hand and mind at creative tasks in a simple, naturalistic setting. The rich and stimulating environment afforded by the camp, the matter-of-fact contact between teacher and learner, the previously unknown informality and intimacy of group living, all enhance personality growth as do the numerous community services performed. Finally, the happy anticipation with which children from the formal school approach their camping experience insures a maximum of interest, effort, and cooperation, all of which are so essential for educational growth and civic development.

2. **Fosters intimate appreciation of Nature.** Daily living close to Nature brings a close personal awareness of soil and stream, cloud and

rock, sunrise and evening star which may immeasurably enrich one's intellectual and spiritual life. The true naturalist is never a neurotic. There is profound psychology in the Biblical maxim: "The heavens declare the glory of God and the firmament showeth His handiwork."

3. Promotes health through developing outdoor interests. Physical vitality, pulsating energy, radiant good health all demand regular outdoor physical activity. Camping brings a depth of personal satisfaction with outdoor activity, and a deepened appreciation of physical fitness; together, these values become purpose which motivates enduring participation in outdoor recreational and service activities of many kinds.

Camping introduces the child to the world beyond the city streets, to the world of Nature and the world of personal work. In very real fashion, creative camping bridges the gulf between city and country, as well as that between school and community. Camping is thus a potent instrument of social democracy as well as of functional education.

What Kinds of Camping Are There?

Camping projects may best be differentiated in terms of their *primary purposes*. Although practically all camps will stress various purposes or values, it is usually possible to distinguish in each camp one fundamental purpose which subsumes all others. Perhaps the following classification will illustrate this fact. Let us note that there are at least these four chief purposes among camps:

1. Recreational—"Have Fun." This is the typical summer camp. Three kinds of activities receive major emphasis: (a) *sports* such as archery, boating, fencing, fishing, hiking, riding, shooting, swimming, tennis, and volleyball; (b) *arts and crafts* like dancing, dramatics, music, weaving, woodworking; and (c) *campcraft* including cooking, fire making, tent-pitching, use of axe and knife.

2. Health—"Develop Strength." In this group are the various welfare summer camps, including the "fresh-air" camps for underprivileged city children, special camps for cardiac and tuberculosis cases, and rest camps with light activity for convalescent adults. Both mental and physical health are stressed, with the camp program built chiefly around (a) *body-building* in terms of improved physical strength, stamina, and weight increase or reduction; (b) *social adjustment* through group experiences; and (c) *emotional stabilization* through guided living in a wholesome atmosphere.

3. Work-service—"Help People." This is the newest kind of camp in terms of basic purpose. Sometimes called a "work camp" and sometimes a "service camp," its primary goal is to develop individual character and skill through organized and socially-motivated manual labor devoted to community improvement. Such a camp thus combines elements of both service projects and work experience. In this country, the Civilian Conservation Corps Camps and the American Friends' Service Camps are typical examples of this emphasis in camping; abroad, the German youth work camps which operated under both the Weimar Republic and the Nazi regime were most prominent. Major activities in work-service camps usually center around such work projects as those of agricultural service, the construction or remodeling of buildings or public facilities, forest and soil conservation, landscaping, land reclamation, park improvement, reforestation, social settlement service, swamp draining, and trail building.

4. School Camp—"Outdoor Living." Here is the school camp, operating during the summer or the entire year, either as a strictly day camp or with overnight facilities in addition. It may be intended chiefly for elementary school children, high school pupils, college or university students, or for adults engaged in scientific research work. Among the many subjects or areas of study commonly approached in the school camp are these: art, biology, botany, camp crafts, conservation, designing, food service, foreign languages, forestry, gardening, geography, geology, nature study, physical education, remedial teaching, safety skills, stagecraft, wild life, zoology.

Camps may also be classified according to their *sponsoring agency* (commercial camp owner, public welfare organization, philanthropic individuals or groups, religious organization), their *clientele* (children, adolescents, youths, adults), their *type of program* (rigidly fixed in all details in advance, broadly prearranged, but flexible in daily program, unplanned by the staff in advance, but planned cooperatively by staff and campers from day to day) or their *duration* (day camp, week-end, full-time for a week, a month, or a season). Since at least these five variables must be considered— purpose, sponsor, clientele, program, duration—it is evident that a very wide variation in camping experiences can and does exist today. In this chapter, however, we shall confine attention to the last-mentioned of the four main types of camps, that is, to the academic or school camp. Discussing this school camp as it might well operate upon either a day-camping basis or a full-time basis, we shall stress basic principles in democratic planning and programming, rather than administration of technical details such as construction of huts and the like.

Why Inaugurate School Camping?

Since there are already thousands of private and public welfare summer camps in operation, what justification is there for proposing that school-sponsored camps be established? The question is natural, and must be answered in terms of the fact that summer camping represents a *most valuable educational development*. President Eliot of Harvard once said that organized camping is "the most significant contribution to education that America has given the world." The potential learning values inherent in adequate camping opportunities are so manifestly great that they should be available to all the children of all the people as part of their general educational experience. That is why the school camp constitutes another necessary bridge between school instruction and community living.

How May We Develop a School Camp?

Several significant cautions are in order for those schools and school systems which contemplate establishing school camps as part of their total educational problems. Among these cautions are several which merit special consideration at this point.

1. DEFINE THE PURPOSES OF SCHOOL CAMPING

Just *why* should school camps exist? Shall we use them as media for enriched academic learnings? For outdoor recreation? For physical hardening, emotional release, individual socialization? For community service and work experience? Any or all of these possible purposes are fully legitimate for the modern school camp. Until such purposes are clearly defined and delineated in the specific situation, no satisfactory camp program can be planned.

Regardless of the specific objectives sought, however, it is essential that the entire camp program be built directly around the needs, interests, and problem-purposes of young people, *not* around the academic requirements of the traditional school curriculum. It would be ridiculous and fatal to take children into the woods and there have them study in formal fashion about Eskimos or deserts, algebra or Roman history, Addison's essays or aerodynamic theories. Campers need continuous challenge to satisfy their creative interests through artistic media close to Nature, to carry forward emerging interests in the natural and social environments, to stabilize their emotional lives through new aesthetic appreciations and personal associations, to develop useful practical skills, strong and healthy bodies, and a deep respect for the simple, yet essential, requirements of individual and group living close to Nature. All this requires that the camp program be both informal and functional, and that pupil-teacher relationships be comradely and human, rather than officious and strict. If such a camp program is to be achieved, it will have to be built around the democratic and life-centered philosophy in education. As this is done, school camps can become vital laboratories for rigorously testing the validity of that philosophy in actual "real-life" outdoor situations.

2. DEVELOP ADMINISTRATIVE ARRANGEMENTS

The organization of a school camps program entails a considerable amount of preparatory work. In some localities, this work may be undertaken by an already existing bureau, within the local board of education—such as that of Health Education, Extension Activities, or Community Service. In other communities, it will be necessary for the local board to establish a school camp bureau by designating a responsible supervisor to direct and administer the proposed program. This supervisor should thereupon engage a staff of selected assistants, research workers, and clerks. The following diagram suggests such an administrative plan, with major lines of executive responsibility indicated.

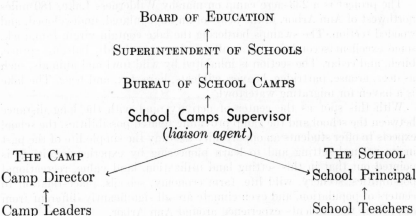

BOARD OF EDUCATION
↑
SUPERINTENDENT OF SCHOOLS
↑
BUREAU OF SCHOOL CAMPS
↑
School Camps Supervisor
(*liaison agent*)

THE CAMP   THE SCHOOL
Camp Director ←   → School Principal
↑   ↑
Camp Leaders   School Teachers

Having achieved some such administrative organization, even though on an initially experimental basis, the Camps Supervisor and his staff should then proceed to explore the many problems involved in planning and establishing a successful school camping program. Chief among those problems is that of how extensive the projected camp project should be.

3. DECIDE EXTENT OF THE CAMP PROJECT

Full-time camping experience is far superior in educational value to occasional day-time camping episodes. Best thinking stresses the great desirability of the sustained camping program since this offers whole and continuous experiencing on a round-the-clock basis in a completely new and unbroken environment.

The ideal school camp is therefore one which carries on a full-time program throughout the calendar year, and which operates in intimate coordination with the all-year community school. Is this ideal purely visionary? No. Despite its administrative difficulties, it is already receiving experimental application in some communities. The possibilities of such expansion are presaged by such camps as that at Wilderness Lake in Michigan. This camp is owned by the Ann Arbor Board of Education and is operated by the faculty and students of one junior high school of that city's public school system.

WILDERNESS LAKE CAMP

The really unique feature of the Tappan (Junior High School) program is the inclusion of a camp, owned by the Ann Arbor Board of Education, in the school program. . . .

The project is a 233-acre camp on marshy Wilderness Lake, 180 miles northwest of Ann Arbor, in the heart of an unpopulated, undeveloped, and wooded section. The swamps bordering the lake contain virgin tamarack, some excellent second-growth conifers of various kinds, balsam, spruce, birch, and cedar. The section is inhabited by wild fowl and animals, such as deer, grouse, partridge, beaver, wildcats, hare, fox, and bear. The lake is a haven for migrating waterfowl. . . .

With this spot as the center of activity, and with the long distance between the school and the camp providing related possibilities, the school expects to offer students an opportunity to study the simple life of the past in its natural setting and to learn pioneering by experiencing it. It is pointed out that in this setting land utilization, land value, recreational possibilities, scenery, wild life, farm economy, schools, place-relation to centers of population, and even climate are all significantly different from conditions the students experience around Ann Arbor.

The distance of the camp from the school building proper adds to its educational possibilities. Every step of the project, from the original purchase down to the planning of each trip to Wilderness Lake, has been one of co-operation among pupils, parents, and teachers. A group of junior-high-school pupils anticipating living together three or four days in the woods, 180 miles from home and 8 miles from the nearest town, face a possible growth situation which demands purposeful planning. Under the direction of the student council, a Lake Committee was formed for the supervision of the project.

The problem of transportation was first met by the purchase of an old truck, which was made over into a modern covered wagon by the practical arts classes. Long boxes served as seats and as lockers for supplies. Later the Parent-Teacher Association, through its interest in the project, supported the student body in the purchase of a new bus, which now provides safer transportation on each excursion, with each pupil protected by insurance.

The success or failure of each trip made to the camp depends upon previous planning by the students and teachers. This planning is not done before or after classes, but becomes the curriculum in the social-studies class, the mathematics class, the shop, and the home-economics class. There are the problems of finance, food preparation, equipment preparation, social living, and itinerary which act as centers of learning. The experiences of the trips are brought up in class in the planning of each subsequent trip. The students learn planning by planning, and the experiences of the excursion act as a real test of such preparation.

Once the students are back, the experiences carry over into the school, determining the curriculum in class after class. The work of the art classes reveals the impressions of the trip. Social-studies classes are the seat of discussion concerning the wide differences which exist within the state, the social problems of each locality, and the attempts made by the state to meet these. Experiences in group living present material for social-studies consideration. The leaders of the school, boys on probation, the bold, the timid, and those who seem to be disliked by the group have all engaged in the planning and the experiences of the excursion. In the sharing of blankets and other possessions on a trip, social differences are lost. The fellowship of teacher and pupil on the trip strengthens the guidance program back in school. A teacher becomes also a comrade to the student, and in turn the activities enable the teachers to become better acquainted with the individuals in their classes. . . .

School pride in Wilderness Lake Camp and appreciation of its inherent educational possibilities have grown with increased participation. The major part of the development of the site has been done by the students, under the guidance of faculty and parents. This endeavor has included the improvement of a shack to act as kitchen and storage room, the construction of platforms for sleeping tents, the improvement of the grounds, and the provision for sanitation. A janitor with well-drilling experience was of value in providing a driven well which would stand the state test each year.

Experiences are varied. A trip may include the study of beaver dams and abandoned log houses, conversation with old settlers, cooking in the open, building roads and bridges, a visit to a coal mine, and listening to the bobcats at night. Possibilities reveal themselves as the development of the program moves forward. A unit of work built around the project will include opportunities for writing a history and studying the geography of the area about Wilderness Lake. A general survey of the resources of the property, such as lumber, will be estimated, while written and oral expression will function around the folklore which students have discovered in their conversations with lumbermen and settlers of the region. . . .

Work at the camp is carefully organized, each student sharing responsibility for the whole undertaking and making his individual contribution to group welfare. Individual interests are cared for through nature study.

historical exploration, and similar activities, but seldom is endeavor individual. The group, either large or small, is always noticeable.

As the school sees it, the elements of importance in this camp project, as related to curriculum development, are its experience in reality, learning through doing, the fusion of departments in a study approach more natural than subject matter, opportunity for guidance through the natural situation, social integration of individuals through the solution of common problems, and the possibility for the individual's growth and experience. Such provision for individual interests and abilities automatically removes the unnatural barriers set up by the academic angles of the educational system. "Instead of training for living, students are trained by living." [2]

In larger cities where a full-time camp is not immediately feasible, it may be desirable to experiment with limited day camping. Under this plan, much less equipment and consequent expense is involved since no overnight facilities are necessary. Children come to the camp during a stated daytime period, just as they might otherwise go to school. While such "camping" may be little more than excursion picnicking, it nevertheless is far better outdoor experience than is none at all.

The individual day camp should be equipped to handle several school classes each day. Attendance at school day camps should begin with the fourth grade and extend perhaps through high school. In large cities, many such camps would have to operate simultaneously in order to permit each child to enjoy even one day per month in camp. Eventually, the program should enable each child to live at least one day out of each school week in camp. A day in camp and four days in the school building might come to characterize the new school week of the future. A glimpse of its potentialities was recently given in New York City, where a school day-camping program was in operation from 1935 to 1941 under the auspices of the Board of Education and the Works Progress Administration.

Camp sites for as many as ten camps, during one period, were made available to the schools through the cooperation of the New York State Park Commissioner. Shelters, tables, benches, storage facilities, lavatory facilities were also furnished by this source. Park maintenance workers were instructed to take an active interest in the school camps by keeping the sites and lavatories clean, disposing of garbage, and assisting in removing all hazards. Food for

[2] Harold Spears, *The Emerging High-School Curriculum*, pp. 153–57. New York: American Book Company, 1940.

lunches was prepared by the city's central kitchen, and its delivery was facilitated by the Board of Education. Food dispensing staffs and lunchroom workers were assigned to each camp by the W.P.A. Teaching staffs and clerical workers were also furnished by the W.P.A. project, the Field Activity Program, under Board of Education supervision. The Field Activity Program, through its Managing Project Supervisor and his staff, supervised and administered the whole school camps program.

In approaching the question of how extensive the school camping program ought to be, one is thus confronted at the very outset by the ancient dilemma of quality vs. quantity. Specifically speaking, the camping issue is this: Is it better to begin by providing occasional daytime camping for all the children from the beginning, and work gradually into an eventual full-time camping program for all? Or is it more desirable to start with a full-time program limited to a selected few, and thus demonstrate the real values of camping as a basis for gradual extension of this program to all the children? One alternative distributes lesser value among greater numbers and hopes to increase that value progressively; the other alternative stresses maximum value first and plans to increase coverage later. This dilemma lies at the very heart of the whole school-camp question, and must obviously be resolved in terms of each particular school's philosophy, size, and budget.

Other important questions involved in that of extent may merely be suggested as follows:

1. Should day camping be confined to the elementary school level, and full-time camps provided for high school and even college students?

2. Should school systems operating day-camp program also experiment with control groups attending a full-time camp?

3. What is a satisfactory minimum period of attendance at a full-time camp?

4. By what criteria shall students be chosen for full-time camp experience?

4. OBTAIN A CAMP SITE

A thorough survey should be made to discover whatever large tracts of land are possibly suitable for development as school camp sites. An ideal land tract would provide an interesting variety of terrain and a markedly different physical environment. No undue physical hazards should exist or be incapable of removal. Wide, grassy fields, dotted with flowers and trees, wooded areas, haunted by small forest animals and birds, a clear lake, an ocean front, a turbulent meadow stream or creek, a hilly or mountainous section —these are the physical elements which in varying proportions go to make up our ideal camp site. In addition, the site should be historically significant if possible, desirably containing within its limits some realia of early America. Finally, it must be readily accessible by common forms of transportation.

Such sites are not always hard to obtain, since they often exist adjacent to both large cities and small towns. Once a tentative choice of site has been made, the necessary legal steps should be taken to purchase or lease the specifically demarcated areas. Purely day camps may often be established in the picnic areas of publicly-owned city parks, as was done in New York City and in many other places.

5. PROVIDE EQUIPMENT AND SUPPLIES

Adequate housing is of paramount importance. Even in day camps, some sort of shelter is essential to protect campers from sudden storms. Sometimes wooden shacks, pavilions or other buildings, suitable for this purpose, already exist on the camp site; in such cases, be sure to secure written permission for their use. On day camp sites where no shelter at all exists, giant tents should be erected over raised wooden platforms located on high ground, close to drinking facilities and lavatories.

In the full-time camp the problem of shelter becomes that of providing housing proper. From the very first, full-time campers should be encouraged, under expert guidance, to plan, design, and erect their own living quarters. Many types of shelter are feasible. The most common and convenient is the ordinary tent for summer camping or the wooden hut for either summer or winter use. Using the tent or shack as the basic type of shelter, campers should be allowed to build, live in, and continually keep in repair a variety of "early men" shelters such as tree-houses, lean-to's, long-houses, tepees, or covered wagons.

Food is always a problem and an opportunity. In the full-time camp, where school campers live together for a week or more on a 24-hour basis, the problem of securing, preparing, and eating food becomes a matter of very fundamental firsthand experience. Here school campers and teachers may cooperatively develop their own menus, discuss their values with the school camp dietician, make trips to the village or camp store to purchase stocks, keep records of the costs incurred, develop ideas for improved refrigeration, build ovens and fireplaces, cook, serve and eat their own meals. Such is the ideal culinary process from the perspective of educational growth.

At the school day camp, however, feeding the campers is mainly a question of the noon meal. Each school day camp should be equipped, and its staff prepared, to distribute sufficient lunches daily. The day camping program experience in New York City suggests one practical method of solving this problem. Financially needy children were given their lunches without charge; others paid from one to eight cents for the regular camp lunch. The schools from which they came were requested to forward specific requests, with money orders to cover the paid lunches, to the central office of the camp project at least a week in advance of the projected camp visit. At the central office, the order was checked against class lists, the money was accounted for, and a copy of the order was forwarded to the city's central kitchen in Long Island City. On the day of the trip, the ordered lunches were sent in special steel containers, by auto trucks, directly to the specified day camp. With the delivery, came a list of the number of children from each school to be served at the camp. This procedure enabled the camp authorities to check the actual amount of food received each day, against the amounts ordered from the school. Thus, discrepancies were avoided, and every child had his lunch. In addition, a pint of milk was regularly served to each child, free of charge, upon his arrival at the park.

Special provision should be made in both daytime and full-time camps for adequate first-aid measures. With the cooperation of the local Board of Health, a registered nurse may be assigned to each school camp just as she would be assigned to a school building. Complete medical kits and other needed equipment should be readily available in every camp. Children displaying any symptom of illness must be referred to the nurse, at whose discretion the child might either be isolated for observation or else escorted directly home. Nurses should be required to fill out detailed reports of all accidents for referral to the local board of education.

6. Choose a Competent Camp Staff

The average classroom teacher knows little about either camping or learning by direct field experience. It is therefore not usually practicable to assemble a camp counsellor staff by the simple expedient of transferring school teachers to camp assignments. The school camp program, particularly if it is operated upon the full-time basis, requires professional leadership, trained to meet the wider responsibilities of education through camping. Teacher-education for camping education is prerequisite to successful operation of any school camp.

Such a training program for teachers as that sponsored by National Camp, Inc. needs widespread development in our nation. National Camp was established in 1940 for the purpose of training advanced leadership in the field of camping and outdoor education, to the ultimate end that camping might be incorporated as an integral part of the school curriculum. National Camp is now actively working with eighteen state teachers colleges, helping them to develop camping and outdoor education within their professional programs of teacher education. This organization is also rendering field service to a number of other teacher-educating institutions, as well as to some local communities. Especially significant are the institutes on camping and outdoor education which are conducted by National Camp upon invitation from boards of education. These institutes introduce teachers and administrators to the philosophy and methods of school camping, and provide firsthand experience in discovering teaching materials from the world outside the classroom.[3]

7. ENLIST COMMUNITY, PARENTAL, AND STUDENT SUPPORT

Special emphasis should be placed upon making the school camp an integral part of the community and school program. To this end, a meeting might be called by the school camps bureau for the purpose of establishing a community camp advisory committee composed of parents, teachers, and potential campers. This committee should discuss tentative plans for organizing a school camp program, set up objectives to be sought, and list proposals for achieving them. The following are some suggestions for enlisting the active participation of the community in the school camps program, once that program has begun to operate. These suggestions are obviously most pertinent to elementary school camping projects.

1. Send speakers with motion pictures or slides to address student assemblies about the school camp program.
2. Do the same for faculty meetings, and organize Saturday and weekend trips for teachers to typical school camps.

---

[3] For further information, write to National Camp, Life Camps, Inc., 14 West 49th St., New York 20. N. Y.

3. Explain the camping values and program at parent association meetings; invite parents to join the teacher on a camp-inspection trip.

4. Invite parents to accompany their children on school day camp excursions to see for themselves how such camps function.

5. Welcome newspaper representatives to the camps.

After a full-time camp has been actually established, a series of planned meetings with the teachers and children who will attend camp, and the latter's parents, if possible, should be arranged. At these sessions, camp objectives should be analyzed and discussed. Time schedules should be established and definite dates assigned to specific groups or classes. Extended consideration should be given to such aspects of camp preparation as the nature of the camp program and its routine, safety factor and facilities, and necessary clothing and equipment.

A week or more before the contemplated arrival of any class at camp, a camp teacher should visit the group with which he will be associated during the camping experience. This camp teacher should come prepared with films and slides featuring the high lights of the camp and camp life. His visit thus enables the camp teacher and the future campers to become acquainted with each other. It also provides an exciting, intimate opportunity for children to ask their own questions about what to expect in camp. In these ways, the preparatory program operates to give the children a good "mental set" toward the camping experience they are about to enjoy.

What Kind of Camp Program Is Desirable?

The program of the school camp must be derived from a careful activity-experience analysis of the daily camp life at its best. In short, superior camp living itself becomes the curriculum pattern. Thus the "curriculum" of the school camp will center in many broad and varying areas of camp activity such as nature exploring, healthful living, social relationships, recreation, working.

8. PLAN DAILY ACTIVITIES

In the smaller, full-time camps, the daily activities should be planned cooperatively by the campers and counselors together, as was done in Life Camp Raritan, already described. Such a program is at once simple, flexible, and decentralized. While complying with certain broad time divisions, full allowance is made for varying conditions such as new interests, unforeseen discoveries, in-clement weather, and the like. Furthermore, the camp program should be arranged on a sensible stagger basis, so that while some groups engage in sports, others will be occupied in nature activities, service projects, campcraft instruction, and so on. Such a system of rotation will enable the entire camp to run smoothly without taxing any of its facilities unduly. Many informal activities such as the following will offer worthwhile and highly interesting learning experiences:

1. Compile a scrapbook of leaves from the camp trees
2. Make leaf-prints (spatter, smoke, shadow or blue prints)
3. Construct paraffin leaf friezes
4. Arrange an exhibit showing the various uses of wood to man
5. Collect and preserve flowers, rocks, seeds, cocoons
6. Plant seeds experimentally in different types of soil
7. Discover effects of sunshine and darkness upon plant growth
8. Help build a camp nature trail
9. Identify and label camp trees and rocks
10. Make an insect collection
11. Build bird houses and baths for camp birds
12. Keep a bird diary
13. Learn to recognize birds and reproduce their calls
14. Cultivate a camp vegetable garden
15. Harvest crops on neighboring farms
16. Build a terrarium for camp nature room
17. Help destroy poison oak or ivy growth
18. Study and sketch various types of clouds
19. Analyze the plant and animal life in one cubic foot of soil
20. Plant flowers and trees to beautify the camp
21. Construct a sun-dial
22. Help conserve natural resources
23. Make a weather calendar and diary
24. Study life cycle of tree from its stump
25. Observe life cycle of a frog or a caterpillar
26. Compare different birds, nests, and eggs
27. Start fires by friction, and by flint-and-steel
28. Lay various types of fires: Indian fire, star fire, hunter's fire
29. Signal by smoke, tom-tom, heliograph
30. Pick berries and learn to recognize the edible ones
31. Knot and splice ropes
32. Construct simple pottery and bake it
33. Master use of jackknife and hand axe
34. Blaze a forest trail
35. Photograph wild life in natural habitat

For the larger day camp, with its more numerous and shifting clientele, a somewhat more formal "curriculum" may have to be planned. In such instances, the program or curriculum might well consist of two distinct sections. The first should be of general character and should yield a set of units dealing mainly with the first-hand types of experience so inherently a part of the camping picture. These units should be centered about the basic social processes already described in Chapter 3:

Utilizing natural environment	Maintaining health and safety
Appreciating the past	Improving family living
Adjusting to people	Securing education
Exchanging ideas	Meeting religious needs
Making a living	Enjoying beauty
Sharing in citizenship	Engaging in recreation

In each case these processes should be observed and analyzed as they currently operate within the camp community in relation to the larger communities outside.

9. DEVELOP UNITS OF WORK

The second part of the curricular program should be of a more specific nature, consisting of units dealing directly with the historical, geographical, physiographical, anthropological, and architectural features of the immediate camp site and vicinity. Example: a school camp located in Inwood Park, New York City, would doubtless develop units of work treating such phases of that region as these: ·

Historical—The life and story of Henry Hudson; his landing at the Tulip Tree
Geographical—The Hudson River as a tidal river; the Palisades
Physiographical—Native and imported flora and fauna
Anthropological—Inwood Indian tribes; history, organization, artifacts; typical Indian caves.
Architectural—The George Washington Bridge; the Cloisters

To discover the educationally vital aspects of each particular day camp site, it is desirable that a prior series of camp area surveys be undertaken. Research should be done on the local history, geography and natural features of each camp site. Frequent conferences and discussions should be held by all camp staffs, together with members of the school faculties participating in the school camp program. This material should then be organized into units of work and submitted to the school camps bureau for approval and distribution. The completed units, when combined with the regular school syllabi units, thus form the basis of the day camp curriculum, and the resource materials upon which both the camp teacher and the school teacher may draw in anticipating and preparing specific lessons. The following nature study outline is one sample of such a resource unit.

TREES IN SPRING

Aims:

>To teach children to recognize the common trees
>To stimulate appreciation of man's relationship to trees
>To foster awareness of the beauty and harmony in nature
>To develop a conservation viewpoint and attitude

Leading Themes:

>*Trees in Spring:* the growing buds; the flowing sap; the appearance of green leaves (chlorophyl); blossom time; the appearance of fruit; seed dispersal; return of the birds; the leafy season.
>*Trees in Myth:* the tree of good and evil; Christmas trees; the English oak; the tree of life; historic trees.
>*The Tree's Parts:* trunk, roots, branches, twigs, leaves and their functions; where trees grow; the bark, types of fissures.
>*The Leaves:* parts of the leaf; texture of leaf.
>*Types of Trees:* deciduous and evergreen trees; their various families.
>*The Forest:* what makes a forest? Type of soil found in a forest; the soil as source of food and moisture; the forest as barrier against floods; forest fires; other forest enemies such as borers, beetles, aphids, fungi; the conservation movement.
>*Value of Trees to Man:* shade and windbreak; source of wood for building and heating; soil conservation and replenishment; air purification (oxygen-carbon dioxide cycle); food bearing (fruits, dates, cocoanut, etc.); sugar; rubber; turpentine; homes for birds and smaller animals.

Activities:

1. Sketch a tree; label its various parts
2. Sketch a leaf; label its various parts
3. Make leaf-prints, spatter prints; leaf plaster casts, etc.
4. Make a collection of leaves; mount and label them
5. Make a model exhibition of the various uses of wood to men
6. Draw posters urging campers to prevent forest fires
7. Make an insect chart, showing those insects that are tree enemies
8. Draw a relief map of the U. S. showing where government reforestation is going on
9. Make box-lid constructions of a lumber camp. Show the chopping down of the trees, their hauling to the river, the saw mill, transportation of lumber to the city
10. Organize a tree guessing contest
11. Print small identification labels for trees

12. Learn how to start and extinguish a fire correctly
13. Construct a sand table model of a forest before and after a fire
14. Model in clay an exhibit showing the life of a forest ranger
15. Divide the class into two groups. Let Group A construct a model of a well-wooded forest with a model log cabin in it. Let Group B model a rocky hillside cleared of trees, with dry gullies, flooded lowland, a turbulent stream, and an abandoned shack. To emphasize the difference between the two exhibits, label: Fires cause floods, wasteful lumbering ruins forests, floods carry away top soil, floods are prevented by trees, trees break the force of the wind, forests shelter animal life.

Reference Books for Teachers:
1. Keeler, H. L., *Our Native Trees and How to Identify them*
2. Lounsberry, A., *A Guide Book to Trees*
3. Mathews, F. S., *Familiar Trees and Their Leaves*
4. Pack, C. L., *The Forest Primer*
5. Pack, C. L., *School Book of Forestry*

Books for Children:
1. Brown, E., *Woods and Fields*
2. Curtis, M. I., *Stories in Trees*
3. Meyer, Z., *Field and Tree*
4. Rogers, J. E., *Trees Every Child Should Know*

Nature exploring in the school camp is of paramount importance. The outdoor camp obviously presents numerous opportunities which are seldom available in the classroom; it permits concrete experiencing to supersede the vicarious imagining demanded by the limitations of the school building. Customary teaching procedure should therefore be reversed when in camp; that is, it should proceed from the specific to the general, rather than from the general to the specific. Instead of studying about scientifically *classified groups* of birds, trees, rocks, plants, etc., as such, the camp situation encourages examination of *whatever individual* plants, rocks, trees and birds are encountered on hikes and nature walks. Nature, from the camp perspective, thus becomes an integral aspect of living in the open and of close communion with one's fellow-creatures. All this means that a heavy responsibility devolves upon the school camp staff, all of whose instructional members should be nature specialists regardless of their other educational functions.

10. MAKE A TIME SCHEDULE

While each day camp's program will necessarily vary somewhat, the following general time schedule is suggested for daily use by such camps, particularly if the numbers of children involved are so great as to require such formal organization.

9:00 to 10:00	**Travel:** from school to camp, under school escort.
10:00 to 10:30	**Orientation:** Children arrive at school camp, are checked in, attend to wants, receive a bottle of milk, and are assigned to a definite location on the camp site. A short rest period ensues during which camp hazards are reviewed and all pertinent camp instructions are issued.
10:30 to 11:15	**Nature Exploring:** This may consist in a variety of nature activities such as nature walks, work on nature collections, gardening, and the like.
11:15 to 12:00	**Recreation:** Organized and free play; active and passive games; storytelling; calisthenics; woodcraft; hiking; singing; folk dancing.
12:00 to 12:30	**Lunch:** Classes eat together, with their teacher, as units.
12:30 to 1:00	**Rest:** Sunbathing, napping, story-telling.
1:00 to 1:45	**Unit Study:** Units of work or lessons begun in the formal school and now given concrete exposition and application.
1:45 to 2:15	**General Assembly or Town Meeting:** Group singing, dramatics, discussions, reports, announcements, evaluation, exhibitions.
2:15 to 2:30	**Afternoon Milk:** then clean-up, preparation for dismissal, rechecking of campers.
2:30	**Dismissal:** and carefully-supervised escort back to school building for final dismissal to homes.

11. BE DEMOCRATIC

There is one thing more. The desirable program of the camp school, whatever the nature of its curriculum, will be fundamentally democratic in its conceptions and operation. *Democracy,* which is a rather vague concept in the minds of many, cannot be taught on the verbal level alone. If democracy is to take shape and assume definite meaning in the lives of children and youth, it must be vividly lived and concretely experienced. If we want our children to learn democracy, we must give them continuing opportunity to live, plan, and work together in a simple, dynamic, democratic environment. It is in the free atmosphere of the well-run school camp that our children can come to feel an essential regard for each other's origins, to respect each other's opinions, to share in vital group planning, to develop a feeling of personal responsibility for group welfare, to work cooperatively together for democratically chosen ends. The opportunities for such democratic experiencing are legion in the good school camp, and in this very fact lies the ultimate significance of camping education in our democracy. If we would really build democracy into the daily behavior of our American youth, we must do so by giving our youth continuous democratic experience in meeting their problems intelligently. Nowhere are the constructive possibilities for democratic individual-school-community relationships more apparent than in the emerging school camp of tomorrow.

What Are the Limitations upon School Camping?

The great educational values of school camping, even at its best, are still limited by two factors, neither of them necessarily inherent in camping itself:

1. **Academic tradition,** which includes public opinion concerning the proper functions of schools. By long-established practice, schools are operated in schoolhouses, not in the woods. The latter is likely to be identified among the "fads and frills" and therefore not properly worthy of tax support.

2. **Societal isolation.** Although the camp group is itself a society of sorts, it is not a realistic one since the whole atmosphere is isolated from the rest of the world. Granted that such periods of retreat are exceedingly desirable at times, continuous living in such retreat is both socially and psychologically undesirable.

Isolated living, even isolated group living, is not basically satisfactory for long, particularly for older adolescents and youth. Education is a social process as well as an active one; at its best it requires constructive participation by youth in the ongoing life of adult society; education must therefore be framed in the crowded market place as well as within the deep woods. But could such actual participation in community processes be arranged for students by the school, as a part of the general education of all? Yes indeed! It could, and it should be! The next chapter will describe one method of individual education through social participation.

SELECTED REFERENCES

Allen, Hazel K., *Camps and Their Modern Administration.* New York: The Womans Press, 1930. Practical, detailed suggestions for such camp administrative matters as those of staff selection, budgeting, rates, business procedure, food and its service, sewage disposal, specifications for camp cabins, etc.

"Camping Education." *The Phi Delta Kappan* Vol. 21, No. 4 (Dec. 1938). The entire issue is devoted to the philosophy, problems and procedures of camping education.

Carr, Lowell J., and Others, *Integrating the Camp, Community, and Social Work.*

New York: Association Press, 1939. A suggestive study of actual and needed coordination between these agencies for improved education.

Character Education in the Summer Camp. New York: Association Press, 1935—. A series of annual monographs dealing with such aspects of camping as character education, guidance and supervision, setting standards, putting standards into operation, appraising the camp, frontier developments in camping, relation of camping to democracy, etc.

Extending Education. New York: National Camp, Life Camps, Inc. 14 W. 49th St., New York 20, N. Y. Occasional monographs, each treating "some significant demonstration of camping education in action." Free to school administrators and youth leaders.

Grubb, Gena, "Camping Is Education." *Journal of Health and Physical Education* 14:266–67, 288–90 (May 1943). General account of educational values, types of camps, desirable characteristics of counselors, camping activities, and recommendations for camping programs.

Hammond, Maurice, "School Camping Education." *New York State Education* 30:18–19 plus (Oct. 1942). Analyzes experiences with a democratic school camp, listing the important needs of youth and suggesting how these needs may be met through educational experience in the out-of-doors.

Johanna M. Lindlof Camp Committee for Public School Children, "Adventures in Camping." 10 Park Avenue, New York City: The Committee. Describes in some detail a school camping experiment by New York City schools, some typical camp programs, the relation of camping to democracy, an objective appraisal of the experiment, etc.

Kilpatrick, William H., "The Role of Camping in Education." *Camping Magazine* 14:14–16 (Feb. 1942); *Education Digest,* March 1942. The nature and psychology of effective learning as it proceeds in camp living.

Mason, Bernard S., *Camping and Education.* New York: The McCall Company, 1930. Through hundreds of interviews with campers, the author secured and here reports their reactions to camp problems, particularly those of character and personality development, camp leadership, types of camp program, and camping activities.

Masters, Hugh B., "A Community School Camp." *Elementary School Journal* 41:736–47 (June 1941). Three Michigan communities started in 1940 a community school camp program as an integral part of the community and school. Each community organized a camp committee, and the program of the camp was divided into a pre-camping, a camping, and a post-camping period. The program for each period is described.

National Camp, Life Camps, Inc., "Adventures in Camping Education at National Camp." 14 West 49th St., New York 20, N. Y. Illustrated description of camp life in the outdoor school for advanced leadership of camp directors and counselors.

Otto, Henry J., "A Camp Program for Children." *Educational Method* 28:287–91 (March 1939). Describes the W. K. Kellogg Foundation's camps for underprivileged children. The camps, the children, the camping objectives, and the summer and winter programs are characterized.

Pittenger, A. O., "School Camps: A Needed Postwar Development." *Curriculum Journal* 14:215–18 (May 1943); *Education Digest,* Oct. 1943. Needs and possibilities of greatly extending school camping for all pupils.

"Role of Camping in America." *Camping Magazine* Vol. 14, No. 2 (Feb. 1942). The entire issue is devoted to pertinent discussions by outstanding leaders in the field.

Sharp, Lloyd B., "Schools Go Out of Doors." *School Executive* 63:24–26 (Jan. 1944). Describes the Life Camps' philosophy of camping education.

Sharp, Lloyd B., and Ernest G. Osborne, "School and Camping." *Progressive Education* 17:236–41 (April 1940). Reviews recent developments in the relationship of schools to camping projects. Work camps are mentioned, and a few basic problems posed.

Van Til, William, "Schools and Camping." In *Toward a New Curriculum: 1944 Yearbook*, Department of Supervision and Curriculum, National Education Association, Ch. 7. Washington: The Association, 1944. Values and recent developments in educational camping, with suggested criteria by which to evaluate a school camp.

Ward, C. E., *Organized Camping and Progressive Education.* Nashville: the Author, 1935. The history of organized camping in America, a case study of one camp over a period of years, and an analysis of the camping movement in the light of modern social science and educational thinking.

CHAPTER 12

Service Projects

DEMOCRACY IN LIBERTY

The Liberty Consolidated School is pioneering new patterns of rural community living. Faculty, students and local adults are growing in their awareness of what these times mean—this century of such fundamental change that only a rethinking of basic direction can suffice. Old values are being reappraised. Education for a new kind of civilization is being evolved. Increasingly the entire group is coming to realize that social disasters such as floods, depressions, plagues, wars are only the ultimate consequence of social blindness. The civic result of all this group concern and action at Liberty Center has been startling in its boldness and in its direction. Economic democracy, for example, is becoming a very real thing in that community. A new form of group life is emerging as the community utilizes for its own improvement three great instruments of human progress:

a. **Social planning.** Social drifting is over as far as Liberty can control its destinies. Planning is based on continuous surveying, which is itself a service enterprise, carried forward by adults and children together. There is a program which constantly extends five years ahead, and in which both adults and students share as their needs and interests suggest. Examples: the adults are now chiefly concerned about problems of postwar economic adjustment; the youth, meanwhile, are measuring the effectiveness of economic production and distribution within the community at the present time. Both youth and adults consider broken doorknobs and unpainted homes as essential symptoms of social maladjustment and as direct challenges to improvement through group action, appropriately planned and carried out.

b. **Cooperative movement.** Through "Study-Action" groups a definite change of social-economic philosophy has occurred. Beginning with a single cooperative "buying club," almost all the business enterprises have now changed into cooperatives. Community cooperative enterprises now include a general store, credit union, cannery, barber shop and beauty parlor, hatchery, sweet potato curing and storage house, saw mill, filling station, grist mill and flour mill, burial society, general repair shop and garage, community pasture, apiary, group ownership of farm machinery, purchase of electric power, and insurance protection. The growth of all these cooperatives has been gradual. Organization has kept pace with expansion, and no one is required to give undue time to these enterprises which are giving new, profound meaning to Liberty Center, and even to the whole concept of democracy itself. The community sees the relationship between giant reservoirs of capital autocratically controlled, political chicanery, and social disaster. The primary motivating force behind the development of these cooperative enterprises is therefore not the saving of money through patronage dividends, but rather the group desire to establish Liberty Center as one local unit in a cooperative commonwealth.

c. **Functional education.** Doing and thinking are recognized as twin aspects of the growth process. Interest is the only motivating force utilized, and the interrelatedness of individual and social interests is fully understood. Problem solving in real situations is the occasion for thinking. Facts are the instruments of such thought. But facts, ideas, effort, discipline are all secondary to the function of defining and solving individual and group problems. Growth is the natural consequence of hopefully attacking and eventually solving one felt problem after another. The rewards of success are courage, resourcefulness, understanding. Temporary failures teach modesty, sobriety, tolerance. Such is the educational philosophy at Liberty Center.

Community-wide utilization of these three social instruments—planning, cooperatives, functional education—has led to a great variety of service projects in the local community. Several illustrations follow:

In each home, each church, each school room there is a copy of Liberty Center's five-year plan. Regular public meetings are held to consider aspects of that program, such as developing the community-owned forest, improving the community layout, bettering the water supply, creating a folk museum and a museum of science to dramatize social changes, building a recreation center, organizing cooperatives.

The recommendations of a state forester were followed in thinning, planting, pruning and harvesting the community forest. This forest is now a model which visitors from considerable distances come to see. The school shop is abundantly supplied with lumber from the 900-acre tract which guards the town's water supply. Proper care of this area has already raised the low point in the water flow several per cent.

A 9 by 12 foot map has been made of Liberty Center. This map has upon it photographs of all the buildings in the community, photographs which were taken, developed, and printed by the students. There is also a map of Liberty as it might become, showing areas desirable for industry, commerce, social life (including churches, school, health center, etc.) and residences. Each year new pictures are made as the buildings are renovated or replaced. The students help directly in effecting many of these improvements.

The school has taken on such continuing service projects as (a) building a health center, which includes a special reading room with books supplied by the traveling bookmobile, (b) gathering data for the ongoing community survey, (c) studying the stock of the cooperative store to recommend changes of brands, local production to replace purchased goods, or discontinuance of items such as most patent medicines, (d) direct attack upon emergency situations wherein the services of school pupils would be helpful.

It is realized in Liberty Center that many of these projects are similar to those engaged in by other functional schools. The essential difference, however, lies in the deep purpose which motivates every effort: that of learning through personal experience how man can move into tomorrow as master and not servant of the machines his hand and mind have made.

What Are "Service Projects"?

Service projects are cooperative group activities organized and carried out by students as specific contributions to civic welfare. Being primarily *civic* in both purpose and motivation, such projects never include financial remuneration although they always provide for deep personal satisfactions of other kinds. Involving individual activity of an integrated mental-physical-emotional-spiritual nature, service projects eventuate in genuine educational value to the student as well as in significant social value to the community.

Service projects repay the learner-doer by a no less elevated reward than the identification of self with group in solving social problems. This would be distinctive education in any historic period, but in our era it is socially imperative that genuine service activities be widely developed to attack the source of our civic confusion. That confusion is now so great that mere "busywork" becomes an even more dangerous waste of time and effort. Simply to follow blindly accepted patterns of "spectator education," or to study uncritically the social processes which have led to disaster, is clear indication of failure to comprehend the essential social need of our times.

Why Are Service Projects Advantageous?

Service projects lift education from the dull routine of leading each generation in the footsteps of its predecessor to a deadly earnest yet joyous adventure in cooperative social improvement. Service project values are most clearly perceptible among youth who have sensed the transition crisis of our times and are devoting themselves to local community betterment, work camps, to improving intercultural relations, to building cooperatives, to fostering international organization, to other progressive movements. Thus service projects:

1. **Give hope and courage** to youth who are in danger of demoralizing frustration. They promote change from despair at the thought of a "world like a hog trough already too full of feet," to an eager desire to help build,

for all men, that kind of truly civilized community which this earth could become.

2. Effect definite social improvements and thereby enable youth to contribute in significant fashion to the social progress of his group.

3. Promote status for youth by enabling adults of the community to understand and approve the contributions being made by youth to the common civic welfare. Such social recognition is deeply prized, for it is among the most desired of all achievements during the adolescent period.

4. Stimulate all-around growth and development of the students, since the projects undertaken are of such nature as to necessitate sustained and integrated effort of intellect, emotions, and physique.

5. Create more functional patterns of education. Each century, each generation, we have outgrown our previously prevailing notions about formal education. Just as our scientific researches into the psychology of the learning process moved us, during the 1920's, from support of the traditional school to that of the activity school, so our scientific insights into the sociological nature of human relationships are now drawing us forward to uphold the community, life-centered school.

6. Help to make world citizens out of provincial youngsters because they lift the imagination from petty matters of the moment to the enduring life concerns of all peoples everywhere.

Thus do service projects advance education to the social frontiers in a manner so constructive that the learner grows in character, personality, insights, and civic skills through actual participation in the slow creation of world sanity, security, and civilization.

What Are the Types of Service Project?

Service projects may include a tremendous range of discrete activities as even a quick perusal of Hanna's *Youth Serves the Community*[1] and Mitchell's *Youth Has a Part to Play*[2] will indicate. Yet for practical purposes, most of these varied activities can properly be classified into one of three general categories, depending in each case upon the ultimate objective sought. These three categories —which are by no means mutually exclusive since they represent dominant emphases only—may be characterized as follows:

Civic Improvement Projects: Activities of this type include such diverse general contributions to community welfare as those of area surveying, exterminating rats, revising bicycle ordinances, having a street closed for play hours, helping initiate a housing project, developing urban

---

[1] Paul R. Hanna and Research Staff, *Youth Serves the Community*. New York: Appleton-Century, 1936.

[2] Morris R. Mitchell and Others, *Youth Has a Part to Play*. Progressive Education Association Service Center Pamphlet 6.

recreation centers, mapping a town for expected growth, planting a community forest, aiding in local beautification. All such projects are intended to improve the functioning of community processes through social planning for future development, as well as for present needs.

Consumer Welfare Projects: Protection of the ultimate consumer is the basic goal toward which activities of this group are directed. Stress, therefore, falls upon such closely related contributions as these: insuring pupils against their breakage of cafeteria dishes, organizing student buying clubs for the more economical purchase of supplies by many local fraternities jointly, studying and encouraging the extension of noncommercial rural electrification lines, establishing cooperative stores in schools, colleges, and local communities, developing credit unions, furthering community understanding of the cooperative movement as the social basis for economic democracy in an age of potential material abundance.

Scientific Thinking Projects: Here are elementary research activities designed to promote the habit of rigorous and objective thinking about all community elements—physical setting, population, social processes and problems, agencies and organization. Research projects ultimately intended for public enlightenment may vary from experiments in the manufacture of inexpensive cosmetics or wall paints, to gathering folk music, to analyzing wastage of natural resources, to assembling the scientific conclusions concerning racial differences and similarities. Such scientific enterprises seek to extend the scientific way of thinking, to arouse admiration for the great contributions of the scientific mind in all areas of living, and to deepen popular awareness of the threat to civilization which arises primarily from the fact that man's social institutions lag far behind his technical achievements. And it is understood that great concepts such as these are not likely to become effective guides to social action unless one basic requirement is met: that the teachers themselves develop confidence that scientific thinkers are more likely to be produced through a continuously guided series of research projects than by any formalized, subject-matter approach. The first approach nurtures creativity and in so doing, fosters practical attitudes and skills while teaching needed factual knowledge. The second approach, beginning and ending with knowledge *per se*, often dulls the imagination, subdues the emotional drive to serve through discovery, and fails to stimulate confidence in one's own ability to pioneer.

Service projects are thus varied enough to include all the elements of any truly functional program of education. Being deeply concerned with human society and its progressive improvement, they tend to further consciously the three great and relatively new instruments of social progress: civic planning, cooperative organization, and functional education.

How May We Develop Successful Service Projects?

The purposes, curricula, and methods of our schools inevitably reflect our profit-seeking social order as well as our cloistered academic tradition. Both philosophies are challenged by the basic orientation of the service project which stresses voluntary group action outside the classroom to help meet existing human needs in times of peace as in time of war. Schools today confront no greater obligation than to promote this truly democratic spirit which is so desperately needed in society at large as well as within the school itself. Yet it is wise to proceed slowly and with caution; indeed, it is almost necessary that an entire school move toward the service-project orientation, for if one teacher proceeds alone he will be regarded as an eccentric by many of his colleagues and students, as well as by the community. Gradual experimentation with service projects is advisable, with full discussion always carried on in faculty meetings and informally elsewhere.

Service projects are most apt to become a vital part of the school program if the teachers and administrators of the school identify themselves with the constructive forces of the community. Even by joining luncheon clubs and engaging in other conventional social activities, teachers are sure to bring more freshness of purpose and perspective to the classroom. Today there are newer moving forces: groups interested in promoting better interracial relations, the co-operative movement, postwar planning, internationalism, decentralism, local, regional, national, and world planning. Educators should be leaders in such groups, and where no such groups now exist, should lead in stimulating local thinking along such lines to the end that a "current of true and fresh ideas" may hasten right transition in these troubled times.

The first essential therefore is that the teacher himself live constantly in an atmosphere of responsible social participation. Most teachers are the product of generations of academic inbreeding. Many are teachers, despite the low salaries, because teaching offers institutional protection against the hazards of most other careers. Too many of us teach for immediate and selfish reasons solely, rather than from long-range professional and social considerations. Under such circumstances, classroom instruction is not likely to be very influential.

Of course there are limitations upon student participation in social processes and problems. There are handicaps of physical strength and of mental and emotional immaturity, but we are often apt to exaggerate these limitations. Student immaturity, for example, has too often been made the excuse for not meeting a profound professional responsibility. Because children cannot participate completely, cannot wholly solve a problem, is no reason for their not taking such part as they rightly can. Psychologists know that the vivid imagination of the normal child easily carries his emotional participation far beyond the confines of the real. A child may have placed one brick in a wall and thereafter sincerely believed that he had, with some help, built the entire structure. Such a child is not dishonest, he is merely the victim and the rich possessor of an alert imagination. The child who is never introduced to social-civic problems until he is relatively mature is not likely then to develop the desired breadth of vision and social sensitivity.

Guided social participation is the essence of true educational method. Schoolroom walls will largely melt away, home and school will work together, and student-community enterprises will function much more fruitfully when we teachers come to view education as broadly as it must be conceived if it is to meet the challenge of its enormous responsibilities in and for the postwar world.

Toward that end, it is essential that the service projects undertaken by the school be planned, executed, and evaluated with extreme care. There is no surer way to discredit the newly emergent life-centered educational philosophy among colleagues, students, and townspeople generally than to undertake and fail in some hastily and ill-planned community service project. As with all other vital educational techniques, the service project must be administered with care and discretion.

Planning the Service Project

Cooperative group discussion, analysis of proposals, and democratic planning of policy is the essential procedure to be followed in undertaking the service project. Certain major steps and decisions should thus be taken; let us therefore examine each of them briefly.

1. DISCOVER THE SOCIAL NEED

Exhortation to social action is the wrong approach. To be sure, the teacher may invite his students to join in civic projects in which he is already active—in planning for slum clearance, street improvement, smoke nuisance abatement, malarial control, interreligious fellowship, and the like. But, for the most part, the students should discover their own service projects through a growing personal awareness of social needs as they actually exist. In some communities real courage is required to plumb the open or secret economic greed and political chicanery. Much can be done, however, if a constructive enthusiasm is maintained, and if emphasis is constantly placed upon the importance of positive and democratic civic responsibility by all good citizens, including the school students. This psychological atmosphere, surrounding the students' discovery of social needs, should enable them to sense right directions, kindle group purpose, and act with responsible vigor.

2. Select the Project

If the projected experience is to be of maximum educational and civic value, it must be selected with considerable care. Children can never experience more than a sampling of possible service projects; it is therefore highly desirable that those chosen serve also as types for interpreting broad areas of human concern. They should also be selected with reference to safety, and to the willingness of the community to cooperate in carrying forward the project. Furthermore, the enterprise chosen should be one which will insure wholesome relationships among all its participants, including adults in and outside of the school, as well as students. Too often a project may nurture a condescending attitude, or even an arrogance, which destroys rather than fosters a sense of responsible comradeship in facing mutual problems.

It is evident that all proposed service projects must be appraised in terms of specific criteria if their educational and civic quality is to be maximally assured. Because this point is so highly important, the standards developed in *Youth Serves the Community* are now reproduced in full for the guidance of those without access to that excellent volume.[3]

Individual Educational Criteria

1. The youth who participate in a project must sense its social significance. No matter how worthy the project may be from a social utilitarian standpoint, unless those engaged in it appreciate that their effort in cooperation with others will contribute to the improvement of some aspect of community life, much of the educational value is lost. On the other hand, no project should be termed *socially useful* if its major purpose is primarily a stunt to enhance the prestige of the adult leader or the organization, or to raise funds for some objective beyond the concern of the children or youth. A project lacking social significance in these respects should not be saddled on young people with the exhortation

---

[3] *Op. cit.*, pp. 35–40.

to participate, because such practice dulls the sensitivity of youth to the finer characteristics of enterprises which are truly socially useful.

2. Youth must have a part in planning the project. In a democracy, probably no learnings are more significant than those which result from social experiences in which a group need is faced cooperatively, analyzed, possible solutions projected, tentative plans agreed upon, and the task eventually culminated. If we would prepare our youth to take over the responsibilities of a democratic way of life, such experiences at collective planning are indispensable. Whenever a project is planned in broad-outline and/or in detail by the adult leader, two indiscretions have been committed: (a) the project may never appear to have significance to the young people, and their efforts will undoubtedly be half-hearted and the outcomes disappointing; and (b) the adult deprives youth of the most important learnings that will come with participation in the planning phases of the enterprise. It seems trite (but probably a necessary precaution) to state, however, that this must not be interpreted as implying that children and youth alone should plan the project; it is clear that the more mature experience of the adult leader must contribute to the formulation of the plan, but this contribution should be made in a democratic manner of sharing decisions.

3. Youth must have some sporting chance of carrying the project proposed through to more or less successful conclusion. Young people should undertake socially-useful work within the range of their physical strength and endurance. Youth must confine its projects to realms where their social maturity permits success rather than predicates failure. No task should be planned which is clearly beyond their capabilities. It must be said, however, that this criterion is more restrictive than constructive in the hands of leaders who are overconservative or lacking in vision, or who are looking for excuses to keep young people from attempting to improve conditions from which the leaders profit at the expense of the general welfare. If the project is possible from the standpoint of the physical materials and physical power to carry it out (an illustration might be the elimination of traffic hazards at a street corner where children's lives are in danger), and the only inhibiting factors are the inertia or corruption of the social, economic, or political arrangements and institutions, then no better learning situation can be staged than to have young people fail to achieve an obviously needed improvement and strikingly discover the reasons why they were foredoomed to failure. In such a failure, it is clear that the ground has been cultivated for future success in that an intimate knowledge of the forces retarding social progress must be included in any plan for betterment.

4. Youth must accept the responsibility for success or failure of a project. Any vital learning experience is incomplete until the plan and its execution have been evaluated in terms of successes and/or failures in the social environment. Whenever children and youth are denied this culminating experience by the leaders of a project, they have been allowed to "prepare the food, but not to taste it." So often the adult teacher will shield the young when the project fails or when reactionary forces in the community object to having children and youth engage in constructive work which may undermine their vested privileges. Of course, the leader has the responsibility of protecting the mental and emotional stability of those in his care, but in the long run, more harm is often done by shielding than could possibly be done by facing frustration frankly and intelligently and learning how to cope with it. Probably more general, however, is the situation in which the project is eminently successful and wide acclaim is given it. The leader who is conscious of the educational values to the young will give all the credit where it is due. If the satisfaction that comes from social approval of work which betters the social situation will lead on to more activity of the same worthy nature, then the wise leader will be jealous that his young co-workers share fully that satisfaction with him.

5. **Youth must actually grow in total personality as a result of the work undertaken.** Projects directed toward socially-useful work offer a host of avenues to the enrichment of the intellectual, social, emotional, and physical personality. Any comprehensive planning of a project must involve such intellectual pursuits as research into the (a) origin of the problem, and (b) how costly in time, materials, and human effort the accomplishment might be, etc. In addition, many projects entail experimentations of a wide range; a project to improve the agricultural practices would involve laboratory and seed-plot experiments in seed treatment, soil content, fertilizers, etc. A project may include much study and creative effort in the arts; a landscaping project will necessitate familiarity with many art principles and techniques. Similarly, each project must be explored to the fullest in order that (a) the best plan may result from wide study and experimentation, and (b) the young will have the enriching experiences of "study" in terms of problem-solving. No experiences can be any more significant than the opportunities utilized to enrich broadly that indefinable thing we know as *personality*. No project can be justified on its contribution to social welfare alone; unless the young who participate in the work gain in personality, then the project might well be classified as exploitation of youth.

Significant Social Value Criteria

1. **Any project must culminate in the actual improvement of living in the community.** Projects are not completed when a "proposal" is formulated and then carefully filed in the archives. Only when proposals are effective in changing the environment for the better can they be considered satisfactory from a pragmatic viewpoint. Whenever a project terminates in a plan which is not carried through to application, there is an unfortunate hiatus between thought and action. This hiatus, if continually repeated in situation after situation, may well lead to the development of habits of social inertia and general ineffectuality in applying knowledge to human progress. Further, the world is so desperately in need of *action* for improvement that intelligent leadership of the young cannot permit the youthful energies to be dulled by endless *discussion* about action.

2. Projects must clearly be an obligation of youth as well as adulthood. Many areas of social living are the direct concern of children and youth because these areas vitally affect their well-being. There are, however, aspects of community life needing improvement which are unquestionably the responsibility of adults, and youth should not be made responsible for righting these wrongs or for the unpleasant task of cleaning up social festers which adults would like to leave to more eager hands. If the fault for social inadequacy lies entirely on adult shoulders, there is a salutory effect in having to remedy the situation ourselves. This criterion must not be interpreted too narrowly, however. Throughout this volume we are urging projects in which all members of the community—children, as well as youth and adults—together tackle a problem of cooperatively improving living. In such a conception of a project, naturally the adults would perform those duties that are clearly their responsibility, and the young would find their field of contribution in tasks appropriate to their maturity and ability.

3. In so far as possible, projects must get at the basic problems of improving social welfare. Projects must not contribute to the further entrenchment of a social practice which is obviously evil. As an illustration: a project of providing Thanksgiving baskets for the poor, while lessening suffering for the moment, does not get at the root of the evil—the inadequate income of the majority of our families. Not only may the Thanksgiving-baskets-for-the-poor type of project contribute to the notion that we should hold a class of citizens in economic slavery in order that those of us who are more fortunate may annually have the smug satisfaction of "sharing" but, in addition, time and energy given to such superficial betterment could much more effectively be spent in getting at the basic inhibiting influences which perpetuate a scarcity economy in the midst of abundance. Probably no other criterion in the social category is more often violated by project leaders who intend to do the best possible thing for youth and society, but fail to see that the project really contributes little even to the immediate amelioration of the evil and may even further crystallize it. If project leaders would guide the planning phases of projects more carefully and thoroughly and, through research and experimentation, drive the roots to deeper soil, many projects which have been insignificant *might* be made significant in community improvement.

3. Gain Background and Insight

Most of the specific suggestions already advanced in Chapters 4 through 9 are fully applicable as the group seeks preliminary orientation to its chosen project area. Without amplification in this section, therefore, let us simply summarize the essential steps which may be taken in gaining the requisite information and appreciations necessary to the development of a successful service project:

a. **Utilize documentary materials** as a primary source of data concerning the problem-area chosen.

b. Employ relevant audio-visual aids to dramatize the need and to illustrate significant approaches to it already made in this or other communities.

c. Invite resource visitors to explain the need and the problem, and to suggest possible courses of action toward solution.

d. Arrange interviews to gather data and suggestions, advice and aid, and to enlist cooperation and support of key adults.

e. Conduct field trips to develop common insight and to stimulate group purpose.

f. Make surveys to assemble data, define and refine the problem, and then to evaluate results after the service project is completed.

In using any of these varied approaches, it is essential that they always be organized and carried forward with the special needs of the service project foremost in mind. For the goal now sought is the successful completion of the chosen project, and all the other "bridges between school and community" are, in this instance, merely means to that end. Their use is now warranted only to the extent in which they do actually develop intellectual, emotional, and ethical background for the selected service project itself.

4. CLEAR WITH ADMINISTRATION

The teacher who senses a social cause in some community problem—such as mosquito control, or the need to demolish an adjoining "lung-block" to gain space for a playground—should always approach his school administrator before engaging in any general discussion of the project. This precaution is professionally courteous, and also avoids the possibility of jealousy at headquarters, of conflict or overlapping of plans among various teachers, and of the embarrassing necessity of retracting, should the proposed plan prove administratively unfeasible. Besides avoiding these negative possibilities, preliminary consultation with the administrative officer will often result in the project receiving his full support from the very outset.

5. ORGANIZE THE CLASS

Effective group organization now becomes essential. In stimulating such organization, the astute teacher will take steps as follows:

a. Sense student interests. Assuming that the project which the teacher has in mind is appropriate for school sponsorship, he should be able to find, in the diverse interests of the boys and girls, some adequate opportunity to lead them in the desired direction. But in so leading, the teacher should not pretend merely to follow the students' interests when he is actually guiding the group thinking toward some preconceived plan or program. To do that is to be fundamentally dishonest. The desirable alternative is for teacher and students together to recognize the importance of having proposals presented for group analysis, and then to work together for the improvement of those proposals. Good rapport between instructor and class is the heart of this problem; where it exists it avoids the antinomy of either domination from above or of sentimental overemphasis upon the validity of students' suggestions.

b. Condition the psychological atmosphere. Pupil attitudes are highly responsive to environmental changes. The teacher can therefore do much to direct students' feelings and expressions of interests by a judicious choice and use of pictures, charts, posters, books, slides, recordings, radio programs, motion pictures, scientific exhibits, and the like.

c. Observe conditions of effective organization. Whatever specific plans are made, the procedure followed should always be:

(1) *Democratic:* Because our schools have so long patterned after the autocratic European systems, it is now crucially important that we deliberately bring America's finest political tradition into our everyday classroom planning.

(2) *Efficient:* Political democracy will not endure in the machine age unless we can adapt its basic concept to the rational demands of our technical era. Technology is efficient precisely because it recognizes and utilizes special talents and training. These qualities are not identified by a system of selection based upon popularity won through emotional oratory, appeal to prejudice, joviality, or pre-election generosity. In the scientific world, it is results that count, and superior results are not expected from people of inferior ability or education. We should lead our students to recognize this principle, to apply it in the world of human relationships, and therefore to choose democratic leaders in terms of such factors as natural aptitude, special training, demonstrated efficiency, motives of social service, ability to stimulate cooperation, loyalty to the highest ideals of human brotherhood, and the like.

(3) *Creative:* Designated leaders and committees should be allowed as much initiative and responsibility as discretion will permit. The teacher who is changing from more traditional forms of instruction to the use of service projects must remember that he can no longer expect to dominate in every assignment and to check up on every achievement. His older responsibility for these items must now be gradually and increasingly shared with the students. In the best service project programs, pupils are often working on projects located blocks or miles away from the school. The sharing of responsibility—which is so strong a characteristic of the service project type of teaching—actually releases the teacher from much burdensome detail in working with large numbers, and makes possible far more individual attention where guidance is especially needed. Thus, service projects may be carried on with as great a number of students as is customary in more formal methods.

6. Approach Community Leaders

Real service projects deal with community problems and thereby involve community sensibilities. For this reason, let it be said frankly that service projects may sometimes involve an element of social danger. But this danger must be faced and not escaped, else we shall accumulate such unsolved social problems as will bring increasing suffering and perhaps eventual destruction in civil strife and renewed international conflict.

Our community leaders are often far from receptive to proffered aid from schools. Sometimes they fear intelligent scrutiny of their inefficiency, their dishonesty, or both. Sometimes they are merely contemptuous of teachers for their academic-mindedness, and of students for their immaturity. Yet thousands of American teachers are shouldering civic responsibilities, and doing so with public gratitude. In hundreds of school systems, children are winning the increased respect of adults by the initiative they show, by the hard work they are eager to do, and above all, by their demonstrated capacity to understand civic problems and to act upon them constructively. In the light of extended experience, however, we can say that unless community leaders are first approached and their confidence gained, most ambitious service projects will probably be doomed to failure. Jealous officials can find many quiet ways to discredit and thwart the best-planned service project program. Conversely, however, community leaders whose cooperation is sincerely sought, will often do much to smooth the way and promote the success of projects in which they are interested.

1. Work Through Community Groups

To the parents through the children, and directly by personal contacts, the teacher should enlist the support of such organizations as parent-teacher associations, civic clubs, churches, newspapers, and the like. The service project should always be the community's project, never the teacher's nor even the school's. Let the teacher be not too greatly concerned about personal credit for achievements made; far more will be accomplished if major credit is attributed to community leaders and organizations who have given their aid. But be sure that the students know their successes have been appreciated, and that even their mistakes were considered to be fruitful aspects of worthwhile learning.

8. Secure Needed Supplies

Service projects often require some technical equipment and supplies. The group must therefore think ahead and arrange for the procurement of such materials. Example: red oxide of iron (at five cents a pound) mixed with burnt motor oil was found to be a suitable material for painting homes and barns in a rural area where many of the buildings had had no protective covering whatever. Again: to change the quality of native nut trees to the most superior varieties calls for a few simple tools and such other items as strips of linen, beeswax, rosin, and linseed oil. Unless such materials are made available at the needed time, student interest may lag or even die. In a sense, then, the service project must be planned to operate somewhat on an assembly line basis; all necessary tools and supplies should assuredly be made available at the exact time they become necessary in the progress of the project.

9. Plan Essential Safeguards

Necessary physical safeguards depend largely on the type and location of the service project undertaken. When fighting forest fires in the Rockies, for example, adequate precautions must be taken against injury from the fire, against the fever tick, and against poisonous snakes. By contrast, the safeguards necessary to the construction of toys for the community's lending library would be simple. In any case, it is usually desirable for the teacher or administrator to contact the parents of elementary and high school students to discover in advance the existence of any possible parental objections. Sometimes parents ignored at such times have later injected emotionalized barriers into a project even after it has been well advanced.

The group should also be sure to ascertain the existence of any legal barriers to any aspect of the proposed project. If this is not done, the group may unwittingly violate the law—as one class did when it trucked an apiary across a state line and thereby incurred the possibility of a $500 fine and the imprisonment of the group's leader for six months. Legal barriers are not usually obscure, but in case they are, it is better to be informed in advance rather than in retrospect.

Executing the Service Project

No definite line should divide the preparatory from the executing aspect of the service project, for these two aspects are merely progressive phases of one ongoing process. Yet it is important, when appropriate, to move out of the planning and into the practicing stage, else the project itself will never mature. In this second stage also there are certain fundamental procedures which may well be followed.

10. Give Definite Initial Direction

Many service projects have failed because of the seeming lack of responsiveness among the pupils. A class may show great interest in planning a project, but when the actual work in the field begins, may lapse into a disappointing indifference. Sample: a group has decided to repair a pig house and then to raise pigs to get funds to give to the Red Cross. The pigs have been purchased with money borrowed from the school's credit union. The necessary carpenter tools and the whitewash ingredients are all on hand. Students are aglow with anticipation, but when they get to the scene of supposed activity there is only indifference; the children fool around chasing one another, while conversation is devoted to quite irrelevant affairs. Teacher urging does no good.

What is the trouble? Many factors may be in the picture, but among them all, there is probably one of dominant influence: the pupils have planned their general policies well enough, but they have not adequately planned their *precise techniques*. Perhaps none of them have mixed even lime with water to make whitewash, to say nothing of the more complicated formula involving also soap and alum. They may never have seen a fence built, nor helped to build one themselves. And so with troughs, storage bins, and other aspects of the project chosen—they do not know precisely where to begin or how to start. Under such circumstances, preliminary planning should have provided for very specific initial directions, both for the exact sub-jobs to be done and for the particular pupils who were to do them. With such definite initial direction, otherwise reluctant groups have been known to grow greatly in both self-direction and technical competence.

11. Let Emotional Satisfactions Attend Each Step

The first law of learning is that activities which bring personal satisfaction tend to be both repeated and fixated thereby. Nowhere is this psychological principle more apparent than in the development of genuinely successful service projects. Specimen: In one rural school, long given to formal instruction, a propagating house for ornamental shrubbery was developed upon the basis of textbook teaching of botany. Now, a score of years later, that school is enjoying the use of its third propagating house. Its nursery covers three acres. Fifteen hundred shrubs beautify the school grounds, and a half million ornamentals add to the charm of nearly every home within a six-mile radius. The example of this project has spread to fifteen or more schools within that state, and even to schools in other states.

The real success of this initial botanical service project was due to the fact that from its very inception, care was taken to see that each step in its progressive development brought emotional satisfaction to the pupils and the patrons of that school. This fundamental satisfaction led to widespread community approval, and as a consequence dozens of other service projects followed—a cooperative hatchery, cooperative curb market, student-built gymnasium and baseball park, school apiary, pupil-operated public library, and the like. School and community approval of such projects was further stimulated by the judicious use of public meetings wherein such activities were discussed, and the point was always made that from service projects like these the students were constantly achieving highly worthwhile learning values. Through such precautions, community support was assured, and no serious criticism has ever been encountered in that area because of the now-phenomenal extension of service project enterprises in the school.

12. BE CONSIDERATE OF OTHER TEACHERS

Administratively it is important that the principal and all affected teachers know of any disruption to the regular program which the projected service project will occasion. In many schools, a majority of the faculty have joined in coalition against a minority who favored service projects, largely because their classroom teaching of the students involved had been often interrupted with little apparent concern. We must never forget that the difference between the routine procedures of formal schooling and the vigorous challenge of learning through social action is so basic that the utmost tact, patience, and unfailing goodwill must ever be observed by those engaged in service project work.

13. KEEP PERMANENT RECORDS

Sufficient records should be kept to enable teacher and students to review their course of effort and to evaluate it at its conclusion. Such records should be as complete as necessary to enable one group to profit from a previous group's experience. Somehow, a nice balance must be maintained between the extremes of keeping no written records and keeping too many. The former course fails to make adequate provisions for the later sharing of experience with other groups; the latter becomes burdensome and frequently degenerates into an end in itself. An illustration of the latter extreme: a college seminar class spent a year making an exhaustive and exhausting survey of a community; when it finished the task, its members had no strength or enthusiasm left for directing an attack upon the community needs thus revealed. The written report of its findings was filed away in a bookcase, whereupon the discovery was made of the report from an exactly similar survey made twenty-five years before, and which revealed almost identically the same problems about which neither group had done anything. Records, like service projects themselves, should be guides to action, not ends in themselves.

14. SECURE APPROPRIATE PUBLICITY

Publicity is important and necessary, but it should be sought and used for constructive educational purposes, never as an agency of personality projection or of student exploitation. It is unworthy of the great purposes of community-centered education for personally aspiring teachers or administrators to seek advancement of their own status by advertising their small part in this democratic movement for social betterment. Publicity can and should be used only as an educational means of acquainting the general public with the purposes, plans, procedures, findings, and activities of the projects undertaken, and to interpret fairly the whole philosophy of the modern, life-centered school.

Interpreting the Service Project Experience

If greatest educational growth is to occur and thereby validate the first purpose of the service project, it is essential that the whole experience be critically evaluated. This evaluation will be continuous throughout the project, but it should also serve as final interpretation of it. In planning this critical summary, there are three areas which should surely be examined with care. The first two relate to the fundamental objectives of the service project technique itself; the last is concerned with using the present procedural experience as a basis for planned improvement in the future.

15. Identify the Learning Results Achieved

There is real danger that many of the nonintellectual learnings inherent in the service project may go unrecognized, even by the teacher. The notions of external discipline and of learning as a dull chore are so deeply ingrained in our consciousness that it is hard for many to comprehend how enjoyable the most wholesome growth experiences can and should be. Teachers and students alike need to realize that it is educationally as important that they learn to work together, to integrate their thinking, to compromise their differences, to develop social sensitivity, and the like as it is that they acquire an increasing fund of factual information. A helpful way of clarifying the actuality of such varied growth through service projects is through recounting the problems met and solved, or met and still unsolved. For true development is the by-product of a succession of problems constructively met with all the intellectual, emotional, spiritual, and physical resources at one's command.

16. Summarize the Social Contribution

The second major purpose of service projects, it will be recalled, is to advance community welfare. Just how is the community now a better place in which to live because this particular project has been completed? To what extent and in what manner has this project actually penetrated into a real civic defect, rather than merely ameliorated a surface symptom? Thoughtful group consideration of such queries as these is another essential aspect of the final evaluative process.

17. Analyze the Group's Procedure

Evaluation should now go one step further to include a critical analysis of the part played by each participant in the group enterprise. While this process is sometimes carried to such an extreme that the students become too self-conscious about their own development, it is well that they do not ignore such factors and their opposites as cooperativeness of spirit, the willingness of each to accept suggestions, the endurance of purposefulness, creativeness of suggestion, promptness of action, resourcefulness in suggesting feasible means to the attainment of desired ends, and the like. These factors, after all, are likely to have been central to either success or failure. If democracy is to work, our youth must have opportunity to make considered judgments upon their own and others' growth toward competence in the basic skills of democratic action.

Our schools have traditionally been the academic counterpart of a society dominated by purposes of exploitation. Our times demand change to an era of cooperative enterprise for the full release of human energies in a truly democratic social order characterized by material abundance and international harmony. This change must come, but it must come slowly, through education. We teachers must change ourselves during this process. We must courageously acquaint our students with the factors that have led to world discord. We must permit students, under guidance, to define their own purposes and programs of constructive civic action. We must seek the new materials needed for the execution of these purposes and keep our colleagues informed of newer educational purposes and unavoidable administrative conflicts, and we must win the good will of our communities.

What Are the Limitations of Service Projects?

Many indeed are the limitations which impose themselves upon all who would extend and enrich education through the use of service projects. The essence of service lies in the confidence that cooperative effort will, in the long run, prove more remunerative to all than does individual self-seeking. In such cataclysmic times as these, confidence in our fellowmen, especially in those beyond the pale of our own major group, is at its lowest ebb. Our kindlier impulses are submerged in an outburst of harsher sentiments. Teachers pressing for service projects may therefore encounter a widespread indifference or even hostility toward the philosophy underlying such effort. Besides this special limitation of our epoch are all the handicaps which an outworn, relatively nonfunctional school system imposes—traditional curricula, credits, promotions, grades, assignments, methods, examinations, and the lack of community-competent teachers. More specifically, these are the chief limitations just summarized:

1. **Popular prejudice is strong.** Even in this period of vast social upheaval, there is widespread callousness toward many social problems challenging democracy and thereby offering opportunities for constructive service projects. He who would promote school-community projects of a civic nature must therefore overcome great inertia as well as strong prejudice in most local situations. Illustration: racial segregation is not a practice confined to the South, or even to Negro Americans. Indians, Mexicans, and often Spanish-Americans suffer segregation in various states in both the North and South. Yet there is general public emotional support of this conspicuously undemocratic institution. Any service

project directed against racial segregation would doubtless meet with considerable disfavor in many localities.

2. Our schools are aloof from life. "Culture" has long been considered an ethereal value acquired through certain disciplines, largely memoriter, and is often particularly centered in relatively remote fields of study. Consequently, it is difficult to persuade parents or even students that true culture involves the intelligent meeting of current problems, both personal and social. We accordingly find our schools still placing great emphasis upon curricular subjects of traditional prestige, and upon intellectual tasks carried on in the classroom and within regular school hours. Service projects, on the other hand, do not lend themselves to the regimentation of standardized assignments, grading, state-adopted textbooks, paper-and-pencil examinations, and other ritular aspects of traditional school education. There is an element of daring, an adventuresome challenge in learning through service projects that calls for a different set of educational procedures than those still characteristic of our American schools.

3. Competent teachers are few. As a nation, we are utterly inexperienced in educating teachers to guide students in the planning, executing, and interpreting of successful civic service projects. Such guidance-teaching calls for professional resourcefulness and imagination of a high order—abilities which can only develop out of rich, varied, and predominantly first-hand experience in significant community processes and problems.

In these thunderous times, teachers of great foresight and boundless patience are needed to help develop functional, democratic education, based upon cooperative service in attacking the fundamental ills of modern life. Perhaps fortunately, the very desperateness of our world strife is today shaking schools out of their historic complacency with the traditional pursuit of knowledge as an end in itself. Today we realize as never before that practical citizenship must be the very heart of democratic education, and that this citizenship must be initially learned through personal experience in working at it during the period of formal schooling.

Democratic citizenship requires something more than the voluntary performance of significant service projects, fundamental as these are. This "something more" is personal vocational competence, including especially the development of that sustained self-discipline which free men find essential to vocational success. The development of that competence through improved school-community cooperation is therefore worthy of special consideration in the chapter which follows.

SELECTED REFERENCES

Anderson, L. W., "Biology Class Led Fight Against Mosquitoes." *Clearing House* 17:267-70 (Jan. 1943). Students in a mosquito-infested town studied the problem and then campaigned for the fight that brought a more healthful community.

Bretnall, R. J., "Welfare Workers at Millburn High School." *Clearing House* 16:329-31 (Feb. 1942). Throughout the year, students do actual work on special welfare problems of their own community. The school is legally an established administrative unit in the Welfare Department, and its services are subject to call at any time.

Chase, Stuart, "Bring Our Youngsters into the Community!" *Reader's Digest* 40:7-10 (Jan. 1942). A dramatic account of what young people are doing in and for their communities.

Davidson, Leone, "Consumers' Cooperative of Centerville." *Progressive Education* 19:203-06 (April 1942). A one-room elementary school established a school consumers' cooperative store, wrote articles of incorporation, issued stock, elected a board of directors, sold goods, declared a dividend—all as a class project. Learning values were marked.

Educational Policies Commission, *Learning the Ways of Democracy*, Ch. V. Washington: The Commission, 1940. Numerous challenging accounts of how schools across the nation are studying and serving their own communities.

Hanna, Paul R., and Research Staff, *Youth Serves the Community*. New York: D. Appleton-Century, 1936. Classic description of several hundred varied service projects, classified by their chief types.

Herkness, Walter W., Jr., "Philadelphia's Student Volunteer Service Corps." *School Executive* 62:15, 38 (Dec. 1942). Pictures a summer work-experience program for senior high school students.

Kilpatrick, William H., "The Underlying Philosophy of Cooperative Activities for Community Improvement." In Paul R. Hanna and Research Staff, *Youth Serves the Community*, Introduction. New York: D. Appleton-Century, 1936. A definitive statement, simply yet profoundly written.

Mitchell, Morris R., and Others, "Youth Has a Part to Play." *Progressive Education* 19:87-109 (Feb. 1942). Association Service Center Pamphlet 6. New York: The Association. A hundred and sixty-seven case-study examples of youth service to the community.

Nelson, Lowry, "Planning and Organizing Cooperative Community Projects." *Social Education* 7:68-70 (Feb. 1943). Analyzes various types of community problems which may be attacked by cooperative service projects, and offers step-by-step procedures for developing such projects.

Sims, Verner M., "Education Through Community Improvement." *Progressive Education* 19:332-35 (Oct. 1942). Critical analysis, stressing desirable manner of approach, points of emphasis, ways of working, and evaluation principles.

Smith, Estelle S., "Community Living Isn't Extracurricular." *School Executive* 62:38-41, 46 (March 1943). Summary sketch of many community service activities carried on by schools in an Alabama town.

Spence, Lucile, "Block Beautiful: Pupil Club Changes a Community." *Clearing House* 16:3-7 (Sept. 1941). A high school for girls in an overcrowded city tenement district decided to clean up the neighborhood. Parents, teachers and students cooperated with marked success.

Troyer, Maurice E., "Educating Through Community Service." In *Toward a New Curriculum:* 1944 Yearbook, Department of Supervision and Curriculum,

National Education Association, Ch. 4. Washington: The Association, 1944. Describes several types of service projects currently carried on by American schools, and lists eight criteria by which such projects may be evaluated.

United States Office of Education, "Together We Serve." Education and National Defense Series Pamphlet 24. Washington: Government Printing Office, 1942. Local, state and national agencies offer varied opportunities for service projects with educational implications.

CHAPTER 13

Work Experiences

EDUCATION THROUGH WORK AND STUDY

The Atwater School is nation-renowned for its richness in program of work experience. Serving a rural area of some three hundred square miles it has touched almost every farm and home helpfully. The soil has responded to an awakened interest in its conservation. In driving through that district one encounters innumerable SOS signs bearing sub-title, "Save Our Soil." These are the contribution of fourth and fifth grade children. Even first-graders have participated in various types of check dams in gullies. Once one gully contained a series of twelve such dams illustrating as many forms of construction. Each dam basin had become filled with sediment which was being held in place by an over-covering of kudzu planted by seventh and eighth graders. There are demonstration permanent pastures dotted over the district created by high school students in cooperation with adults. Likewise there are demonstrations of winter cover crops, unknown until recently in the Atwater area. The school owns three tractors, and equipment for sub-soiling, terracing and power spraying; also a combine and power mower. Last year the school, through this equipment and otherwise, rendered twenty-eight thousand dollars' worth of service within the district. Cooperation of the school and farm owners with such other constructive agencies as the Farm Security Administration, the County Farm Agent, the Soil Conservation Service, the State Forest Service, have related this work experience to a broad agricultural program which is clearly holding the soil in place and enriching it. Farm yields have conspicuously increased.

Right use of the land is demonstrated in the school's use of its own property. There is a school garden of nine acres worked cooperatively by the students and parents. It is a model in planning and care. Its products are canned and dried through further work experience. For this purpose the students have constructed a cannery which is available to the entire community and which processes one hundred thousand cans annually. Other food for the school and community (for there is little distinction at Atwater) is perfectly kept in an eighty-unit zero locker planned and operated entirely by students. One-third less food has spoiled in the Atwater district since these means of preservation have been in use. Besides the curing of meat in cold storage the students constructed a pisé de terre smoke house which has cured thousands of hams and shoulders and sides. Part of the school grounds are in forest. This forest is a model for the area. Undesirable trees were cut out under recommendation

271

of a forester. The branches were used to fill gullies. The cord wood was used in the community. There is a saw mill at the school, used by the school and community. Farmers bring loads of logs to be sawed for a service fee in lumber, thus obtaining boards for additions to their homes according to plans recommended by the Home Economics students. The mature trees from the school forest are harvested, and the resulting lumber affords ample supply for the well-equipped wood-working shop. Varied work experiences result in the making of furniture for remote as well as nearby homes, as also for brooders, feeders and the like. In connection with the health program, incident to the control of hook worm, lumber was sawed from the community's ninety acre forest (separate from the school forest, sometimes called the arboretum) for the making of ninety-six sanitary pit toilets which were trucked to the individual farms and properly installed.

On the school grounds, too, are two sweet potato beds, each of which produces about fifty thousand slips which in turn produce around eight thousand bushels. About the school grounds are bird houses and bird feeding stations, one bearing a sign, "all birds welcome to eat here"— signed, fourth grade. The whole area is dotted with such evidences of concern for bird life that the area has become an unofficial bird sanctuary. The school too is a center for the beautification of the homes, churches and other public buildings of the district. More than one-half. million ornamentals have been grown in the school's three-acre nursery. For nineteen years this project has added greatly to the beauty of the area without a penny's cost. In the year the nursery was started a planting of six thousand loblolly pines was made on an eroded corner of the grounds. The resultant forest, now thirty feet high is called Atwater's Arden, and one may hear Shakespeare read under its shade. The school museum, exhibiting a surprising array of handcraft implements and products, dramatizes to the school's constituency the period of transition we experience from an economy of scarcity based on handcraft to a future economy of abundance based on industrial production. The interesting exhibits range from hand-made waffle irons with long handles, once used in open fire places, to home-spun hand-quilted covers, still sturdy, warm, lovely.

As a work project of a mechanical nature the children trapped a stream, carried it in an earthen and then a wooden flume to a large waterwheel which they constructed and which in turn produces electricity for a log cabin which they built for school use in recreation. A related pond is treated with commercial fertilizer with the result that from four to five hundred pounds of fish are produced annually for school lunch use.

Besides clerking in the school's own cooperative store the children assist in local competitive stores by trimming windows, dusting and sweeping, and even arranging shelves. They have conducted research experiments in connection with the study of the items in their store. For example they make for sale their own brands of library paste, tooth paste and ink. In the same library where these products were developed and tested was evolved a highly satisfactory formula for making interior paint from local native clays. Related to self-grooming there are in the school a barber shop and a beauty parlor, and the students installed their own shower and water-heating equipment.

Atwater School is in fact a hive of industry in which, however, doing is always related to thinking, study to action. Far too many examples of study-action have become a part of the program to permit even mention. The children helped to tear down the minister's dilapidated home, helped design a new one, made a model of the proposed home, and helped in constructing it. They installed a public address system in the school; built their own gymnasium, fifty by seventy feet, having a high ceiling without central support. They built their tennis courts, out-door volley ball courts. With two other parties, each of whom with the school have third interests, they constructed a ball park. One owner furnished the lumber, another the grounds, they the work. The students helped create a town park; have built and operated a materials' bureau; operate their own apiary, the honey from which is used in the school lunch room. They operate a hatchery of twenty thousand egg capacity. They built a ceramics' laboratory and large kiln. In this kiln they make of local clays, and glaze in fiesta style, all the dishes used in the school lunch program. And many are found in the homes of that area.

What Are "Work Experiences"?

Work experience is sustained and interrelated activity of body and mind, carried on for purposes which are primarily prevocational in nature. More specifically defined, it means "practical activity in the production or distribution of goods or services exercised in a normal way in business, industrial, professional, and institutional fields."[1] In contrast with the Service Project, therefore, work experience is likely to be somewhat more regularized, routinized, and formally organized. Student clerking in a store at Christmas time is thus a form of work experience; so is after-school service in a social settlement, and a summer assignment as a farmer's helper. So, too, is the daily activity of many students at home. Such experience may often eventuate in a genuine civic contribution, and should always be infused with the spirit of cooperative service for social welfare, rather than that of grasping exploitation for personal gain. Yet, fundamentally, the aim of work experience is to help young people to acquire the vocational orientation, the specific skills and interests, and the sustained self-discipline essential to their individual success in some vocational career. Work experience, moreover, may or may not include financial remuneration for work done.

---

[1] Warren C. Seyfert and Paul A. Rehmus (eds.), "Work Experience in Education." Harvard Workshop Series No. 2. Cambridge: Harvard University Graduate School of Education, 1941.

What Values Have Work Experiences?

In the world's most difficult period of readjustment now ahead, our comprehensive human need is neither for "heroes of speech" nor for "muted toilers"; it is rather for a new generation of youth inspired by clear vision of an efficient, harmonious world society, yet ever sobered by an intimate acquaintance with the workaday world and with the patient, painstaking kind of effort that lasting social progress requires. To the development of such youth, planned work experiences can contribute enormously in both inspiration and realism. Work experiences, in addition to the basic values resident in any community-centered educational approach, possess several special advantages of their own. Work experiences:

1. **Offer occupational orientation and exploratory vocational experience.** In this realistic vocational laboratory setting, the student can more clearly define his career aspirations, evaluate his previous expectations, discover the specific nature of further training needed, and decide in which particular occupational area his life will prove most useful to society and most satisfying to himself.

2. **Stimulate a healthy attitude toward work,** including the desire to secure needed occupational information, skills, habits and discipline—not the least of which is a growing ability to "take it" in doing responsibly the necessary work of the world.

3. **Deepen civic insight as it brings first-hand contact with varying social-industrial conditions** in their relation to problems of employment, wages, conditions of work, unions and employers' associations, government regulation, consumer income, and the economic meaning of wealth production.

4. **Identify the adolescent with the adult group** through their cooperative attempts to meet a real need in a real situation. This psychological identification can be highly satisfying to both adults and adolescents, for as it develops adult status for the adolescent, it promotes genuine cooperation between the two generations in the accomplishment of socially useful work.

5. **Meet a social need as students are progressively inducted into the labor force** and ultimately achieve full personal competence in their chosen careers. If the chosen areas of work experience are of genuine value to human society, there will, in those instances, be little logical distinction between work experience and service projects. The twenty-five million school children and youth in this nation are an almost untouched reservoir of eager, potentially capable energy. This reservoir could and should be educationally utilized in a determined, democratic effort for postwar security and abundance.

6. **Relate doing with thinking.** Excessively verbalized education is not adequately functional for the modern world. The mind and the body

are one, and must be educated as a unit. Broad work experience, based on sound values and devoted to the development of marketable vocational skills, employs mind and body in one functional interrelationship.

Thus does work experience, of a cultural as well as prevocational nature, vastly enrich our educational program. Work experience can help prepare youth for the postwar reconstruction by bringing greater realism into their lives, by building personal character, generating wholesome attitudes toward self and society, developing useful career skills, and by actually contributing to the general welfare. Suitable work experience thus becomes more significant as one vital aspect of *general education,* as well as a means of vocational placement. Providing as it does for continuing firsthand experience with the vocational world, work experience should be made a primary avenue for the development of sound social, economic, and civic insight and responsibility.

How May Work Experiences Be Characterized?

Home and school will benefit children greatly if both require of youngsters all of the educative labor experience which is appropriate to their individual maturity and opportunity. Participation in various community service projects will itself provide considerable measure of such experience. For older children and adolescents, at least, we must go much farther in the direction of more specialized, sustained, day-after-day-after-day systematic work training. More systematic training may be provided through at least four major types or sources of work experience:

1. **Work activities at home.** Many students are forced to work within the home, on the farm, in the family store, etc. Such "work experience" is important, but is not likely to develop fullest educative value for the adolescent unless it is carried on with personal interest .and insight. The school's responsibility is to stimulate that insight and interest by continuous official recognition of the student's work at home, and of its genuine significance to him, his home, and to society in general.

2. **Part-time jobs.** Enterprising young people always find remunerative minor jobs for themselves—selling newspapers, shining shoes, delivering groceries, picking fruit, caring for children, Saturday clerking in stores, and the like. Such "normal" work experience by children was enormously extended during the manpower shortage occasioned by the war, when scores of thousands of high school boys and girls secured part-time and summer situations in industry, agriculture, and business. These war jobs usually carried adult status with adult pay. Paid work experience of all these varieties is tremendously valuable to youth, providing always that

they labor in jobs which permit growth in initiative, responsibility, and skills, and also that they are not physically, financially, or morally exploited in the process.

3. **Group service-work projects.** Here and there is a local community which has so fully integrated the school program with the life of the community, the service project with the work experience, as to make the two approaches almost indistinguishable. In communities such as that which centers in the Atwater School, sustained, responsible vocational training is functionally inherent in the school-community service activities in which adults and children mutually cooperate for common ends.

4. **Individual vocational training.** Sometimes systematic and specific occupational training is given by community industries and offices working in close cooperation with the school's vocational education program. As in the Jacksonville plan, students study part time, work part time, and are supervised throughout by officials representing industry and labor as well as the school. On the college level, cooperative work-and-study plans are well exemplified by the "Antioch Plan," whereby students alternate periods of work off campus with periods of study on campus. Yet regardless of the specific administrative plan, this type of work experience stresses the integration of vocational and social thinking with vocational skills as a fundamental, shared responsibility of school and community.

In varying degrees and in diverse ways these and other sources of work experience may contribute much to the genuine education of American youth. Some situations place chief emphasis upon the development of specific vocational aptitudes; others stress social service; still others consider only the wages to be earned. Whatever the primary emphasis, all such programs are much concerned about the obvious and often desperate need of modern American youth: to develop, through guided practical experience, those essential qualities of character, hand, and mind without which enduring vocational and civic success is improbable at best.

How May Successful Work Experiences Be Arranged?

Whatever its basic type, any substantial educational work experience must be carefully planned, supervised, and evaluated. The school obviously can have little or no control over the home or part-time job type of work experience, although it should surely be fully informed concerning the nature and extent of such work or jobs being carried by its students. Group service-work projects and individual vocational training, however, are both officially sponsored and primarily controlled by the schools. Suppose that we therefore notice certain broad principles of operation which should be observed in administering such programs of work experience.

Planning the Program

Careful planning is particularly important in the area of community-centered work experience. Although resource visitors, interviews, field trips, surveys, and service projects all involve considerable public cooperation, all of those "bridges" are fairly brief in terms of time; that is, each individual project is planned and completed in relatively short order. But an ongoing program of sustained work experience requires the development and maintenance of cooperative and cordial relations with the same community groups, for identical purposes, over an indefinite period of years. The best assurance of maintaining such cooperation is to use every care in planning for it, both initially and continuously.

1. DEVELOP A SOUND PHILOSOPHY

Work experience should not be advocated through any ascetic concern for the inherent value of severe or prolonged physical activity. There are sounder reasons than that for introducing curricular work experience of a socially useful nature.

Physical toil has been so arduous, yet so necessary during the three thousand centuries of mankind's existence within a handicraft age of economic scarcity, that even our religious writings have referred to the "sweat of his brow" as man's inescapable fate. His efforts to escape that toil have been constant and profound. The more intellectual sought means of substituting mental for physical labor; one result of these efforts was the progressive emergence of technological short cuts, such as machines. Another common form of escape was through exploitation of the weak and less gifted by the strong and the ruthless. A third escape was through the rendering of professional services such as preaching and teaching. Formal education thus often became an instrument whereby people might further refine their techniques for escaping the exigencies of physical toil.

Naturally, there arose an exaggerated distinction between physical and intellectual activity, with a greatly emphasized prestige and hence formal stress upon the latter. Our traditional schools, with their tendency to divorce curricular programs from vital life needs, are merely the educational reflection of this artificial yet deep-seated dualism. Many such schools, especially on the secondary level, have maintained curriculums which were fundamentally unsuited to most of the children "educated" within them. Adolescents of limited mental ability cannot cope successfully with the traditional book-learning, and in consequence are usually directed into narrowly vocationalized trades; there they attain limited personal skills, but without adequate insight into their social and civic responsibilities. An equally dangerous consequence of the traditional school program, however, is that to the mentally gifted children. Many of these children, commonly considered too "superior" or too "promising" to work with their hands, go through school on a basis of planned inexperience with various kinds of physical labor. Emerging from school as "intellectuals" or "artists," their concepts and attitudes toward society are founded almost entirely upon vicarious rather than direct experience with the hard realities of the working world. Yet these children also, like those of lesser mentality, will each have his vote in helping to shape the political, economic, and social policies of the community. Neither group is apt to be *adequately* prepared for democratic citizenship in this critical era; the first because its members often work without thought about the social implications of their labor; the second because it becomes easy to think grandly yet often impractically through lack of direct appreciation of what human toil means and must mean to the world. Nowhere is the virtual immorality of disassociating social thinking from vocational doing more apparent than in many schools and factories of this twentieth century. That separation has left many intellectuals out of sympathetic touch with the people, while business managers, technicians, and laborers often show little concern for the promotion of general human welfare.

Any educational program designed to bridge this gap must therefore include as an essential aspect an integrated program of thought-in-work experience for all students, regardless of their mental abilities and future prospects. No other approach can harmoniously stimulate a unified development of our youths' physical, mental, and emotional potentialities.

It is apparent also that such an integrated program, to be effective, must be built upon a new conception of the significance which socially-useful work must have in our developing civilization. Increasingly, it is clear that the traditional ethics of work must be revised under the impact of this current Power Age. For as we move forward from an economy of inevitable scarcity into one of relative material abundance, the historic economic problem changes from that of getting *technical production* to that of securing *social distribution*. With this change in primary economic emphasis, should properly come corresponding alteration in our thinking about the moral virtue of work. From an uncritical acceptance of all production and work as valuable *per se,* we need now to discriminate increasingly between types of production on the basis of their particular *social consequences.* Illustrations: millions of people "work" at many enterprises (such as growing and processing tobacco or manufacturing and selling liquors) which are, on the whole, harmful to human health and vigor. Millions more labor to produce products and services which are quite unessential or even entirely unnecessary to human living at its highest and best. Much war production is engaged in by "workers" on both sides of combat; from a broadly human viewpoint, however, the labor on one side is worse than useless if that on the other is justifiable at all.

The point is simply this: if human civilization is to make genuine advance, we must increasingly judge the social value of production and work in terms of their ultimate human consequences. We shall do well, therefore, to begin by insisting that any work experience to which we give school approval shall be carried on in productive areas that are of *true value to human society,* as well as of manifest educational worth to the participating students.

2. Arrange Work Opportunities

It is advisable to proceed slowly in developing the commercial, industrial, agricultural, and institutional contacts which may provide suitable work experiences. No wholesale solicitation of such opportunities should be made, for to do so, is likely to cause administrative complications, difficulties in personality adjustment between the center's personnel and the working students, and even some likelihood of requests for student help under conditions which would endanger or exploit them. It is much better to add one or at most a few placement centers at a time, and to do so only after quiet but thorough investigation. Such centers should be chosen with an eye to affording a wide range of learning experiences suitable to the different aptitudes and interests of the students. The danger that work experience selections may be limited by the special vocational interests of the teachers involved, should be clearly recognized and provided against. And every opportunity should be sought whereby urban youth may secure rural working experience, and vice versa.

3. ADAPT THE SCHOOL SCHEDULE ACCORDINGLY

Extra-class activities, service projects, work experience, and other less formal aspects of education are constantly—*and properly*—impinging upon the traditional school program of arbitrarily scheduled learning periods. Specific suggestions for meeting this problem are given in Chapter 15 of this volume. Here we shall simply note that teachers who desire to develop such vital learnings must be patient with those other teachers who are still satisfied with the formal disciplines, and that every care must be taken to arrange a reasonable balance between educational values sought through field projects and those obtained within the academic classroom. Actual details must obviously be settled in terms of each school's particular situation. It is well to note, however, that under stress of a broadening curriculum, both the school day and the school year tend to be considerably lengthened.

Supervising the Work Experience Program

Adequate supervision by qualified adults is an essential aspect of any successful work experience program. Without going into minor details, let us therefore examine several significant considerations which must be observed as the program moves from the planning and into the active phase.

4. PROVIDE COMPETENT SUPERVISORS

Supervision of work experiences can provide admirable opportunities for guidance at its best. So often guidance has been a periodic affair, designed to meet crises rather than to prevent them. Work experience requires constant adjustment. Sound adjustment means personal growth. The teacher should therefore meet regularly with the students working under his direction, should maintain close contact with the employers involved, and should be regularly in touch with the students' parents.

Sometimes an outsider can best be called in to supervise work experience. In such cases, however, the wise teacher will not dismiss his own responsibility for the safety and educational growth of his students. He will make sure, for instance, that the learners enjoy a flow of changing purposeful activities; that they demonstrate capacity to carry through their purposes despite wearying repetition; that they do not become content with mere perseverance after growth has ceased; that they are relatively free from periods of rush or overstrain, and of slack times and even idleness.

5. Associate Study with Action, Thinking with Doing

Various work programs divide the school day into a formal, closely scheduled morning (to insure "mastery of fundamentals"), and a free afternoon of diverse practical activities. This is like separating flavor from food. Flavor has a function in digestion. Thought without action is futile. Action without thought is unethical. Functional education does not consist in mornings devoted to thought and afternoons dedicated to action. Thinking and doing are inseparable aspects of sound human growth. This basic principle is the veritable foundation and keystone of educational advance during recent decades; it has already given us both the activity school and the community school. The functional program of work experience will therefore relate thinking and doing—planning, organizing, executing, and judging—in organic unity, rather than in artificial sequence.

6. Adjust the Work to the Student's Needs

Youth enjoys hard work if he feels that the job is his own. Work that is too easy, offends. Yet work that is too hard may cause serious overexertion, particularly if the worker is stimulated by a new environment, by the presence of spectators, or by the prospect of high material reward. A nice balance must be maintained between the physical condition of the student and the physical demands of the job-situation. We must remember how completely most city children are accustomed to a life involving little sustained physical effort. In most instances, their muscles are flabby and their body tissues are soft. When such a child spends several hours or a whole day in driving a tractor, in haying, in helping build a house, a dam, or the like, a severe strain is thrown upon him as a physical organism. When high school and college youths attend work camps, it is sometimes impossible to constrain them sufficiently during the first few days of "hardening," and as a result they sometimes develop dysentery, vomiting, and other less obvious symptoms of excessively severe and rapid adjustment. Every possible effort must therefore be made to prevent work experiences from causing undue fatigue or excitement at the outset.

7. Beware of Excessive Monotony or Stimulation

Guard against both excessive monotony from repetitious work (most such work can be done better mechanically in any case), and against undue stimulation from a new environment. Children new to the city will not concentrate upon planting, along streets, the trees they have brought from the country; neither will city children mend a pig fence until they have made friends with the pigs. If work experience is to be successful, the learner-worker must be challenged by the situation, and at the same time find himself purposefully identified with it.

8. Be Cautious but Not Over-Protective

Avoid extremes of over-concern for the students' safety and of unwise disregard of danger. There should be a nice sense of challenge and courage, but never of recklessness. Furthermore, we must be careful neither to under-estimate nor to over-estimate the learner's technical knowledge. The former is resented. The latter leads to frustration. Every supervisor of work experience should know first-aid, and should have adequate first-aid equipment constantly on hand in the work center itself. Comfortable work shoes, loose clothing, and gloves for soft hands are important. Sunburn should be avoided, and so should overheating. In the case of a prolonged job, involving strenuous exercise, it is well to begin with a work period of an hour or so the first day, and then lengthen each day's work by an hour or two until a proper balance between work, study, play, and rest has been achieved.

9. Remain Alert against Exploitation

Public desire to safeguard children against exploitation has led to regulations which often make difficult the provision of needed, vital, and hand-work experience. What is desirable is not a complete exclusion of children from work until they reach some given age such as fourteen, but rather a gradual introduction of children into work situations on a guidance basis. Such a program would be practically impossible to administer on any other than an educational basis, and even here it is difficult to organize, particularly in urban situations where work opportunities for the immature are far fewer than they are in rural areas.

A more immediate consideration is that of making certain that students are not exploited through school approved or directed work experiences which are inexpertly directed, that are not socially useful, that demand exertion beyond the capacity of the young people involved, or that endanger them physically, emotionally, or morally.

10. KEEP ADEQUATE RECORDS

Think through the problem of records in terms of the educational purposes of the work experience itself. Avoid becoming enslaved to the time-consuming task of filling in unnecessarily detailed forms. In planning the needed records, ask such questions as these: Will this item assist the student, the employer, the parent, or the school in better guiding student growth? Will this item help us to appraise the real value of this particular work experience? Will this information be useful to the administration in deciding whether to continue this work experience opportunity? Under such practical scrutiny as this, every recorded item of information is assuredly functional in considerable degree.

Interpreting the Work Experience

Concern for the student's educational growth through work experience requires that he, as well as the school and the cooperating community organizations, be led to evaluate that experience constructively. Such appraisal, to be adequate, must be continuous, and it must make provision for such evaluative procedures as presented in the following five paragraphs.

11. ENCOURAGE CONSTRUCTIVE CRITICISM

Encourage the student to evaluate his own work; encourage the group to appraise each individual's work; and encourage the group to judge its own work. The best evaluative approach emphasizes favorable points first, and then goes on to discuss the unfavorable factors. A truly objective viewpoint will not offend learners accustomed to such evaluation; on the contrary, they may even want to wave aside compliments in their desire to learn how best to improve their efforts in the future.

12. ANALYZE THE PROCEDURE

There is real need to analyze the procedure in work experience in order to make clear to the learner, and often to his parents, that genuine educational growth has occurred. Extraneous rewards and punishments have so long and so often been used to exaggerate the value of formal learning, that the highly significant values of a *doing* program may be obscured by the less important items upon which pencil-and-paper examinations are based. That is why we must analyze the learning process with our students, and thereby help them to understand that in an activity program, many valuable learnings are achieved even though these learnings are often not of the traditional type. Socialized attitudes, new personal interests, deepened appreciation of labor, ability to "take it" in completing a contractual task—all these are learnings of tremendous significance to the individual as well as to society at large.

13. SUMMARIZE THE VALUES

Measure the learner against his former self and against the problems still ahead. There should thus emerge a rising sense of confidence and of reasonable hope. In case there has been partial or complete failure, by individual or group, determine the cause; carefully select a new course; then move forward toward the original purpose. But if that purpose was itself unworthy or too difficult, judge it accordingly and develop new purposes for the future. In such ways, even failure may hasten and strengthen educational growth.

14. SEEK IMPROVEMENTS

One of the more important aspects of guided work experiences is a needed sensitivity to suggestions from the students and from those with whom he works. By all means invite everyone concerned with the work experience program to criticize it constructively and in detail. Such desire for criticism is but one aspect of that cooperative (and hence democratic) relationship that should increasingly characterize all group effort. Honest criticism, pointing forward to future improvements, is the surest guarantee of genuine progress.

15. PUBLICIZE THE PLAN

The public is so aware of the need to make education more functional that it will welcome the inclusion in the school program of properly organized and directed work experiences. The community status of the school will therefore be strengthened as sound publicity is given to those broader opportunities for learning which confront our youth through fruitful work experience in industry, agriculture, commerce, social welfare agencies, and the like. The school has both duty and opportunity to keep its community informed concerning work experience programs, developments, and needs. In preparing such publicity, stress should be laid upon the civic contributions made through student work experience, as well as upon the extended learning values thus available to the individual students.

*

Work experience, at its best, will not be a fitful, infrequent interruption of an otherwise "normal" curriculum. On the contrary, such experience will be an integral and habitual aspect of the regular educational program in the life-centered school. Yet there must always be careful preparation, competent supervision, and constructive evaluation of each individual work activity and program.

What Are the Limitations of Work Experience?

Work experience, as we have seen, is an indispensable aspect of well-rounded youth education today. Yet various important obstacles to its widespread development are evident. Among the several handicaps, the following three are perhaps the most noteworthy:

1. **The dominant economic system is not designed as an educational agency.** Its purpose is to produce for profit, and all other considerations are subordinated. This is no more the fault of capital than it is of labor or of the consumer; it is simply the basic characteristic of the system itself. Management, bent on maximizing profits, disfavors interruptions by immature students. In the business and industrial world of rapid pace, there is little place or patience for the inefficiency of a beginner, especially if he is handicapped by lack of physical strength or general maturity, and does not expect to stay with the company. Trade secrets are sometimes a further barrier, as are some laws relating to employers' legal responsibility for injuries to workers. Organized labor is often fearful of newcomers in a given field of work, and is frequently opposed to "productive" labor; it is nearly as much enslaved by a restrictive philosophy of business as is management. Both groups, therefore, tend to remain indifferent, if not opposed, to general and extensive vocational training as a form of work experience for youth.

2. **Competent supervision is difficult to find.** If the work experience is of the group-service type, the lack of teachers really prepared to guide and supervise it is a frequent obstacle. Unless a teacher is living a richly varied life himself, he will hardly possess sufficient practical competency in enough fields to be able to follow the expanding interests of students, even to the point of securing satisfactory lay or professional assistance.

Should the work experience program be of the individual vocational training type, the difficulty is that of finding supervisors who are both master technicians and master teachers. Vocational coordinators of requisite dual ability are by no means plentiful.

3. Distance and expense are factors. Yet this is an age of increasingly rapid transportation in both rural and urban communities, and it is still axiomatic that people will find means to afford what they think is worth buying. In any event, it should be remembered that many opportunities for excellent work experience exist within the local community itself, and that among these opportunities there are likely to be some which may quite properly become financially self-liquidating.

Despite these limitations, work experience must be widely developed during the next generation. A youth is never fully mature until he is self-supporting in his own job. Society must now stand ready to provide jobs for all who wish to work, and must initially offer adequate opportunity for personal, sustained and carefully-supervised working experiences as a part of general education for all young people. Thus will the last of our ten bridges unite school and community as together they establish a more functional educational program in a democratic world.

SELECTED REFERENCES

Abernethy, George L., "The Volunteer Work Camps." *School & Society* 56: 482–86 (Nov. 21, 1942). The story of the Quaker Work Camp movement, with emphasis upon its philosophy, program, activities, costs, and values.

American Youth Commission, American Council on Education, *Youth and the Future*, Ch. IV. Washington: The Council, 1942. The Commission's statement of principles that should govern relations between youth work programs and the schools.

Andreé, Robert G., "Six Errors About Work Experience." *Clearing House* 16: 518–20 (May 1942). Six major mistakes are analyzed, and four constructive proposals presented.

Barton, Florence W., "Youth on the Job." *Parents Magazine* 14:23 + (Jan. 1939). Popular description of how some schools and communities are working together to provide cooperative vocational education.

Bostwick, Prudence, "Education Takes to the Fields." *Progressive Education* 19: 328–31 (Oct. 1942). Potential values of work experience on farms for enriched social studies, science, literature, and art.

Chase, Stuart, "Young Men in Tunbridge." *Survey Graphic* 31:229–33 (May 1942); *Reader's Digest*, May 1942. How some Harvard students established a volunteer work camp in Vermont, and what came of their venture.

Cocking, Walter D., "A Program for Work Experience." *Bulletin of the National Association of Secondary-School Principals* 27:27–31 (Jan. 1943); *Education Digest*, Feb. 1943. Objectives, values and requirements of effective work experience for youth.

Couper, George P., "California Student Harvest Crops." *Bulletin of the National Association of Secondary School Principals* 28:42–52 (April 1944). The program whereby 3500 students were enrolled in California harvest camps in 1943. History, values, training, leadership, camp operation, recreational provisions are among the topics treated.

Cross, Henry A., "Work Experience in Secondary Schools." *Bulletin of the National Association of Secondary-School Principals* 26:36–43 (March 1942); *Education Digest*, April 1942. Types, objectives, and suggested procedures for supervising and recording school-sponsored work experiences.

Douglass, Harl R., "Youth, School, Work and Community." *School & Society* 50:65–71 (July 15, 1939). *Education Digest* (October 1939). Make the school more life-like by centering it in the community, and provide extensive work experience for youth through half-time participation in school and in work.

English, Horace B., "Education Through Work in a Time of Social Change." *Educational Method* 15:67–71 (Nov. 1935). A closely reasoned analysis of the growing need for constructive work experience as part of the educational heritage of American youth.

Evans, Louise, "Work Camps for 1,500,000 High-School Youth." *Clearing House* 15:515–19 (May 1941); *Education Digest* (Sept. 1941). Reports on the 1940 summer work camps operated by the Associated Junior Work Camps.

Girault, Willia S., and Stewart T. Walton, "We Gave Them Experience." *Educational Method* 18:262–65 (March 1939); *Education Digest* (May 1939). Reports a plan whereby high school students are actually interviewed for "jobs," and then placed in such jobs for work experience if they appear suitable to the potential "employer."

Holland, Kenneth, "Work Camps for College Students." Washington: American Council on Education, 1941. Illustrated pamphlet analyzing several operating work camps and reporting upon the values therein which might be translated into the structure of general education.

Holland, Kenneth, and George L. Bickel, "Work Camps for High School Youth." Washington: American Council on Education, 1941. An Illustrated pamphlet describing several junior work camps and suggesting how similar camps might be made a valuable aspect of many community programs.

Jacobson, Paul B., "Adolescents Need Experience in the Work of Their World." In North Central Association of Colleges and Secondary Schools, *General Education in the American High School*, Ch. 11. Chicago: Scott, Foresman, 1942. Social need, examples, types, obstacles and future of work experience.

Jacobson, Paul B., "Educating Through Work." In *Toward a New Curriculum:* 1944 Yearbook, Department of Supervision and Curriculum, National Education Association, Ch. 5. Washington: The Association, 1944. Philosophy and levels of work experience, current experiments through schools, problems, suggestions, and values.

Jacobson, Paul B., and B. L. Dodds, "Work Experience and Secondary Education." *Bulletin of the National Association of Secondary School Principals* 28: 75–81 (Feb. 1944). Report of a conference on work experience. Defines basic assumptions, objectives, related school activities, proposed administrative techniques, evaluative procedures, and work-experience standards.

McClusky, Howard Y., "A Philosophy of Work Experience." *Progressive Education* 19:72–75 (Feb. 1942). Biological and psychological bases, with educational implications.

Mann, George C., "Value of Work in Education in the Secondary Schools." *Bulletin of the National Association of Secondary-School Principals* 25:77–83 (March 1941). The importance of work as a part of education, the NYA's type of work experience, and the basic principles which govern successful NYA work programs.

Mitchell, Morris R., "The Importance of Socially Useful Work in Childhood Education." *Childhood Education* 16:201–04 (Jan. 1941); *Education Digest*, Feb. 1941. Emphasizes the significance of socially useful work experience for social reconstruction as well as for personal growth.

Mitchell, Morris R., "Socially Useful Work." Democratic Education Series, Bibliography No. 4. New York: Progressive Education Association. Scores of brief case-illustrations, with sources of each.

Moe, M. P., and L. O. Brockman, "Utilizing Community Resources for Vocational Guidance and Training." Helena, Montana: The Authors, 1937. Pamphlet description of a successful program wherein community resources are widely used in vocational guidance, part-time cooperative training and education on the job, adjustment of the worker, placement, and continued training.

Out-of-School Guidance Committee, National Vocational Guidance Association, "Organizing the Community for Vocational Guidance." *Occupations* 22:102–08 (Nov. 1943). Suggested steps, organization plan, publicity and financial measures, etc. for pooling community resources to aid vocational adjustment of youth and adults.

Phelps, Seth, "Making Farm Work an Education Experience for City Boys." *School Review* 51:144–49 (March 1943). Describes the experiences of the University of Chicago's Laboratory School's faculty in planning, organizing, supervising and evaluating a farm work project for city boys.

Robinson, Ormsbee W., "Youth in the Nation's Service." *Frontiers of Democracy* 8:202–05 (April 15, 1942). Summary of work camps, farmwork experiences, and child care opportunities as desirable sources of work experience.

Seyfert, Warren C., and Paul A. Rehmus (eds.), "Work Experience in Education." Harvard Workshop Series: No. 2. Cambridge: Harvard University, 1941. A Workshop report upon work experiences, stressing the administration, supervision, evaluation, and coordination of such experiences.

Smith, Leo F., "Implications of Cooperative Work for Secondary Education." *School Review* 50:17–23 (Jan. 1942). Discusses present programs of work experience and some of the difficulties inherent in them; then describes practice at the Rochester Athenaeum and Mechanics Institute where general education and work experience are alternated in four-week intervals.

Thompson, Dorothy, "The Patriotism of Work." *Survey Graphic* 31:233–34 (May 1942); *Reader's Digest* (May 1942). The work and value of the Volunteer Land Corps in New England.

Warren, Curtis E., "A Work-Experience Program for Youth." *Bulletin of the National Association of Secondary School Principals* 27:69–78 (Nov. 1943). The San Francisco program, explained in considerable detail. Purposes, planning, administration, supervision, credit, evaluation, job specifications, the coordinator's functions, etc. are discussed.

Weber, C. A., "Rotary Gives Youth Vocational Experiences." *Occupations* 21:464–68 (Feb. 1943). Describes a Chicago Rotary club project through which youth receives practical vocational guidance and well-organized work experience. Reports from students, employers, teachers and parents are reproduced.

"Work Experience in Secondary School." *Bulletin of the National Association of Secondary School Principals* 27:No. 111 (Jan. 1943). A special number. See also "Youth and Work Opportunities," another special number under date of April 1940.

PART IV

PROBLEMS TO BE FACED

ALTHOUGH bridges between school and community vary widely in purpose and design, their construction and use involves many problems which are significant to them all. Almost regardless of the particular approaches chosen, school workers will need to take adequate account of such matters as those of program-planning, scheduling, transportation, expense, legal liability, evaluation techniques, public relations, clearing house facilities, community coordination, and the professional training of personnel. We shall therefore now consider each of these general problems in practical terms.

◆

BOOKS ARE ARTIFICIAL, LIFE IS REAL

THE school must understand that its main material, books, are poor substitutes for experience; that truth is life and not a knowledge of books; that we learn from books really only when their contents are interpreted by life and experience. Books interpret and expand experience, but they do not supply it. Books are artificial, life is real.

—HERMAN H. HORNE

The Philosophy of Education. By permission of The Macmillan Company, publishers.

INTELLECTUALLY CRIPPLED PEOPLE

AS educators, then, we must understand that the capitalist who knows only his markets, the engineer who knows only his machines, the teacher who knows only his books, are all intellectually crippled people. The fatal weakness of their education and training is that it makes them incapable of dealing with the real world: they are helpless except in dealing with the series of abstractions in which they have achieved a minor competence.

—LEWIS MUMFORD

In "The Social Responsibilities of Teachers and Their Implications for Teacher Education." *The Educational Record*, October, 1939.

LIFE AS WELL AS BOOKS

TO guide the present experiences of learners effectively, teachers must know life as well as books. They must learn as well as teach. They must be citizens as well as school teachers.

—PAUL J. MISNER

In NEA Department of Supervisors and Directors of Instruction, *Mental Health in the Classroom*, p. 226. Thirteenth Yearbook.

THE FINEST TEACHING

THE finest teaching is that which best adjusts the child to his own total life problems. Because of this the child's real community provides the most important teaching situation. It is imperative that each teacher develop the utmost skill in utilizing the community as a natural laboratory. Basing the children's activities upon the realities of the social situation is the surest, most understandable, and most effective way of making the curriculum "modern"—or rather, functional.

—MICHIGAN DEPARTMENT OF PUBLIC INSTRUCTION

In "Instructional Guide for Elementary Schools." Quoted in the NEA *Research Bulletin*, November, 1937, p. 227.

A SIMPLE THESIS

THAT which ought and can best be taught inside the schoolroom should there be taught, and that which can best be learned through experience dealing directly with native materials and life situations outside the school should there be learned.

—L. B. SHARP

In "Outside the Classroom." *The Educational Forum*, May, 1943.

personnel," Yearbooks and journals of teachers' organizations often
publish examples of such units, and give many practical suggestions for selecting and preparing them. Excerpts from one such
unit in the area of community relations are presented by way of illustration.

CHAPTER 14

Program Planning

Community study and participation is valuable even if carried on
independently of any school affiliation, direction, or control. Most
community experiences with which we are concerned, however,
will be part of school programs developed because of their potential educational value to school students. Teachers everywhere
—in traditional and activity schools, as well as in definitely community schools—are therefore faced with the problem of including
community projects within the curriculum, or of vitalizing their
existing courses by incorporating community experiences. Three
pertinent and closely related questions immediately arise:

1. *How much advance preparation should a teacher make for a projected
class experience in the community?*
2. *To what extent should students share in planning community experiences?*
3. *By what criteria should community experiences be evaluated and chosen?*

These three problems are fundamental in planning any community
study or experience. We shall therefore discuss each one in its turn.

How Much Advance Preparation Should a Teacher Make?

A teacher's role at any school level is largely that of stimulating,
guiding, and coordinating the school-sponsored learning activities
of students. This requires of him some definite decisions concerning the values and purposes of specific community experiences, a
wise selection, or at least approval, of certain such experiences from
the total number possible, some preplanning of the community
activities tentatively chosen, and a preliminary organization of the
available resources. Equally important is the cooperative planning
of such community experiences by the pupils with the teacher. But
these preliminary steps of the teacher must come first. The quality
of the community experience is likely to be in direct proportion to
the amount of previous planning done by him.

A noticeable curriculum trend in recent years is that of planning
pupil learning in terms of "units of work" or "units of learning ex-

perience." Yearbooks and journals of teachers' organizations often publish examples of such units, and give many practical suggestions for selecting and preparing them. Excerpts from one such unit in the area of community study are presented by way of illustration.

COMMUNITY LIFE—A RESOURCE UNIT
FOR ELEMENTARY SCHOOLS

From Bertha Frances Carr's "Illustrated Unit of Work" in *The Instructor*, June, 1940. Used by permission of F. A. Owen Publishing Company.

OVERVIEW

In order to be valuable members of our community we should be conscious of the factors that help to make it a satisfactory and comfortable place to live. We should know something about its government and its civic problems, and try to do our part in solving them. Even young children can be taught to feel a certain amount of civic responsibility, and to realize how much the community does for them.

Since earning a living forms the basis of community life, it is important to familiarize children with the principal types of occupations. Therefore interesting places of business are suggested for study. Communities vary in nature; for example, some are agricultural, some industrial; and this difference will be reflected, of course, in the occupations that are chosen for study.

In his home the child first learns the meaning of interdependence and the value of intelligent co-operation. This knowledge he later extends to include the entire community. As he grows older, he will be interested in the origin of its name, why particular events are observed, who were the earliest families, why a settlement grew up at that particular place, and which is the oldest building of historical significance.

From such beginnings as these, children will become curious about their community. There will gradually develop a feeling that they are a part of it. These are early steps toward loyal and desirable citizenship.

OBJECTIVES

1. To create interest in the community.
2. To show how people are dependent upon one another.
3. To find ways of improving the community.
4. To recognize progress made by the community.

METHOD

Before starting a unit on community life, the teacher should make a survey of the community. She should list the activities she wishes to study, and the points about each which she wants to discuss. It would be wise to consult the leaders of the various community activities to obtain historical information and pictures.

•   •   •

The work for the primary grades should be centered around the children's activities. Pupils should visit industries, stores, farms, and other places where members of the community work. The unit offers an opportunity for informational reading. Provision should be made for expression of the children's ideas.

The plans for middle and upper grades give a broader view of the community. Through excursions and reports, the recreational opportunities, occupations, and safety conditions are studied. In each phase of the unit, an appreciation of the community's progress up to the present should be developed. Through reports about other localities, feasible plans for improvements may be considered.

Upper-grade pupils should show noticeable growth in knowledge of, and right attitudes toward, the community. The unit provides an excellent opportunity for vocational guidance as the children study various types of work.

POINTS TO EMPHASIZE

1. Regardless of size, there are certain factors common to every community, such as the home, the school, the church, the store, and the post office (Primary Grades).

2. Schools are supported by the community because they are essential to its welfare (Middle Grades).

3. Like other community facilities, the public library is for everyone, and no individual has the right to do things that hinder others from using and enjoying it (Middle Grades).

. . .

6. There are variations in the size of communities because of climate, topography, and industry (Upper Grades) . . .

7. The more dense the population, the greater is the need for efficient police and fire protection (Upper Grades).

8. For the physical safety of the people, attention must be given to the water supply and to sanitary methods of handling waste matter (Upper Grades).

ACTIVITIES

For Primary and Middle Grades

CONSTRUCTION

What can give a child more pleasure than building a grocery store, a post office, or a miniature of his own house? When these buildings and others are finished, the children can assemble them to form a complete scene of a village or a section of a city.

Community life offers a broad field for children who like to draw and paint. A frieze showing the group on a tour, for example, gives an opportunity for the children to develop and express their ideas.

An activity that demands close observation and careful planning is a large pictorial map, which shows the school or the public library with the surrounding streets.

. . .

Middle-grade pupils will enjoy making posters to emphasize safety rules.

For Upper Grades

TOPICS FOR STUDY

Let the pupils choose from the following list the topics which particularly interest them. Reports may be written and given as each phase of community life is discussed by the class. They will serve to bring attention to the needs of the community.

1. Why banks are organized.
2. In small communities, how do banks take care of their surplus money?
3. How is a state bank different from a national bank?
4. How news reporters receive the last-minute news.

15. Regulations concerning garbage in your community.
16. State regulations concerning dairies.
17. The history of pasteurizing milk.
18. What are the safest and most satisfactory lights for streets and highways?

For All Grades

EXCURSIONS

The children should prepare for an excursion by talking about the things they want to see and the questions they want to ask. Transportation, suitable dress, and correct conduct can also be discussed.

When visiting a post office, the children will see the division of labor that makes for efficiency. Another important realization which they may gain is that it is necessary to be accurate when addressing mail if rapid communication is desired.

When upper-grade pupils are studying the industries of a community, excursions are one of the most obvious and necessary methods of obtaining information.

DRAMATIZATION

A unit on community life provides varied possibilities for dramatic play. . . . A child who plays at mailing a package at the classroom post office should know that packages must be wrapped well and addressed clearly.

Upper-grade pupils may dramatize interviews between employers and prospective employees. Courtesy, appearance, and preparation should be emphasized.

A series of very short scenes showing the work of the policeman, the fire department, and so on, can be used for an assembly program.

BIBLIOGRAPHY

A selected list of references was given under each of these topics: *Primary Grades, Middle Grades, Upper Grades, Teacher.*

It will be noted that such units of work are broadly outlined by the teacher in advance, and are in the form of "resource units"— that is, a kind of file of ideas and materials from which functional learning activities may quickly be developed with the class as the need arises. Those who plan to assemble such units as part of their own preparation for directing community activities by students would do well to organize unit outlines around these three essentials:

1. **Objectives**—the teacher must know what he hopes his students will achieve, and how to evaluate their success. These aims will be expressed as skills to be attained, attitudes to be developed, and knowledge to be gained.

2. **Activities**—the teacher must tentatively plan a variety of pupil experiences to achieve the objectives sought. These experiences should be both interesting and educationally profitable, and should consist of three types: (a) *initiating activities* to give students a broad overview of the problem and its relation to the pupil and to his community; (b) *research activities* to provide opportunity for digging rather deeply into the data related to the problem, organizing the data, interpreting their meaning, and then acting upon findings for community improvement; and (c) *culminating activities* which tie together the work done and make the whole experience intellectually as well as otherwise fruitful.

3. **Materials**—the teacher must be familiar with numerous materials of instruction which contribute to the activities and thereby help to produce the desired modifications of pupil behavior. He will know how to gather various types of data, to see how particular data must be interpreted in terms of the sampling done, to draw valid conclusions from the information available, and he will know what specific sources of information are likely to yield what types of needed help.

All this planning by the teacher is not in any sense a substitute for pupil planning, but is done in order to make pupil planning more effective when that occurs. The teacher's previous development of resource units will serve to facilitate pupil planning, and also to anticipate or guard against many difficulties which might discourage the students if they approached a problem for which careful preparation had not been made by the responsible director of learning, their teacher.

To What Extent Should Students Share in Planning?

Young people are actually educated in the direction of their own real purposes, rather than according to a teacher's specific aims. Particularly in the field of community study it is important to remember that the child learns what he sets himself to learn, whether that be an understanding of an industrial technique, the procedure for earning an "A," or the enjoyment of temporary escape from school. If students are to gain most from their community experiences, they must have personal interest in undertaking them, a clear knowledge of what they wish to gain, and some standards by which to evaluate the true worth of those experiences.

Pupil-teacher planning means *cooperative planning;* it is not a process by which pupils are "motivated" to do what the teacher already wants to do, or are fooled into accepting the teacher's total plan as being really all their own. It should be a real give-and-take situation. All the teacher preplanning described above is merely wise preparation by the most mature member of the democratic group to anticipate possible procedures, difficulties, and alternatives. The less mature the student group, the more essential such preliminary teacher planning becomes.

As the cooperative planning progresses, the teacher and the class members should be alert for suggestions of possible community experiences, techniques of approach, and likely problems to be encountered. If students evince no ideas for community projects, the teacher should suggest several suitable alternatives as a basis for class analysis and possible choice. However the arrangements are made, the students should feel that the community project is really their own, and that they are responsible for planning and carrying it out. Much of its value will be lost if the group feels that it is developing a project merely to please a teacher who happens to be interested in community study.

The thoroughness of group planning will depend on the maturity level of the class with which the teacher is working. With younger pupils the teacher's leadership must be more evident and definite; with older students, the teacher should continue to guide, but do so increasingly from the background. At any level, however —even in the lower elementary school grades—the students will at some time share in planning each major phase of the community project. Its purposes will be stated by them in words meaningful to them. They will examine the different possible ways of carrying out the project and will choose the ways they prefer. The teacher will act always as a resource person, aiding when necessary but never dominating the group procedure.

Students should actively execute the community project as well as merely plan it. They can run down sources of material in the school and community libraries, call on agencies for published information, cull newspapers and magazines, search for audio-visual aids, and look for new sources of information. If resource visitors are to be invited to the classroom or assembly, the students should make the arrangements, write invitations and letters of thanks, and act as hosts and chairmen. All interviews, questionnaires, and field observations ought to be carefully planned and arranged by the student group. On excursions, surveys, and extended field studies, and in service projects, work experience, and camping, the students should assume the responsibilities wherever possible. In doing all these things, however, the students should be led to recognize their need for technical instruction in methods of approach to the community and in public relations generally. Finally, students should have personal responsibility for publicly presenting the story and results of their community experience or project. A report to some local organization, an exhibit placed in the school or community library, an assembly program, a written statement for the newspaper—all of these are typical culminating activities which will conclude the community project with a fine challenge to the best abilities of the students concerned.

By What Criteria Should Community Experiences Be Selected?

Any community experience is worthwhile only if it contributes *in greater degree than would otherwise be likely* to the educational growth of youth and to improvement of the community. Four general admonitions are in order whenever it is proposed to utilize the community as a field laboratory:[1]

1. Use the community only when there are good *a priori* reasons to believe that it provides a better sort of learning experience than could be moulded within the four walls of a school.

---

[1] These suggestions are slightly adapted from Stephen M. Corey, "Utilization of Community Resources in Pupil Guidance." In William C. Reavis (ed.), *The School and the Urban Community*, pp. 76–78. Chicago: University of Chicago Press, 1942.

2. Use the community only when the time available is adequate to permit advance planning and subsequent follow-up of the experience.

3. Use the community only if the group is small enough to permit effective learning by all pupils at all times.

4. Use the community for field studies only when it would be less effective to bring the community to the school through the medium of documentary materials, audio-visual aids, and resource visitors.

Assuming that these suggestions are carefully observed, the next need is to appraise the proposed community project in terms of specific evaluative criteria, in order to assure maximal educational growth and civic improvement. By such evaluation, it will be found that some proposed activities will be decidedly worthwhile, that a great many others must be considerably revised in order to promise full value, that a few would be worthless or even definitely harmful. In this way, valid standards or criteria should save the time and energy of both teachers and students.

No set of standards can be entirely valid. Each item in the list may have to be reworded to be fully meaningful in a particular situation. Most important, no single community project will be likely to measure up in full degree to all the criteria offered. Nevertheless, some general directives are in order, and are presented here to suggest the kind of evaluative thinking that needs to be done about every proposed community project.[2] The criteria below are grouped under three heads: (a) levels of difficulty, (b) social value, and (c) educational value.[3]

A. CRITERIA IN TERMS OF LEVELS OF DIFFICULTY

There are several levels of difficulty that must be recognized in working out community studies. The criteria below are arranged so that one class may undertake studies which meet only the first groups; more advanced classes may attempt activities which meet a larger number. While a good community activity may not meet all of these criteria, the activities may be improved as they are revised to meet as many as possible.

1. *Does the activity acquaint the pupils with the resources of their own community?*

---

[2] These criteria were first presented by the writer, Julian C. Aldrich, in his mimeographed *Guide to Cooperative Community Study* (St. Louis: St. Louis County Commission on the Teaching of the Social Studies, 1937), and later reproduced in the Ninth Yearbook of the National Council for the Social Studies, Ruth West (ed.), *Utilization of Community Resources in the Social Studies*, pp. 23–25.

[3] See also the Service Project criteria in Chapter 12, pages 255 ff.

a. Does it relate to a phase of community life?

b. Is this phase of community life typical? If not, is it recognized by teacher and pupils as an atypical phase?

c. Is the study based on a fair picture of this phase of community life, and would it be considered fair by a person engaged in the activities relating to it?

d. Does the study show the relationship of this phase of community life to other phases in this community and in other communities?

2. *Does the activity permit the pupils to envision the community as a social organism with human interrelations?*

a. Does it permit the pupils to see as many of the social and economic forces which cause community life, as is possible with this age group?

b. Does it offer contact with persons who are seen as human beings with needs, desires, and ideals?

c. Can the activity be related to several phases of community life?

d. Does it offer opportunities to observe conflicts between individuals and groups in the community?

e. Does it offer opportunities to observe differences between professed aims and objectives of individual and group conduct and real aims and objectives?

3. *Does the activity encourage the pupil to acquire a relatively objective and well-balanced point of view toward all communities?*

a. Does it approach the community on an objective plane, or can prejudice be reduced to a minimum? (See 2d, e, above.)

b. Can it be related to ways of living in other communities?

c. Can safeguards be developed against romanticizing about the community?

d. Can it be related to social processes at work in all communities?

4. *Does the activity utilize the immediate community as an illustration of broader and basic contemporary problems and trends?*

a. Can the activity relate a local problem, to a broad national or international problem, or to a problem typical of all communities?

b. Does the activity relate to a basic problem or trend rather than to superficial aspects of it?

c. Does the activity make concrete and real the trends and tensions of American life?

5. *Does the activity give the pupil opportunity to participate co-operatively in community movements?*

a. Does the activity enable the pupil to participate actively in community life?

b. Does the activity permit the pupil to assume the responsibility of citizenship himself?

c. Can the activity actually affect community life?

d. Is the activity within the power of the pupils to complete with minimum of adult dominance?

B. Criteria in Terms of Social Value to the Community

While a good community activity may not meet all of these criteria, the activities may be better as they are revised to meet as many as possible.

1. *Does the activity relate to a basic continuing problem rather than to superficial aspects of it?*

2. *Does the activity lead to a desire to participate actively in community life, rather than to withdraw from it?*

3. *Does the activity relate to the normal and usual functioning of community life, rather than to the abnormal and unusual, or is it recognized as abnormal or unusual?*

4. *Can the community be brought to accept the activity as a legitimate phase of the school program?*

5. *Does the activity seek to learn realities about the community, rather than to search for reasons for bolstering community self-esteem?*

6. *Does the activity develop a recognition of the inevitability of social change?*

7. *Does the activity cultivate a disposition to act for the general welfare?*

8. *Does the activity provide for cooperation with community agencies?*

C. Criteria in Terms of Educational Value to the Pupil

Community activities which have been placed in their general educational perspective, and which have social value, must also have educational value to the pupil. A good community activity may not meet all of these criteria, but activities improve as they are revised to meet as many as possible.

1. *Can the activity be related to the present living experiences of boys and girls?*

2. *Is the activity interesting and challenging to boys and girls?*

3. *Can the pupils be led to understand the social significance of the activity?*

4. *Do the pupils participate in planning the activity?*

5. *Does the activity provide for differences in abilities and interests of pupils?*

6. *Can the activity provide for attempts to seek answers, realizing that final answers may be years or decades in the future?*

7. *Is the activity on a level of maturity in keeping with the abilities of the pupils?*

8. *Does the activity contribute to the growth and development of habits, skills, knowledges, procedures, and ideals which are normally used by boys and girls in the important activities of life?*

9. *Does the activity promote critical thinking?*

Adequate preplanning by the teacher, cooperative group planning by students and teacher, intelligent selection of specific activities and projects—these are the basic needs of constructive program planning in the area of community study and participation.

SELECTED REFERENCE

H. H. Giles, *Teacher-Pupil Planning*. New York: Harper, 1941. Much practical advice on promoting effective cooperation and mutual planning. Many actual case studies are included.

CHAPTER 15

Administrative Concerns

It is one thing to educate students by having them quietly read prescribed textbooks at designated times within specified classroom walls; it is quite another matter if those students are to travel about the actual community in search of education through first-hand interviews, field trips, surveys, service projects, work experience, and the like. Such ventures immediately raise difficult administrative problems, among which are those of (1) class scheduling, (2) transportation facilities, (3) extra expenses, and (4) legal liability. Under traditional school conditions, these problems either hardly exist at all, or have long since been roughly defined and settled through official regulation. But when extensive community study and participation is undertaken, all of these matters become pressingly significant to teachers, students, and administrators alike. That is why these four major problems need to be squarely faced before any field study program is authorized by the school or undertaken by any class.

What about the School's Schedule?

The first problem confronting the teacher who attempts active community study (and the excuse given most often by teachers wishing to evade it!) is the school schedule. As ordinarily planned, the schedule of classes is designed to make maximal use of classrooms and teaching staff. The use of time for field study, or even for use of radio, motion pictures, and other such resources, has generally been of little concern in most schools. Although community study in some form is possible within the limitations of any conventional school schedule, the interested teacher should be aware of desirable administrative changes which might enhance its possibilities.

THE UNPLANNED SCHOOL SCHEDULE

Suppose we first consider the school schedule which is *unplanned from the viewpoint of life-centered education,* although thoroughly planned from the book-centered point of view. Under such traditional scheduling, the teacher has classes scattered through the school day without regard to needs for extended visits outside the school. There will be little difficulty in arranging interviews or excursions which do not involve more than one school period, and no hindrance to the utilization of documentary materials, audio-visual aids, and resource persons in the classroom. There will be difficulty, however, in arranging field trips to last more than one class period.

Longer excursions can be planned, however, even within such traditional class schedules. The easier arrangement is to have trips lasting more than one class period scheduled for late afternoons and Saturdays. In such cases conflicts may occur with out-of-school activities of some pupils, but these are usually easier to readjust than are rigid school schedules themselves.

Many schools will allow classes to leave for several consecutive periods, even when other classes must be missed by some students. Frequently an administrator will permit trips to be scheduled upon a central office chart, and from this information, will send notice to all teachers listing students to be absent, the periods for which they are excused, and requesting for these pupils the privilege of "make-up" work. The teacher wishing such special privileges for his students will ordinarily include his own class period among those utilized. He will also be solicitous for the feelings of other teachers, especially of those who have previously demonstrated little enthusiasm for what he is trying to do. It will help to have students arrange in advance for making up the work to be missed, and to assume personal responsibility for seeing that this is done. Notes of appreciation to the cooperating teachers after the event will never be amiss.

In the unplanned schedule there may be only limited opportunity for effective field study. There will be no time barriers, however, to the use of community documents and visual aids such as reports of governmental and service agencies, specimens and models, books and periodicals, photographs and pictures of the community "then" and "now," and the raw data gathered by students as a part of their out-of-class observations.

The Partially Planned School Schedule

Between such an unplanned schedule and one consciously designed for effective life-centered education lies an intermediate stage. This stage, for want of a better term, might be called a *partially planned* school schedule. In it some provisions for curricular enrichment and hence for field study are made, even though a fairly rigid class scheduling program is maintained. To illustrate: teachers are encouraged to exchange rooms in order to utilize special equipment; study periods may be used for special purposes in or outside of the school building; classes meeting during the same period may work upon common projects of mutual interest; interschool visitation may be permitted.

In most American schools, only a few classrooms are equipped to utilize films, slides, recordings, and radio programs. If such classrooms are temporarily unoccupied, or if the teachers using them for other purposes will exchange rooms, these media for community study may be more widely used. Sometimes dark rooms for photographic work may be made available to nonscience classes wishing to use their facilities. Laboratories are frequently opened for experiments or research studies when not in use by science or technical classes. It is often possible for several classes meeting in one period to join for studies of consumer needs, social agencies, family welfare, and similar community problems which may properly be approached from the standpoints of various subject fields. Joint assemblies may be held by several classes to hear a speaker or to see an exhibit.

In such schools, too, it is likely that study periods may be utilized for work on joint projects or for special studies outside of school. Thus, if the members of a given class have a good distribution of study hall time, they may find it possible to make a complete survey throughout the daytime hours.

Some school schedules are suitably arranged for teachers who wish to make occasional trips. In such cases, there is usually no general change in the total schedule, but special adjustments are made. Example: in one school the teachers desiring opportunity for excursion work were assigned classes and free periods alternating at the beginning and end of the school day. It was thus possible for these teachers to take a morning trip which could include a short time before the opening of school, the homeroom period, and the two following class periods without affecting their other classes. This plan might affect one other class taken by the pupils, but this constituted a minimum of schedule disturbance in view of the total time thus made available for field work. It was also possible to arrange joint excursions with other classes whose teachers had similar schedules.

Another plan is to limit formal examinations perhaps to the fifth, tenth, fifteenth and final weeks of the semester, and to allow excursions during other weeks. Such an arrangement prevents the necessity of giving special "make-up" examinations for a few students, one of the major sources of irritation among affected teachers.

Sometimes students are placed in permanent groups whose personnel remain together for several of their school subjects. Where two or three such subjects are scheduled at successive hours, it is possible to arrange a trip which is the joint project of the several instructors concerned with the group. Sample: the biology and the social studies teachers could arrange for the class to visit a local meat packing plant during their two class periods, and to utilize relevant findings in both subject fields. If these class hours are separated by assembly or lunch periods, the consecutive time available would be proportionately lengthened.

THE FULLY PLANNED SCHOOL SCHEDULE

Here and there is a school whose time schedule is *planned to meet student needs in flexible fashion,* rather than to maintain a permanent system of time allotments for various subject fields. In such schools, vital education is considered more important than is habitual routine and the schedule, accordingly, is organized to permit the broadest possible pupil experiences with many activities and many persons. An activity program and block-scheduling of classes are the chief methods used to promote such vital education, whether it be of the older child-centered or the present community-centered type.

Block scheduling is used in both junior and senior high schools, as well as in some colleges. Arising out of the need for reducing the number of pupils facing the teacher at any one time, it has proved valuable for group work of all kinds, including community activities by pupils and teachers. In the junior high school, it is not unusual to have pupils assigned to a "core" teacher for three hours of class time in which are included the "subjects" of English, social studies, and mathematics or general science. In the senior high school, American history and American literature classes are often taught by the same teacher during two consecutive class periods. It is often possible to schedule a study period for such a group either before or after their "integration" class, thus providing an entire morning or afternoon for class excursions or other field activities.

Another arrangement of somewhat similar nature is to schedule both science and social studies as double period laboratory courses, with the same students assigned to both courses. Such arrangements may as easily be made for other subject fields, and with the same result so far as providing consecutive hours for field work activities is concerned.

Whatever the form of block-scheduling used, the plan eliminates schedule conflicts with other subjects and other teachers. The one teacher is solely responsible for the utilization of the time assigned to his student group, and in this extended period, can make excellent use of most of the community study techniques described in Part III. In addition, joint assemblies, recreation, excursions, and other such activities may easily be arranged with other teachers in parallel blocks.

If block scheduling is not used, it is still possible to carry on a variety of activities which cut across time lines, providing the school operates on one of the several group study plans. The Dalton and Winnetka Plans permit individual study and group work to be so arranged that contracts or projects can be completed on a flexible time schedule. Arrangements by the teachers in conference could provide for almost any type of community study and participation. The Morrisonian Plan can be adapted to permit a wealth of community activities during the assimilation periods.

How Shall We Travel?

A second administrative difficulty is that of transportation. To be sure, resource people will usually drive their own cars or use public transport facilities such as planes, trains, busses, streetcars, or taxicabs; so also will individual students and small committees going into the community for interviews, surveys, service projects, work experience, or camp living. But when entire classes take excursions or engage in extended field study, they may find that transportation becomes a real problem requiring special consideration. Let us therefore suggest what may be done in this connection.

THE SCHOOL BUS

Schools which own one or more busses and have a licensed driver can arrange transportation that is both convenient and inexpensive. If the available bus is used primarily to transport students to and from the school, the excursions will have to be scheduled with this necessity in mind; that is, the field study class will be unable to leave the school until the bus has discharged its morning load, and must return in time for the afternoon dismissal. But if a bus is assigned specifically for excursions and extended field study purposes, then its use may be planned just as needed for most effective results.

In either case, some center for traffic control should be established. This will probably be located in the superintendent's office or in that of the Community Service Center's director. Here should be kept a master list of bus assignments for the information of the office, the driver, and the teachers and student committees. Other information to be recorded at the same time should include:

> Name or number of the class
> Name of person in charge
> Number of students involved
> Outline of trip itinerary
> Starting and returning times

After transportation arrangements have been completed, the class group should be notified, the place of meeting posted, and the starting time noted. Before boarding the bus, the accepted rules for behavior on trips should be summarized and stressed as needed.

PUBLIC CARRIER

When no school bus is available, transportation may have to be by public carrier. If distances are short and transfers few, the subway, suburban train, bus or trolley car may be used. In such cases, the trip itself should be chosen with due regard for the availability and convenience of the transportation facilities. Except in special cases such as Nature hikes, walking should be limited to a few blocks. If the group numbers more than a dozen, it will usually be wise to communicate in advance with the transportation officials in order that they may plan for the increased load. Should the number desiring transportation approximate the normal capacity of a bus or streetcar, a special vehicle may often be arranged without extra cost. Under this arrangement, however, the regular franchised route must be followed.

Should the schedule or the route of the regular carrier be inconvenient, the group might well consider hiring a special bus. The cost of a chartered bus is likely to be reasonable, and may be little more than the cost involved in using the regular lines. For relatively short distances in the city, where temporary crowding is not too inconvenient, several taxicabs can often be utilized to good advantage.

In the case of an extended field study trip over a considerable distance, the class group will need to choose carefully among the various available forms of transportation: train, bus, boat, or plane. Considerations of time, expense, distance, and objectives of the trip will obviously determine the decision. Whatever the means chosen, it will often be possible to secure special accommodations for a sizable group: a special bus, a separate coach or Pullman car on the train, a section of a boat or ship, an entire plane. Obviously, it is essential to make travel arrangements well in advance, particularly if such special accommodations are desired.

Individual Transportation

For many trips, even some of extended duration, bicycle transportation may be desirable. While comparatively slow, travel by bicycle possesses great flexibility of itinerary, and also permits travel costs to be kept at an absolute minimum. It offers healthful exercise, recreation, and desirable social stimulation, particularly if youth hostels are utilized by the party for overnight accommodations on longer trips.

Private automobiles are convenient to use for group travel, and possess the further advantage that they do not make the group as conspicuous to the general public as does the use of bus transportation. Only experienced and fully competent adult drivers should be permitted, however, and no car should be accepted which carries less than $100,000/$300,000 public liability insurance. If this amount is not carried by the owner of the private car desired for school use, the school should request that such insurance be purchased at its own expense for the period of time necessary. Unless adequate liability insurance is carried, the legal risk of utilizing private automobiles is too great for both driver and teacher. And in any case, it is well never to use student drivers who are not of legal age; while they may be quite capable, any accident regardless of cause might bring upon the teacher and the school a charge of negligence that would be difficult to answer.

Who Will Pay Our Expenses?

In most school systems, public funds are available for classroom instruction, for some documentary materials, visual and auditory aids, and for mimeographing or duplicating, as well as for limited postage and telephone calls. It is not yet common practice, however, to finance in similar fashion the school use of resource people, field interviews, excursions, surveys, extended field studies, camping, service projects, or work experience. Yet all of these vital educational approaches to the community involve some expense, and in this factor, lies the third important obstacle confronting the community-minded teacher and class.

FREE AND INEXPENSIVE MATERIALS

The teacher who plans a community study program should thoroughly canvas all agencies and activities which might aid the program with little or no expense to the school. Some suggestions: state and local governments will usually supply official publications to schools without charge, as will numerous business corporations, advertising concerns, propaganda agencies, national committees or organizations, and the like. Senators and Representatives can often send United States government publications free. University libraries and research centers are generally open to interested students. The United States Office of Education and the National Education Association can both provide many helpful materials, either as gifts or on a loan basis. Most resource people will gladly come to the school at their own expense, and many worthwhile field activities may involve only the cost of carfare.

State universities and state Departments of Education will loan motion picture films, still pictures, slidefilms, and recordings for only postage costs; so will many federal government bureaus and large business organizations. If the school has no projector, one may probably be borrowed from a local resident or organization. Students are usually pleased to bring from home a portable radio or record player if one is needed for temporary class use.

Valuable as such materials and services may be, they are not always adequate for a satisfactory program of community study and participation. If a social research map is to be shown to the city council, for example, the students may prefer printed map symbols to homemade ones. Many films are not available except on a modest rental basis or through purchase. If speakers come from a distance or have to stay in town overnight, it is only fair to pay their expenses. Excursions and the like usually involve some extra expenses for transportation, and perhaps for food, lodging, and entrance fees. How, then, can this needed extra financing be arranged?

Three policies are commonly followed to provide such funds. We shall examine the practices and merits of each.

INDIVIDUAL FINANCING

Among these three policies the least desirable is that of individual financing. Generally speaking, this policy should not be followed, although there may be some exceptions to the rule. If students are engaged in hobbies for which they habitually provide their own finances, the school might well utilize their interests and materials. For instance, pupils who make or collect photographs, pictures, books, and maps might bring them into the class for group study. Likewise, students who own motion picture equipment or belong to photography clubs might properly be encouraged to center their recreational activities upon community themes. Care must always be taken, however, not to exploit these students in the process.

Another exception would involve trips which are planned for vacation periods, or which could be enjoyed by only one or a few persons. Example: a teacher spends his vacation with some of the boys from his classes; they combine a camping trip with excursions to historic sites. Or a few students may pay all or part of their own expenses as school representatives at a national conference in a distant city. It is naturally preferable for the school to pay all such expenses as these, but it would be unfortunate if interested students, willing to finance themselves, were not allowed to be delegates simply because the school could not pay their way. Thus, students who take a camping trip during vacation, or who attend a conference during the school year, might well find their experiences the center of a class project, even though they paid their own expenses throughout.

It may also be reasonable for students to pay their own way on general class trips, service projects, work experience, and the like providing that such expenses are low in relation to their economic status as individuals, and providing further that such expenditures are planned and announced well in advance. College students, for example, can usually pay proportionately more for personal field activities than can high school students, while the latter are probably better able to finance such experiences than are elementary school pupils.

The real objection to individual financing, however, is that it is basically undemocratic. Any activity planned for a whole class should be freely available to every member of that class. Some students in almost every class find it very hard or even impossible to pay extra expenses for field activities. Teachers sometimes try to meet this problem by having a special fund, supplied by the Parent-Teacher Association or by a service club, from which the cost for needy students may be defrayed. Although the motive is commendable, the result is unfortunate. In such schools, a needy pupil will seek to protect his pride by giving every reason except the true one for not participating in the group project, or he may manage to pay his share at the cost of tremendous personal or family sacrifice.

GROUP FINANCING

A somewhat better although still unsatisfactory policy is that of group financing. Under this arrangement, the field activity in question is conceived of a *class* project which should therefore be planned and financed by the class as a whole, rather than by its members as individuals. The financial responsibility is thus assumed by the entire group for the entire group, and all members share in carrying it, each according to his ability and each in the service of all.

When a class field activity is planned under this policy, the class convenes as a ways and means committee to consider the cost, ways of keeping it down, and methods of raising money. In considering costs, all possible corners will be cut, within the limits of safety and adequate service. Fund-raising campaigns, whatever their nature, should always be planned with due regard for the ethics of good citizenship.

In some schools, the "kitty" is begun by having each student make such contribution as he is able. If this is done, it is important that each contribution be made directly to the teacher, that it be unquestioned, and that the amount given be kept absolutely confidential. Most teachers prefer that there be no such individual payments for the reasons outlined in the previous section.

Much better practice is to divide the class into teams which compete in raising funds through group activities. Possibilities: one team might conduct a candy sale, another present a dramatic performance, another wash cars or tend babies, and all turn in the proceeds for class use. In one school, a parking lot is maintained, manned by students during after-school hours and on week-ends. In other schools, a sum of money (ten cents to a dollar) is invested by each student, and he who makes the greatest return on the investment receives recognition and a small prize. Whatever money-raising means are used, begging ought not to be condoned. Raffles are obviously in this category.

School Financing

In a few but steadily increasing number of schools there is now official recognition of the changes which have occurred in educational philosophy and method in recent years. Not so very long ago, most schools considered instructional and maintenance costs as about the only legitimate charges against the school budget. But today free textbooks and writing materials are provided in a number of states, while in many communities, visual and auditory equipment and aids are considered a proper cost of modern school education. Sometimes such equipment and materials are paid for by Parent-Teacher Associations until school boards become willing to assume the expense. In all schools which have achieved this broader vision of educational method, it is common to find that the school will assume also the major expenses of community studies, including excursions, surveys, extended field study, service projects, work experience, and even summer camping.

Teachers in such forward-looking schools will do well to plan for probable field activities well in advance, and to discuss their financial aspects with the principal, superintendent, or finance officer at the beginning of the school term. Then plans can be made to finance the projected program through appropriate measures. Such costs can be budgeted and an allotment provided, or they can be assigned to existing budgets. Funds for visual and auditory aids may be earmarked for community study materials; subsidies may be granted to the physics class or the photography club to cover community projects, extra funds may be included in provisions for public relations, speakers may be provided by the teachers' institute fund or the general assembly fund, and documentary materials may be provided by increased appropriations to the school library or the classroom library.

The school may easily provide for excursions and other field activities if their major cost is that of transportation. If the district owns a school bus or a fleet of busses, it is relatively easy to arrange a schedule of trips which will utilize these facilities during their free hours. One or more busses may even be reserved solely for such trips, as is sometimes done for athletic and musical activities. Some schools engage public carrier busses on a contract basis, and are willing to assume extra transportation cost in order to provide for desired excursions. Under these circumstances, school trips are not nearly as expensive as when special arrangements have to be made separately for each occasion.

The obvious advantage of school financing is that it assumes the educational values of an organized community program, and makes those values freely available to all interested students and teachers as a matter of course and right. With these educational and social advantages comes a financial one, since the cost of these extended school services will be at a wholesale rather than a retail rate. Thus, in the long view, the actual cost to the students and their parents is less while at the same time, they enjoy the benefits of an enriched and vitalized school program.

Is There Danger of Damage Suits for Accidents?

Legal liability on the part of teachers and school boards is not confined to the field of community study and participation. Liability exists in the case of all school activities, whether in the classroom or laboratory, on the playground or athletic field, or in the community outside. In most states, liability is based upon the rules of common law, and these rules might be summarized thus:

    a. All persons are liable for their own negligence, and
    b. A governmental division or subdivision cannot be sued for negligence in the performance of established governmental duties.

A few states have modified these rules by statute, and some others have changed them by judicial decision. It is not possible to say generally what is the law because that is specific to each state. Only the general lines of legal liability may be indicated here; reference to the school law or the Education Department of one's own state should always be made by interested teachers and administrators.

THE TEACHER'S LIABILITY

In all states, teachers are legally liable for their negligent acts, just as are all adults generally. It is true that there are fewer opportunities for the operation of negligence within the classroom than in the shops, on the gridiron, or in the community. Yet even the stay-at-homes run risks unless care is taken during the use of motion-picture projectors, special equipment, and during the dismissal of the class. Some greater risks are run when students are taken on excursions and when they are in the presence of natural hazards and moving machinery. But so long as the teacher acts as a prudent person, exercising as much care as a parent would, he cannot be held for negligence in the event of an accident.

The occurrence of an accident, in itself, is not proof of negligence. The fact of negligence could not be established until it was proved that the teacher exercised less care than he should have done as a reasonably prudent person in those particular circumstances, and that he should have anticipated the accident, but did not do so— neither of which is easily proved before a court of law. Since the teacher is acting with a parent's responsibility (*in locus parentis*), he must be more diligent than an ordinary bystander would be, even to the extent of protecting the child from his own acts of negligence. But, having exercised this degree of care, the teacher is not liable for accidents which involve students under his supervision.

Even where the negligence of the teacher can be proved, there are still some defenses which might be offered. Unless the negligent act of the teacher is an important factor in causing the injury, there is no liability. If the negligence of the student is greater than that of the teacher, the latter may sometimes not be held liable. Where the parent consents to the presence of the child in specific situations, the ordinary risks inherent in that activity are thereby acknowledged and assumed by the student and the parent.

In most states, teachers may not be reimbursed for damages which they may be forced to pay. New York and New Jersey, however, have changed this law so as to guarantee rather than prohibit reimbursement to their teachers.

The School District's Liability

In the absence of a body of judicial decisions relating to excursions and other school trips, it is impossible to speak with certainty concerning the liability of school districts in this regard. In general, the common law rule already cited applies; this has been well summarized by Punke:

"The weight of authority holds the district not liable for injury to a child in connection with school-bus transportation, unless a statute specifically provides for liability. The doctrine here, in brief, is that 'negligence cannot be imputed to the sovereign, and for this reason, in the absence of a statute, no private action for tort can be maintained against the state.' Hence, suit may not be brought against agencies performing governmental functions, and therefore exercising sovereignty within a limited sphere. Although functions necessary for maintaining schools are in general considered governmental functions, a question may arise concerning the specific aspects of a school program. In determining whether a particular activity is governmental or proprietary, an Oregon court recently said: 'The underlying test is whether the act is for the common good of all without the element of special corporate benefit or pecuniary profit.' "[1]

This doctrine of nonliability on the part of the school district has been recognized by statute in the states of New York and Washington, and should doubtless be accepted in similar manner by other states in the future.

PROTECTING TEACHER AND DISTRICT FROM LIABILITY

In all school situations, teachers and administrators must be sensitive of their responsibility to exercise great care. All school work, and especially all occasions for leaving the supervision and routine of the school grounds, should be planned with full regard for all physical hazards and safeguards. All possible dangers should be investigated. Areas of special hazard, such as traffic, machinery, excavations, and bodies of water should be prepared against well in advance. Thorough group discussion of such dangers, together with the development of a sound personal safety program and code, is always desirable, even with adults, under many circumstances.

Particular vigilance must be maintained when selecting travel facilities. Only reputable companies should be considered, and always the teacher or other school official should investigate the matter of insurance. In no case should student-driven automobiles be used, and considerable reserve should be maintained in the utilization of any private cars whatever.

In every case where students are to leave the school grounds, the parents should first be informed and their written permission obtained for the trip. Often a courteous letter from the school to each student's parents may serve the double purpose of securing consent and of informing the parents of the general excursion program. A useful letter of this type is reproduced below.[2]

My dear .... :
         (Parent's name)

Your (son, daughter) .... is enrolled in our
                        (Pupil's name)

.... class. We earnestly wish to make this course
  (Subject)

---

[1] Harold H. Punke, "Liability for Injury in School-bus Transportation." *American School Board Journal,* September 1940, pp. 38 ff.

[2] This letter (excluding its lower section) is reproduced from Henry C. Atyeo, *The Excursion As a Teaching Technique,* pp. 105–06.

as valuable as possible, and we believe that the value can be increased by giving opportunity to pupils to acquire a firsthand acquaintance with places and objects about which we are studying. We are therefore offering to your (son, daughter) the opportunity of visiting, under our supervision, some of the buildings, museums, and other places of interest, where such firsthand knowledge can be obtained.

We hope for your cooperation in this study-plan, and ask you to give written permission for .... to take part in the
(Pupil's name)
proposed visits. Your permission for (him, her) to accompany us on any one occasion at a specified time does not imply that you are granting permission for (him, her) to take part in all the excursions that are planned—although we hope that you may be willing for (him, her) to share in all.

The only cost for the supervised visits will be that of transportation and, in some instances, for small incidental expenses. It is estimated that the total cost for all trips will not exceed $ ..... for the term.

If you are willing to let .... share in this first
(Pupil's name)
supervised trip made by the class, will you please sign and return to me the accompanying waiver, without which the school authorities cannot allow any pupil to participate in any excursion.

Yours very truly,

....
(Teacher's signature)

PARENT'S CONSENT FOR AN EXCURSION

I hereby consent to allow my child .... to be
(Pupil's name)
taken on an excursion to .... on ....
(Destination)   (Date)
This permission is given on the understanding that (he, she) will be under school supervision throughout the time of the excursion itself.

Signed ....
(Parent or Guardian)
Date ....

It would be unwise and of no legal value to have the parent sign a waiver of school responsibility. No parent can sign away a minor's right to have suit brought in his name should occasion warrant, and any request for such a waiver appears both ridiculous and irresponsible. The value of the parental consent slip lies solely in its documentary evidence that the parent knew and approved of the activity in question, and thereby assumed with and for the child the ordinary risks inherent in such activity. Because of their possible legal significance, all parental consent slips should be preserved for some time.

As further protection for both parties, the teacher should keep his principal or other administrative official fully informed regarding his plans for student activities off the school grounds. Such advance consultation is itself presumptive evidence of prudence, and to that extent a negation of negligence.

Crux of the Matter

When all is said and done, these problems of legal liability, transportation, scheduling, and finance are relatively minor in significance. The school that really wants to develop a more effective program through community study and directed participation will have little difficulty with administrative details. What is all-important is the willingness of administrators and teachers to experiment together, even at the cost of a changed routine.

SELECTED REFERENCES

SCHEDULING

Culley, Benjamin H., "School and Work Experience in Los Angeles." *Progressive Education* 20:181–82 (April 1943).

Dix, Lester, *A Charter for Progressive Education,* Ch. 10. New York: Bureau of Publications, Teachers College, Columbia University, 1939.

Gelinas, Paul J., "School-Industry Contact." *Clearing House* 16:302–04 (Jan. 1942).

Neuman, Charles E., "Helping the Farmers—Without Missing a Class." *School Executive* 62:16–19 (April 1943).

Turrell, A. M., "Not School *or* Work but Work *and* School." *School Executive* 62:19–20 (May 1943).

LIABILITY

Edwards, Newton, *The Courts and the Public Schools.* Chicago: University of Chicago Press, 1933.

National Education Association, "Teacher Liability for Pupil Injuries." Washington: The Association, 1940.

Punke, Harold H., *Law and Liability in Pupil Transportation.* Chicago: University of Chicago Press, 1943.

Rosenfield, Harry N., *Liability for School Accidents.* New York: Harpers, 1940.

—— "Liability." In Harry N. Rivlin and Herbert Schueler (eds.), *Encyclopedia of Modern Education,* pp. 456–57. New York: The Philosophical Library, 1943.

CHAPTER 16

Evaluation

How are we doing? To what extent are we achieving our goals? Wherein are we succeeding and failing, and what shall we do about it? These fundamental queries should persistently accompany any program of community study and participation. For unless objective evaluation (how are we doing?) is an integral part of such activities, they may easily become ineffective, distorted, or even subversive of the purposes envisioned.

How does evaluation occur? The process may be simple or complex, limited or extensive, but in any case, it centers around four basic steps, as follows:

1. **Define the goals.** Decide exactly what you want to accomplish—what specific understandings, attitudes, and skills you wish to achieve through the project at hand.

2. **Collect evidence of achievement.** Assemble all possible data indicating relative success and failure in achieving the goals as defined.

3. **Decide degree of present success.** Formulate conclusions, based upon the evidence, concerning the extent to which sought goals are actually being realized.

4. **Draw inferences for future policy.** Recognize the implications of present success or failure for future activity; describe those implications in terms of adjusted or expanded purposes, thereby returning to step 1 of the evaluative process and proceeding again through steps 2, 3, and 4. Thus, the whole process of evaluation is continued as long as the project itself may last.

Careful evaluation ought to be a part of any cooperative community project. No matter which of the ten bridges between school and community are being used, the evaluative process should begin when the project begins, and should remain an integral aspect of that project from beginning to end. From preliminary planning through final culmination, the persistent question is this: *How are we doing now, and how might we do better in the future?*

A Case Study

The Place of Science in Our Community was the topic being studied in Miss Warren's ninth-grade science class. Today one of the students brought in a newspaper clipping telling about the prevalence of undulant fever in the nation. Some pupils raised the question of whether undulant fever occurred in their own local community. No one knew. Discussion of where such information might be obtained brought out the fact that undulant fever is usually spread through milk. Presently Tim volunteered, "I think Mr. Barker out at the Dairy Products Company would know. He knows a lot about milk."

Miss Warren replied with enthusiasm, "That's a good idea, Tim! Do you know Mr. Barker?" When Tim said that he did, Miss Warren continued, "Could you ask him about undulant fever here in town? Whatever you find out will be a real help to our discussion."

At this point Harold exclaimed, "Say, why don't we take a field trip to the Dairy Products Company?" Class interest mounted at once. Miss Warren reminded the class that they did not take excursions just for fun, that most of them had been to the Dairy Products Company when they were in the sixth grade, and that the decision about an excursion must be made on the basis of what could be gained from it. The class then adjourned with the plan of discussing field trip purposes on the following day, and also to hear Tim's and Harold's report of their interview with Mr. Barker.

After school, Miss Warren thought through the question of the proposed excursion. She got out the list of course objectives which she had drawn up at the beginning of the year. That list, and her thinking about its several items, now went something like this:

WHAT STUDENTS SHOULD BE ABLE TO DO AT THE END OF THIS COURSE

1. **Attitudes and Beliefs:**
    a. A student should believe that the good of the community depends upon the individuals within the community.
    b. . . .

    The field trip could emphasize the fact that public health depends upon the willingness of dairy men to have their cattle tested regularly for undulant fever, and infected animals destroyed . . .

2. Interests:

   a. A student should become increasingly interested in exploring his environment.

   b. . . .

   Certainly experience in getting acquainted with one of the important food processes carried on in the community should increase interest in learning about other community enterprises . . .

3. Appreciations:

   a. A student should appreciate the beauty of buildings and apparatus which are well designed to serve their purposes.

   b. . . .

   The question of functional design would be brought up when the class enters the milk-bottle doorway of the Dairy Products Company. Inside the plant, attention could be directed to such apparatus as the cooling coils . . .

4. Skills:

   a. A student should be able to interview successfully an adult who is well informed about some phase of a scientific or social process.

   b. . . .

   By careful planning, it should be possible to have students who are inexperienced in interviewing, like Tim, share responsibility with students of more experience, like Johnny. Furthermore, each student should gain confidence by asking a question or two of the guide on the trip . . .

5. Habits:

   a. A student should have desirable and well-established health habits.

   b. . . .

   The field trip ought to initiate or strengthen the habit of drinking only pasteurized milk. Evidence about this habit could easily be obtained. Students could write a statement about "What Kind of Milk I Drink," and then could revise it later on in the light of the excursion experience. The difference between the original and the revised statement would indicate whether change in the habit had occurred. Towards the end of the semester, we could make a further check on the use of pasteurized milk . . .

6. Information:

   a. A student should know the content material and the basic generalizations suggested in the course syllabus.

   b. . . .

   Now let's see what important information required by the syllabus might be mastered as a result of this excursion. Oh, here is something—"Steps in processing milk." We could learn those facts very easily . . .

7. **Critical Thinking:**
   a. A student should be able to apply scientific generalizations to immediate situations.
   b. . . .

   Earlier in the term, we developed some generalizations about the effect of heat and cold upon bacterial life and vitamin strength. We stressed the fact that cold prevents bacterial growth, that heat kills bacteria, and that heat also destroys vitamins. Now we can see if we are applying these generalizations in thinking about the purpose and technique of pasteurization . . .

8. **Personal-Social Relations:**
   a. A student should develop a feeling of belonging to the group, and of desiring to contribute his utmost to common group projects.
   b. . . .

   The trip would offer plenty of opportunity for the class to plan, organize, execute, and evaluate, and would thus give them valuable experience in democratic and cooperative methods of work. And if each student had some definite, personal responsibility for the trip, his sense of belonging would be increased. My anecdote file will be a help in figuring out what sort of thing each student could do—things that would contribute to the excursion itself and at the same time promote individual growth. I'll take a look at the list of student term projects, too, and see which ones might be furthered through this trip . . .

9. **Social Sensitivity:**
   a. A student should become increasingly aware of the interrelation between scientific processes and social welfare.
   b. . . .

   Interrelationships between the producer, the processor, and the consumer of milk could be emphasized. We could go into the problem of costs, and agreements, at each point that the milk changes hands. Social sensitivity to such problems ought to be increased through talking with some people who are concerned with these problems . . .

10. **Philosophy of Life:**
    a. A student should value physical health as a prerequisite to other values in human living.
    b. . . .

    The trip certainly would emphasize this viewpoint, especially if we afterward discussed some of the diseases you can get from drinking contaminated raw milk . . .

This thinking led Miss Warren to conclude that the proposed field trip might contribute markedly to student growth, and would therefore be a legitimate use of school time. Her next concern was what specific objectives the class would agree upon for the trip. Accordingly, she thought through that problem in preliminary fashion, so that the class discussion of the following day would neither go off on a tangent nor ignore important considerations.

The next class hour was spent in planning the mechanics of the excursion, and in developing a list of major questions to be answered by the trip:

1. *How is undulant fever spread through the milk supply?*
2. *What other diseases may be transmitted in the same way?*
3. *What are the various steps in pasteurizing milk?*
4. *How does what we have learned about the effect of heat and cold upon bacteria and vitamins apply to milk processing?*
5. *What does the money for a bottle of milk really pay for?*
6. *What other big ideas are important in milk processing and distribution?*

Besides these informational objectives, the students also listed three others, as follows:

7. *To improve our interview technique since we will need it later when we make the community survey we are planning.*
8. *To show that we know how to conduct ourselves better than we did on our last excursion.*
9. *To get ideas and materials for some of our individual term projects.*

The general question was then raised: "How will we know whether we each can answer the questions listed, and how well we have accomplished our other purposes?" Discussion of this problem led to suggestions for some student committees. One committee was to work with Miss Warren in devising a test through which class members might see if they knew the answers to questions 1, 2, 3, and 5. Questions 4 and 6 could be answered by having each student make a written report outlining the science ideas he had seen utilized in the processing of milk. A second committee of students and teacher was given the responsibility of appraising the written reports when made. It was further agreed that later interviews would indicate whether or not purpose 7 was accomplished, that group discussion about excursion behavior would be adequate for evaluation of objective 8, and that number 9 would have to be appraised at the end of the term when individual project reports were turned in.

The report of Tim and Harold about their talk with Mr. Barker launched further planning for the trip. The day for the excursion was decided. Would Tim and Harold let Mr. Barker know the date chosen, and also the questions the class wanted answered? What arrangements were best for transportation, and what conduct was desirable en route? Committees on transportation, conduct standards, and other problems were organized, and, before the session ended, each student in the class had a place upon some committee.

On the day of the trip the advisability of all this careful planning was evident. Each student was aware of his personal responsibility, and Mr. Barker had in mind the questions raised by the class, as well as the larger purposes of the trip which Miss Warren had discussed with him the day before. As he conducted the group through the plant, Mr. Barker made appropriate explanations, and answered the questions asked by members of the class in keeping with their group and individual objectives.

A necessary intermission during the excursion gave the class about ten minutes for an extemporaneous evaluative session. "How are we doing?" the students asked as they checked the purposes they had formulated earlier to see which had already been achieved, and which still remained to be accomplished. They listed questions which shy members had thought of, but had not asked Mr. Barker, and encouraged those members to ask at least one of their questions later on. Students who had asked questions especially well, and who had been particularly thoughtful of others on the trip, were commended. The committee on conduct pointed out that the group's behavior on this excursion was already an improvement over that of the last field trip; the test committee reminded the class of a written review of answers to the questions formulated by the class; and the committee on reports recalled for the group that written reports were to be handed in the following day and were to be appraised in terms of the number and quality of applications of scientific principles noted.

On the following day, the class period was begun with reports from the various committees. As each reported, it was commended upon those aspects of its work that were particularly well done. Suggestions were made for improved operation of such committees in the future. The interviewing experience was discussed analytically. Thus, part of the period was devoted to an informal evaluative session. Then the latter part of the time was spent in taking the test prepared by the student committee in cooperation with Miss Warren. The papers were scored in class so that students could thus appraise themselves and, at the same time, clear up any misunderstandings they may have had.

A general, summarizing discussion of the whole excursion experience was carried on the next day. This gave Miss Warren considerable opportunity to see whether the class now believed that the health of the community depends upon practices of its members, had developed greater interest in exploring its environment, had increased its appreciation of functional design, had become more aware of the interrelation between scientific processes and human welfare, and had come to value personal health more deeply. The discussion was finally summarized by Miss Warren as she briefly explained how the trip related to the work of the unit and the purposes of both the course itself and the school in a democratic nation.

Even now the excursion experience was not ended. A few days later it was further reviewed when the committee on written reports pointed out what science concepts and their applications students had noted in the milk processing. That review was also a springboard to greater emphasis upon science principles, and to further consideration of their applications in the unit currently studied. Under these arrangements, the field experience was made a definite and integral part of the immediate unit and of the term's work as a whole.

Perhaps the most important aspect of the excursion evaluation program was the inferences and the plans that Miss Warren then formulated. She thought over the evaluative discussions, the data secured by analyzing the student reports and from scoring the tests, and the anecdotal incidents noted. What individual strengths and weaknesses were disclosed? What personal interests were evident? What had the class as a whole accomplished, and what further achievements were needed? In terms of her answers to these questions, Miss Warren then began to plan future class activities and appropriate student responsibilities. In so doing, she was careful to keep in mind the fact that her appraisal of the excursion experience was only partial, since some aspects of student learning could not be properly judged at this time. Miss Warren therefore made only tentative judgments about individuals and the group, and looked forward to additional opportunities for appraisal in the future. These further opportunities, she knew, would enlarge her understanding of each child and of the class as a whole. Meanwhile, however, she concluded that in terms of its varied goals, this particular excursion had been genuinely successful, and was therefore as practical a use of class time as could have been made under the circumstances.

How Can We Evaluate Our Program?

This brief sketch of how a field trip might be appraised is intended to illustrate several important aspects of modern evaluation in relation to community study. Suppose we now summarize and further interpret those aspects in the form of six basic principles:

1. EVALUATION SHOULD BE AN INTEGRAL AND CONTINUOUS PART OF THE COMMUNITY PROJECT

In the case-study just analyzed, evaluation was an important aspect of every step in the process, from the initial planning of the trip through its final follow-up. This procedure is in flat contrast to the more common afterthought, "Well, we had an interesting excursion! Don't you think we ought to stop now and evaluate it before we go on with our regular work?" Evaluation should never be such an isolated activity, apart from the project itself. Objective appraisal should be continuous throughout the progress of every community project, every unit in community study, every program of school-community relationships. Fortunate are the students of that teacher who, at the start of the school year, has access to a cumulative record summary of each pupil's community studies and experiences during his previous school years. Factual information concerning expressed interests, community contacts and achievements, peer relations in the field, and other such factors enables the teacher to plan more effectively for maximum pupil growth and development during the coming year. By analyzing the community-experience records of his students as a group, the teacher will be able to foresee activities that will be of most worth to the class as a whole, as well as to the individual members.

Another valuable aid to planning is a class log or diary, reporting the group members' community experiences of previous years, and noting those activities which were especially interesting and particularly well done and worthwhile. This kind of informal student record enables teachers, in succeeding years, to plan activities to supplement and extend earlier community experiences, thereby stimulating interest and providing challenge without likelihood of either boredom or frustration.

Child and Curriculum I

Made a survey of my own community to discover how the school cooperated with other agencies working for welfare of children.

Visited Franklin Rural School to talk with principal about the way in which a Central School can become a community center.

Visited N.Y.A. Residence center to find out about the kind of education provided for older youth.

During participation in the fifth grade, went to the Sheffield farm distributing company in Oneonta. We were told how many farmers and the radius of farmers sending milk and the importance of the company to Oneonta.

Participated in a class discussion when Mr. Huntington, agriculture teacher from Westford, talked to group about land classification and its effect on school support.

Participated in group discussion when Mr. Polson from Cornell talked on some of the techniques of community surveys.

Junior Child and Curriculum II

Took a field trip to Table Rocks to see how geographic factors affected the agricultural industry in this area.

Visited the Stamford Central School with Miss Hodgdon, to get overview of central school set up. Spent day there.

Participated in a panel discussion on Health, at the Tri-County Conference.

Student Teaching
Off-Campus

Made a community study of defense efforts of the community.
Attended the Sunday and Wednesday evening services in church.
Participated in the Easter cantata rehearsal.

On-Campus

Participated in program of the Womans Home Mission society of the Methodist church. Helped show slides on problems of migratory workers over the country.
Participated in sugar and gas rationing.
Attended a P.T.A. meeting.
Participated in a room mothers meeting. Helped interview some of the fourth-grade mothers.
Participated in activities for MacArthur day - guided children in making posters.
Visited the homes of some of the children.
Attended the Young Peoples society regularly.

PART OF A STUDENT'S PROFESSIONAL LOG. Prospective teachers at New York State Teachers College (Oneonta) systematically record their community experiences as one basis for self-evaluation of professional growth.

2. The Objectives of a Community Experience Are the Basis for Its Evaluation

Any appraisal is begun by specifying objectives. These goals must never be forgotten during the evaluation process, especially since the final step of that process is the interpretation of findings in terms of the original objectives sought. It is therefore desirable in planning any extensive community program to use some such form as this:

OBJECTIVES	COMMUNITY EXPERIENCE	SOURCES OF EVIDENCE	DATA–GATHERING DEVICES
1. *Attitudes*			
. . . . .			
2. *Interests*			
. . . . .			
3. *Appreciations*			
. . . . .			
etc. etc.			

A form like this keeps the teacher constantly aware of the interrelation between educational objectives and community experiences, and furthermore serves to remind him that evidence must be collected through definite procedures and must be interpreted in terms of the listed objectives.

If objectives are to be most fruitfully used for evaluative purposes, they must be stated as types of behavior changes desired in students. "A student should believe that the good of the community depends upon the individuals within the community." This objective, like the others on Miss Warren's list, tells how a student is expected to *act,* and thereby suggests the kinds of learning experiences necessary to produce such action in life situations. Since any community project or program is presumably designed to bring about desired changes in student's *behavior,* it seems clear that instructional success will have to be estimated in terms of the extent to which such desired changes in student behavior have actually occurred. We must beware of mistaking word glibness about the community for better citizenship within the community!

3. Evaluation Should Be Comprehensive

In planning how to evaluate the excursion, Miss Warren considered ten different phases of desired behavior. Certain factors of time and measuring instruments limited appraisal to some aspects of behavior and ignored others, but the teacher kept these limitations in mind and was careful to interpret the value of the trip accordingly.

The teacher who wants to evaluate his efforts comprehensively will need to plan for the year or semester as a whole, consciously considering desirable changes in every phase of student behavior. However, he will be wise if he attempts only limited evaluative studies at any one time. He may acquire some evidence about attitude changes and informational achievements tomorrow, more

---

PART II

SOCIAL SITUATION INTERVIEW

Are you becoming more sensitive to the social importance of facts and ideas? Below are descriptions of four common social situations. These descriptions are easily understood. You should express yourself concerning the way you feel twoard this situation. React in terms of your beliefs as well as your ideas. For each social situation presented, list all of the thoughts that occur to you which are of importance. Consider the implications the situation has for you personally, for your community, and for society in general.

EXAMPLE:

Recreation in the village of B_____ is described in part as follows:

> "On Saturdays the village street is lined with cars from the country, whose owners attend the picture show after their trading is completed. The manager reported, however, that the country attendance has dropped more than one third since the depression."

Among the responses that one might include are the following:

1. Life is drab for the farmer and his family, so they need some kind of recreation.

2. With the coming of the automobile, farmers have been able to get to town more easily.

3. During a depression farm prices are low.

TESTING COMMUNITY UNDERSTANDING. Direction page with example from a test used at the Central Michigan College of Education.

data three weeks later, and further evidence a month after that. He may obtain scores on comparable forms of a standardized test, given as a pretest and again as a post-test, in order to measure changes in various aspects of behavior. By the end of the semester, if he has kept adequate records, he should be able to combine these many bits of evidence into a fairly comprehensive picture of individual student's behavior, and will thereby *know* a great deal about what the class has really accomplished through its utilization of community resources.

4. EVALUATION SHOULD MAKE USE OF VARIED TECHNIQUES OF APPRAISAL AND UTILIZE MANY SOURCES OF DATA

It would be impossible to understand a child's complex behavior, or to obtain data bearing upon each objective of a community course or program, if only a single data-gathering device were used. This was obvious in the case of the field trip, wherein the appraisal of different objectives required the employment of different techniques. In order to appraise changes in personal-social relations, the teacher had observed individual reactions within the group sphere, and recorded them in anecdotal form. To estimate changes in beliefs, interests, appreciations, and social sensitivity, she watched student reactions and listened carefully to statements made during class discussions. To appraise ability to apply generalizations, committee members and the teacher studied the written excursion reports made by each student. To evaluate skill in interviewing, each student observed critically the response he and his classmates secured from adults questioned on the field trip. Factual information was tested in a written examination. Thus, a variety of sources was tapped by various means in an attempt to obtain a more nearly complete and well-rounded picture of individual and group accomplishment.

In appraising any one kind of behavior, more than one evaluative technique may often be appropriate. In the excursion cited, student attitudes were judged through careful analysis of what students said or implied in a free discussion period. But a more reliable study of attitude changes might have been made through a number of other approaches. To illustrate: Fraser used a self-made *Opinions Test* and also the *Kelly-Remmers Attitude Test* in evaluating the Tennessee and Georgia extended field studies made by New York City's Lincoln School seniors a few years ago. He was thereby able to find out that those students, as a result of their field study experience, became less favorable to unlimited individual initiative in farming, and more inclined toward private ownership of utilities, than they had been before.

Robbins appraised the Antioch field study course in sociology through the use of pretests and post-tests of opinion and thinking, anecdotal records, free-response tests on social problems observed, a library-reading check list, a check-list evaluation of group experiences, and a questionnaire. In evaluating an eleventh-grade field study of the coal industry, Raths used not only pencil-and-paper tests, but also excerpts from correspondence, conversations, and parental interviews. Diary records proved most helpful when a group of instructors at Oneonta State Teachers College made a study of two contrasting communities which were home towns for some prospective teachers and future teaching locations for others.

Another easily used means of evaluating behavior changes is that of analyzing students' community notebooks, posters, cartoons, scrapbooks, slides, essays, themes, debates, and other such personal exhibits. All of these items, assuming that they have been conscientiously done, should reveal to the discerning teacher most of the ten kinds of behavior considered in this chapter.

5. Evaluation Should Be Concerned with Both Immediate and Ultimate Changes in Student Behavior

Too frequently evaluation is limited to appraisal of immediate, and often temporary, changes in students. The teacher who finds delight in the high scores made by his students on a factual test of community information might be surprised at the low scores received on a retest several months later. Obversely, the teacher who has developed a test of ability to apply basic principles may be gratified to find that student scores months later compare very favorably with scores made at the time the principles were first learned. Both immediate and delayed outcomes should be appraised.

6. Evaluation Should Emphasize Self-Appraisal, Both Group and Individual

Much group self-appraisal was integral to the dairy products field trip previously described. The class as a whole identified its purposes for that trip, and planned for appraisal with respect to those purposes. The student committees, with the teacher's aid, gathered data about achievement of certain objectives, analyzed the evidence, and, in cooperation with the whole class, used their findings as a basis for drawing valid inferences about future activities.

Extensive experience in individual self-evaluation is also most important. Students are expected to grow toward mature and intelligent adulthood in the community. They need to develop facility in appraising their own personal accomplishments and deficiencies, and in proposing and executing plans for improving their strengths and overcoming their weaknesses. Guided experience in critical self-evaluation will help them to develop such abilities.

The question is sometimes raised as to whether evaluation should be student self-appraisal or teacher-appraisal of students. Probably no evaluation program is ever exclusively one or the other. The extent to which evaluation centers in students or in teacher will

EVALUATION OF GROUP MEMBERS Is the member	Very	Somewhat	Little
Responsible for attendance at meetings?			
Willing to contribute to discussions?			
Willing to do outside reading and report to the group?			
Willing to do field work?			
Willing to help assemble, interpret, and write up findings?			
Willing to listen to others?			
Capable of doing satisfactory field work?			
Able to stick to the point in discussion?			
Skillful in presenting his ideas to the group?			
Original in contributing to group plans?			

EVALUATION FORM USED IN SURVEY PROJECT. Students at the Central Michigan College of Education appraise each other's participation at the conclusion of a group survey of the local community.

vary from class to class, and will necessarily depend upon the maturity of the students and upon their previous experience in self-
appraisal.

No matter what the proportion of self-appraisal and teacher-
appraisal, mutual cooperation in evaluation should be as great as
can possibly be developed. Both students and teacher should assume real responsibility for evaluating learning progress in the
community program. The extent to which mutual cooperation is
a fact can quickly be determined by analyzing evaluative plans in
the light of these criteria:

a. **Objectives:** Did the purposes grow out of the needs, interests, and
   problems of the students? Are they in keeping with student abilities?
   Are students fully and constantly aware of what objectives were
   agreed upon?
b. **Opportunity for Choice:** Did students consider alternative possibilities before final selection was made by the group?
c. **Flexibility:** Were changes made in original plans as subsequent
   events indicated the need for such changes?
d. **Full Experience:** Was there adequate opportunity for every student
   to have rich experiences with the dramatic, the novel, the thrilling,
   the inspiring—both emotionally and intellectually—to reflect quietly
   upon their experiences—to pursue individual interests by themselves
   —to exchange ideas with their classmates—to analyze the total experience in a spirit of mutual, yet critical, helpfulness?

Finally

Although only a field trip has been offered by way of case-study
illustration, the six basic principles of evaluation would apply with
equal validity to any other fundamental technique of cooperative
community education. Whether students are promoting their community understanding by observing the community around them,
by participating experimentally in some of its activities, or by
sharing deeply its processes, they can and should make evaluation
an integral part of their experience. If they are to do that, we,
their teachers, must, with them, think clearly about the *real values*
to be sought in connection with every projected school-community
experience. Together, we shall have to ask and tentatively answer
the generic question: *Does the proposed activity seem likely to
stimulate maximum educational growth* as judged in terms of
the community education criteria proposed in Chapter 14?

As we examine proposed life-centered projects and programs in
the light of these standards, we may be able to summarize our
thinking in terms of three basic evaluative queries, as follows:

a. **What are the real purposes of this project?** Are they in keeping with the purposes of democratic education and with the objectives of the course as a whole? In what specific ways do we want to behave differently as a result of having this experience?

b. **What evidences of achievement may there be?** In what situations will behavior changes be most apparent? Just how, specifically, can we expect students and cooperating adults to act differently because of this project? How will the community be changed?

c. **How can valid evidence of behavior changes be obtained?** Can this be done in such a way that students learn from the process? What are the simplest and most fruitful techniques and measuring instruments? In what ways can students share in using them?

Throughout the progress of every community education project, both the teacher and the class will want to ask, "How are we doing? Are we accomplishing our purposes?" At the conclusion of the experience, they will inquire: "Just what was accomplished? How effectively did we work? What did we learn from this experience that we can use in the future?" Such, in brief résumé, is modern evaluation in the democratic manner. Its result will be to improve teaching effectiveness, vitalize curriculum content, and demonstrate worthwhile learning to the community itself.

SELECTED REFERENCES

Atyeo, Henry C., *The Excursion as a Teaching Technique*, Ch. VI. Contributions to Education 761. New York: Bureau of Publications, Teachers College, Columbia University, 1939. Reports a controlled experiment comparing learning values in history achieved through excursions, with those achieved through classroom instruction.

Fraser, James A., *Outcomes of a Study Excursion*. Teachers College Contributions to Education 778. New York: Bureau of Publications, Teachers College, Columbia University, 1939. Reports scientific measurements in attitude changes among Lincoln High School students as a result of their extended field study in Tennessee and Georgia.

Jones, William J., "Measuring Some Outcomes of a Field-Study Experience." *Educational Research Bulletin* (Ohio State University) 19:31–47, 58 (Jan. 17, 1940). Evaluates objectively the educational results of a ten-day field study made by West Virginia high-school students in New York City. Measurement procedures, findings, and students' reactions are given.

—— "Some Further Evaluations of a Field-Study Experience." *Educational Research Bulletin* (Ohio State University) 19:99–104, 116 (Feb. 14, 1940). A sequel to the previous report, which was expressed in terms of group tendencies. The present article studies the scores, records, and impressions made by two individual students on the trip.

Meshke, E. D., "The Effects of Utilizing Selected Community Resources in Ninth-grade and Tenth-grade Homemaking Classes." *Journal of Experimental Education* 12:1–9 (Sept. 1943). Summarizes a doctoral study of the use of community resources in connection with home economics study, and the relative effectiveness of study in the community and in the classroom.

Phelps, Seth, "Urban High-School Boys on the Farm." *School Review* 52:293–98 (May 1944). Reports "an experiment conducted to determine the effectiveness with which teachers could judge the ability of students to 'make good' in an actual work situation." Tells how evaluation was secured, indicates comparative ratings by teachers and farmers, analyzes work habits and attitudes, and suggests general findings.

Price, Roy A., and Robert F. Steadman, "Testing for Community Information." In Ruth West (ed.), *Utilization of Community Resources in the Social Studies:* Ninth Yearbook of the National Council for the Social Studies, pp. 213–25. Cambridge, Mass.: The Council, 1938. Briefly discusses the testing of students' knowledge of the community, and then describes the construction of an informational test on community affairs for the Regents Inquiry into the Cost and Character of Public Education in New York State. This "Cooperative Community Affairs Test, Form R," is now published by the Cooperative Test Service, 15 Amsterdam Avenue, New York City.

Raths, Louis, "Some Evaluations of the Trip." *Educational Research Bulletin* (Ohio State University) 27:189–208 (Oct. 1938); *Education Digest*, Dec. 1938. Reports a controlled experiment on interpretation of data, consistency in social attitudes, and changes in liberalism-conservatism, as result of a Lincoln School field study in coal and steel communities.

Robbins, Irving, "An Evaluation of the Field Course." *Educational Research Bulletin* (Ohio State University) 20:64–78 (March 12, 1941). Summarizes the participating group's evaluation of an Antioch College field course in sociology. Explains procedures, performance on tests, responses and records of various kinds.

Smith, F. Tredwell, *An Experiment in Modifying Attitudes Toward the Negro.* (Contributions to Education, 887.) New York: Bureau of Publications, Teachers College, Columbia University, 1943. A doctoral study which measured attitude changes among white students as a result of four days of favorable experiences in Negro Harlem.

Taba, Hilda, "General Principles and New Practices in Evaluation." In William E. Young (ed.), *The Social Studies in the Elementary School:* Twelfth Yearbook of the National Council for the Social Studies, Ch. XII. Washington: The Council, 1941. Presents purposes of evaluation, and many examples to show techniques for evaluating clear thinking, democratic social attitudes, and social interests.

—— "The Evaluation of Critical Thinking." In Howard R. Anderson (ed.), *Teaching Critical Thinking in the Social Studies:* Thirteenth Yearbook of the National Council for the Social Studies, Part IV. Washington: The Council, 1942. Purposes, characteristics, principles and problems of evaluation of critical thinking are discussed at length, and numerous illustrations are given.

Van Til, William, and Louis Raths, "The Influence of Social Travel on Relations Among High-School Students." *Educational Research Bulletin* (Ohio State University) 23:63–68 (March 15, 1944). A study of the extent to which a week's field trip changed the participating students' attitudes toward each other.

Wilson, Howard E., "Developing Skill in Critical Thinking Through Participation in School and Community Life." In Howard R. Anderson (ed.), *Teaching Critical Thinking in the Social Studies:* Thirteenth Yearbook of the National Council for the Social Studies, Part III. Washington: The Council, 1942. Techniques for developing skill in discovering problem-situations in school and community life, in finding and evaluating information about school and community life, and in group planning and social action.

CHAPTER 17

Public Relations

The democratic school draws upon and also contributes to the community. Such a school cannot hope to maintain a successful program if community resources are not available for instructional purposes, or if the community itself is not open to students and teachers as a work-service laboratory. It is therefore essential that administrators, teachers, and students alike understand how every interview, excursion and survey, every extended field study, service project and work experience is a venture in public relations— a situation through which they interpret the school and its program to parents and community groups. Every such contact which brings commendation of school personnel and policy creates also the basis for increased appreciation and public support and, conversely, every dissatisfactory incident experienced by cooperating adults provides ground for community criticism of school affairs. Amiable public relations are essential to the successful building of bridges between school and community life.

As practical psychologists, teachers must know and apply the fundamental principle of successful public relations: *If you want somebody to support your program, be sure that he fully comprehends its values and shares with personal satisfaction in its development.* Thus you may build both passive *consent* and active *support* for that program.

Any comprehensive policy for securing public tolerance and support must include several major aspects, each vital in itself, as well as in its relationship to the whole. For convenience in analysis, let us therefore identify and examine four such aspects, each in turn.

How May We Secure Community Consent and Support?

Three general groups of people must always be considered in all plans for improved relations between the school and the community. These groups are the students themselves, their parents, and the public at large. Suppose we examine some successful approaches to each of these groups.

Build Better Student Attitudes

As the curriculum becomes increasingly life-centered in scope and function, it will doubtless become necessary to give students definite help in adjusting to this changed emphasis in education. The resistance or confusion which teachers sometimes find in their classes often arises out of traditional attitudes toward education, and out of student insecurity in dealing with new problems and new techniques. Teachers need not think for a moment that parents and community will accept a pattern of education that is not understood and accepted by the boys and girls in the classrooms. A few guideposts for such teachers to follow may therefore be useful in this connection:

a. **If the student is insecure without assigned tasks or definite reading,** then give some help with the assignment, but move steadily toward a learning situation in which the pupil sets his own tasks, formulates his own problems, and seeks his own sources of information.

b. **If the student relies entirely upon books for building concepts,** then use books, but make sure that concepts become meaningful and realistic through utilization of firsthand experiences also.

c. **If the student is accustomed to teachers who determine all purposes and make all plans,** then help him to identify his own purposes and formulate his own plans until eventually he can plan cooperatively with others in terms of both immediate and long-term goals.

d. **If the student is timid in interview or excursion situations,** then give the assistance necessary for making this a pleasurable, successful experience, but gradually give enough directed practice in field work techniques so that he may come to attack such activities eagerly and independently.

e. **If the student is too immature to cope with a given situation,** then keep him out of it. Recognize his age and degree of social maturity, and help him plan projects which, in the judgment of sensible but not over-cautious adults, are suitable for him.

Through these and other similar measures, democratic teachers may gradually lead students out of their traditional academic dependency into that self-reliant independence which is itself an evidence of social competence today.

Secure Parental Cooperation

The best way of getting parents to support cooperative educational projects is to develop a demonstrably effective program. If the school faculty has thought through its philosophy of education and agrees upon the dominant purposes of the democratic school, and if students have realized these purposes and have participated in planning activities which are meaningful and vital to them, it will not be difficult to convince most parents that the program of community-centered student experiences is really worthwhile.

Just as we find insecurity on the part of boys and girls faced with a new kind of educational situation, so we can expect to find doubt, and at times open hostility, on the part of parents whose concepts of "good education" were traditionally built in a book-centered school. That is why a program of parent education must run parallel with, and often gear into, the program of education for children and youth. This requires that we demonstrate to parents the real values of life-centered education today. Let us therefore:

a. **Assure parents that community experiences are part of the total education of the child,** and actually facilitate his learning of reading, writing, language, mathematics, science, social studies, home economics, commercial education, and other subject fields. An objective evaluation program which furnishes test data to support this position is almost essential by way of proof.

b. **Make it clear that the child's life and health are fully safeguarded,** and that when off the school grounds he will be carefully supervised by responsible persons. Field work hours should be sensible and time schedules for community activities planned in such a way that the ordinary routines of family life are not broken into unduly. The cost of field work should be reasonable and in proportion to benefits received.

c. **Contact parents of elementary and high school pupils well in advance** of any excursion, survey, extended field study, service project, or work experience. In each school, establish a uniform procedure for handling this problem. Suggestion: call a parents' meeting or devote a P.T.A. session to the question of field study by students. Explain the values, schedules, costs, programs, safety measures, and supervision steps. Throughout the school year, send informational bulletins and general reports upon actual field experiences to the parents.

d. **Secure parent participation in school-community projects.** Often parents can be used as liaison persons to gain entrance into plants, business establishments, and agency offices. As parents help to direct excursions, grant interviews, observe students as they visit and labor in various enterprises, these parents come to know the school program better and are able to judge it in action.

Through such approaches, the adults most directly concerned with the school's program—the children's parents—are kept fully informed of both values and techniques. The ultimate goal, here as elsewhere, is *consent and support,* and the key to success is *informed participation.*

STIMULATE PUBLIC INTEREST

Cooperative community projects inevitably result in either praise or blame of the school by influential groups. That is why the general public, as well as the parents and the students themselves, must be favorably influenced toward the school-community program if it is ever to achieve real success. Three considerations are highly significant in this connection:

a. **Plan the program carefully and in detail.** Informal conversations between teachers and townspeople easily pave the way for the more formal interviews in which specific problems and carefully formulated plans are presented. A functional index of community resources and service opportunities should be built up in each school and made available to townspeople, students, and teachers. Excursions, surveys, service and work projects should be well organized; arrangements made in a businesslike way; purposes stated clearly; and records kept so that there will be neither duplication nor undue demands upon the time of any individual or agency. Sincere appreciation should always be expressed for help received.

b. **Be sure the students master field work techniques.** Fumbled or ineffective interviews, excursions, surveys, and the like will inevitably produce criticism of both students and school. Students who plan to do field work must therefore learn how to approach people by telephone, how to make appointments and meet them promptly, how to state problems for study clearly and concisely, how to prepare interview schedules, the best methods of taking notes and recording data in the field, the need to obtain permission before quoting information secured, and the ways in which to show appreciation for help received. The underlying qualities which, in the last analysis, determine whether students succeed in establishing good community relations are sensitivity to people, their attitudes and problems, the ability to plan and work cooperatively, and an appreciation of others' contributions. These personality traits can be developed through well-selected experiences providing a conscious and continued effort to build meanings and attitudes is made. In conjunction with the general aim, students should set up acceptable standards of behavior which they carefully observe in all community relationships.

c. **Publicize notable programs.** Let the community know what special projects are planned, in progress, and completed. Invite suggestions and solicit aid from the townspeople. Send newsletters to parents, stories to local newspapers, suggested programs to radio stations. Plan for student and faculty talks to be given before business and luncheon clubs, civic groups, women's groups and church organizations. Let school administrators and Board of Education members discuss special school-community projects with community leaders. Make public some "progress reports" from time to time, and at the project's conclusion give appropriate publicity to its major findings, conclusions, and recommendations.

Through such well-planned programs as these, the students and their parents, as well as the public generally, may come to understand, approve, and actively support any reasonable measures for closer cooperation between the school and its community life. It must never be forgotten that public consent and support is forever essential to lasting school success.

How Shall We Publicize Community Study Findings?

Collected data would be valueless unless organized in terms of the purposes which it is intended to serve. It is here that students will learn how to make tables, graphs and maps; to take and arrange photographs; to plan sequences for school-made movies; to draw sketches, organize speeches, write radio scripts, or prepare articles for publication. The preparation of such exhibits will naturally prove much more interesting and significant to the students if they plan from the outset to share them with a wider audience.

Classroom groups may wish to use relevant information for better planning of their own future activities, or in furthering some all-school project. Example: a tenth-grade investigated the question, "What kinds of help do people in our city need this Christmas?" The information secured was passed on to the other eleven grades in the school so that their Christmas planning might also be more realistic and helpful. Again: a women's club asked a college class to cooperate in planning for better integration of the community's service facilities. The students thereupon surveyed the services rendered by various public and private agencies in the community's child welfare program, and then presented their findings before a meeting of the club. The service duplications which they discovered and reported, both orally and in writing, led to immediate consideration of plans for a coordinating council in that community.

USEFUL AVENUES OF PUBLICITY

Many are the media which can be used to keep the community informed concerning school-community activities. Among the most appropriate and practical channels of information are the following:

a. **School publications**: articles in school newspaper and magazine, a summary in the annual yearbook, booklets and leaflets depicting community-centered projects, statement of policy and program in the school's official catalogue.

b. **Newspaper stories**: well-written articles in local newspapers describing cooperative community projects of general public interest.

c. **Parent-Teacher Association, mothers' meetings, American Education Week programs** and similar organized sessions for discussion of educational developments and needs.

d. **Photographic exhibits** of service activities: housing surveys, soil erosion control, home and farm projects of all kinds.

e. **School-made movies and slides**: Victory Corps, school lunch facilities, school-community recreation, service and work projects.

f. **Dramatizations and pageants**: local history, community planning, the school in a democracy, intercultural relations.

g. **Fairs and festivals**: flower shows, harvest festivals, exhibits of agricultural and homemaking projects, health activities, hobby displays.

h. **Hospitality committee**: office staff, teachers and students receive visitors during school hours, interpret school to the public, welcome visitors at school functions.

i. **Publicity committee**: send or make announcements before farm and business groups, luncheon clubs, women's organizations, church groups.

j. **Joint parties for youth and parents**: revive old-fashioned music and dances, plan play days, sports, picnics.

k. **Speakers' bureau**: make teachers and older students available as speakers at meetings of educational and civic groups, church organizations, farmers' clubs, and business groups.

l. **Participation in civic enterprises**: students and faculty to work together in cooperation with the community chorus, little theater, art workshop, book clubs, and in all projects for community improvement.

m. **Graphic exhibits** in public buildings, store windows, schools: charts, graphs, sketches, posters, photographs.

n. **Community calendar**: kept up by a faculty-student committee, published in parents' newsletters, local newspapers, posted in the school corridor.

o. **School-community meetings** to discuss community service projects, work experience plans, school excursion policy, cooperative community activities generally.

Those community projects which enlist the energies of all age groups, and which are planned and carried out cooperatively by the school and other community agencies, are the ones which serve best to demonstrate and publicize the functional program of the modern school. Such projects represent democracy in action.

How Can We Avoid Exploitation of the School Program?

The public schools have long been considered a kind of "happy hunting ground" by special interest groups and individuals. This problem is not so serious as long as school education is confined within traditional classroom walls, where it is relatively easy for the school to safeguard pupils against the blandishments and pressures of such exploiting interests. As soon as the community at large becomes the school laboratory for social living, these special interests find their opportunity to influence youth's ideas and behavior tremendously increased.

How, then, can students utilize the community as a laboratory in which to study and participate in social processes, and still be protected against the influences of the many commercial, political, religious, and other agencies which may seek to exploit youthful minds and energies? Three safeguards may be used, and all are important. We shall consider each of them briefly.

Help Students to Recognize and Analyze Propaganda

Although it is impossible to keep propaganda out of schools and homes, it is not difficult to counteract it. Our best weapon against the propagandist in any field is to see that our students can detect and analyze the great volume of propaganda with which they are constantly bombarded. They should know that pressure and propaganda by social, economic, political, and religious interests is a basic characteristic of modern life, and that they need to be able to identify the propagandas which impinge upon their lives. Students should be taught to recognize the various propaganda techniques, and should learn to differentiate between competing propagandas in terms of their long-range social and personal effects upon human living.

Establish Criteria by Which to Select Cooperative School-Community Projects

The policy committee of each school system and each college should develop criteria to serve as a guide in evaluating the projects which may be proposed by patriotic, economic, religious, commercial, and other interested groups. Some such standards need to be established, maintained, and publicized by every school for the protection of its students and its life-centered educational program. In the formulation of these standards, such questions as the following might very well be kept in mind:

a. *Would the proposed project contribute to the basic purposes of the democratic school, or would it ignore or negate them?*

b. *Is the desire to cooperate with the school based upon a genuine concern for improved education, or is it motivated by essentially selfish interests?*

c. *Would the project increase cooperation between the school and other community groups, or might it diminish cooperation in the future?*

d. *Would the project result in more effective social thinking and action, or would it end in academic sterility?*

e. *Would the project help to liberalize thinking and increase human freedom, or might it ultimately threaten intellectual integrity?*

Stand Ready to Suggest Legitimate Projects

Some pressure groups have a sincere interest in education and a strong desire to be of service in its behalf. While the intentions of such groups may often be laudable, their conception of modern educational objectives and programs is frequently very limited. In such cases, the alert educator will be quick to channel such interest into really worthwhile activities which the group in question can sponsor or in which it can participate constructively according to the criteria suggested above. Thus, exploitation of students is avoided, community interest in the school is capitalized constructively, and pressure group members experience some re-education of their own motives and outlooks.

Through judicious use of these three devices, the informed teacher or administrator should be able to make full use of community resources as desired, and, at the same time, safeguard the school program against the pressures of selfish interests seeking to spread dogmatic ideas. Success in this area obviously requires that the teacher know his community and know it well.

How Can We Preserve Freedom to Learn?

No school can build a realistic program closely related to community processes and problems unless there is adequate freedom of thought and discussion, freedom of inquiry, freedom to depart from traditional teaching methods, freedom to deal frankly with controversial issues, and freedom to utilize the community as a laboratory for learning. Yet in most communities there are groups and individuals who will seriously interfere with these freedoms if they see any possibility of success in doing so. Every school in a democracy has therefore the professional and civic responsibility of dealing with all issues and problems of community life which are of vital importance to the pupils at their maturity level, and of protecting its basic right to make fair-minded study of such problems without interference. All classroom teachers, as well as all administrators, are involved in this social obligation, since an attack upon any one curriculum area is essentially an attack upon the democratic educational process itself.

Educational freedom calls for a vigorous, honest program of school publicity, and for the organization of adult groups in which the techniques of free discussion are used to deal with school and community problems. Illustration: in some school systems, a school-community deliberative council is formed for the general consideration of education problems. Such a council is composed of parents, teachers, taxpayers, business men, labor and farm leaders, and others representing influential community groups. The democratic discussion thus carried on helps keep the public informed, enlarges common understanding, and builds sympathetic support for the school program. Frequently, delicate issues can be recognized and settled through such a council before serious trouble begins.

The astute teacher will not rely solely upon cultivation of general public understanding, important as that is. He will think also of his own personal situation, and of what he alone can do to improve and strengthen it. Realizing that *academic freedom is basically an earned privilege rather than an automatic right,* he will take professional measures whereby that freedom for himself and his students may be both secured and increased.[1] Yet there may still be times when the teacher must take a resolute stand against

---

[1] Ten practical methods of safeguarding educational freedom are outlined by Edward G. Olsen, "Preserving Academic Freedom," *National Education Association Journal,* 26:3–4 (January 1937).

unwarranted interference from pressure groups. At such times, he will be far better equipped to give battle if he has also developed an enduring faith in those freedoms which underly our whole system of democracy and public education—freedom of thought and of speech, freedom to learn and to teach the truth, freedom to attack undemocratic policies and practices, freedom to ally one's self with any group supporting democratic purposes. Even then, of course, personal sacrifices may sometimes be demanded if principles like these are persistently upheld. Yet sacrifices to preserve intellectual integrity are often individually, and always socially, preferable to acquiescent acceptance of intellectual tyranny. Martyrdom may enlighten a people as slavery never can.

SELECTED REFERENCES

American Association of School Administrators, *Schools in Small Communities.* Seventeenth Yearbook, Ch. 12. Washington: National Education Association, 1939. Guiding principles for the development of better public relations. Discusses methods of learning interests and needs of the community, how to enlist the interests of lay groups, public relations procedures. Illustrations are given of school newsletters, local newspaper releases, exhibits, etc. designed to promote community interest in the school program.

Anderson, L. W., "Conservation Fair: A Wartime School-Community Project." *Clearing House* 18:329–31 (Feb. 1944). Tells how a school used a Fair as conscious public relations by inviting the community to participate, including Negro schools, despite some early opposition.

Charters, W. W., "Community Obligations to Teachers and Administrative Officers." In William C. Reavis (ed.), *The School and the Urban Community,* pp. 158–70. Chicago: University of Chicago Press, 1942. Discusses selection of school trustees, the teaching of controversial issues, salaries, tenure, old-age security, teaching morale, transmission of community ideas to the school.

Cook, Lloyd A., "Community Action and the School." Columbus: The Ohio State University Press, 1941. Deals generally with school-community relationships and specifically with the democratic processes of social planning, particularly with procedures that schools might follow in furthering a deeper sense of community and in carrying on social action projects.

Fine, Benjamin, *Educational Publicity.* New York: Harpers, 1943. Public relations policies and procedures, especially through the newspaper. Examples of both good and bad techniques are given.

Greenhoe, Florence, "The Community Contacts and Participation of 9,122 Public-School Teachers Selected as a National Sample." *School and Society* 50:510–12 (Oct. 14, 1939). Reports an extensive study covering teachers in every state in terms of four factors in their community relationships: teacher mobility, "social fitness" for teaching, teacher reaction to community mores, teacher participation in organized community life. A longer account by the author appears in the *Elementary School Journal* for March, 1940.

Haley, George P., "Vocational Guidance: A Community Responsibility." *School Executive* 62:32–33 (March 1943). Community committees, acting in an advisory capacity to the school, render yeoman service in promoting cooperative vocational guidance programs.

Koopman, George R., and Others, *Democracy in School Administration*, Ch. 8. New York: D. Appleton-Century, 1943. Deals with the school as a focal point of unification in community life, and with ways in which to secure participation of adults in the formulation and administration of the educational program.

Lafferty, H. M., "The Social Status of the Teacher." *Educational Administration and Supervision* 27:641–54 (Dec. 1941). Descriptive analysis of the community's attitude toward teachers, and the latter's consequent restricted behavior. Ample quotations from the literature of this field.

Moehlman, A. B., *Social Interpretation*. New York: D. Appleton-Century, 1938. Comprehensive treatment of the principles and practices of community and public school interpretation.

Saunders, Carleton M., "Teachers as Interpreters." *School Executive* 62:41–42 (Oct. 1942). Teachers in a New Jersey community increased their friendly contacts with the community, to their own social advantage as well as for improved school-community relationships.

Southeastern Workshop, *A Handbook in Community Development*, Ch. IX. Greenville, South Carolina: Furman University Press, 1941. Presents basic principles in school-community relationships, and discusses the chief barriers to better relationships with suggestions for overcoming each.

Stout, Dorman G., *Teacher and Community*. New York: World Book Company, 1941. Techniques of leadership whereby teachers may promote better understanding and cooperation between school and community.

Weller, Gerald M., "75 Visits from Community Leaders." *Clearing House* 16: 26–28 (Sept. 1941). How a junior high school established cordial public relations with its community by carefully selecting and entertaining 150 key people in the community, representing among them 100 local organizations. Two visitors only were entertained on any one day.

Wilson, Elizabeth K., "Schools Learn from Industry." *School Executive* 63:40–41 (Nov. 1943). An occupational study by ten school districts in one city area generated unusually good feeling between the schools and industry. Detailed procedures of the survey are outlined.

Yeager, William A., *Home-School-Community Relations*. Pittsburgh: University of Pittsburgh Press, 1939. Emphasizes the social necessity of more cooperative relationships between these three agencies, and suggests varied means of developing them.

CHAPTER 18

Community Service Center[1]

"Direct experiences in the community are certainly desirable," said the school superintendent to the president of the local teachers college. "But what are you going to do when a lot of your teachers want to invite speakers into the school or to schedule excursions outside? Sometimes so many of my teachers ask to visit the same agency or factory that the place is swamped with requests and in sheer self-defense refuses them all! Other times, many worthwhile centers of interest, which I know would welcome student visitors, are quite neglected simply because many teachers just don't know about them."

"That's what happens, all right," answered his friend. "We've had exactly the same experience at State College. And we find the same kind of confusion arising in connection with other kinds of community activities, too. For example, some of our instructors who happen to be better known are almost overwhelmed by local requests that their classes undertake this survey or that service project—while other professors, equally competent and interested, would welcome many more such opportunities than they now have. It certainly is a headache!"

"Well, I know one thing," returned the superintendent, "and that is that my teachers desperately need more direct experience with community life in all its areas—local, regional, national, and even international. They ought to go outside their books and really participate in significant community processes and problem-situations. If they don't do that, if they just stay in their academic ivory towers, they're only mental and emotional cave-dwellers!"

"That's precisely the problem which bothers me most," answered the college executive. "All future teachers, regardless of subject

---

[1] This chapter is based upon an earlier article in which the writer proposed a much more restricted "Office of Excursions." See Edward G. Olsen, "Acquainting the Teacher with the Community," in Ruth West (ed.), *Utilization of Community Resources in the Social Studies:* Ninth Yearbook of the National Council for the Social Studies (Cambridge, Mass.: 1938), pp. 36–48.

field, certainly ought to have basic experience in using all the various 'bridges between school and community.' If they don't know how to do that, they can't be really competent teachers no matter how much subject matter and educational psychology they know. Sometimes I actually long for the old days of academic seclusion! It was so much easier to teach that way! But of course I realize the futility of that isolation today, so—what *can* we do to control some of this confusion? I wonder—could we work out some kind of a centralized community study office or service center that would act as a clearing house for field arrangements, and also perhaps offer some practical training in field study techniques? Maybe *that* would be our answer! What do *you* think?"

Why Is a Service Center Essential?

A well-organized, administered, and financed community service center must eventually become an integral part of every modern school program. Indeed it *must*, for without it the new educational program can never really succeed. Lacking such a central office, that program at best will remain limited in effectiveness as various teachers overwork some resource centers and speakers while neglecting others, as they compete for dates and materials, as they promote community projects independently and even in ignorance of other groups' plans. And at worst, such failure to coordinate and control difficult school-community relationships will discredit the whole community emphasis because of cumulative irritations upon the community and recurrent frustrations among teachers and students. The ten "bridges" between school and community are *two-way* avenues of public relations, as well as important media for realistic learning. In every case, the prerequisites to continued and increasing success in public relationships are judicious handling, careful organization, and guiding control on the part of some one responsible agency.

What Would a Service Center Do?

The functions of any community service center would naturally depend upon many factors such as those of purpose, structure, size, and personnel. The constructive possibilities are many. By way of throwing them into sharper focus, we shall examine the basic structure and primary functions of such a center as would meet modern educational requirements. Since schools and their programs vary widely, we shall describe this service center as it might be organized to operate upon three distinct levels of complexity. Each subsequent level should be thought of as including all the aspects of its predecessor, even as it takes on some additional functions of its own.

Service Center — Minimum Program

Here and there across the nation, limited steps have already been taken to overcome such difficulties as those identified by the superintendent and the president who were quoted in the opening paragraphs. Typical of good practice on this *minimum level* are the programs developed in Seattle and in Minneapolis.

SEATTLE EXCURSIONS

The public schools of Seattle have developed an extensive excursional study program under the direction of Mr. Joseph T. Hazard, a teacher in one of the local high schools. He has prepared a brief set of mimeographed instructions for planning and conducting an excursion, together with an attached list of fifty local excursion points and ten extended field study centers. This bulletin is circulated among the schools of the city. Teachers who wish to ask help in planning class excursions may telephone to Mr. Hazard, who will then make the necessary arrangements, and may sometimes conduct the trip himself. During recent years, however, the pressure of increasing calls has necessarily diminished this personal service, and emphasis now is upon the desirability of teachers arranging and conducting their own trips insofar as that is possible.

Mr. Hazard personally arranged or conducted nearly 700 vocational, science, social studies and literary trips for over 20,000 students during the four academic years preceding Pearl Harbor. This he did on the proverbial "shoestring," for besides carrying three-fifths of a normal teaching load in his own school, Mr. Hazard worked without a secretary, without adequate office space or records, and without the prestige of a formal administrative title. Yet even under such conditions, much interest in school excursion possibilities has developed among teachers and school patrons in Seattle; an excursions textbook is in preparation by a local committee of teachers; and neighboring communities are considering the inauguration of similar programs.

It is interesting to note that the Seattle program places heavy emphasis upon the study of governmental functions and of local industries such as lumbering, agriculture, and general manufacturing. Chief concern, moreover, centers upon the operation of these agencies as ongoing social *processes;* their related social *problems* (except those of conservation) receive less attention.

Minneapolis Field Trip Office

Since 1923 the Minneapolis public school system has included an official Field Trip Department. This Department has a separate administrative status, although its basic policy is determined by the Board of Education administrative staff in conference with the Superintendent and the Assistant Superintendent of Schools. The Field Trip Office is now directed on a part-time basis by Barbara H. Wright, Supervisor of Counselors, assisted by a clerk whose duty it is to book excursions desired by applying teachers.

A community resources file is maintained in the form of alphabeticized cards listing possible excursion points of interest, including information about the most suitable days, times, and seasons for visiting them. At the opening of the school year, a mimeographed list of a hundred such centers is sent to each school in the city. Appropriate suggestions for planning and arranging trips are included, as is a special form on which each school is asked to list trips and trip arrangements desired for the current semester. After this form is returned, the requested arrangements with excursion centers are made by the Field Trip Office.

After the completion of each excursion, an evaluative report is returned to the Field Trip Office by the school in question. These reports enable the Office to collect data on all excursions taken, to determine which particular trips have been judged most valuable, and to receive suggestions for improving the service in the future.

This Office does not itself conduct trips for schools; neither does it demonstrate the techniques of successful excursion-conducting. It rather acts solely as a clearing house for teachers requesting listed trips. This service, however, makes possible the satisfaction of study interests in both social processes and social problems as they appear in any academic field.

A minimum service center similar to the two just described can be maintained by small individual schools as well as by large city systems. One drawer in a filing cabinet, if manned by an enthusiastic and competent teacher, even on a part-time basis, may be like the proverbial acorn in its promise! Yet however organized and staffed, the service center's primary function is clearly indicated. Such a center will

Operate as a Clearing House for the Systematic and Intelligent Linking of School Programs with Community Life

All instructional projects involving school-community relationships should be arranged, or at least cleared, through the service center. To facilitate such cooperation and administrative efficiency, the Center will necessarily carry on several specific activities relating to its role as clearing house. Suppose we look now at three of these activities or functions in turn.

1. CATALOGUE AVAILABLE COMMUNITY RESOURCES

A comprehensive and itemized card file of community resources and needs is essential to any community service center. In this file, there should be many standardized cards which provide summarized data concerning each particular resource—data which can reveal, at a glance, the suitability of that resource to the specific educational purposes sought. Such data should therefore be organized and classified to indicate whichever among the many possible factors are significant in each instance. Provision should thus be made for recording upon the file card the significance of any among these several factors:

COMMUNITY SETTING: GEOGRAPHY AND PEOPLE

Climate

Size

Topography

Soil

Water resources

Mineral deposits

Forest and animal resources

Population number

Age and sex composition

Educational status

Occupational status

Nationality pattern

Racial groups

Class and caste structure

Land use

COMMUNITY PROCESSES

Utilizing natural environment

Appreciating the past

Adjusting to people

Exchanging ideas

Making a living

Sharing in citizenship

Maintaining health and safety

Improving family living

Securing education

Meeting religious needs

Enjoying beauty

Engaging in recreation

COMMUNITY PROBLEMS

Faulty use of land

Waste of natural resources

Ancestor worship, cultural imperialism

Social instability

Personality conflicts

Racial, national, class hostility

Stereotyped thinking and action

Evil propaganda

Unemployment

Poverty and insecurity

Exploitation of labor

Capital-labor conflict

Inadequate production

Public indifference

Political corruption and graft

Crime, vice, delinquency

Physical unfitness
Mental unfitness
Slums
Marital discord and divorce
Neglected children
Consumer exploitation
Illiteracy
Waste of intellectual resources

Superstition
Bigotry and intolerance

Community ugliness

Poor use of leisure time
Exploitation by commercial agencies
Etc.

COMMUNITY AREAS

Local   Regional   National   International

COMMUNITY LEVELS

Material   Institutional   Psychological

COMMUNITY TIME PERIODS

Historic   Contemporary   Future

COMMUNITY AGENCIES

Governmental   Commercial   Noncommercial

TYPE OR APPROACH

Documentary material
Audio-visual aid
Resource visitor

Interview
Field trip
Survey
Extended field study

Camping
Service project
Work experience

ITEM NAME

New York Times
Huntington Museum
A fireman

Y.M.C.A. secretary
Chinatown
Venereal disease conditions
Paleontological excavations

Nature study
City beautification
Dental receptionist

LOCATION AND CONTACT DIRECTIONS

Post office and street adddress, telephone number, names and positions of officials

RATING GIVEN

Probable value generally, date rated and by whom, date rating was reviewed, general comment upon rating, notation concerning any special features to be stressed

TIME REQUIRED

Total approximate time necessary, itemized according to probable time needed for travel, program, meals, and the like

EXPENSES

Total expenditures required for various items such as rental of equipment or materials, admission fees, travel, meals, speakers' honoraria, etc.

TRAVELING DIRECTIONS

Accurate, specific, and detailed instructions concerning most suitable travel route

LIMITING CONDITIONS

Fragility of items, size of exhibit, time required for borrowing, hours, days and seasons for visiting, maximum number of visitors accommodated, suitability for children, proper clothing to be worn for comfort and safety, attitudes of officials, activities of pressure groups, use of cameras, etc.

GENERAL COMMENTS

Additional desirable information which should be known or would be useful

CROSS–REFERENCES

Notations concerning cards of other available resources of similar character and interest

RECORD OF PREVIOUS USERS

Names and addresses of those who have utilized this particular resource already, together with the dates of such use

No community service center can function with full efficiency unless all appropriate data about resources is systematically recorded on some such standard card form as that pictured on the adjoining page. Cards of this nature can easily be filed in any one of numerous useful ways: by type of community setting, by social process, by kind of problem, by community area, by basic approach or technique of experience, or even alphabetically by item names. If cross-filing by two or more of these categories seems desirable, this can easily be arranged by filling out the forms in duplicate, triplicate, or further multiple copies, and then filing them accordingly. In such instances, efficiency will be increased by using different colored cards for each separate file.

COMMUNITY RESOURCES FILE CARD

COMMUNITY SETTING	COMMUNITY PROCESS	COMMUNITY PROBLEM

COMMUNITY AREA	COMMUNITY LEVEL	COMMUNITY TIME PERIOD	COMMUNITY AGENCY
Local_____	Material_____	Historical_____	Governmental_____
Regional_____	Institutional_____	Contemporary_____	Commercial_____
National_____	Psychological_____	Future_____	Non-Commercial_____
Intern'l_____			

TYPE OR APPROACH

Document_____ Audio-visual Aid_____ Resource Visitor_____ Interview_____ Field Trip_____
Survey_____ Extended Study_____ Camping_____ Service Project_____ Work Experience_____

ITEM NAME_____

ADDRESS_____ TELEPHONE_____

OFFICIAL (1)_____ TITLE_____

OFFICIAL (2)_____ TITLE_____

OFFICIAL (3)_____ TITLE_____

RATING: Excellent___Very Good___Fair___Poor___Unsuitable___ SPECIAL FEATURES:_____

DATE RATED_____ RATER_____ RATER_____ _____

DATE REVIEWED_____ COMMENT_____ _____

TIME REQUIRED: Travel_____Program_____Meals_____Other_____Total_____

EXPENSES ITEMIZED_____

TRAVEL DIRECTIONS_____
_____

LIMITING CONDITIONS_____
_____

GENERAL COMMENTS_____
_____

SEE ALSO CARDS:_____

USERS & DATES:_____ _____ _____

   " " "_____ _____ _____

   " " "_____ _____ _____

   " " "_____ _____ _____

A SERVICE CENTER RECORD CARD, front and back sides. Russell Sage College, Troy, New York.

2. Discover Additional Community Resources

However comprehensive the resource file, it will often not include precisely the type of item needed or desired by particular teachers. Furthermore, many items listed will quickly become obsolete as newer materials appear, as resource persons leave the community or are otherwise no longer available, as excursion centers change their public relations policies, as additional service-project or work-experience opportunities become available. It is therefore necessary that the resource file be constantly extended and revised through systematic routine procedures.

Alert perusal of current newspapers, along with regular canvassing of teachers, students, and interested laymen, will provide up-to-date information at relatively slight cost and trouble. Needless to say, every new community resource of whatever type must be critically investigated as a basis for making a preliminary critical rating of that item's potential educational value and most feasible approaches.

3. Coordinate the School-Community Program

A third important function of the service center as a clearing house is to act as coordinating agency for the entire school or school system's utilization of community resources. Coordination by such a central body is necessary so that:

a. **Limited resources may be utilized to best advantage** through careful planning, sharing, and scheduling.
b. **Popular resources will not be overworked** through the unwelcome pressure of undue calls or numbers, thus discrediting the community-life approach in that situation.
c. **Lesser-known resources may be publicized** sufficiently to attract a wider use commensurate with their educational values.
d. **All available resources may be widely utilized** at full productive capacity for mutual benefit of school and community.
e. **Good public relations may be maintained** with the community, and not undermined because too many people are trying to make individual arrangements.

All of these factors—both educational and personnel—are of crucial importance to the success of the school's total program. They must therefore be carefully planned for the entire school in a coordinated fashion.

Minneapolis Public Schools
Field Trip Office

School_____

Person Reporting _____

Date_____

Place Visited_____

Grade_____ No. of Pupils_____ No. of Teachers_____

Method of Transportation_____ Hours of Starting _____Returning _____

How much time was spent in traveling to and from place visited?_____

Arrangements: Were transportation plans satisfactory?_____If not, how (under

the war restrictions) could they be improved?_____

_____

_____

Were arrangements made in the Field Trip Office regarding dates, guides, etc.

satisfactory?_____What suggestions can you give for improving this service?

_____

_____

_____

Value of Trip: State the specific values of the excursion. (If an Art Institute

Trip, also state lecture topics.)_____

_____

_____

_____

_____

Would you recommend it for other pupils of this grade?_____

What suggestions can you give for improving the experience?_____

_____

A FIELD TRIP EVALUATION FORM. Minneapolis Public Schools.

Service Center — Expanded Program

The minimum service center just described will be of much more practical value if its primary clearing house function can be developed to an *expanded level* and thereby encompass additional functions. The Philadelphia program illustrates some such further possibilities.

PHILADELPHIA'S DIVISION OF VISUAL EDUCATION

The Philadelphia school system has long maintained a well-equipped Division of Visual Education, adequately staffed and ably directed. The Division has a materials library, from which motion picture films and slides are loaned to local teachers upon application. This service has recently been extended to include other types of community-centered educational experience, particularly in the field of the social studies. In cooperation with the local United War Chest, the Division now arranges for school classes to utilize many kinds of resource speakers and excursions, as well as documentary material, motion pictures, and electrical transcriptions.

To publicize these opportunities, a printed folder describing them has been sent to every social studies teacher in the public schools of the city. This folder summarizes the topics upon which expert speakers are available, characterizes some of the social and welfare agencies which may be visited, and suggests types of research material, photographs, films, recordings, and advisory helps which are available.

Provisions for utilizing these community resources are simple. Speakers are booked by a letter or telephone call to the Visual Education Office, which then forwards the request to the Speakers' Bureau of the United War Chest. Field trips, including guides, are arranged in a similar way. Requests for documentary materials and for personal advisory aid are sent direct to designated social work offices.

Perhaps it is interesting, in contrast with Seattle's primary emphasis, to note that this entire program centers about the city's social and welfare *problems*, largely ignoring their constituent *processes* as such. This preoccupation with problems is well reflected in the leading statement of the publicity folder mentioned above: "Young people studying the general problems of social living in the modern world, should hear about and inspect at first hand some of the causes and effects, RIGHT HERE IN PHILADELPHIA, of poverty . . . delinquency . . . crime . . . ignorance . . . neglect . . . racial conflict . . . disease . . . bad housing . . . dependency . . . and study concrete examples of what is being done to offset these evils in our society and to make Democracy work for the benefit of every citizen."

On this expanded level, the desirable community center provides the three services already outlined and in addition two others of real importance to the vital school-community program; it enforces necessary standards, and promotes the program itself.

4. Enforce Necessary Standards in Utilizing Community Resources

Educational efficiency and public goodwill both require that the clearing house establish and enforce certain minimum standards of planning and public relations. It may therefore properly:

a. **Insist that definite reservations be made** for borrowed audio-visual aids, resource speakers, excursions, etc., and that such reservations be given, as well as asked, in advance.
b. **Send both preliminary and last-day reminders** of scheduled interviews, excursions, service projects, etc. to the centers to be visited, together with accurate lists of expected visitors.
c. **Issue distinctive tickets or other tokens of admission** to all persons going on excursions involving considerable numbers. Such tickets, checked on frequent occasion, constitute a useful device to prevent unauthorized persons from joining the group, as well as an easy means of enabling guides and other helping adults to identify members of the party.
d. **Extend official thanks** to those individuals and organizations whose efforts helped to make the community project possible, meaningful, and worthwhile.

Standards such as these are the minimum criteria of courtesy and efficient operation. Sensible as they are, their observance is frequently neglected with consequent deterioration in both educational results and general public relations.

5. Promote the Community-School Program

A final clearing house function is that of constantly promoting a reciprocal school-community relationship, whereby the school utilizes to the full the varied resources of the community and, in turn, applies its own resources to the problems of community improvement and progress. Promotion of this nature involves several specific activities on the part of the service center.

a. Distribute Lists of Possible Projects

Catalogues of possible projects in the field of community study and participation should regularly be compiled and distributed. These catalogues might list many suggestive opportunities for community exploration and service through various of the ten basic "bridges" or approaches, and also include summarized data concerning each cited resource to cover:

Classification according to fundamental type or value

Recommendations concerning the curriculum areas and grade levels with which each community study aid or opportunity might be fruitfully correlated

Suggestions for combining separate though similar resources in a more extended unit of study or experience

These lists or catalogues should be distributed principally to each school or department, so that they may be readily available for consultation by all teachers, students, and others interested.

b. Provide Requested Information

Another important aid in promoting the new program would be that of answering requests for information about community resources and projects previously utilized and therefore now critically rated. Evaluative data of this kind might well include reference to:

The curriculum areas and grade levels in which the particular resource item or project has been found most worthwhile by others

The specific educational value of the item or experience as an introductory overview, a motivating device, a technique of study, an emotional experience, an integrating medium, a culminating activity, and the like.

The critical rating given it by previous users, opinions as to its value, criticisms heard, suggestions for improvement, etc.

Informative and evaluative information of this kind is obviously semi-confidential in nature, and should therefore be available from the Center only at the discretion of its Director.

c. Assist with Community Projects

Many teachers are initially hesitant or incompetent to conduct field trips, surveys, or extended field studies. Again, community agencies and organizations may desire expert advice or aid in planning their own educational efforts and programs. In all such cases, the Center staff should stand ready and eager to assist in every way possible, both in planning and in cooperatively carrying out the desired field project.

Service Center — Comprehensive Program

In large school systems and in universitites, the community service center may readily be extended to a really *comprehensive level,* and thereby prove even more educationally worthwhile. Recent developments in two teachers colleges may be cited in this connection.

MONTCLAIR'S BUREAU OF FIELD STUDIES

In 1937 the New Jersey State Teachers College at Montclair established an official Bureau of Field Studies, with Professor Edgar C. Bye as full-time director. Financed through tuition and special travel fees for students, and by the income from an endowment fund, this Office was designed to conduct for the College several regular-credit field study courses in social science. One such course consisted of ten all-day excursions in the New York metropolitan area, each preceded and followed by appropriate classroom study; another of a ten-day extended field study trip through New England and French Canada during the summer period; a third of a similar tour through the Central Eastern Region of the United States; and a fourth was a sixty-two day trip through Continental United States to the West Coast and return.

As documentary materials for these various courses, the Bureau published several bulletins dealing with excursion philosophy, techniques, and problems; with excursion programs operating in New Jersey; and with detailed syllabi and bibliographies for the four respective field study courses. Steel cabinet files and an alphabetical card index of community resources are maintained by the Bureau.

Rather than acting as a general service center for the cooperative improvement of instruction in all academic departments, the Bureau operates almost entirely within the social science area. It is set up and equipped, however, to act as a general service center whenever the policy of the college permits.

THE COMMUNITY SERVICE CENTER AT TEACHERS COLLEGE, COLUMBIA UNIVERSITY

The idea of a college-wide Community Service Center was launched at Teachers College in the Spring of 1942. A faculty committee composed of representatives of all departments and divisions was appointed to act as a steering committee. This group, known as the Coordinating Council, helped to delineate both the functions and pattern of operation of the Center. Another group of key persons in various organizations—national and local, and urban and rural—were invited to become members of the Advisory Council. This group offers advice and information, and also serves as a means of communication between the work of the Center and that of community agencies.

The chief responsibility of the Center is to implement, in as many practical ways as possible, the concept of community-centered schools. The importance and the use of community resources by educational workers is given considerable emphasis. The procedures developed for working in the desired direction are:

1. Courses and seminars, viz:
   Community Resources for Curriculum and Teaching.
   Study of Community Problems.
2. Field trips.
3. Visual and other materials showing the work of many community agencies in many parts of the nation.
4. A bulletin whose purpose is to bring information to those most concerned in the promotion of community-centered schools.
5. Monthly exhibits, the chief purpose of which is to bring to those in the college not only the work of community agencies but also suggestions by which schools can become more community-centered.
6. Conferences on problems such as group work, youth councils, etc. to which are invited lay and professional leaders.
7. List of schools and colleges, together with a description of their work, which have some or many phases of worthwhile community-centered education.
8. Bibliography on all topics pertinent to understanding and developing a community integrated school.
9. Consultation service on school and community problems related to education in the community.

There has been a steadily increasing demand for the varied services offered by the Center. Some of the services rendered include:

1. Advisory service to professional community workers.
2. Requests for exhibits within the city and other places.
3. Many types of literature for students majoring in the various departments.
4. Leadership for discussion groups within the college.
5. Community groups seeking to coordinate the activities of the community.
6. Requests for information and literature on camping and other subjects.
7. Descriptions of community work of colleges, high schools, and other community agencies.
8. Special trips—to courts, maternity and foster homes, and the like.
9. Requests for introduction to agency heads to obtain information and ideas.

The truly adequate service center is that which can concurrently offer three major services: (A) a clearing house, (B) a resource library, and (C) an instructional agency. Having already discussed the first of these three functions, let us now proceed to examine the other two.

Maintain an Extensive Resource Library of Information and Aids Pertaining to All Community Types, Areas, Levels, and Time Periods

Research documents and audio-visual aids of many kinds will constitute the desired library materials. Research documents include suitable books, periodical and newspaper articles, old diaries and similar records, original and speciman deeds, charters, receipts, tax forms, and the like. Audio-visual aids maintained in the library should include appropriate charts, graphs, and maps, with requisite materials for making them; objects, specimens and models; flat pictures and stereographs; slides, slidefilms, and motion pictures, together with necessary portable equipment for making, projecting, and repairing them; recordings and broadcast transcriptions; dramatic scripts; and portable television receivers.

All of these items—both documentary and audio-visual—must be methodically sought, assembled, mounted, catalogued, and stored. Under appropriate safeguards, all of them must be easily and quickly available for instructional use through some simple yet reliable circulation procedure.

Serve as an Instructional Agency Whereby Educators in All Fields and at All School Levels May Receive Expert Training in the Effective Relating of School Programs to Community Life

The Community Service Center should be an instructional medium in its own special field as well as a service agency *per se*. Through various means, the Center should offer systematic training in all the varied techniques of community exploration and contribution through the schools. More specifically, the Center should carry on, as needed, seven types of instructional work.

1. Sponsor Conferences

Discussion meetings, short conferences, and longer workshops should be arranged wherein interested teachers, mature students, and cooperating laymen may share community project experiences, evaluate present progress, and plan future activities.

2. Offer Courses

Regular university and extension courses dealing with the philosophy, programs, procedures and problems of community study and participation should be offered in cooperating universities and in the supporting school or school system.

3. PROVIDE CONSULTANTS

Expert consultative service should be made available to such workshops, professional conferences, and other interested group sessions as may desire it. The Center's Director would doubtless be the expert consultant in such cases.

4. PUBLISH BULLETINS

Various service bulletins and information sheets of practical value to those wishing to develop increased competence in this whole area should be prepared and issued from time to time as demand indicates.

5. INVITE TEACHER PARTICIPATION

Interested teachers and competent laymen should be permitted to participate, under guidance and upon a voluntary basis, in the Center's various activities. Such participation is the best source of widespread enthusiasm and support for the Service Center's work.

6. PROVIDE STUDENT EXPERIENCES

Selected prospective teachers should be encouraged to serve part-time in the Center and to share actively in its operations as part of their regular practice-teaching program. Teacher-education of this nature might fruitfully precede as well as follow the period of conventional practice teaching in the classroom.

7. FOSTER COOPERATION BETWEEN SCHOOL AND NON-SCHOOL EDUCATIONAL WORKERS IN THE COMMUNITY

A final important responsibility of the Service Center is that of bringing about greater understanding and more cooperative effort among social workers, community organizers, group work leaders, museum personnel, teachers, and many other educational workers in both the school and the community at large. All these officials, regardless of their other functions, should consciously be *educators* in the best sense of that term, for the cooperative effort of all is required to provide really effective *education* for the youth and adults of today.

A SERVICE CENTER BULLETIN—first page. Teachers College, Columbia University.

These, then, are the prime functions of the *adequate* community service center: to operate simultaneously as a two-way clearing house for the systematic linking of school program with community life, as an extensive resource library of aids and information pertaining to all community areas and levels, and as an instructional agency whereby prospective and in-service teachers in all academic fields and at all school levels can receive expert advice, demonstration, and guided personal experience in mastering the basic procedures of life-centered education.

How Should an Adequate Service Center Be Organized?

The operation of any school-community agency such as a comprehensive community service center involves careful planning for both democratic policy-making and efficient administration. This requires, primarily, that basic policies of the Center shall be cooperatively determined through full discussion by appropriate representatives of the school and of the public at large. It requires, secondly, that the Center's administrative personnel be technically competent and properly free to organize and execute efficient programs of action within the general framework of policy thus determined. More specifically, then, the Service Center might well be organized somewhat as described in the following three sections.

Policy-Making

A Service Center Advisory Committee should be formed to determine basic policy concerning school-community learning situations and projects. The composition of this central advisory Committee should directly reflect the interests and outlooks of classroom teachers, school administrators, local community groups, and the Center's own administrative staff. If an entire school system or a large university is sponsoring the Center, this Committee will be proportionately extensive in scope. If the sponsor, however, is a single school or a small college, then the Committee will be less diverse geographically, but just as representative democratically. Suppose we note who might thus become Committee members under all four types of sponsorship, as indicated in the following table.

Regardless of type or size of school, the Service Center Committee members should be responsible for cooperatively formulating a broad framework of general policy within which Center activities

SUGGESTED MEMBERSHIP ON COMMUNITY SERVICE CENTER COMMITTEE

By Types of Schools and Interested Groups

Large School System	Single School	Large University	Small College
CLASSROOM TEACHERS			
One instructor from each constituent school or geographical group of schools	One instructor from each major department or instructional field	One instructor from each major academic and professional division	One instructor from each major subject field
SCHOOL ADMINISTRATORS			
The superintendent or an assistant superintendent of schools	The principal or an assistant principal	The president, vice-president, or academic dean	The president or the dean of instruction

LOCAL COMMUNITY GROUPS

Selected representatives of parental, professional, public welfare, governmental, industrial, commercial, religious, racial, cultural, and other significant groups or associations in the local community.

THE CENTER'S ADMINISTRATIVE STAFF

The Executive Director, together with all associate directors who may have been appointed.

shall proceed. This fundamental responsibility naturally requires Committee members to be fully conversant with newer educational philosophy as well as with present school programs and community resources and needs. An additional function of the Center will therefore be to see that all Committee members have ready access to professional literature and other sources of philosophic enlightenment.

In the event that the central Committee represents a large school system, it would be well for each classroom teacher member of it to act also as a community service leader within his own particular school. Under such circumstances, he himself would doubtless have been chosen by that school's local committee on community exploration and service.

ADMINISTRATIVE PERSONNEL

A well-qualified administrative and technical staff is essential to the successful execution of any school-community instructional program. That staff should therefore include at least three types or categories of personnel:

An executive director should be appointed on a full-time basis. He would be directly responsible to the superintendent of schools, the principal, or the university or college president for the successful operation of the Service Center. Associate directors could be added as they became necessary for the effective functioning of the Center. Such assistants should be chosen by the executive director and be responsible only to him.

Specialist teachers and other educational experts should be available for extended consultations as needed. These consultants would represent many fields—physical and biological science, geography, social studies, literature, foreign languages, industrial arts, homemaking, psychology, the creative arts, religion, library service, visual education, youth-serving agencies, etc.—and would provide summarized information, technical data, expert interpretation, and constant evaluation of community-centered materials and experiences as these pertain to their own fields of special competence.

A clerical staff should include the secretaries, filing clerks, librarians, visual aid makers and any other office technicians that may be necessary. This staff should be fully competent to assist the director in carrying out the several functions of the Center previously described.

The personal and technical qualifications for all of these staff positions should be carefully drawn and fully observed when employing persons to fill them. The Executive Director, in particular, must be selected with utmost care, for in large measure the ultimate success or failure of the Service Center will hinge upon his ability, enthusiasm, technical competence, and tact.

OFFICE AND EQUIPMENT

The Service Center should be centrally located so as to be easily accessible from all schools in the system or all buildings on the campus. It would need to include office space, conference and work rooms somewhat as follows:

A private office for the Executive Director

A conference room for the Center Committee and other conferring groups

Several small workrooms for the technical assistants and the clerical staff

A combined library and showroom for "live" books, bulletins, magazines, photographs, charts, card indexes, etc. dealing specifically with current school-community achievements and opportunities

Shelving, filing, and storage space for documentary materials and audio-visual aids, together with all necessary supplies and equipment

If a large city school system develops such a central office, it would be desirable for each individual school in the system to provide in its own building an office for its local community service leader, who is also his school's representative on the central Committee. In this local office there should be adequate facilities for filing or storing documentary and audio-visual materials owned by the school, duplicate records and reports, and other similar items of immediate interest and concern.

These are intended to be suggestive proposals and not in any sense a final blueprint. Although the principles outlined are believed to be sound, much actual experimentation will have to be done before final judgment can be rendered. The important need now is for wiser professional recognition that some kind of functional service center becomes imperative for every school as that school begins to expand its concept and practice of life-centered education. Initial organization may have to be simple, equipment meager, leadership inexperienced—yet even such leadership, equipment, and organization will be welcomed as a beginning by all students, teachers, and administrators who today are searching for means whereby to develop more lifelike programs of education.

There is no city or county school system, teachers college or university school of education anywhere which has to date established anything like a *truly adequate* service center. Here indeed is a fertile field for significant educational experimentation!

SELECTED REFERENCES

Engelhardt, N. L., and N. L. Engelhardt, Jr., *Planning the Community School.* New York: American Book Co., 1940. Architectural planning for the building which is designed to operate as a community center for adults as well as a community school for children.

Minty, C. C., "How Minneapolis Schools Conduct Field Trips." *Business Education World* 18:810–14 (June 1938). Describes the advantages of a centralized excursions office, and illustrates the local program with a detailed description of a field study in industry.

Reller, Theodore L., "Procedures in Identifying and Appraising Community Resources Having Educational Values." In Twenty-sixth Annual *Schoolmen's Week Proceedings*, pp. 220–28. Philadelphia: University of Pennsylvania, School of Education, 1931. Indicates what community resources are available as materials for each of the Seven Cardinal Principles of Secondary Education, and how the school might lead the community in cooperating in their use.

Teachers College Community Service Center, *Community News and Education.* New York: Teachers College, Columbia University. Occasional bulletins dedicated to the commmunity approach in education.

CHAPTER 19
Community Coordination

Underlying all modern programs of education is one fundamental principle: *the child is a whole being who is educated by a total environment.* Educational psychology has disclosed the essential unity of personality as it develops through interaction of mind and body, beliefs and emotions, thinking and doing. Thus we know today that a student's mind cannot be abstracted and educated apart from these other vital aspects of his total existence. Educational sociology, meanwhile, has revealed the essential unity of one's life experience, showing that all influences which impinge upon the individual educate him in some manner and some degree, for better or for worse. We therefore now assert with confidence that the educational process can neither be confined to the school nor concentrated therein. Thus do the psycho-sociological findings of our time compel us to recognize this truth: When the school seeks to promote the constructive *education of the whole child in relation to his total environment,* the school thereby commits itself to a conception of *education as a community-wide function and enterprise.*

Out of this conception have emerged two divergent trends in school policy. One trend is toward the centralization of all educational activities within the school itself; the other, in contrast, seeks to decentralize even the educative activities now carried on by the conventional school. Perhaps we may best appreciate the implications of these two policies through the medium of two statements illustrating their respective possibilities:

THE SCHOOL AS A COMMUNITY CENTER

"The school should be the center of everything in the community except the religious activities, and it should be a very vital, contributing factor to these. . . . Public school buildings should be open every weekday in the year for at least twelve hours. It should be a place where children may both play and study; where they may learn to work with their hands as well as study books; where people may continue their education throughout life; where business women may enjoy exercises after the day's grind; where people may read and talk; where parents may meet to learn their task of supplementing education in their own homes; where citizens may discuss the vital problems of the day; where the housewife may learn how to do her work more efficiently. . . .

"Most cities want libraries. Why not make the city library a part of the school? Most cities desire municipal au-

ditoriums. Why not build this in with the local school building? . . . Let the school be the center of everything in the community."[1]

Centralized Education!

EDUCATION AS A COMMUNITY FUNCTION

"The community health officials should also be the teachers of health. . . . If the community is ready for better household arts, what is needed is not a set of special school equipment but visitors who can demonstrate in the homes . . . A consumer's cooperative can serve as the town's method of consumer education. . . . The music leader will be not primarily a school person but an addition to the community life. The introduction to literature can best be handled by the staff of the public library. . . . The

factory will be the gateway of contact with economic life. . . .

"All of this varied program should be the concern of an educational director, whose business it will be to keep all of life as educative as possible. . . . School will go on in homes, the library, the hospital, the cooperative store, the dairy barns, the little theatre, and in all the museums, shops and studios which can be set up to facilitate the pursuit of worthy interests."[2]

Decentralized Education!

Both of these orientations obviously seek to bridge the gap between school and community through structural reorganization of the school. Proponents of each viewpoint would doubtlessly claim that theirs is a true "community school." Perhaps each policy has chief merit under different community conditions. It is possible, for example, that *centralized* education is more appropriate to sparsely-inhabited rural regions where the material and institutional resources of the community area are few, and that the *decentralized* pattern is more suitable to urban communities possessing a rich variety of readily-available resources. In any event, there are very few schools which fully epitomize either position today. Most schools now seeking to relate themselves to community life are merely striving in one of these two directions, and sometimes in both directions at once.

What, then, is the desirable role of the school in the community? How shall we conceive its proper function as one among many educational agencies, yet of them all that one specifically maintained by society for the effective education of youth? Today the answer to that query is clear: The school's proper role within the total educative process is strictly a residual and a coordinating one. Its function is *residual* in the sense that its primary obligation is to

---

[1] From D. Harley Fite, "Making the School a Community Center." *Education,* February 1940, pp. 362–72.

[2] From Goodwin Watson, Unpublished manuscript. Used by permission.

teach all those abilities, appreciations, ideas, skills, attitudes, and ideals which are essential to the student's effective living and which he does not learn elsewhere. Its function is *coordinating* because both efficiency and economy require that the school neither duplicate what other agencies are doing, nor fail to utilize all their educational offerings to the fullest practicable extent. Maximum individual development through democratic social participation is our fundamental educational goal for each person. This goal is possible to attain only through the carefully coordinated educational efforts of all communities agencies concerned with the welfare of youth, including the school. The school's special obligation is therefore obvious: it is to analyze the minimum educational needs of its students, survey the community to discover to what extent those needs are already being satisfactorily met through non-school educational agencies, provide a curricular program to meet the remaining needs, and lead the community in more effectively coordinating its total educative resources for the increased benefit of all its members, adults as well as children.

The organized agency through which such coordination can best be achieved is the community coordinating council. As a social device, this is nothing new; nearly all of our larger cities have had councils of social agencies for many years. The war, meanwhile, has given tremendous impetus to the whole coordinating council idea. Nearly every American community has recently had intensive experience in cooperatively developing and administering its local Office of Civilian Defense, its War Council, its United Service Organization center, and other similar community-wide agencies occasioned by the war. Councils on community defense, committees on the care of children for working mothers, citizens unity associations, youth councils, adult education councils, religious instruction councils—all these and many more such *coordinating councils* are now personally familiar to Americans in every section of our nation.

Most prewar community coordinating councils originated in the essentially negative, though highly commendable, purpose of ameliorating poverty or of preventing juvenile delinquency. The war focused primary attention upon problems of home defense, of providing recreational facilities for service men and women, of caring for the children of employed mothers, and of combatting wartime delinquency. In pursuing these essential ends, local citizens, agencies, and organizations of many kinds learned to *work together* as they had never done before. It is essential that this war-born community cooperation be maintained and even increased after hostilities cease. Improving racial and intercultural relationships is one obvious problem with which practically every American community must seriously grapple during many postwar years. Providing adequate work opportunities for youth is another that is equally fundamental to American democracy. Problems such as these will demand the best thinking and cooperative planning of every community.

Another, and perhaps more significant, conception of community coordination is now emerging. This view holds that the community council should be the agency through which school personnel and community citizens may maintain active, critical, and continuing cooperation in the planning of the basic school policy itself. Educational cooperation of this nature is highly desirable in a nation which prides itself upon local control of its schools, and is particularly important when the school's program involves widespread use of resource visitors, interviews, field trips, surveys, service projects, work experiences, and other activities outside the classroom.

In all such programs—whether for the prevention of delinquency, the promotion of better race relations, the provision of work experience, or the planning of field trip opportunities—the fundamental key to success is community *coordination*. Neither the school alone, nor any other agency alone, can do these things to best advantage. When homes, churches, welfare organizations, police departments, courts, clinics, youth agencies, service clubs, professional groups, women's clubs, business associations, labor unions, veterans organizations *and schools* plan and work together, much can be accomplished. When education is conceived as experience, when the community is recognized as the matrix of that experience, when the community's responsibility for promoting better experience for its youth is widely affirmed, and when the school actually develops a residual and a coordinating function—then, but not until then, will education for life become truly functional.

What Is a Coordinating Council?

A coordinating council is a cooperative organization of groups and individuals who work together to improve social welfare within a given local community. A council is primarily an advisory and catalytic influence, rather than a super administrative agency. Its purpose is to clarify community problems and needs and to stimulate existing individual agencies to more intelligent and cooperative efforts in meeting those problems and needs. Even more specifically, the general purposes of community coordination have been au-

PUBLISHED BY ADULT EDUCATION PROGRAM
UNIVERSITY OF MICHIGAN, ANN ARBOR

653.1 3-44
TOPIC: YOUTH RECREATION

COMMUNITY ACTION

COMMUNITY
PROGRAM
SUGGESTIONS
NO. 3 MAR. 1944

MICHIGAN YOUTH CENTERS

A STUDY OF PROBLEMS AND PRACTICES

Many questions:

There are many questions concerning youth centers. One town wants one, another does not. One group thinks they are good for nothing, another sees in them the millennium for youth. Some are successful, some fail. Communities are asking what they should do. The answer is, of course, no one can arbitrarily say what any individual community should do.

The information tabulated here covers some of the present practices of community youth centers. These tabulations are best considered as guideposts

MICHIGAN'S STATE UNIVERSITY is stimulating community consciousness and activity through its department of adult education. *Community Action* is published regularly and distributed widely.

thoritatively stated in that excellent little bulletin, *A Guide to Community Coordination:* [3]

1. **To promote Cooperation** among organizations and citizens interested in making the community a more wholesome place in which to live.
2. **To foster the Coordination** of efforts of the foregoing organizations and individuals in order to meet the needs of the community more effectively.
3. **To sponsor the Study** of resources, conditions, and needs.
4. **To advance the Education** of the general public regarding conditions to be improved.
5. **To secure Democratic Action** in meeting local needs through existing agencies, organizations and institutions.

Well over a thousand local coordinating councils have been organized under a variety of names—"community council," "neigh-

[3] Coordinating Councils, Inc., 145 West 12th St. Los Angeles, California, 1941.

borhood council," "youth council," "community welfare council," "human relations council," "community coordinating council," and the like. The first group to use the present term *coordinating council* was organized in Berkeley, California in 1919. Since then the movement has developed far enough to establish *Coordinating Councils, Inc.* as a national informal advisory service and clearing house for exchange of experience.

Who belongs to a typical coordinating council? The *Coordinating Councils'* bulletin quoted above states that

"Councils in small cities and towns usually invite into their membership representatives of all organizations interested in the welfare of children and youth or in making the community a more wholesome place in which to live. The following organizations are usually represented on these councils.

GOVERNMENTAL SERVICES	PRIVATE SOCIAL AGENCIES	CIVIC ORGANIZATIONS	RELIGIOUS ORGANIZATIONS
City, County, State and Federal	Children's Protective Agencies	Veterans Organizations and their Auxiliaries	Catholic
Health	Community Centers	Chamber of Commerce	Jewish
Juvenile Court	Family Welfare	Junior Chamber of	Protestant
Libraries	Agencies	Commerce	Church Federations
Police and Sheriff	Organizations for Boys	Men's Service Clubs	Ministerial Associations
Probation	Organizations for Girls	Parent-Teacher Asso-	Church Youth Organ-
Public Schools	Youth Organizations	ciation	izations
Recreation	Others	Women's Clubs	Others
Welfare		Youth Organizations	
Others		Others	

"This list is frequently supplemented by adding representatives of industrial groups, trade unions, and professional bodies such as the Bar Association, Medical Association, and others.

"In addition to the representatives of organizations, many councils invite to membership individual citizens who may not officially represent any group, but whose interest and ability are so well known that they make valuable additions to the council in their own right."[4]

What Does a Council Do?

PROJECTS INSPIRED BY COUNCILS

"Councils function as counseling, coordinating or planning groups but not as agencies. A council usually discovers that if it takes on an administrative function and acts as an agency it is forced to give so much time to this service that it functions less effectively as a coordinating or planning group. It also runs the risk of encroaching on the territory of a member agency. Since this is true the question may well be asked as to how results are secured. How do councils get action?

"The councils work through the many organizations, agencies and departments included in their membership. If a council discovers a serious lack of recreational facilities in a certain area, it takes up the subject

[4] Coordinating Councils, Inc., *A Guide to Community Coordination*, p. 3.

with the recreation department, the public schools, or whatever group is in a position to do something about it. A solution to each problem is sought through the agencies or organizations already rendering service in the general field of the problem in question. Through cooperative planning, through the pooling of ideas and resources, a way is usually found to meet the needs which all agree are urgent.

"The following list gives some conception of the improvement councils have made in their communities through cooperative planning:

1. Recreation facilities.

Practically all councils report more activity in this field than in any other. They report the lighting of playgrounds; securing of new playgrounds, new facilities, equipment, club houses, swimming pools, community centers; extending present programs, securing directôrs, promoting back-yard playgrounds, improving life guard service, and securing the use and control of streets for play.

2. Improving public service.

Councils frequently discover ways by which public service can be extended to areas not yet reached or new forms of service introduced. This applies to every type of public service, particularly health, sanitation, fire protection, probation, police, libraries, and public schools.

3. Health and safety programs.

Clinics for children and mothers have been promoted, medical treatment provided for individual cases, health education stimulated, and hot lunches provided. Councils also have secured crossing guards and have improved traffic conditions.

4. Organizations for boys and girls.

Councils assist in the extension of boys' and girls' organizations through a variety of activities: leadership training and promotion; securing leaders for individual groups; assisting in organizing new Boys Clubs, Boy Scout troops, Cub Packs, Girl Scouts, Camp Fire girls, Y.M.C.A. and Y.W.C.A. groups, toy loan centers, and vacation church schools. The councils are particularly interested in extending these organizations to areas and to groups not hitherto served.

5. Employment for youth.

The councils recognize this as one of the major problems facing practically all communities. They have assisted by increasing the school facilities for vocational training, counseling, and placement service. A number of councils have provided special employment bureaus for youth.

6. New youth groups organized.

Councils have endeavored to meet social and educational needs of youth by assisting in the organization and supervision of community dances, social outings, drama classes, youth forums; courses on the preparation for marriage, home-making and parenthood; young married peoples' clubs, music clubs; clubs to promote athletics, gardening, study of radio, bicycle and automobile safety.

7. Educational opportunities for adults.

Councils have realized the need of assisting adults as well as youth and have played a prominent part in encouraging Americanization classes, public forums, adult education courses, citizen education centers, consumer education classes, parent education classes, mothers clubs, mothers educational centers, nursery schools and leadership training. In rural districts councils have assisted in providing recreational counseling for school teachers, teacher-training in service, and county school trustees' institutes.

8. Improving community conditions.

Councils have found it necessary in many communities to use their influence in preventing the sale of liquor to minors, the circulation of salacious literature, the use of gambling machines, the showing of undesirable motion pictures, and unwholesome conditions in dance halls and skating rinks. They have also played an active part in improving housing conditions.

9. New organizations and agencies formed.

When a council discovers that a new organization is needed it takes steps to create it and then leaves it to function quite independently of the parent council. Councils have thus launched community choruses, community theaters, motion picture estimate service, farm produce markets, and cold storage facilities. Several councils have successfully organized community chests and social service exchanges. Junior councils are now putting in their appearance in a number of cities.

PROJECTS SPONSORED BY COUNCILS

"The projects for which councils can safely assume responsibility are usually in the nature of special events, which may require intensive effort for only a short period. The following projects are typical of those sponsored by councils:

1. Special activities for children.

"Many councils sponsor special activities and events for children who ordinarily have few opportunities for such participation. These events include Christmas parties, fiesta programs and carnivals, Hallowe'en parties, soapbox derbies, miniature boat regattas, hobby and handicraft shows, industrial education tours, pageants, pet shows, patriotic programs, and free admission to athletic events.

2. Assisting summer camps.

"Councils participate in the summer camp programs by assisting in raising funds to send to camp children who could not otherwise go, assisting stay-at-home camps, and promoting camp parades.

3. Raising standards of home life.

"Through a number of different methods councils have sought to assist parents in improving the standards of their home life and in providing better supervision of their children. They have arranged community programs in school auditoriums, in which talks to parents have been combined with entertainment. Other councils have sponsored conferences on family relations, conferences on the home and the community, and fireside conferences.

4. Community events.

"In recent years many community events have been sponsored by councils which have brought relaxation, entertainment, education and uplift to thousands of people of all ages. These events include Clean-up Campaigns, Community Picnics, Farmers Days, Community Festivals, Community Christmas Celebrations, Community Hallowe'en Carnivals, Community Easter Services.

5. Social welfare.

"Councils have assisted the welfare program of their communities in many ways. They have raised money for milk funds, have assisted the Red Cross drives, and Community Chest campaigns, have cleared Christmas and Thanksgiving baskets, have established loan closets, and have promoted educational campaigns for syphilis control.

6. Community calendar.

"Many councils have found it advisable to sponsor a Community Calendar of important events in the interest of better programs and community good will. When important meetings of interest to the same people fall on the same day, the attendance at each function suffers, not to mention the hard feelings fostered by rival attractions." [5]

Where Does the School Fit In? [6]

In any community, the school is likely to be the only permanent agency which is supported by all the people and which already serves all the children. As such, the school has—or should deserve to have—the confidence of the community. The school is thus in a strategic position to initiate proposals for community coordination, and to carry a major share of the responsibility for developing proposals into plans, plans into policies, and policies into action.

It is inconceivable that a community council should be organized without the school being represented. Most school people recognize the council as a force having great educational potentialities, and hence are eager to support it. School people can clearly see the deep significance to democratic living inherent in the work of a good council. Here, people of divergent background and outlook meet together with common purposes to work for the common good. Thus does the educator see in the coordinating council a new area

---

[5] Coordinating Councils, Inc., *A Guide to Community Coordination*, pp. 9–12.
[6] This section was written for this book by Anne Wright, Principal of the Horace Howard Furness Junior High School, Philadelphia.

in which he may serve by giving a definitely educational direction to its activities.

School people who participate in a coordinating council would do well to keep in mind their particular responsibility as professional educators. Among those special obligations which are also opportunities are these:

1. To provide leadership and to act with others in making and keeping the Council a potent educational force in the community.
2. To maintain the democratic values of group discussion, group planning, group decision, and the scientific values of objective thinking about controversial issues.
3. To guide the Council in the use of evaluative procedures so that results may be reliably appraised, and purposes adjusted to changing needs.
4. To aid in sensitizing the Council's membership to youth needs, youth interests, and youth problems.
5. To endeavor to widen the base of Council membership so that young people are included in the deliberations and are encouraged to participate actively in both planning and executing of policies.

The last two of these five responsibilities merit more extended analysis. Young people now in school need to participate actively in community affairs, and the community itself benefits when they do so. A recent radio program featured four high school students from different parts of the country. These young people discussed their problems of the future with a great deal of intelligence and feeling. During the question period, the adult chairman of the program inquired of these youth representatives, "What do you want of us older folks? What can we do to help you solve your problems, to face your future?" The reply came without hesitation. It was forceful, honest, almost pleading in its sincerity: *"Let us work with you now in the solution of your problems.* Your present problems are part of our future problems. Don't make us wait to be of use. We can think. We can plan. Don't push us to one side with the comment, 'He is only a boy.' "What a picture of youth's energy, enthusiasm, vision of service—being patronized by adults with the smiling comment "He's only a boy!" We must not forget how other countries have seized upon the energies of youth and rallied them to their national purposes while we have forced our young people to stagnate while waiting for the day when they will be considered "old enough" to work with adults on projects affecting the common welfare.

If the young people of today are to fulfil their proper role as adequate citizens they must have every opportunity to study, to criticize, and to contribute to the constructive life of their local communities. Such opportunities are a challenge to the initiative and the creative thinking of young people, for they require youth to work on equal basis with adults in the development of intelligent programs for community action. In some cases, the schools will initiate such action—as in the form of service projects and work experience —but in others the schools will cooperate with other community agencies, enlisting youth in the coordinated program. The source of stimulation to action is not important. What is important is that communities become deeply aware of their problems, their responsibilities, and their resources for meeting both. To that awareness the school can contribute much.

How Is a Coordinating Council Started?

Just how does one go about starting a community coordinating council? To answer this practical question in a practical and detailed manner, let us follow a school principal as he tells the story of how one successful council originated, expanded, and functioned.[7] Within his statement we shall interpolate ten basic principles which were observed and which thereby assured the council's success.

"It is difficult to identify the origin of the organization which has come to be our community council. It may have been the yard of the Benson School which urged the new principal to go beyond the school gates to solve the problems of the free play period. It may have been the constantly recurring fights among pupils on their way home from school. Perhaps it could be traced to the numerous complaints from neighbors who were annoyed, from storekeepers whose goods were upset or stolen, from parents whose children were beaten or 'shaken-down' for money. It may have been the pressure under which teachers were forced to work to meet the instability and poor habits which pupils brought into school with them. It may have been the findings of a survey of neighborhood recreational facilities conducted by the Council of Social Agencies. Without a doubt, the presence of Tasker Homes, a federal housing project, played a part. It may have been the faith that the majority of parents want the community in which they raise their children to be a place of good influences, or the faith that the majority of parents want their children to receive a better education than they themselves received. Then, again, it may have been that the 'times were ripe,' that all of us who engaged in the enterprise felt the need for action too long delayed.

---

[7] Harry S. Ward, Jr., "The Development of the Grays' Ferry Community Council." Unpublished manuscript. The present statement is somewhat abridged and adapted from the original account. Used by permission.

Perhaps no one factor should be singled out; our council may be the result of all of these factors as well as others not identified. . . .

(1) Study the problem situation

"The new principal had spent the school year 1939 to 1940, his first in the school, in making observations of pupils and neighborhood, in asking questions of teachers, parents, and residents, and in noting reactions. He came to the conclusion that much of what was built up in children in the school was broken down by conditions in the out-of-school environment; that teachers and parents were working against great odds. He also felt that improved conditions outside the school were needed to increase the effectiveness of teachers and parents in their efforts toward child welfare. The problem seemed to center outside the school and home as much as it did inside these social institutions.

(2) Analyze the limitations and resources of the community

"On the negative side the community appeared to shape up as follows:

Racial antagonisms (the school population was 50% Negro, 25% Italian, 15% Irish, 10% others): frequent fights between Negroes and Whites; beatings of individuals by gangs of white or vice-versa; segregation of Negroes; prevention of Negroes from using recreational centers, motion picture theaters, etc.; discrimination in the renting of houses on certain streets; etc.

Low economic status: between 30 and 40% of families on relief; inadequate food and clothing for at least 20% of the pupils in the school.

Poor housing conditions: sub-standard plumbing and heating; absence of bathing or indoor toilet facilities in many homes; inadequate protection from weather; overcrowding.

Poor sanitary conditions: filth in alleys, backyards, empty houses, vacant lots; children playing in filth; scavenging rampant; streets littered with refuse, particularly on garbage collection day.

Poor social conditions on streets and in homes: loiterers in gangs on many corners and lots; open gambling; annoyance of pedestrians; streets on which residents would not walk at night; organized looting of stores and trucks by teen-age boys; adults purchasing stolen goods from children; protection for the law-breaker by 'covering-up' or using the 'close-mouth' policy; children on streets from early in the morning to very late at night; children living under 'broken-home' conditions.

Harmful recreational facilities: many tap-rooms and 'candy' stores; exploitation of children through sale of cigarettes, use of pin-ball machines, and issuing of chance cards; admission of children to tap-rooms to shine shoes, to dance and sing for money, etc.; admission of school-age children into moving picture houses during school hours; parents' expenditure of money for alcoholic drinks resulting in the neglect of children's needs; adults loitering in tap-rooms while children were left to do as they pleased.

Numerous 'social' clubs: these listed, observed conditions seemed to reflect a number of adverse attitudes; these attitudes were found present in adults and were brought into the school by children.

Sectionalism (a hang-over of many years' standing): certain sections 'belonged' to certain residents, to move or travel into these sections meant 'taking what you get'; 'superiority' among those who lived on one side of the railroad; unwillingness to accept the Negro as part of the community; resentment because Negroes would not stay 'where they belonged.'

Irresponsibility: attitudes of 'pass-the-buck'; 'get all you can but do nothing to get it'; 'what are you going to do to help me'; and 'this is what should be done for me.'

Lethargy: a feeling of doing nothing about conditions because nothing would help ('what's the use?'); fear of consequences if one tried to do something; lack of confidence in trying to bring about improvement because social and intellectual levels seemed too great a handicap.

Lack of community consciousness: little appreciation of difficulties faced by others; lack of understanding and, as a result, much misunderstanding; lack of respect for authority ('the cop's a rat'); lack of respect for property.

No neighborhood organization which held as its purpose the improvement of the entire community.

"But on the positive side there were encouraging factors:

Self-respecting residents: a number of groups, including 'old timers' and their families who stayed on in the neighborhood when others moved to the suburbs; property well kept; pride in Grays' Ferry as it used to be—all potential helpers in a program of improving conditions by getting at causes.

A number of fine churches: some energetic leaders and a social point of view.

A cooperative police captain: but the police activities could have been more effective if more police were available to handle the problems, and if they did not have to cope with the subtle 'grapevine' tactics of many of the residents.

A group of business men: an expressed willingness to go along with someone who would 'start something' but doubting that much could be done.

Cooperative teachers: doing much for children whose parents could not or would not care for them as they should.

Cooperative principals in other schools: helping with problems arising as pupils shifted from school to school for industrial arts and home economics.

The school district superintendent: experience, vision, and advice—an invaluable source of help.

School provisions for compulsory attendance: the home and school visitor who, though handicapped by the frequency and urgency of needs, faced the problem with courage and earnestness.

A fine social settlement house: well-organized and serving up to its capacity (clinics, mothers' groups, recreational groups, etc.); but limited in its total neighborhood influence because it was forced to serve a very large area.

Two recreational centers: one privately endowed and one operated by the Municipal Bureau of Recreation.

A federal housing project: opportunities for better physical conditions and a program of education for residents and nearby families.

Active social agencies doing fine work.

"It seemed to the principal that this array of positive forces for improvement was sufficient to organize a cooperative movement—the need lay in the direction of bringing them together. However, he chose to start in a small way with a small group to attack problems in the local school environment and to reserve the larger community organization until such times as progress in this small group could be developed. Here, he felt, was a good proving ground for community activities. Hence the reason for first organizing a Parents Association.

(3) Call together a few key people to face the facts

"The Parents Association developed in an interesting manner. First, a group of twelve parents, white and Negro, were called together early in the fall of 1940. The principal presented a picture of neighborhood conditions and attitudes and requested the parents to check on its accuracy. The parents not only verified the data but offered additional proof. The principal then developed the effects of these conditions on children and on the work of teachers in the school and parents in the home. This was followed by a proposal for some kind of organization to enlist cooperative effort on the part of parents to do something to improve conditions. The result was a decision to try to form a Parents Association. A date for holding a meeting of parents for this purpose was set.

(4) Develop a small cooperative program

"The meeting was held. The district superintendent, the director of the local settlement house, and our school doctor participated. Only 40 parents came. Some missionary work to arouse more interest was needed. The original 12 parents responded to meet the need. After a second meeting brought only 50 parents, this group of 12 parents went door-bell pulling. It is a fine tribute to the interest and effort of these women that this door-to-door visitation was made during a stretch of bitter cold weather. The next meeting went over 100 in attendance. Then came a proposal to hold an evening meeting in order to get fathers as well as mothers to attend. The evening meeting produced results which surprised all—an attendance of over 200; a request to have the school open every Thursday night for activities of the Parents Association; a request to organize a Boy Scout troop; many volunteers to help the Mothers Assistance group to care for the clothing needs of poor children; a request to do something about a summer recreational program. With the cooperation of our Board of Education, the W.P.A., active individuals among the parents, and others, the program went ahead.

(5) Expand the program carefully

"The school was opened on Thursday nights; sewing leaders were provided by the W.P.A. to help in the problem of clothes for the needy; the Boy Scout troop was organized, one of the parents becoming the Scoutmaster; crafts, dancing, and dramatic groups were formed; a home visiting group to look into needs went into action; community leaders including clergymen, the police captain, and others came to speak to parents; a summer recreational program developed. By the end of May, a fund had been built up, children were clothed, families helped, and a spirit of cooperation between neighborhood groups started to develop. When schools closed in June, the recreational program was responsible for having the basement and yard of the Benson School open and accommodating a total attendance of 3000 children during the months of July and August. Responsible parents, serving as members of a committee of supervision, appeared daily in the school during the summer to make sure that the school building, equipment and supplies received proper care. It is interesting to note that, in contrast with previous summers, not one window in the school was broken. Meanwhile, small lots were cleaned up, and small play areas were made available to the younger children. Thus, in the fall of 1941, the Parents Association was a reality and was functioning well. The response and activity had been such that now the principal felt he could safely venture forth into a larger community organization.

(6) Call together representatives of all community agencies

"The preliminary steps toward the organization of a coordinating council were taken by the first of October. Contact lists were prepared, letters sent out, telephone calls made, and personal interviews held. An initial meeting of all interested community leaders was called near the end of October. The response was gratifying. Leaders from 38 organizations attended. Representatives came from local schools, churches, social agencies, law enforcement groups, and city-wide welfare organizations. Negro and white, Hebrew and Christian, Catholic and Protestant, participated through the leadership of pastor, priest, rabbi, district superintendent, principal, home visitor, executive secretary, president, director, and the like. The meeting climaxed with the formation of two committees and the decision to have them make a study of what councils in other parts of the city were doing, what principles they were following, and what purposes they sought. In addition, the committees were requested to define boundary lines for the operation of the council. A second meeting date was set.

(7) Develop a permanent organization

"The response to this second meeting was greater than to the first. The Council organization was accepted by the group as the means of improving community conditions. Basic principles, purposes, practices, and possible boundary lines were agreed upon. Officers were chosen.

(8) Call public mass meetings

"Plans were made to bring the Council to the attention of the general public. One of the principles which had been adopted in the second meeting of assembled leaders was, 'the enlistment of interest and co-operation of lay members of all community groups is basic.' This principle served as the keynote of a large mass meeting set for December 9, 1941. In spite of the fact that war came just before the meeting and our mayor called a public mass meeting for the evening of December 9, an audience of over 200 people came to the school auditorium for our own scheduled meeting. The leaders in our community had advertised the council meeting in pulpit, school, community house, and neighborhood groups. The response to the meeting reflected their interest and effort. The results of the meeting reflected the response of the interested public. Thirty-two specific suggestions for community action and improvement were made by the audience. The meeting adjourned with the understanding that an executive committee, selected during the meeting, would review all suggestions and report back to the public in a future mass meeting.

"The review of suggestions and the preparation of a program for the second mass meeting proved a very enlightening experience for the executive committee. The suggestions made indicated the need for attack in two areas: Housing, and Delinquency and Recreation. In a series of six sessions, the executive committee contacted the city Housing Association, the Hale America Program, the Inter-agency Council for Youth, the Education and Recreation Division of the W.P.A., the local recreational centers and local settlement houses. On the basis of what was learned and discussed, two programs were organized for presentation at the second mass meeting. Both programs involved lay participation including air raid wardens, auxiliary police, local real estate agents, mothers' clubs, youth groups, etc. A voluntary questionnaire for use by all local organizations was prepared to determine what activities were already under way in the community, and to summarize information about available facilities and leadership.

(9) Undertake constructive programs of social action

"The second mass meeting resulted in the acceptance of both programs and the participation of volunteers from the general public as members of the two committees. Various civic projects were thus launched, among them being these: a survey of fire and health hazards by air raid wardens to be used by the council as a basis for later action if the wardens could not enlist enough cooperation to eliminate such hazards; a reorganization of activities in local recreational centers to make more opportunities for the Negro; a survey of vacant lots for the purpose of increasing the recreational facilities; a campaign to get leadership for summer activities since previous leadership supplied by the W.P.A. was no longer available; a youth organization in public and parochial schools to improve pupil actions on the streets; the relating of such organization to the war and defense effort.

(10) Constantly evaluate results

"The results of all this effort—from the Parents Association to the Community Council—may be summarized in terms of the following outcomes:

I PARTLY OR ENTIRELY DUE TO THE PARENTS ASSOCIATION:

A. **Better pupil-pupil and pupil-neighborhood relationships.** The cooperation of parents has played an important part in bringing about:

1. Substantial reduction in fighting among children at dismissal; in disciplinary cases involving racial antagonisms; in complaints from neighbors, store-keepers, and parents; in annoyance from outsiders during play periods in the school yard.
2. More wholesale participation in free play in the school yard.
3. Better attitudes toward authority; more willingness to accept direction from pupil leaders.

B. **Improved parent-school relationships:**

1. Less antagonism toward correction of pupils, particularly in instances where the parent used 'color-discrimination' in the defense of children's actions.
2. Expressed opinion, in open meetings (almost testimonials) that pupils were treated fairly, irrespective of race, color or creed.
3. Expressed appreciation, in open meetings and in the neighborhood, of what the school was doing to help the community.

C. **Increased participation in activities influencing children:**

1. Organization and installation of a Boy Scout troop.
2. Functioning of a home-visiting group, keeping in touch with extreme needs and making it possible for children to be in school and for agencies to be notified before acute hardships had developed; relieving conditions by sharing time, materials, and effort.
3. Creation and use of a money fund to care for needs not met by organized social agencies.
4. Supervision of summer recreational program in the school through daily inspection of equipment, supplies, and relationships.
5. Clean-up and preparation of small lots for use as play space by children.

D. **Increased use of school building by the community:**

1. Average weekly attendance of over 125 adults and youths on Thursday nights since March, 1941.
2. Classes in sewing (repairing and renovating for community use), dressmaking, crafts, dramatics, dancing, Boy Scouts, etc.
3. Education through orientation with the work of social and civic agencies, and the problems faced by groups and individuals in the neighborhood, etc.

4. Discussion, planning and carrying out of activities for combating negative influences.

II PARTLY OR ENTIRELY DUE TO THE COMMUNITY COUNCIL:

A. **Increase in community consciousness:**
   1. Suggestions given by the public in mass meetings, their purposes reflecting a desire for improvement and a willingness to cooperate; acceptance of a council as a means of improvement.
   2. Publicity given in pulpit, school, and settlement house indicating the need and advantages of cooperative effort.
   3. Intervisitation of leaders and groups among various institutions in the community; understanding of the work done by social agencies and other groups.

B. **Creation of a means for clearing problems and planning action to solve them:**
   1. Establishment of a Housing Committee and the collection of data relative to safety and health; enlistment of cooperation by air raid wardens, local real estate agents; distribution of information to householders concerning care of homes and procedures to take if difficulties arise.
   2. Development of a Delinquency and Recreation Committee; definition of various phases of the problem; survey of programs and facilities available in the community; enlistment of cooperation by the local police, auxiliary policemen, local volunteer leadership; planning of a summer recreational program on an extensive scale.

C. **Specific action taken:**
   1. Against tap rooms for admission of children.
   2. Against motion picture theaters for admission of school age children during school hours.
   3. Against neighborhood gangs.
   4. With agencies who might supply leadership for recreational activities.

D. **Publicity for local organizations, programs, and activities carried on by the Council:**
   1. Projected monthly publication for distribution to community."

Such is the story of one American community, led to definite civic improvement by the social vision and tactful management of its school principal. What a dramatic demonstration of the power and potentialities inherent in constructive community coordination! Even when the confronting social situation is markedly deteriorated —as in the present instance where racial conflict and slum housing were characteristic—cooperative effort, intelligently applied, can work veritable wonders. And far greater success has attended many communities where the original social conditions were less depressed and consequently less formidable.

Education Is a Community Function

For generations we maintained the book-centered school in its social isolation. Then we discovered the community and eagerly sought to use its varied resources to enrich and vitalize our academic programs. In recent years teachers have done much to bring the community into the school and to take the children into the community. But in that very process of *academically* bridging the gulf between community and school we have discovered that community conflicts and disorganizations are reflected in our students' behavior, that mere information about the community is insufficient to influence personal living or community improvement, that active student participation in community processes is both educationally and civically inadequate as long as dominant community influences oppose the work of the school or even remain indifferent toward it. Thus, we have been driven to recognize the inescapable truth: that *the education of the whole child in his total environment is and must remain a community function* despite the existence and development of the school. Education cannot be identified solely with schooling, nor learning with formal instruction. That is why "education for democracy" cannot be much more than a delusive verbalism unless it is everywhere *grounded in appropriate, community-wide, and community-guided action.* Such action may and should be stimulated by the school, but never confined within it. For in the classic words of Joseph K. Hart:

"The democratic problem in education is not primarily a problem of training children; it is the problem of *making a community* within which children cannot help growing up to be democratic, intelligent, disciplined to freedom, reverent of the goods of life, and eager to share in the tasks of the age. A school cannot produce this result; nothing but a community can do so." [8]

There is our professional challenge! There also is our inescapable responsibility as creative teachers of youth in democratic America.

SELECTED REFERENCES

Association for Childhood Education, Committee on Teacher Preparation, "Making Use of Community Agencies." *Childhood Education* 14:261–63 (Feb. 1938).

[8] *The Discovery of Intelligence,* p. 383. New York: Century Co., 1924.

Lists typical social service agencies whose aid might be enlisted to help solve pupils' problems, and indicates a variety of school situations in which the aid of community agencies might well be used.

Beam, Kenneth S., "Coordinating Councils in California." California Department of Education Bulletin 11. Sacramento: State Department of Education, 1938. Shows the development and functioning of councils in California.

Brunner, Edmund deS., *Working with Rural Youth*. Washington: American Council on Education, 1942. Reports a three-year project involving 15 counties in 5 states, the purpose being to work through existing community agencies for the development of strong community cooperation in the building of a permanent rural youth program.

Coordinating Councils, Inc., "A Guide to Community Coordination." 145 West 12th St., Los Angeles: Coordinating Councils, 1942. Principles and suggestions for the development of coordinating, community, and neighborhood councils in cities and towns under 25,000 in population.

Dickson, Virgil E., "The Coordinating Council and the School." *California Journal of Secondary Education* 13:21–23 (Jan. 1938). The philosophy of the movement, and seven guiding principles.

Fenton, Norman, "The Coordinating Council Offers a Solution." *California Journal of Secondary Education* 15:32–37 (Jan. 1940); *Education Digest*, March 1940. Social and educational achievements of coordinating councils.

Fite, D. Harley, "Making the School a Community Center." *Education* 60:362–72 (Feb. 1940). Comprehensive analysis of the kind of school needed as a genuine community center for learning activities.

Goodykoontz, Bess, "Leadership in the Coordination of Social Agencies." *Curriculum Journal* 13:257–60 (Oct. 1942). Five basic principles to be observed, as indicated by the literature and experience.

Hurt, H. W., "Relation of the School to Other Educative Forces in the Community." *Clearing House* 8:526–31 (May 1934). Four alternatives confronting the school: oppose community organizations, ignore them, tolerate them, use them.

Journal of Educational Sociology, special issues as follows: February, 1936, "Schools That Serve the Community"; April, 1936, "Education and the Community"; September, 1936, "Community Coordination and Social Programs"; March, 1937, "Community Agencies and Character Growth"; October, 1937, "Proceedings: National Educational Conference on Community Coordination"; January, 1938, "The Yonkers Plan of Community Coordination"; April, 1938, "Cooperation of Schools and Community Agencies."

Mayer, Jane, and Miriam Sutherland, "The Community—A Laboratory." Progressive Education Association Service Center Pamphlet 1. New York: The Association, 1941. The story of how schools and other community agencies developed effective cooperation in Glencoe, Illinois.

McClusky, Howard Y., "School in the Community." *North Central Association Quarterly* 15:363–67 (April 1941). A positive philosophy of school-community relationship, stressing the catalytic and coordinating function of the school.

Moffitt, J. C., "Community Cooperation for Health." *Educational Method* 22:175–78 (Jan. 1943). The advantages and possibilities for increased public health through school and community coordination.

Nelson, Lowry, "Planning and Organizing Cooperative Community Projects." *Social Education* 7:68–70 (Feb. 1943). Types of community problems, with specific suggestions for procedure in attacking them cooperatively.

Nisonger, Herschel W., "The Role of the School in Community Education." Columbus: The Ohio State University, 1940. How the school may serve its community through such projects as an adult school, aid to new voters, encouragement of library usage, better recreational opportunities, vocational education, parent education, community forum, community council.

Peyser, N., "School as the Center of the Community." *Journal of Educational Sociology* 9:354–58 (Feb. 1936). How a metropolitan public school set out to help prevent delinquency, and became an educational center for the whole community.

Prall, Charles E., "Community Organization and Cooperation." In *Toward a New Curriculum:* 1944 Yearbook, Department of Supervision and Curriculum, National Education Association, Ch. 10. Washington: The Association, 1944. Illustrations of recent community councils and other cooperative activities, a listing of derived principles, and a brief discussion of the role of school personnel in community cooperation.

Riggs, Lawrence, "An Opportunity for the School in Community Cooperation: The Coordinating Council." *School & Society* 51:598–603 (May 11, 1940). Comprehensive description and analysis of the community council movement. Includes principles and trends in organization, and cites examples of local, county, and state councils.

Sheffield, A. D., "Techniques of Cooperation Between Community Groups and the School." *Educational Method* 17:335–41 (April 1938). Methods whereby the democratic school may stimulate local community leaders and groups to cooperate with it in discussing vital social questions. Illustrations of desirable procedure are offered, and major principles are drawn.

Southeastern Workshop, *A Handbook in Community Development*. Greenville, South Carolina: Furman University Press, 1941. Manual of tested suggestions for beginning, developing, organizing and evaluating cooperative community improvement programs.

United States Department of Commerce, "Small Town Manual for Community Action!" Washington: Government Printing Office, 1942. Suggestions for local war service and improvement of business conditions.

University of Virginia, Extension Division, *New Dominion Series*. Charlottesville: The University, September, 1941. A series of leaflets describing experimental approaches to democratic living in various communities.

Works, George A., and Simon O. Lesser, *Rural America Today: Its Schools and Community Life,* Ch. XV. Chicago: University of Chicago Press, 1942. General description of community planning in typical rural situations, and therefore valuable in contrast with other reports which stress urban conditions.

CHAPTER 20

Teacher Education

Education can be a powerful force in shaping the quality of human relationships. No blunter truth than this is implicit in world events of the past two decades. Totalitarian regimes initially seized upon education as their primary tool for moulding the hearts and minds of men; their success in using that tool for evil purposes is still too evident for comfort. But now—in America, Britain, China, Russia, and others among the United Nations—there is growing recognition that education can and must serve the cause of democracy with even greater effectiveness than it has done in the past.

If new vitality is to produce and permeate a democratic world civilization, it will have to be developed out of a new education for all age groups—an essentially democratic education which will develop in each individual a driving interest in bettering group living, together with personal mastery and devotion to the social techniques necessary for democratic organization and control. This requires that we free the intelligence of children and youth; that we constantly challenge them to *extend* democracy, as well as to protect and preserve it; that we continually practice them in the skills of cooperative group action. Is it not evident today that democracy can be based only upon education, and that true education will produce democracy?

A democratic social outlook and a sound psychology of learning together demand that functional programs of education be speedily and generally developed. To anyone who perceives the great social trends of our time, it is clear that the improvement of human living and the extension of the democratic way of life will depend, in large measure, upon the development of public education centering in community processes and problems as they impinge upon the lives of children and of youth today. This means that the life-centered community school must come to supplant both the book-centered and the child-centered patterns of formal education, at least through elementary, high school, and junior college levels,

This fundamental need in education presents very real problems to both the prospective teacher and the teacher in service, as well as a basic challenge to teacher-educating institutions. *How is the alert teacher to prepare himself for effective work in the community school of tomorrow?*

What Community-Centered Teacher Education Programs Are Available?

To what extent do our college and university programs of teacher education now emphasize community study and its relation to effective teaching? To answer this question, Olsen recently made a national survey covering all fully-accredited American institutions engaged in teacher education.[1] From the data secured it was concluded that "approximately one-third of America's fully accredited institutions now educating teachers make available to them some type of experience with the philosophy, procedures, and problems of community-centered education." Quoting Olsen further:

These programs are of three chief kinds: (*a*) special courses which emphasize community study methods and techniques, community structure and organization, or community relationships of the school; (*b*) aspects of conventional courses whereby community study is given limited attention in General Methods, Educational Sociology, Rural Education, etc.; and (*c*) informal and extracurricular experiences such as those involved in scrap collection, gasoline rationing, service in social settlements, leadership of youth groups, and the like. . . .

The special courses offered are themselves of four chief types: (*a*) community study methods, techniques, programs, and philosophy; (*b*) community organization, structure, and problems; (*c*) community relations of schools, involving both teacher-community and school-community situations; and (*d*) community study workshops.[2]

The complete report of this survey includes specific descriptions of numerous special courses being offered by institutions located throughout the United States. This national survey was essentially *quantitative;* that is, it sought to discover the extent (how much?) of professional preparation for community study leadership.

It is interesting to note that a *qualitative* study (how good?) was made in the same year by Blackwell for the Commission on Teacher Education.[3] This inquiry sought to describe in some detail

---

[1] Edward G. Olsen, "National Survey of Teacher Education in Community Study Techniques." *Educational Record,* October 1943, pp. 421–35.

[2] *Ibid.,* pp. 425–26.

[3] Gordon W. Blackwell, *Toward Community Understanding.* Washington: American Council on Education, 1943.

how community study programs actually operate in selected institutions purported to be doing outstanding work in developing community understanding among prospective teachers. A number of prominent educators were first asked to name those institutions which they thought were doing unusual work in the field of preparing teachers for community-centered education. The fact that almost four score colleges and universities were thus suggested bore out Olsen's finding that considerable emphasis is now being given to this area of study. Among the sixteen institutions finally selected for intensive, firsthand investigation were colleges and universities of all types—public and private, large and small, white and Negro, sectarian and nonsectarian, universities, teachers colleges, and liberal arts colleges. In these varying institutions, all types of approach to community understanding were found—special courses, documentary fact-finding, audio-visual aids, resource visitors, interviews, excursions, surveys, extended field studies, service projects, work experiences, student government, use of the arts. After analyzing the sixteen programs, Blackwell concluded that no one approach to the community is sufficient, but that the various techniques of developing community understanding can all be helpful if judiciously used.

By What Standards Shall We Judge a Teacher-Educating Institution?

Students and teachers who have chosen education as a profession, and who desire superior preparation as prospective workers in community schools, are often puzzled by the question of where to go for their college and professional training. Such young people are advised to study the actual programs of various possible institutions, and to judge the professional advantages offered by each in the light of these criteria which follow.

CRITERIA FOR SELECTING A SUPERIOR PROGRAM OF TEACHER EDUCATION

1. Does the college offer experiences through which the student will learn democracy through its philosophy, history, aspirations, and practice?
2. Does the college provide for much sharing and cooperation, so that the area of common concern will be widened and students behave in a way consistent with democratic values?
3. Does the college help each student to understand the relationship between the community school and the maintenance and extension of a democratic society?

4. Does the college guide the student in building a personal ideal of service whereby he will desire to promote democracy's essential instrument of progress—education?

5. Does the college stimulate free social interaction, interchange of views and mutual interaction, so as to break down provincialism, cliques, class and race discrimination?

6. Does the college foster a quality of human relations which will contribute to the integration of personality among both staff and students?

7. Does the college encourage participation in social groups by all students, so that they may develop a healthy sense of collective loyalty and security?

8. Does the college sponsor a wide range of creative experiences through which the student can develop interest, skill, and satisfaction in the arts, in recreational activities, and in social relationships?

9. Does the college recognize that effective learning comes through active participation of students in the actual affairs of a real world?

10. Does the college give students adequate opportunity to develop the skills of communication in situations of use?

11. Does the college provide "homes-away-from-home" in which students can have the experience of cooperative group living of the highest quality under the guidance of a wise and sympathetic adult?

12. Does the college encourage a socially responsible student leadership capable of respecting the individuality of others, yet possessing increasing psychological insight, civic understanding, and social vision?

13. Does the college facilitate general student responsibility for solving everyday problems which arise in college and community, and thus furnish direct instruction in the techniques and processes of democratic group life—consulting and cooperating, setting group standards, determining policies, resolving conflicts, judging the results of group actions?

14. Does the college permit a major part of the professional program for teachers to be centered in the study of children and youth, how they grow and develop, and how one works and lives with them in home, school, and community?

15. Does the college stimulate critical study of American and world culture, and of the relation of the individual's life to the surrounding social processes?

16. Does the college offer experiences through which students will develop skill in community study, will come to comprehend community life and processes, will identify conflicts of values and resultant community problems?

17. Does the college, in principle and practice, stress education through social participation and through socially useful work on the campus, in cooperating schools, and in the community at large?

18. Does the college program as a whole, as well as the teacher-education aspects of it, emphasize reflective thinking and experimentation in problem situations which are of genuine concern to the student, his group, the college, and the community?

No institution will completely measure up to all of these criteria. Marked divergence will be found in the degree to which various institutions preparing teachers meet these standards, even though such institutions all satisfy existing state certification regulations. That is why both the alert young person entering college and the enterprising teacher in active service will look beyond minimum legal requirements and glowing catalogue statements; they will also interview administrators in community schools, college students and teachers, and community workers who know the institution by its practice. They will search out and attend that institution most devoted to a democratic, experimental philosophy—in which administrators, teachers and students are seeking cooperatively for better ways of educating leaders for the functional community schools of today and tomorrow.

How Can Teachers in Service Develop Community Competence?

Little organized provision is as yet being made whereby teachers in service may continue their education toward more effective service in the life-centered, community school. However, some universities and teachers colleges offer summer session courses in this field, and here and there, a community emphasis is being given to the in-service program as well as to the regular professional curriculum.[4] Off-campus laboratory courses and summer workshops have recently been organized, and for these some expert consultants have been secured—mature men and women who have themselves directed community studies and service projects, who are familiar with cooperative group-work techniques, and who can really assist teachers with practical plans for building functional curriculums, utilizing community resources, and organizing the community toward more effective education. Extension classes and workshops of this kind have already been held under the auspices of such institutions as the Alabama State Teachers College at Florence, the University of Arkansas, Central Michigan College of Education, the University of Chicago, Denver University, George Peabody College for Teachers, Los Angeles City and County, the University of North Carolina, the W. K. Kellogg Foundation, the Philadelphia Board of Public Education, and the National Education Association's Department of Supervisors and Directors of Instruction.

[4] For a descriptive listing of typical courses, see Edward G. Olsen, op. cit., pp. 426–32.

The teacher who is doing creative work in building a curriculum for a life-centered school especially needs the stimulation and psychological security which come through working with others having common purposes. Some teachers' organizations, recognizing this, foster group education which includes creative work, recreation, and serious professional study. Frequently, they carry on under their own leadership, bringing in consultants as they are needed. Sometimes they organize laboratory courses or workshops in conjunction with the teachers' association or the board of education, staffing them with instructors from some nearby teachers' college or university. Illustrative of this procedure is a rural teacher's club in northern Michigan which has combined club meetings, Christmas parties, weekly suppers, and a community arts and crafts exhibit with a laboratory course in community survey-analysis and organization.[5]

In addition to the various types of professional group training just mentioned, the enterprising teacher can find innumerable opportunities for personal growth in community life itself. In the last analysis, real ability to function in a community school situation will develop through growing experience in working cooperatively, for the solution of common problems, with boys and girls, parents, community leaders, welfare organizations, pressure groups, etc. from day to day. The following ten suggestions are therefore offered to the teacher in service who desires to fit himself for more effective educational leadership in the future. These suggestions are equally valid for the prospective teacher just beginning his professional preparation.

1. **Study the school and the community.** The teacher who understands the ongoing life of his community, its mores and customs, factions and cleavages, needs and values, will be strategically able to make intelligent professional adjustments. It is well to know community "causes" and their leaders, the important political and business figures, the occupations and prejudices of school board members, causes of previous friction between town and school, the community blocs which support purposes similar and antagonistic to the purposes of the school, and the like. Know your community!

2. **Make a wide variety of social contacts** with people of different ages, races, nationalities, classes, political and religious beliefs. Recognize human differences as normal and desirable in a democratic community. Utilize your experience as a person who has come

[5] See Margaret O. Koopman, "Education for Better Community Life." *Michigan County School Commissioners Bulletin*, May 1944.

perhaps from a rural, working class or middle class home, to enter sympathetically into the lives of people in your present community. Help lessen the social distance between teachers and other occupational groups. Know your people!

3. **Share common interests with a wide circle of friends,** many of whom are outside the teaching profession. Deliberately cultivate personal friendships with people of divergent backgrounds but of common civic and social concerns. Widen your friendships!

4. **Become acquainted with community agencies and their leaders, and demonstrate your interest in cooperating with them.** Every teacher should understand the work of such agencies as the Bureau of Social Aid, Health Department, Welfare Department, County Agricultural Offices, Recreation Department, Juvenile Center, Probate Court, private charitable organizations, church and religious societies, settlement houses, farm and labor organizations, and the like. On many occasions, teachers will need to contact these groups about school problems, and should therefore resolutely break down the inertia or reticence which keeps them from visiting such agencies. Invariably the face-to-face meetings prove both interesting and stimulating, and lead the active teacher to increase the breadth of such experiences. These agencies have their own public relations problems, and teachers should be willing to meet them more than half way. Contact agencies!

5. **Know your state and regional resources.** State and national officials, college extension workers, members of the state department of education, representatives of foundations, medical and research groups, etc. are available to most communities. It is the definite responsibility of teachers and school administrators to know who these resource people are, and to utilize their services at appropriate times. Utilize resources!

6. **Attend public meetings in the community,** talk with people, introduce yourself, express your appreciation of what others do for community welfare. Appear in public!

7. **Participate with others in studying community needs and attacking community problems,** particularly those which bear upon the education of boys and girls. Be more interested in helping groups formulate and achieve civic purposes than in securing personal or institutional publicity. Work with others!

8. **Become well versed in techniques of scientific thinking,** and apply your knowledge to the handling of controversial issues in your classroom as well as in the community outside. Remain objective!

9. **Make careful study of the age group which you are teaching.** Visit pupils in their homes, enter into their recreational life, observe them in public places and in work situations. Know your students!

10. **Become a legal resident of the community** and vote in local, state, and national elections. Understand local community problems and issues, and be prepared to exert your influence as well as to vote intelligently. Be a real citizen!

Scientific studies have shown that often the teacher is a "stranger" in the community wherein he works—that although he is physically *in* the community, he is not psychologically *one of* the community. Although working there, he may not *live* there in the deepest sense, for his fundamental interests and concerns are frequently elsewhere. Putting down no lasting roots in the community where he teaches, cherishing academic interests which are largely remote from the life and needs of the present, and failing to participate responsibly in the cooperative endeavors of lay groups—is it to be wondered that such a teacher remains essentially a "stranger" within the community? But let that teacher earnestly and constantly observe the ten primary principles of educational leadership just outlined, and it is safe to predict that his status of community "stranger" will change to that of community "friend." Then, and only then, will he become also a true teacher of youth.[6]

Who Is Responsible for Promoting Life-Centered Teacher Education?

Community understanding and social competence represent a kind of growth which the teacher cannot achieve all by himself. Social learning is a group enterprise. The education of the socially effective teacher is therefore the joint responsibility of the state, the teacher-educating institution, the local community, the school system, and the teacher himself.

Schools are in position to serve as a powerful force for extending the democratic way of life. Their major purpose is the democratic socialization of the individual. This does not mean standardization through indoctrination, but rather the development of diversity and

[6] For interpretative reports on studies of the community contacts and participation of teachers, see the following:

Lloyd A. Cook and Ronald B. Almack, "The Community Participation of Two Thousand Eight Hundred Seventy Ohio Teachers." *Educational Administration and Supervision,* February 1939, pp. 107–19.

Florence Greenhoe, "The Community Contacts and Participation of 9,122 Public-School Teachers Selected as a National Sample." *School and Society,* October 14, 1939, pp. 510–12.

New York State Teachers Association, *The Social, Cultural, and Economic Status of Public School Teachers in New York State.* Educational Monograph No. 6, 1937.

Harold E. Snyder, *Educational Inbreeding.* New York: Bureau of Publications, Teachers College, Columbia University, 1943.

David M. Trout (ed.), *The Education of Teachers,* Chap 9. Lansing: The Michigan Cooperative Teacher Education Study, 1943.

To the College Faculties of the State of New York:

The undersigned members of the Social Understanding Group of the College Faculty Workshop held at Syracuse in June, 1941, desire to call to your attention the following brief statement of principles concerning the study of community structures and functions. We hope the statement will be considered by faculty groups and individuals concerned with the problems of general education, especially as general education enters into the training of teachers.

---

1. One of the critical needs of a teacher in American schools today, no matter what his special subject or his educational responsibility, is familiarity with the social process as it operates concretely in the community in which he is teaching. This need arises in the increased consciousness of community welfare in the nation today, in the tendency toward closer cooperation of school and community, and in the demands of personal adjustment of the teacher to the community group which he serves.

2. It is important that, within general education at the college level, a prospective teacher be made familiar with the community as a functioning unit in American life, that he acquire basic knowledge of community structure and function, a reasonable objectivity toward community reconstruction, and a reasonable degree of skill and facility in the human relations of community living.

3. Within general education it is eminently desirable that the prospective teacher experience a combination of aloof intellectual analysis of a community organism and immediate, conscientious participation in the life of a real community.

4. Community study must avoid mere isolated and segmented thrusts into community living. The details and fragments of community analysis and experience must be integrated into a conceptual understanding of community patterns. The student must see parts of the community close at hand but must also see the community as a whole.

5. The task of community analysis and of equipping prospective teachers with requisite understandings and attitudes and skills, does not belong to any one segment of the curriculum or to any one subject field. Most of the arts and sciences which enter into general education have ramifications into and implications for the analysis of the contemporary community. This is true of both "academic" and "professional" courses. The development of a full community consciousness is the proper task of the entire college and the responsibility of each member of the college staff.

Harold V. Fagan
Mark Mohler
Alma G. Montgomery

(signed)
Howard E. Wilson,
Consultant

Frederick A. Morse
Edward G. Olsen
Margaret M. Wood

A WORKSHOP GROUP'S STATEMENT OF POLICY for community study in teacher education, College Faculty Workshop, Syracuse, N. Y. Sponsored by the Committee on Teacher Education of the Association of Colleges and Universities of the State of New York.

the freeing of intelligence. It is society's responsibility to educate teachers who are competent to assume this responsibility. Teachers who have not themselves clarified their values, and who do not understand thoroughly the community in which girls and boys live and work, cannot hope to do their part in bettering human relationships and improving the quality of community life. A system of democratic, life-centered education requires well socialized teachers who exhibit in their day-by-day behavior the basic democratic values, and who are adept at social interpretation and leadership.

How are we to assure children and youth of such teachers? *The teacher-educating institutions* will need to be experimental in attitude, creating a democratic atmosphere and providing experiences through which young men and women may develop the insights, understandings, attitudes and ways of behaving which are necessary for leaders in a democratic society. This may necessitate eliminating some of the highly academic materials and formal procedures characteristic of the traditional college, and the substitution of cooperative effort toward the solution of vital problems of modern living. *Public school systems* will need to cut administrative red tape and free teachers' time for cooperative and creative work in school and community—the finest and most effective kind of in-service education. *Local communities* will need to accept the teacher as a productive citizen and allow him freedom to do constructive work, no longer limiting his academic freedom and holding him at arm's length as a stranger. *The teacher,* whether prospective or active, will need to develop an ideal of community participation and service which will lead to continuous personal growth. Only by the recognition and acceptance of such joint responsibility by all concerned, shall we be able to educate socially competent teachers, and thereby develop a truly functional pattern of life-centered education.

How Can One Appraise His Personal Fitness for Community-School Teaching?

All of those who now teach, or who hope to teach effectively in the future, would do well to make periodic examination of personal fitness for that responsibility. To aid in such evaluation, the self-appraisal instrument which follows has been devised.

Appraising My Fitness for Work in a Community-Centered Program of Education

DIRECTIONS TO THE TEACHER:

How well are you fitted for work in a school which is closely related to the life of its community? The following check list will help you determine the extent to which you have developed the social and civic competence which such teaching requires of you. Indicate the degree of growth you think you have achieved by placing an X in the appropriate column opposite each item. Remember that you should evaluate yourself in terms of your *actual behavior in life situations*, not merely in terms of your present ideals.

VIEWING MYSELF OBJECTIVELY, I THINK I HAVE ACHIEVED:

THIS DEGREE OF LEARNING   IN THIS AREA OF LEARNING

MUCH	SOME	LITTLE	NONE	
				I. A Realistic Approach to the Study of Human Relations
				1.1 Understanding the community-school movement and its significance for democratic education and the conscious improvement of human living
				1.2 Comprehending life in various types of communities with regard to such fundamental factors as:
				(a) The land and its resources
				(b) The people
				(c) Utilizing natural environment
				(d) Appreciating the past
				(e) Adjusting to people
				(f) Exchanging ideas
				(g) Making a living
				(h) Sharing in citizenship
				(i) Maintaining health and safety
				(j) Improving family living
				(k) Securing education
				(l) Meeting religious needs
				(m) Enjoying beauty
				(n) Engaging in recreation
				1.3 Understanding social forces at work in the community:
				(a) Caste and class
				(b) In-group and out-group relationships
				(c) Pressure groups and propaganda
				(d) Democratic leadership and cooperation
				1.4 Applying effective methods of community analysis and inventory in relation to basic social processes as they are carried on in everyday life
				1.5 Understanding some of the more persistent problems of our modern social and economic society
				1.6 Comprehending the socio-economic and cultural position of my community in its regional, national, and international setting
				1.7 Understanding methods of community organization, coordination, and planning

THIS DEGREE OF LEARNING				IN THIS AREA OF LEARNING (*Continued*)
MUCH	SOME	LITTLE	NONE	
				1.8 Seeing possibilities for improvement of group life through a knowledge of what some communities and people are doing to enrich and advance life
				II. EFFECTIVE THINKING AND RESEARCH IN THE SOCIAL AREA
				2.1 Awareness of community conditions which give rise to important problems and conflicts
				2.2 Ability to see what might be done to solve or adjust to these problems
				2.3 Ability to define an area for study and to formulate a plan of work
				2.4 Ability to gather significant and pertinent data, using field and library research techniques:
				(a) Observation
				(b) Participation
				(c) Interview
				(d) Questionnaire
				(e) Mapping
				(f) Documentary materials
				(g) Background reading
				2.5 Ability to differentiate between data that are significant, valid, and relevant and those that are unimportant, invalid, and irrelevant, and to interpret findings
				2.6 Habit of suspending judgment until sufficient facts are available for drawing a legitimate conclusion
				2.7 Ability to summarize the results of an investigation and to present findings in vital written, oral, or graphic form
				2.8 Practice of making decisions and of acting on the basis of these decisions where such action is desirable and possible
				2.9 Habit of testing actions in the light of consequences and in terms of the broadest democratic principle: "Has this action promoted the personal development of the people affected by it?"
				III. SOCIAL PARTICIPATION AND SOCIAL ACTION
				3.1 Knowing the people of the community as parents, neighbors, workers, worshippers, consumers, citizens, and formulators of community customs, standards, and beliefs
				3.2 Participating constructively in the ongoing life of the community by:
				(a) Contributing to some community activities such as boys' and girls' clubs, church groups, community council, war service, etc.
				(b) Helping direct some community activity such as Boy Scouts, League of Women Voters, Red Cross work, etc.
				(c) Working in the community at jobs other than teaching

| THIS DEGREE OF LEARNING | | | | IN THIS AREA OF LEARNING (*Continued*) |
MUCH	SOME	LITTLE	NONE	
				(d) Meeting effectively my problems of personal relationships incidental to participation in community life
				3.3 Exercising responsible leadership in significant movements designed for intelligent community betterment
				3.4 Participating effectively in district, state, national, and international group life:
				(a) Functioning as a member of state and national organizations
				(b) Using techniques of communication characteristic of larger group participation, such as petitions and letter writing
				3.5 Creating in students social sensitivity and the inclination and habit of participating constructively in community affairs
				3.6 Utilizing community resources in personal living and professional work
				IV. COOPERATIVE LIVING
				4.1 Understanding democracy as the opportunity for development of maximum capacity of all individuals
				4.2 Expressing democratic values through behavior, attitudes, and beliefs in all the areas and relations of life
				4.3 Recognizing free interaction, cooperation, and sharing as the methods of democratic group life
				4.4 Utilizing effectively in school and community those techniques essential to cooperative living:
				(a) Free and fruitful discussion
				(b) Democratic planning
				(c) Sharing responsibility for group undertakings
				(d) Evaluating the effectiveness of group action
				4.5 Realizing the sterility of much academic procedure and developing in its place effective methods of group work in the classroom

This check list, honestly used from time to time, should serve as a stimulus to any teacher who seriously desires to improve his personal and professional competence. It goes without saying that if the majority of these items are checked in the "none" or "little" columns, that the teacher in question is unfitted to work in any school which relates its program to community life and needs. But if practically all of the items can conscientiously be checked in the "much" column, then that teacher is decidedly the kind America and the world so desperately need today. For as Stout has so eloquently said:

"The supreme need of the American system of education is a body of dynamic teachers who are eager to make the community a place where talent is marketed, where human values are enriched, and where the basic needs of life are satisfied; teachers who are possessed with a zeal for truth about the crucial facts of the community in which pupils live and grow; who are thrilled at the prospect of guiding the relationship of individual and institution so that richer and ever richer personality and culture may be created; teachers who take courage in the thought that whenever one lifts the life of a community, he lifts by just so much also the life of America; finally, teachers who are devoted to the task of giving to the communities of this nation a generation of men and women trained to think their way through the complex ramifications of modern society, charged with the spirit of truth and justice, and ready to meet the situations which tomorrow will bring." [7]

SELECTED REFERENCES

Aldrich, Julian C., "Utilizing Community Resources for In-Service Training of Counselors." *School Review* 48:193–96 (March 1940). Eighteen school districts and certain youth agencies established a County Guidance Council to help counselors understand their jobs better.

Bain, W. E., "Prospective Teachers Learn to Live with Their Neighbors." *Childhood Education* 14:245–51 (Feb. 1938). Describes the former New College community farm maintained in the South for the education of future teachers from the city.

Blackwell, Gordon W., *Toward Community Understanding.* Washington: American Council on Education, 1943. Reports and analyzes the community study and participation programs of teacher education carried on in sixteen outstanding institutions.

Bonney, Merl E., "The Use of Community Resources in Psychology Courses for Teachers." *Educational Administration and Supervision* 30:105–17 (Feb. 1944). Student experiences and learnings as they worked actively with children in social settlements, nursery school, Boy Scouts troops, public schools, churches, etc. Concludes that such experiences greatly vitalize classroom teaching of psychology.

Brown, Harry A., "Student Participation in Institutional Life and Contemporary Culture as an Essential Aspect of Modern Teacher Education." *Educational Administration and Supervision* 24:29–38 (Jan. 1938). Future teachers need extensive community participation for professional understanding and skill, and also for their own personality development. Suggests possible programs.

Buzzard, Robert G., "Educating Teachers for Effective Community Service." In William C. Reavis (ed.), *The School and the Urban Community*, pp. 171–86. Chicago: University of Chicago Press, 1942. Discusses the problem-factors in securing improved teacher-education, and suggests how better community integration may be secured.

Carley, Verna A., "A Venture in Teacher-Education in the Study of a Region." Normal, Illinois: Illinois State Normal University. An illustrated brochure describing the experiences and itinerary of 24 supervisors of student teachers who developed a Traveling Seminar to study the Tennessee River Valley at

[7] Dorman G. Stout, *Teacher and Community*, p. vi. Yonkers-on-Hudson, N. Y.: World Book Co., 1941.

first hand. Essentially the same text, but without the photographs, appeared in *Educational Method* for February, 1941.

Committee on Field Services, Department of Education, University of Chicago, "The School and the Community." Chicago Heights, Illinois: Boards of Education Districts 170 and 206, 1942. Describes a field course and survey, an in-service teacher education project carried on under the auspices of the local boards of education in cooperation with the University of Chicago.

Cuber, John F., "Community Training in the Preparation of Teachers." *Educational Administration and Supervision* 24:382–88 (May 1938). Increased training of teachers should take the form of community experiences. A unit of instruction toward that end is proposed and outlined.

Gans, Roma, "The Teacher in the Community." *Teachers College Record* 43: 100–07 (Nov. 1941). If teachers are to be effective under modern conceptions of education, they must be constructively identified with the problems of living, comprehend the place of children in a complex environment, and be genuinely concerned for the total welfare of each pupil.

Holford, Anne, "The Teacher's Use of Her Environment." *Instructor* 49:12, 75 (Nov. 1939). How teachers in one district surveyed community resources, listed findings in a card file, mapped the hobbies of the community, made an art survey, and established a school museum.

John Dewey Society, *The Teacher and Society*, Ch. IX. First Yearbook. New York: Appleton-Century, 1937. Identifies and analyzes five successive levels of relationship between the teacher and his local community, and recommends extensive community study, participation, and service by every teacher.

Karlin, Jules (ed.), *Field Manual for Teachers*, Ch. V. Chicago: Werkman's Book House, 1941. Describes the excursion and group work program at Chicago Teachers College.

Karlin, Jules, and George J. Steiner, "Prospective Teachers Study and Serve Chicago." *Social Education* 5:339–42 (May 1941). The field trip program at Chicago Teachers College is described, 7 of the 20 trips offered being outlined in full.

Koopman, Margaret O., *Social Processes: An Experiment in Educating College Students for Social Living*. Mount Pleasant: Central Michigan College of Education, 1940. Describes the social education of prospective teachers through community survey-analysis, excursions, study of persistent problems, social action in the community.

Koopman, Margaret O., and A. S. Hatch, "Community Study in Teacher Education." *Curriculum Journal* 12:205–08 (May 1941). Future elementary school teachers survey many aspects of the community as social need arises. A detailed description of a housing survey is given to illustrate.

Low, Camilla M., and Mary Frances Gates, *Handbook of Laboratory Activities for Pre-Service Teachers at the University of Wisconsin*. Madison: University of Wisconsin Department of Education, 1941. Stresses the value of first-hand learning experiences, lists such opportunities in Madison, suggests techniques of studying the child and his community background, outlines essentials of group leadership, gives directions for participants, and indicates methods of gathering and recording data.

Michener, James A., "Teachers in the Community." *Social Studies* 32:219–21 (May 1941). Describes a community study course in which teachers spent a week in each of three New England communities, preparing for and summarizing their field experiences with appropriate campus study.

Mitchell, Morris R., "Teacher Education Through Useful Work." *Educational Method* 20:15–22 (Oct. 1940). A stirring account of how pioneering teacher-educating institutions are beginning to prepare teachers for community leadership by giving them work experience as an integral part of their school education. Reports in detail on what such experience does to the individual in terms of insight and motivation.

New Jersey State Teachers College at Montclair, Bureau of Field Studies, "Field Studies in a Teachers College." Montclair: The Bureau, 1938. Describes the excursions and extended field studies in social science which are given for credit in the college.

New York State Teachers College at Oneonta, "Teachers as Learners." Oneonta: The College, 1942. Describes a two-week group study, under professional guidance, of contrasting local communities. Tells what the group did and why, where they went, how they went at it, what they got out of the experience, and why they were successful. A shorter report on this project appeared in the *Newsletter* of the Commission on Teacher Education for May, 1942.

Olsen, Edward G., "National Survey of Teacher Education in Community Study Techniques." *Educational Record* 24:421–35 (Oct. 1943). Reports on extent of such education, types of programs, major obstacles to wider development, kinds of help desired, and regional differences indicated. Quotes catalogue descriptions of numerous community study courses.

Olsen, Edward G., "Pioneering in Community Study." *Educational Method* 20:236–43 (Feb. 1941). Origin, development, program and values of the Reconciliation Trips, an educational excursion organization extensively used by teachers of the New York area.

Otto, Henry J., and others, *Community Workshops for Teachers in the Michigan Community Health Project*. Ann Arbor: University of Michigan Press, 1942. Detailed descriptions of four summer workshops in which the use of community resources was given major emphasis. Health education, science education, citizenship and health in the community school, and problems in social science, library science, and language arts were the four areas investigated.

Prall, Charles E., and C. Leslie Cushman, *Teacher Education in Service*, pp. 182–96; 215–27; 387–435. Washington: American Council on Education, 1944. Stimulating accounts of how teachers in three different systems discovered community resources, planned how to build the school into the community, and worked cooperatively toward the solution of community problems.

Quinby, Elsie M., "Materials on Community Study for Discussion Groups of In-Service Primary Teachers." *Educational Administration and Supervision* 25:577–96 (Nov. 1939). Lists selected materials on the need for community study, materials for community understanding and for using community resources in teaching, and outlines a plan for a year's study program.

Seeds, Corinne, "The Teacher Learns to Use the Community." In Gladys L. Potter (compiler), "Exploring Your Community," pp. 24–31. Bulletin of the Association for Childhood Education. Washington: The Association, 1940. How teachers may help children utilize community resources to enrich their classroom study activities.

Shimel, Vesta M., "Teachers Study the Community." *Educational Method* 18: 340–44 (April 1939). Tells how a public school system helped its teachers explore their environment and its resources through a series of some 30 excursions.

Taggart, Lelia Ann, "Enriching Teacher Experience." *Childhood Education* 14: 252–55 (Feb. 1938). A supervisory staff made a community survey, and then arranged a series of teacher excursions throughout the school year. Arrangements are described, materials given the teachers in advance are mentioned, and a list of community resources is classified according to social processes.

Trout, David M. (ed.), *The Education of Teachers*, Chapter 9. Lansing: Michigan Cooperative Teacher Education Study, 1943. Suggestions for educating teachers for community service, and for freeing them to participate in community life.

Ullrick, Laura F., and Charles H. Coleman, "The Social Studies Teacher and the Community." In Burr W. Phillips (ed.), *In-Service Growth of Social Studies Teachers:* Tenth Yearbook, National Council for the Social Studies, Ch. IX. Cambridge, Mass.: The Council, 1939. Community-teacher relationships, the teacher's approach to the community, the problem of academic freedom, growth through use of community resources.

Wofford, Kate V., "Teacher and His Community." *New York State Education* 28:20–22 (Oct. 1940). Practical advice to beginning teachers in small communities on how to become "accepted" as effective persons.

Zerfoss, Karl P., and Harriett D. Moore, "The Use of Field Studies in Teaching Educational Psychology." *Journal of Educational Psychology* 33:527–37 (Oct. 1942). Students carried on field work in social agencies, correlating their directed observations with theoretical learnings in the classroom.

PART V

BASIC PRINCIPLES

NOW we have examined the underlying philosophy of cooperative community education, analyzed the community structurally, and noted also its fundamental processes and emergent problems, investigated each of ten vital ways to relate school instruction with community life, and considered some of the general problems involved. All that remains is to summarize basic principles of action and to present a challenge for the future. This we shall do in the final chapter of this volume.

*

CHALLENGE TO STATESMANSHIP

CHILDREN and youth, millions of them the world over, restless with tremendous energies! Communities, thousands of them from Pole to Pole, embracing the conditions and the materials from which we may create a far more ideal environment for better living! On the one hand, the great energy of youth requiring only a dynamic purpose to make that force the most constructive factor in social progress. On the other hand, cultures rich in potentialities, needing a great constructive force in order to realize the abundant human life which they are capable of providing. To coordinate these two mighty resources —to harness the energy of youth to the task of progressively improving conditions of community life— that is the supreme challenge to educational and social statesmanship.

—PAUL R. HANNA

(And Research Staff), *Youth Serves the Community*. By permission of the D. Appleton-Century Company, publishers.

THE OLD BASIC TRUTH

ISN'T the community-centered idea of education in direct conflict with the individual-centered school? Not really. How else
can we have a better society than by having better persons? Any
other conception of democracy is bound to end in regimentation.
Democracy exalts the individual not for his own sake, but for
what he gains from giving. The old basic truth of Christian
morality has got to be rediscovered by the school. 'He that loseth
his life for My sake shall find it.' Only out of competence of the
individual can a competent world be built."

—Burton P. Fowler

In "Education for the Future."
Parents' Magazine, February, 1944.

PREPARATION FOR LIFE

IF the environment, in school and out, supplies conditions which
utilize adequately the present capacities of the immature, the
future which grows out of the present is surely taken care of.
The mistake is not in attaching importance to preparation for
future need, but in making it the mainspring of present effort.
Because the need of preparation for a continually developing life
is great, it is imperative that every energy should be bent to
making the present experience as rich and significant as possible.
Then as the present merges insensibly into the future, the future is
taken care of."

—John Dewey

In *Democracy and Education*, p. 65.
By permission of the Macmillan
Company, publishers.

REALITY AND CHALLENGE

A COMMUNITY activity can have a reality and a challenge
that no lesser activity can properly have. Moreover, it serves
to bring the youthful group into desirable intimate contact with
the surrounding community. To do something which others count
significant ranks very high among the satisfying and steadying
influences in life. For the young to feel that their activities have
community significance is to accord to them a worth and standing
that will call out the best the young have to give."

—William H. Kilpatrick

In the Introduction to Paul R. Hanna and
Research Staff, *Youth Serves the Community*,
p. 18. By permission of the Appleton-Century
Company, publishers.

CHAPTER 21

Ten Guideposts

Owing to the fragmentary character of most school-community programs, little progess has yet been made in determining the basic principles upon which any comprehensive program of life-centered education should be based. Although a score of authentic "community schools" are already operating in various American communities,[1] no two are alike and much additional experimentation will have to be carried on before we can expect general agreement. Yet it is true that recent experience and present thought suggest that the life-centered community school of the future may be based upon a number of practical curriculum principles already discernible. Let us examine ten such principles briefly, remembering as we proceed that the term "principle" here means not some permanent, established, universally-valid "truth," but rather a reasonable "hypothesis with which to experiment" further.

This brief chapter may thus serve both as a kind of final summary and as a means of restoring perspective upon the comprehensive problem of better relating school instruction with community life. Throughout this summary as in the entire volume we take for granted a fundamentally *democratic* frame of reference. For we had better not forget that education in fascist Italy, in Nazi Germany, and in totalitarian Japan was definitely "life-centered" —each within its fascist scheme of social values! *Our conscious concern must ever be that of developing more functional school programs grounded firmly in the democratic faith and process.*

Essential Principles [2]

I

Distinguish three omnibus aims in the area of school-community relationships: (a) social comprehension—developing an understand-

---

[1] For extended descriptions of such schools, see Samuel Everett (ed.), *The Community School;* Elsie R. Clapp, *Community Schools in Action;* Paul R. Pierce, *Developing a High School Curriculum.*

[2] These ten principles were first presented by the writer in the University of Pennsylvania Bulletin, *Education in a Nation at War* (Schoolmen's Week Pro-

ing of the changing culture; (b) *social motivation*—establishing incentives to democratic social improvement; and (c) *social skills*—increasing personal competence in community participation and leadership. Such differentiation (even though it cannot actually be maintained in a functional learning situation) serves to forestall a prevalent belief that community experiences are primarily a device for stimulating intellectual understanding. Knowledge is needed, but without adequate motivation it is sterile. Both knowledge and motivation are futile, even dangerous, unless they are utilized and directed by democratic group skills and values.

II

Define the community as the service area of the school; but relate it directly and constantly with the larger areas of state, region, nation, and world. Such definition eliminates the ever-present danger of fostering those provincial attitudes which sometimes arise when community studies and activities are confined to the immediate locality alone. Since the community is essentially a set of social relationships rather than a geographic area, we must today study the locality more intensively and the world more extensively than we have done in the past.

III

Recognize three major levels of culture to be studied in every community, immediate or remote, contemporary or historical: (a) the *material culture*—geographic factors together with the things people have made or used; (b) the *institutional culture*—the mass habits or customs of the people; and (c) the *psychological culture*—the motivating beliefs of the people. Such recognition safeguards against the common practice of relating community study to the material culture alone, with consequent disregard for the institutional and especially the psychological level which ultimately shapes both of the others.

IV

Emphasize physical setting, social processes, social structure, and social problems; and stress the close interrelationship among these factors. The community must be perceived in its wholeness as well

ceedings, 1942) and subsequently revised for inclusion in Harry N. Rivlin and Herbert Schueler (eds.), *Encyclopedia of Modern Education*, pp. 172–73. The latter statement has been somewhat expanded in each section for this volume. Used by permission.

as in its elements; in its virtues as in its vices. It is therefore well
to concentrate upon setting, processes, and structure, rather than
upon problems, until at least the senior high school level. Young
children are intensely interested in the physical environment and in
ways of living, but they do not become deeply concerned with larger
social issues until later adolescence has brought both wider social
interests and full maturity of intelligence. Such concentration provides initial perspective upon normal social processes, and thereby
avoids that "rotten-spot" preoccupation which often seems to result
in cynicism rather than citizenship among high school students suddenly plunged into "social problems" courses.

V

*Plan a sequential development of student experiences throughout
each year of the entire school program.* Such planning lessens the
possibility of purely sporadic delvings into limited segments of community life, of repeating community activities unnecessarily, and of
giving undue attention to superficial or transitory areas. Comprehensive planning enables each community experience to be functionally related with both prior and subsequent experiences, and
thereby contributes to the child's developing sense of at-homeness
in his world, to his improving techniques of getting vital information, and to his growing ability to generalize abstractly from concrete experiences.

VI

*Begin this sequence with consideration of material culture in the
local community, in particular reference to its geographic and demographic aspects.* Such beginning takes a proper account of the young
child's dominant interests as well as of his natural difficulty in thinking abstractly about the institutional and psychological levels of
human culture. Abstractions will remain mere verbalisms unless
each new experience is made meaningful in terms of related past
experience.

VII

Expand this initial study in three related dimensions: (a) *space*
—in other areas, geographically; (b) *time*—in other communities
and areas, historically; and (c) *scope*—in institutional and psychological culture levels. Such expansion stimulates the child to
think increasingly in terms of symbols as his developing ability to
do so progressively permits.

VIII

Utilize all appropriate techniques for effectively relating the school with the community: (a) *firsthand experience with reality* —resource visitors, interviews, field trips, surveys, extended field study, camping, service projects, and work experience should be used in the local community and, so far as feasible, in the larger areas as well; (b) *representations of reality*—audio-visual aids should be widely utilized in the study of communities remote in space or time; (c) *symbols of reality*—documentary materials ought to be freely used in the intensive analysis of the local community as well as in the study of other community areas through all three levels. Such varied use of relevant approaches avoids the common imbalance of learning resulting from limited use of one or two techniques alone, and also emphasizes the fact that highly worthwhile learning does not always require direct experience on the part of the learner.

IX

Focus attention upon the status, problems, and social contributions of youth who have participated in the basic processes of the various communities and societal areas studied. Such focusing stresses the organic relationship between each individual student's life and the functioning of the surrounding social processes, thus stimulating a psychological identification of youth interests with adult concerns.

X

Direct primary personal loyalties to a people's finest traditions, ethical ideals and social values, rather than to their geographic territory, political structure, or any other segment of their material or institutional culture. The crying necessity of our times is to expand provincial loyalties—political, social, economic, religious— into a broader and deeper devotion to genuine human welfare everywhere. Such direction of fundamental loyalties provides the only assurance of individual and national stability in our world of rapid material and institutional change.

*

Such basic principles, intelligently developed within practical programs, permit full recognition of the central tenet in the life-centered school philosophy: that education itself is inherently a social process which therefore cannot be truly realistic, vital, and defensible unless its curricular program is framed in terms of a well-pondered, first-hand acquaintance with significant aspects of the learner's physical, biological, and social environment.

Perhaps some may assert that this community school philosophy and procedure threatens liberal education. To such critics we would simply suggest that true liberal education is that which liberates a person from blind subservience to the mores of his group as these have been defined by the traditions of a particular people, place and period in history. Liberal education means a freeing of the mind from provincial pettiness in every field. It is perspective at its best. It is to "see life steadily and see it whole" as Matthew Arnold wisely said. *To see life steadily and to see it whole* is also a major value and purpose of life-centered education.

There is more even than that to the educational viewpoint we have outlined. The intellect does not operate in an emotional vacuum. Almost above all else, youth today needs a sense of *belonging*—of being *wanted by society* in times of peace as well as during years of war. If only for psychological maturation and emotional stability, each youth must develop his personal conception of *individual worth* through his achievement of genuine *social recognition*. Particularly in these times of strain and confusion, we must somehow succeed in giving all our children and young people a realistic understanding of their world, extensive opportunity to participate with personal satisfaction and social recognition in its ongoing processes of living, and consequent possibility of developing those feelings of true achievement, personal worth, and social sensitivity which are essential to emotional adjustment and to democratic citizenship. If we cannot, then there is grave danger that the new adults of the postwar world, disillusioned with the social unreality of the linguistic and vocational schools, may express their accumulated frustration in native fascist movements destructive of democracy itself.

The postwar years hold promise as well as hazard for youth and education. If we can succeed in developing widespread educational programs that are psychologically satisfying and socially creative, and which function in all teaching areas at all school levels, we may surely expect to witness during the second half of this century a vital expansion of democratically effective living, both personal and social. This requires that we increasingly relate education to life experience, school instruction to individual and community needs, teaching to living at its highest and best. Whatever the specific nature of such future educational programs, we may even now assert with confidence that their primary purpose must be to channel the splendid energies of youth toward the progressive, cooperative improvement of community life in its local, regional, national, and international aspects. Here looms the supreme educational and civic opportunity of our times. What a challenge to peaceful reconstruction of this war-weary world!

Author Index

Subject Index

A

Academic freedom, 343
Academic school, 6, 10, 19, 268, 277
Activities, student, 297
Activity:
  child, 30
  school, 7
Address, forwarding, 218
Adjustment, 30, 31, 52
Administrative problems, see Chapter 15
Adventure of teaching, 38
Agencies, community, 66
Aims:
  community study, 34, 409
  educational, 10
American Education Fellowship, 8
American School of the Air, 117
Ancestor worship, 52
Antioch field study course, 330
Antioch plan, 276
Appraisal, see Evaluation
Appreciation as objective, 320
Arts, enjoyment of, 64
Attitudes:
  as objectives, 36, 319
  of students, 336
Atwater School, 271
Atypical children, 63
Audio-visual aids, see Chapter 5
  definition, 101
  in school publicity, 339
  limitations, 125
  principles of use, 120–23
  sources, 123–25
  values, 101
Austria, field study in, 13

B

Baggage, traveling, 218
Beauty, enjoyment of, 64
Behavior:
  changes in as aim, 327
  code of, 219
  democratic, 36
Books, 77, 289, 290
Broadcasts, 115
Bus, 306–07
Business agencies and organizations, 56, 67, 80

C

Camps, see School camp
Capitalism, 285
Capital-labor conflict, 58
Census, U. S., 82ff.
"Census tracts," 85
Central Michigan College of Education, 328
Change, social, 3
Character, 37
Child:
  interests, 8
  nature, 30
Children, neglected, 62
Churches, 64
Citizenship, 58
City directories, 80
Civic:
  associations, 80
  improvement, 251
  indifference, 59
  organizations, 92
Class and caste structure, 49
Clearing house, see Community service center
Climate, 47
Community:
  agencies, 66
  analysis techniques, see Chapter 3
  areas, 44
  child's idea of, 43
  coordination, see Chapter 19
  experiences, 297
  handbooks, 81
  improvement, 18
  leaders, 261
  levels, 45
  meaning of, 43, 410
  participation, 4
  planning, 68
  problems, 410
  processes and problems, 50–65
  projects, 357
  resources:
    analyzed, 152
    card file, 350
    correlated with curriculum, 152
    discovered, 151
    file card, 353
    school utilization, 18

417